CENSUS OF THE BLACKFEET, MONTANA, 1897- 1901 EXPANDED EDITION

TRANSCRIBED BY JEFF BOWEN

NATIVE STUDY
Gallipolis, Ohio
USA

Copyright © 2020
by Jeff Bowen

ALL RIGHTS RESERVED.
No part of this publication may be reproduced,
distributed, or transmitted in any form or by any means,
without the prior written permission of the publisher.

Native Study LLC
Gallipolis, OH
www.nativestudy.com

Library of Congress Control Number: 2020913244

ISBN: 978-1-64968-004-4

Made in the United States of America.

This book is dedicated to
all the people within the
Blackfeet Nation,
past, present and future.

"When I was a boy, very few members of my tribe could read or write. But now all our young people are in school. They learn a lot about the Pilgrims, George Washington, Abraham Lincoln. That's fine. But they learn nothing about the history of their own people and their great chiefs. That is American history too."

                              Richard Sanderville

                              The Blackfeet Raiders on the
                              Northwestern Plains

Table of Contents

Introduction	vii
Lame Bull Treaty of 1855	xxi
1897 Census	3
1898 Census	65
1899 Census	135
1900 Census	197
1901 Census	249
Index	299

INTRODUCTION

Census of the Blackfeet, Montana, 1897-1898, was originally published in 2004. In republishing this piece it was felt that there needed to be an expansion upon the work since the earlier volume had attracted such positive feedback. This new census volume now covers the years 1897-1901 and has been given great care for accuracy. These censuses were taken by United States Indian Agents, George B. McLaughlin (1897), Thomas P. Fuller (1898), W.R. Logan (1899), no agent listed for (1900), and James H. Monteath (1901). It needs to be remembered that the Native peoples in general during these times didn't always have their information recorded correctly. In explaining the inaccuracies of record it could have been for many reasons. Individual agents and personnel concerns or lack of, the education of individuals recording the results as well as those giving their information. The knowledge of their age during a time of lesser technologies where life or different cultures had different priorities could also play a factor. In those years many weren't as concerned with what seems important to those of this period. Example, over the years and concern for peoples' research there has been great care taken to transcribe the materials only to find individual's ages or degree of blood changed time and again while losing or gaining years depending on recorders and again individuals offering their information. Hours sometimes have been poured over traveling through records year to year to somehow make sense of inaccuracies (like gaining or losing five years in one census as an example among whole families) only to realize you can't go back there, you can't change what was entered as record long ago but you can try to use it to the best of your ability to assemble that family puzzle. Use the materials at hand to compile what you have with offerings given or possibly found through older family members from previous research or records they might have gathered. Marriage records, birth and death, yearly census, county and state, Soundex, National Archive records, family bible records recorded over the years (which are considered legal documents, of course now there are varying circumstances being statistical (vital) records have been kept for a long time now and it would have to be a situation from long ago before official recordings weren't as abundant and depending on jurisdiction), court records, military, etc.

The Blackfeet are a wonderful people with a lot to share, just reading through James Willard Schultz's [Apikuni], *Blackfeet and Buffalo, Memories of Life among the Indians,* carries you to a time of beauty and innocence where people lived full lives even though they sometimes faced harsh realities but knew how to deal with it without having to make the rest of the world suffer. They handled their own world and didn't suffer fools. They were tough but loving; they opened themselves up to those that deserved it. They defended their world if they had to but never failed to give to others when necessary. They held on to their beliefs and followed their cultures for a better life not only for themselves but for their generations.

"For nearly two centuries the three Blackfoot tribes have been known to white men by their separate names. They are the Pikuni or Piegan (pronounced Pay-gan'), the Kainah or Blood, and the Siksika or Blackfoot proper, often referred to as the Northern Blackfoot to distinguish it from the other two tribes. The three tribes were politically independent. But they spoke the same language, shared the same customs (with the exception of a few ceremonial rituals), intermarried, and made war upon common enemies. So it has been customary to speak of these three tribes as one people, under the general name of Blackfoot or Blackfeet. The former is the more literal translation of the native name, Siksikauwa (black-footed people). Together these three tribes comprised the strongest military power on the northwestern plains in historic buffalo days."[1]

You will find similar but different situational opinions within this introduction but it was felt that you should have different opinions from a couple historical and cultural experts along with their life experiences with the Blackfeet or Blackfoot tribes so you can study the circumstances involved in their world and time.

They moved where the buffalo moved. They were hunter and gathers and lived in teepees that could be disassembled and reconstructed with the speed and skill unmatched by any others except other Plains Native tribes. In the summer months the Blackfeet resided in substantially large encampments and during the winter months lived in smaller camps ranging from approximately 10 to 20 lodges. They usually had a few headmen in each band, but only one was known as chief. To hold this position he had to have extensive ceremonial experience, some wealth, and many triumphs in war.

"Whether the Blackfeet moved west because they were attracted by opportunities for big-game hunting in the open country, or whether they were driven westward by other Algonkian tribes whose growing populations forced them to expand their own hunting territories, we do not know. Possibly both factors encouraged Blackfoot migration. At any rate, it is certain that the Blackfeet entered the plains on foot. It is just as certain that they were accustomed to the plains life when the first white trader-explorers discovered them. The late Clark Wissler, for

---

[1] The Blackfeet Raiders on the Northwestern Plains; Pg. 5, Para 2

many years a thorough student of the Blackfeet, expressed the opinion that they 'were on the plains a long time before the discovery of America.'"[2]

"It is said that one time, long ago, a tribe was traveling and could not find enough food; they were all hungry. The chiefs agreed that the tribe should temporarily divide into groups to make it easier to find food. Later in the summer, they regrouped. The faces and hands of one northern group were stained red because they ate mostly berries: They became known as Bloods or Kainai. Another group had to walk across a large burned-out area, and their moccasins and leggings were black: They are now known as the Blackfeet in the United States and Blackfoot in Canada, where there are three groups, the Northern Piegan, the Kainai Nation, and the Siksika Nation. They share origins, culture, and their native language, which has its roots in the Algonquian language stock."[3]

Again you will read a few redundant statements but from a few different sources so their opinions and knowledge can be shared as quotes from the materials and studies they used.

"The territory of the Blackfeet, at its greatest extent, encompassed a vast area from the eastern Rocky Mountains of Alberta and Montana and extending several hundred miles out onto the Great Plains, around the upper reaches of the Saskatchewan River and its tributaries in Alberta and the upper reaches of the Missouri River and its tributaries in Montana."[4] "The tribes were organized into bands, with each band having its own structure and rules. They would come together in the spring or early summer and camp together as a tribe for sacred ceremonies.

---

[2] The Blackfeet Raiders on the Northwestern Plains; Pg. 7, Para 2
[3] Indian Nations of North America; Pg. 158, Blackfeet Top Introduction
[4] The Blackfeet, Native American Tribes; Pg. [iv], Para 1

Each lodge had its special space in the giant circle of tepees. Drastic change began in 1853 when Isaac I. Stevens was appointed the first territorial governor of Washington and the Superintendent of Indian Affairs. Stevens, who was first in his class at West Point, also spent some time in the Corps of Engineers. On his way to his new post, the ambitious soldier volunteered to survey the northern route for a railroad from Minneapolis to the West Coast. Moving slowly across the prairie, he met most of the tribes and their headmen and had them sign many long-lasting treaties in 1855. His methods were stern and intimidating; some negotiations even involved killings. Most of those treaties, however, are still in effect today. The tribes that signed surrendered their rights to their regions. They promised to live in peace, allow outsiders to travel in peace, and permit the construction of roads and telegraph lines. In turn, the Blackfeet received a huge Montana reservation that still holds great beauty. A decade later, though, the government reduced these holdings, and clashes ensued. In January 1870, forces under Maj. Eugene Baker attacked the peaceful camp of the Blackfeet chief Heavy Runner, killing 173 people, mostly women and children."[5]

"The area of the land most sacred to the Blackfeet is the Sweet Grass Hills, which are located just south of the Canadian border in the central part of Montana. These are a group of buttes forested with balsam firs rising several thousand feet above the surrounding plains and which can be seen for a considerable distance. This was also Napi's favorite resting place in the mythology of the Blackfeet. Young Blackfeet went up into the Hills on their vision quests and, as their predecessors had

---

[5] Indian Nations of North America; Pg. 158-159, Para 4-6

done for several thousands of years, left inscriptions and petroglyphs on the surface of the tall sandstone cliffs. Many of the stories told by the Blackfeet take place there."[6]

"The last buffalo hunt was in 1882, south of the Sweet Grass Hills. The Blackfeet, until recently self-supporting, now often had no other recourse than to try to survive on the meager rations issued to them at the Indian Agency, which, in 1876, had been relocated to Badger Creek near present-day Browning, Montana. In spite of the resident Indian agent's imploring, the rations sent to them were far from sufficient. The weather was poor, and the crops the Indian tried to grow often failed. Over the hard winter of 1883-84, nearly 600 of the Piegans – one-quarter of the whole tribe – starved to death. The victims were buried in mass graves in what is still known as 'Ghost Ridge.'"[7]

Within the front matter of this book you'll notice the Treaty of Fort Laramie of 1855, or the Lame Bull Treaty (the Piegan chief, Lame Bull, was one of the first signers) has been included so you can get an idea of the involvement concerning many of the Plains tribes as well as the Blackfeet of Montana and their boundaries. The Blackfeet were given a very large portion of their own land or what could be considered North Central Montana today, surrounded by the Musselshell, Missouri and Yellowstone Rivers. "At the same time, the Blackfeet's land base was shrinking. In 1871, the U.S. government ceased its long-standing practice of making treaties with Indians as independent nations. In the place of treaty-making, often a long and convoluted process, the President now issued executive orders and the Congress passed laws. 'Agreements' were made with individual Indians that overrode previous treaties and circumvented Indian tribal decision-making processes. Blackfeet

---

[6] The Blackfeet, Native American Tribes; Pg. [iv], Para 1-2
[7] The Blackfeet, Native American Tribes; Pg. 25, Para 2

boundaries agreed upon in the 1855 treaty were cut back again and again. Some of the Blackfeet's best hunting lands were lost in 1874 when an Act of Congress established a reservation across northern Montana to be shared with the Gros Ventres and River Crows. The southern boundary of this new reservation was moved from the Sun River to the Marias River, opening up that whole region to white cattle ranchers. Editorials in the Montana newspapers continued during the 1870s and 80s to push for further reductions in the size of the reservation in the name of 'progress' and for opening up the land for settlers. In 1877, a huge swath of seventeen and a half million acres was taken by the U.S. Congress from the Montana Indians, including the Blackfeet, for the construction of the Northern Pacific Railroad. The next year, Congress passed a new Act that superseded the Act of 1874. Out of the reservation across northern Montana that had been shared by the Blackfeet as a common territory with the other Indian tribes, three separate reservations were created for what the tribes were told would now become their permanent homes. The Blackfeet were left with a reservation in northwestern Montana."[8] "But this was not the end of the story. Now whites looked greedily at the Rocky Mountain part of the Blackfeet reservation, because they thought it might contain minerals to exploit. In 1895, 800,000 acres were sold by compliant individuals among the Blackfeet for 1.5 million. In 1910, after no minerals were found there, this became the eastern half of the new Glacier National Park."[9]

"The Blackfeet Nation also known as the Blackfeet Tribe of the Blackfeet Indian Reservation is an Indian reservation and headquarters for the Siksikaitsitapi

---

[8] The Blackfeet, Native American Tribes; Pg. 26, Para 2
[9] The Blackfeet, Native American Tribes; Pg. 26, Para 3

people in the United States. Located in Montana, its members are composed primarily of the Piegan Blackfeet (*Ampskapi Piikani*) band of the larger ethnic group historically described as the Blackfoot Confederacy. It is located east of Glacier National Park and borders the Canadian province of Alberta. Cut Bank Creek and Birch Creek form part of its eastern and southern borders. The reservation contains 3,000 square miles (7,800 km^2), twice the size of the national park and larger than the state of Delaware. It is located in parts of Glacier and Pondera counties.

The reservation is also east of the Lewis and Clark National Forest in Montana, which contains the Badger-Two Medicine area, sacred to the Blackfeet people. This sacred part of the Rocky Mountain Front was excluded from Blackfeet lands in a Treaty of 1896 but they reserved access, hunting and fishing rights. Since the early 1980s, when the Bureau of Land Management approved drilling rights leases without consultation with the tribe, the Blackfeet have worked to protect this sacred area, where they practiced their traditional religious rituals.

Geography

Elevations in the reservation range from a low of 3,400 feet (1,000 m) to a high of 9,066 feet (2,763 m) at Chief Mountain. Adjacent mountains include Ninaki Mountain and Papoose. The eastern part of the reservation is mostly open hills of grassland, while a narrow strip along the western edge is covered by forests of fir and spruce. Free-ranging cattle are present in several areas, sometimes including on roadways. Several waterways drain the area with the largest being the St. Mary River, Two Medicine River, Milk River, Birch Creek and Cut Bank Creek. There are 175 miles (282 km) of streams and eight major lakes on the reservation.

Demographics

The 2010 census reported a population of 10,405 living on the reservation lands. The population density is 3.47 people per square mile (1.34 people/km^2). The Blackfeet Nation has 16,500 registered members. The main community is Browning, which is the seat of tribal government. Other towns serve the tourist economy along the edge of the park: St. Mary and East Glacier Park Village, which has an Amtrak passenger station and the historic Glacier Park Lodge. Small communities include Babb, Kiowa, Blackfoot, Seville, Heart Butte, Starr School, and Glacier Homes. The nation celebrates North American Indian Days, an annual festival held on pow wow grounds, near the Museum of the Plains Indian in Browning. Adjacent to the reservation's eastern edge is the city of Cut Bank.

History

The Blackfeet are fairly recent occupiers of this area. Until 1600 CE, they resided in an area of the woodlands north and west of the Great Lakes. Pressure exerted by British traders at James Bay in present day Canada on the Algonquin-speaking tribes in the area drove the Blackfeet out onto the Northern Plains. They eventually acquired both fire arms and horses, and became a formidable example of the classic Plains Indian culture. They were a powerful force controlling an area that extended from current day Edmonton, Alberta Province nearly to Yellowstone Park, and from Glacier Park to the Black Hills of South Dakota. Their sacred history became centered in what is now known as the Badger-Two Medicine area, known as their 'Cathedral.'

In the late 19th century, Blackfeet territory was encroached on by European Americans and Canadians, and various branches of the people were forced to cede lands and ultimately move to smaller Indian reservations in the United States and reserves in Canada. Adjacent to their reservation, established by Treaty of 1896, are two federally controlled areas: the Lewis and Clark National Forest, set up in 1896, which contains the Badger-Two Medicine area, an area of 200 square miles (130,000-acres); and Glacier National Park, both part of the tribal nation's former territory.

The Badger-Two Medicine area is at the Rocky Mountain Front of the national forest. The Blackfeet call the Rocky Mountains the 'Backbone of the World'. Their names for peaks include Morning Star, Poia, Little Plume, Running Crane, Spotted Eagle, Kiyo, Scarface, Elkcalf Bullshoe, and Curly Bear.

The Rocky Mountain Front near Birch Creek The Badger-Two Medicine is 'covered by the Treaty of 1896, which gives Blackfeet tribal members the right to hunt and fish in any portion of the area in accordance with state law and cut wood for domestic use. Blackfeet treaty claims as well as spiritual and cultural uses of the Badger-Two Medicine are pre-existing rights... Blackfeet tribal members have used the Badger-Two Medicine and its waters for hundreds of years for vision quests and for other religious and cultural purposes.'

Culture

The tribe has an oral history of 10,000 years in this region. It recounts the sacred nature of their central place, the Badger-Two Medicine area, known as their site of creation and origin.

In 2002, the Department of Interior declared roughly two-thirds (almost 90,000 acres) of the Badger-Two Medicine area along the Rocky Mountain Front as eligible for listing as a Traditional Cultural District in the National Register of Historic Places. This was a recognition of its importance to the Blackfeet. They used an ethnographer to document their oral history of use and practices, and in 2014 used this information to negotiate with stakeholders over leases for drilling rights that had been made in the area."[10]

Piegan Blackfeet

"The **Piegan** (Blackfoot: *Piikáni*) are an Algonquian-speaking people from the North American Great Plains. They were the largest of three Blackfoot-speaking groups that made up the Blackfoot Confederacy; the Siksika and Kainai were the others. The Piegan dominated much of the northern Great Plains during the nineteenth century.

After their homelands were divided by the nations of Canada and the United States of America making boundaries between them, the Piegan people were forced to sign treaties with one of those two countries, settle in reservations on one side or the other of the border, and be enrolled in one of two government-like bodies sanctioned by North American nation-states. These two successor groups are the Blackfeet Nation, a federally recognized tribe in Montana, U.S., and the Piikani Nation, a recognized 'band' in Alberta, Canada.

Today many Piegan live with the Blackfeet Nation in northwestern Montana, with tribal headquarters in Browning. There were 32,234 Blackfeet recorded in the 1990 United States Census. In 2010 the US Census reported 105,304 persons who identified as Blackfeet ('alone' or 'in combination' with one or more races and/or tribes.)

---

[10] Blackfeet Nation; Wikipedia

Terminology

The tribal governments and the US government use the term 'Blackfeet', as in Blackfeet Nation, as used on their official tribe website. The term *Siksika*, derived from *Siksikáíkoan* (a Blackfoot person), may also be used as self-identification. In English, an individual may say, 'I am Blackfoot' or 'I am a member of the Blackfeet tribe.' 'Canadian Blackfoot people use the singular Blackfoot.'

Traditionally, Plains peoples were divided into 'bands': groups of families who migrated together for hunting and defence. The bands of the Piegan, as given by Grinnell, are: Ahahpitape, Ahkaiyikokakiniks, Kiyis, Sikutsipmaiks, Sikopoksimaiks, Tsiniksistsoyiks, Kutaiimiks, Ipoksimaiks, Silkokitsimiks, Nitawyiks, Apikaiviks, Miahwahpitsiks, Nitakoskitsipupiks, Nitikskiks, Inuksiks, Miawkinaiyiks, Esksinaitupiks, Inuksikahkopwaiks, Kahmitaiks, Kutaisotsiman, Nitotsiksisstaniks, Motwainaiks, Mokumiks, and Motahtosiks. Hayden gives also Susksoyiks."[11]

It is hoped that this work will help many find their ancestors along with a little encouragement to read about their own history. It isn't easy trying to be a detective looking into a case over 100 years old. But the answers can be found. Talk to your oldest relatives (parents, grandparents, great aunts and uncles, brothers, sisters, children). Ask questions and learn where they lived, what they did, who they were. Ask if they told stories about their lives, or their parents, or grandparents and what they did during their days?

This effort is dedicated to the people on every page and for every moment they lived to the best of their ability for themselves and those they loved.

---

[11] Piegan Blackfeet; Wikipedia

These censuses were transcribed from the National Archival Film Roll M595 Roll 4. Indian Census Rolls 1885-1940; Blackfeet Agency, 1897-1906.

Jeff Bowen
Gallipolis, Ohio
NativeStudy.com

Treaty of Fort Laramie of 1855 or the Lame Bull Treaty

(the South Piegan chief, Lame Bull, was one of the first signers)

No. 299

Treaty with the Blackfoot and Flathead at the Council Ground on the Upper Missouri near the mouth of the Judith River in the territory of Nebraska, October 17, 1855.

Treaty C. 24. Made & concluded between the United States and the Blackfeet and other Tribes of Indians, at the Council Ground, on the Upper Missouri River, October 17, 1855.

Franklin Pierce
President of the United States of America,
To all persons to whom these presents shall come
Greeting.

Whereas a treaty was made and concluded at the Council Ground on the Upper Missouri, near the mouth of the Judith River, in the Territory of Nebraska, on the seventeenth day of October, in the year one thousand eight hundred and fifty five, between A. Cumming and Isaac I. Stevens, Commissioners on the part of the United States, and the Blackfoot and other tribes of Indians, which treaty is in the words and figures following, to wit:

Articles of agreement and convention made and concluded at the Council Ground on the Upper Missouri, near the mouth of the Judith River, in the Territory of Nebraska, this seventeenth day of October, in the year One thousand eight hundred and fifty five, by and between A. Cumming and Isaac I. Stevens, Commissioners duly appointed and authorized, on the part of the United States, and the undersigned Chiefs, Head Men and Delegates of the following Nations and Tribes of Indians, who occupy, for purposes of hunting the territory on the Upper Missouri and Yellow Stone rivers, and who have permanent homes as follows: East of the Rocky Mountains the Blackfoot Nation, consisting of the Piegan, Blood, Blackfoot and Gros Ventre Tribes of Indians. West of the Rocky Mountains, the Flat Head Nation, consisting of the Flat Heads, Upper Pend d'Oreille and Kootenay Tribes of Indians, and the Nez Percé Tribe of Indians; the said Chiefs, Head Men and Delegates in behalf of and acting for said Nations and Tribes and being duly authorized thereto by them.

Article I. Peace, Friendship and Amity shall hereafter exist between the United States and the aforesaid Nations and Tribes of Indians parties to this Treaty, and the same shall be perpetual.

Article II. The aforesaid Nations and Tribes of Indians parties to this Treaty, do truly, jointly and severally covenant that peaceful relations shall likewise be maintained amongst themselves in future; and that they will abstain from all hostilities whatsoever against each other, and cultivate mutual good will and friendship. And the Nations and Tribes aforesaid do furthermore jointly and severally covenant that peaceful relations shall be maintained with and that they will abstain from all hostilities whatsoever, excepting in self defense, against the following named Nations and Tribes of Indians to wit: the Crows, Assinaboines, Crees, Snakes, Blackfeet, Sans Arcs, and Aunc pa pas Bands of Sioux, and all other neighboring Nations and Tribes of Indians.

Article III. The Blackfoot Nation consent and agree that all that portion of the country recognized and defined by the treaty of Laramie as Blackfoot Territory, lying within lines drawn from the Hell Gate or Medicine Rock Passes in the main Range of the Rocky Mountains, in an Easterly direction to the nearest source of the Musselshell River, thence to the mouth of Twenty five yard Creek, thence up the Yellow Stone River to its Northern source, and thence along the main Range of the Rocky Mountains in a Northerly direction to the point of beginning, shall be a common hunting ground for ninety nine years, where all the Nations, Tribes and Bands of Indians, parties to this treaty, may enjoy equal and uninterrupted privileges of hunting, fishing and gathering fruit, grazing animals, curing meat and dressing Robes. They further agree that they will not establish villages, or in any other way exercise exclusive rights within ten miles of the Northern line of the common Hunting Grounds, and that the parties to this treaty may hunt on said Northern boundary line and within ten miles thereof—

Provided that the Western Indians, parties to this treaty, may hunt on the trail leading down the Muscle Shell to the Yellow Stone, the Muscle Shell River being the boundary separating the Blackfoot from the Crow Territory.

And provided that no Nation, Band or Tribe of Indians, parties to this treaty, nor any other Indians, shall be permitted to establish permanent settlements or in any other way exercise during the period above mentioned, exclusive rights or privileges within the limits of the above described Hunting Grounds.

And provided further, that the rights of the Eastern Indians, or whites, or a part of the Common Hunting Grounds, derived from occupancy and possession, shall not be affected by this Article except so far as such rights may be determined by the Treaty of Laramie.

Article IV. The parties to this Treaty agree and consent that the tract of country lying within lines drawn from the Hell Gate or Medicine Rock Pass in an Easterly direction to the nearest source of the Muscle Shell River, thence down said River to its mouth, thence down the channel of the Missouri River to the mouth of Milk River, thence due North to the forty ninth Parallel, thence due West on said Parallel to the Main Range of the Rocky mountains, and thence Southerly along said Range to the place of beginning, shall be the Territory of the Blackfoot Nation, on which no other Nation shall remain cultivate exclusive control excepting as may be otherwise provided in this Treaty — Subject however to the provisions of the 3d Article of this Treaty, giving the right to hunt and prohibiting the establishment of permanent villages and the exercise of any exclusive rights within One mile of the Southern line of the Common Hunting Grounds; draws from the nearest source of the Musseli Shell River to the Medicine Rock Passes, for the period of ninety nine years.

Provided also, that the Assiniboins shall have the right of hunting, in common with the Blackfeet in the Country lying between the aforesaid Eastern boundary line running from the mouth of Milk River to the 49th Parallel, and a line drawn from the left bank of the Missouri River opposite the Round Butte North to the 49th Parallel.

Article V   The parties to this Treaty residing West of the main Range of the Rocky mountains agree and covenant that they will not enter the Common Hunting Ground, nor any part of the Blackfoot territory, or return hence, by any Pass in the main Range of the Rocky mountains, to the North of the Hell Gate or Medicine Rock Passes. And they further agree that they will not hunt or otherwise destroy the game when visiting the Blackfoot territory for trade or social intercourse.

Article VI   The aforesaid Nations and Tribes of Indians parties to this Treaty, agree and covenant to remain within their own respective Countries, except when going to or from, or whilst hunting upon the Common Hunting Grounds, or when visiting each other for the purpose of trade or social intercourse.

Article VII   The aforesaid Nations and Tribes of Indians agree that citizens of the United States may live in and to pass unmolested through the countries respectively occupied and claimed by them.   And the United States is hereby bound to protect said Indians against depredations and other unlawful acts which white men residing in or passing through their country may commit. ——

Article VIII   For the purpose of establishing travelling thoroughfares through their country, and the better to enable the President to execute the provisions of this Treaty, the aforesaid nations do hereby consent and agree, that the United States may, within the countries respectively occupied and claimed by them, construct roads of every description; establish lines of Telegraph and Military Posts; use materials of every description found in the Indian Country; build houses for Agencies, Missions, schools, ferries, shops, mills, trading and for any other purpose for which they may be required; and permanently occupy as much land as may be necessary for the various purposes above enumerated, including the use of wood for fuel, and land for grazing; and that the navigation of all Lakes and Rivers shall be forever free to citizens of the United States.

Article IX   In consideration of the foregoing agreements, stipulations and services, and in consideration of their faithful observance, the United States agree to expend annually for the Piegan, Blood, Blackfoot and Gros Ventres Tribes of Indians, constituting the Blackfoot Nation, in addition to the goods and provisions distributed at the time of signing this Treaty, Twenty Thousand dollars annually for ten years, to be expended in such useful goods and provisions and other articles as the President at his discretion may from time to time determine; and the Superintendent or other proper officer shall each year inform the President of the wishes of the Indians in relation thereto. Provided however that if in the judgment of the President and Senate this amount be deemed insufficient, it may be increased not to exceed the sum of thirty five thousand dollars per year.

Article X.   The United States further agree to expend annually for the benefit of the aforesaid tribes of the Blackfoot Nation, a sum not exceeding Fifteen thousand dollars annually for ten years, in establishing and instructing them in agricultural and mechanical pursuits, and in educating their children, and in any other respect promoting their civilization and Christianization. Provided however, that to accomplish the objects of this Article, the President may, at his discretion apply any or all the annuities provided for in this treaty, And provided also that the President may, at his discretion, determine in what proportions the said annuities shall be divided among the several Tribes.

Article XI.   The aforesaid Tribes acknowledge their dependence on the Government of the United States, and promise to be friendly with all citizens thereof, and to commit no depredations or other violence upon such citizens. And should any one or more violate this pledge, and the fact be proved to the satisfaction of the President— the property taken shall be returned, or in default thereof— or if injured or destroyed, compensation may be made by the Government out of the annuities. The aforesaid Tribes are hereby bound to deliver such offenders to the proper authorities for trial and punishment, or are held responsible, in their tribal capacity, to make reparation for depredations so committed.

Nor will they make war upon any other Tribes except in self defense, but will submit all matters of difference between themselves and other Indians to the Government of the United States, through its Agent, for adjustment, and will abide thereby. And if any of the said Indians, parties to this treaty, commit depredations on any other Indians within the jurisdiction of the United States, the same rule shall prevail as that provided in this article in cases of depredations against citizens. And the said Indians agree not to shelter or conceal offenders against the laws of the United States, but to deliver them up to the authorities for trial.

Article XII.   It is agreed and understood by all Parties to this Treaty, that if any Nation or Tribe of Indians aforesaid, shall violate any of the agreements, obligations or stipulations herein contained, the United States may withhold, for such length of time as the President and Congress may determine, any proportion or all of the annuities agreed to be paid to said Nation or Tribe, under the IXth and Xth articles of this Treaty.

Article XIII.   The Nations and Tribes of Indians, parties to this treaty, desire to exclude from their country the use of ardent spirits or other intoxicating liquors, and to prevent their people from drinking the same—

Therefore it is provided that any Indian belonging to said tribes who is guilty of bringing such liquors into the Indian Country, or who drinks liquor, may have his or her proportion of the annuities withheld from him or her for such time as the President may determine.

Article XIV. The aforesaid Nations and Tribes of Indians West of the Rocky Mountains, parties to this Treaty, do agree, in consideration of the provisions already made for them in existing Treaties, to accept the guaranties of the peaceful occupation of their Hunting Grounds East of the Rocky Mountains, and of remuneration for depredations made by the other Indians, pledged to be secured to them in this Treaty out of the annuities of said Indies, in full compensation for the concessions which they, in common with the said Tribes have made in this Treaty.

The Indians East of the Mountains, parties to this Treaty, likewise recognize and accept the guaranties of this Treaty in full compensation for the injuries or depredations which have been or may be committed by the aforesaid Indies West of the Rocky Mountains.

Article XV. The annuities of the aforesaid Tribes shall not be taken to pay the debts of individuals.

Article XVI. This Treaty shall be obligatory upon the aforesaid Nations and Tribes of Indians parties hereto from the date hereof, and upon the United States as soon as the same shall be ratified by the President and Senate.

In testimony whereof the said A. Cumming and Isaac I. Stevens Commissioners on the part of the United States, and the undersigned Chiefs, Head Men and Delegates of the aforesaid Nations and Tribes of Indians, parties to this Treaty, have hereunto set their hands and seals at the place and on the day and year hereinbefore written.

Executed in presence of

James Doty
Secretary

Geo. J. Burghton f.l.
R. H. Lansdale, US p. Indpt
Thomas Adams
Special agt. Flat Head Nation
E. W. Sensall Ind. agt.
Flathead Nation
[illegible]
Del Conge the Bay Paris
Blackfoot Interpreters
James Croft
A. Culbertson
[illegible]
Blas Flow—Interpreter
Benj. [illegible] Morin
Witness James Doty
[illegible]
Nell. Broix Autopolis
W Craig
[illegible]
Witness James Doty
[illegible] Crow Chief
[illegible]
Witness James Doty
A. J. Hoecken S.J.
James [illegible]
[illegible]
SS Fulton
Charles [illegible]
Chist. P. Higgins
A. H. Robie
[illegible]

A. Cumming [seal]

Isaac I. Stevens [seal]

——— Piegans ———

Nee-ti-nee—the only Chief now called the Lame Bull
His X mark [seal]
Mountain Chief His X mark [seal]
Low Horn His X mark [seal]
Little Gray Head His X mark [seal]
Little Dog His X mark [seal]
Big Snake His X mark [seal]
The Skunk His X mark [seal]
The Bad Head His X mark [seal]
Kitch-epenistah His X mark [seal]
Middle Sitter His X mark [seal]

——— Bloods ———

Onis-tay-say-nah-que-im His X mark [seal]
The father of all children His X mark [seal]
The Bull's Back Fat His X mark [seal]
Heavy Shield His X mark [seal]
Nah-ton-outah His X mark [seal]
The Calf Shirt His X mark [seal]

——— Gros Ventres ———

Bear's Shirt His X mark [seal]
Little Soldier His X mark [seal]
Star Robe His X mark [seal]
Sitting Squaw His X mark [seal]
Weasel Horse His X mark [seal]
The Rider His X mark [seal]
Eagle Chief His X mark [seal]
Heap of Bears His X mark [seal]

xxix

Blackfeet —
The Three Bulls	his	X mark	18
His Old Kotonnie	do	X do	18
Ser-ah-gue	do	X do	18
Chief Rabbit Runner	do	X do	18

Nez Percé —
Spotted Eagle	his	X mark	18
Looking Glass	do	X do	18
The Three Feathers	do	X do	18
Eagle from the Light	do	X do	18
The Lone Bird	do	X do	18
Yo show no sens	do	X do	18
Jason	do	X do	18
Hah-nah-to-ne-kunk	do	X do	18
White Bird	do	X do	18
Striking man	do	X do	18
Josse	do	X do	18
Flinty Blain	do	X do	18

Flathead Nation —
Victor	his	X mark	18
Alexander	do	X do	18
Moses	do	X do	18
Big Canoe	do	X do	18
Ambrose	do	X do	18
Kootla cha	do	X do	18
Michelle	do	X do	18
Francois	do	X do	18
Vincent	do	X do	18
Andrew	do	X do	18
Adolphe	do	X do	18
Thunder	do	X do	18

Pigan	Running Rabbit	his	X mark	18
do	Chief Bear	do	X do	18
do	The Little White Buffalo	do	X do	18
do	The Big Straw	do	X do	18
Flathead	Bear Track	do	X do	18
do	Little Michelle	do	X do	18
do	Pah-his-ah	do	X do	18
Nez P	The Feather	do	X do	18
do	The White Eagle	do	X do	18

And whereas the said treaty having been submitted to the Senate of the United States for its constitutional action thereon, the Senate did, on the 15th day of April, eighteen hundred and fifty six, advise and consent to the ratification of the same, by a Resolution in the words and figures following, to wit:

In Executive Session
Senate of the United States
April 15th 1856.

Resolved (two thirds of the Senators present concurring) that the Senate advise and consent to the ratification of the Articles of Agreement and Convention made and concluded between the United States and the Blackfeet, and other Tribes of Indians, at the Council Ground on the Upper Missouri River, October Seventeenth, Eighteen Hundred and fifty five.

Attest,

Asbury Dickins
Secretary

Now, Therefore, be it known, that I, Franklin Pierce, President of the United States of America, do, in pursuance of the advice and consent of the Senate as expressed in their Resolution of the fifteenth day of April, one thousand eight hundred and fifty six, accept, ratify and confirm the said treaty.

In testimony whereof I have caused the seal of the United States to be hereto affixed; having signed the same with my hand.

Done at the city of Washington, this twenty fifth day of April, A.D. one thousand eight hundred and fifty six, and of the Independence of the United States, the eightieth.

Franklin Pierce

By the President:

W. L. Marcy, Secretary of State

Miscellaneous Letters - April 1856.

Int. Dept
25 Apl

Department of the Interior,
Washington, April 22d 1856

Sir,

I transmit to you herewith, with the request that it be promulgated as early as possible, a treaty made on the 17" Oct" 1855, by A. Cumming and Isaac I. Stevens, Commissioners on the part of the United States and the Blackfeet and other tribes of Indians, on the Upper Missouri River, said treaty having been ratified by the Senate by Resolution of the 15th instant, a copy of which is herewith enclosed.

I have the honor to be,
Very respectfully,
Your Obt: Servant
RMcClelland
Secretary.

Hon. W. L. Marcy,
Secretary of State.

TREATY

BETWEEN

THE UNITED STATES

AND THE

BLACKFOOT AND OTHER TRIBES OF INDIANS.

OCTOBER 17, 1855.

FRANKLIN PIERCE,

PRESIDENT OF THE UNITED STATES OF AMERICA.

TO ALL PERSONS TO WHOM THESE PRESENTS SHALL COME, GREETING:

Whereas, a treaty was made and concluded at the council ground on the Upper Missouri, near the mouth of the Judith river, in the Territory of Nebraska, on the seventeenth day of October, in the year one thousand eight hundred and fifty-five, between A. Cumming and Isaac I. Stevens, commissioners on the part of the United States, and the Blackfoot and other tribes of Indians, which treaty is in the words and figures following, to wit:

Articles of agreement and convention made and concluded at the council ground, on the Upper Missouri, near the mouth of the Judith river, in the Territory of Nebraska, this seventeenth day of October, in the year one thousand eight hundred and fifty-five, by and between A. Cumming and Isaac I. Stevens, commissioners duly appointed and authorised, on the part of the United States, and the undersigned chiefs, headmen, and delegates of the following nations and tribes of Indians: who occupy, for the purpose of hunting, the territory on the Upper Missouri and Yellow Stone rivers, and who have permanent homes as follows: East of the Rocky mountains, the Blackfoot nation, consisting of the Piegan, Blood, Blackfoot, and Gros Ventres tribes of Indians; west of the Rocky mountains, The Flathead nation, consisting of the Flathead, Upper Pend d'Oreille, and Kootenay tribes of Indians, and the Nez Percé tribe of Indians; the said chiefs, headmen and delegates, in behalf of and acting for said nations and tribes, and being duly authorised thereto by them.

ARTICLE I.

Peace, friendship and amity shall hereafter exist between the United States and the aforesaid nations and tribes of Indians, parties to this treaty, and the same shall be perpetual.

ARTICLE II.

The aforesaid nations and tribes of Indians parties to this treaty, do hereby jointly and severally covenant that peaceful relations shall likewise be maintained among themselves in future; and that they will abstain from all hostilities whatsoever against each other, and cultivate mutual good will and friendship. And the nations and tribes aforesaid do furthermore jointly and severally covenant, that peaceful relations shall be maintained with and that they will abstain from all hostilities whatsoever, excepting in self-defence, against the following named nations and tribes of Indians, to wit: the Crows, Assineboins, Crees,

in the main range of the Rocky mountains to the north of the Hell Gate or Medicine Rock passes. And they further agree that they will not hunt or otherwise disturb the game, when visiting the Blackfoot territory for trade or social intercourse.

ARTICLE VI.

The aforesaid nations and tribes of Indians, parties to this treaty, agree and consent to remain within their own respective countries, except when going to or from, or whilst hunting upon, the "common hunting ground," or when visiting each other for the purpose of trade or social intercourse.

ARTICLE VII.

The aforesaid nations and tribes of Indians agree that citizens of the United States may live in and pass unmolested through the countries respectively occupied and claimed by them. And the United States is hereby bound to protect said Indians against depredations and other unlawful acts which white men residing in or passing through their country may commit.

ARTICLE VIII.

For the purpose of establishing travelling thoroughfares through their country, and the better to enable the President to execute the provisions of this treaty, the aforesaid nations and tribes do hereby consent and agree, that the United States may, within the countries respectively occupied and claimed by them, construct roads of every description; establish lines of telegraph and military posts; use materials of every description found in the Indian country; build houses for agencies, missions, schools, farms, shops, mills, stations, and for any other purpose for which they may be required, and permanently occupy as much land as may be necessary for the various purposes above enumerated, including the use of wood for fuel and land for grazing, and that the navigation of all lakes and streams shall be forever free to citizens of the United States.

ARTICLE IX.

In consideration of the foregoing agreements, stipulations, and cessions, and on condition of their faithful observance, the United States agree to expend, annually, for the Piegan, Blood, Blackfoot, and Gros Ventres tribes of Indians, constituting the Blackfoot nation, in addition to the goods and provisions distributed at the time of signing this treaty, twenty thousand dollars, annually, for ten years, to be expended in such useful goods and provisions, and other articles, as the President, at his discretion, may, from time to time, determine; and the superintendent, or other proper officer, shall each year inform the President of the wishes of the Indians in relation thereto: Provided, however, That it, in the judgment of the President and Senate, this amount be deemed insufficient, it may be increased not to exceed the sum of thirty-five thousand dollars per year.

ARTICLE X.

The United States further agree to expend annually, for the benefit of the aforesaid tribes of the Blackfoot nation, a sum not exceeding fifteen thousand dollars annually, for ten years, in establishing and instructing them in agricultural and mechanical pursuits, and in educating their children, and in any other respect promoting their civilization and christianization: Provided, however, That, to accomplish the objects of this article, the President may, at his discretion, apply any or all the annuities provided for in this treaty: And provided, also, That the President may, at his discretion, determine in what proportions the said annuities shall be divided among the several tribes.

ARTICLE XI.

The aforesaid tribes acknowledge their dependence on the government of the United States, and promise to be friendly with all citizens thereof, and to commit no depredations or other violence upon such citizens. And should any one or more violate this pledge, and the fact be proved to the satisfaction of the President, the property taken shall be returned, or, in default thereof, or if injured or destroyed, compensation may be made by the government out of the annuities. The aforesaid tribes are hereby bound to deliver such offenders to the proper authorities for trial and punishment, and are held responsible in their tribal capacity, to make reparation for depredations so committed.

Nor will they make war upon any other tribes, except in self defence, but will submit all matters of difference between themselves and other Indians to the government of the United States, through its agent, for adjustment, and will abide thereby. And if any of the said Indians, parties to this treaty, commit depredations on any other Indians within the jurisdiction of the United States, the same rule shall prevail as that prescribed in this article in case of depredations against citizens. And the said tribes agree not to shelter or conceal offenders against the laws of the United States, but to deliver them up to the authorities for trial.

ARTICLE XII.

It is agreed and understood, by and between the parties to this treaty, that if any nation or tribe of Indians aforesaid, shall violate any of the agreements, obligations, or stipulations, herein contained, the United States may withhold, for such length of time as the President and Congress may determine, any portion or all of the annuities agreed to be paid to said nation or tribe under the ninth and tenth articles of this treaty.

ARTICLE XIII.

The nations and tribes of Indians, parties to this treaty, desire to exclude from their country the use of ardent spirits or other intoxicating liquor, and to prevent their people from drinking the same. Therefore it is provided, that any Indian belonging to said tribes who is guilty of bringing such liquor into the Indian country, or who drinks liquor, may have his or her proportion of the annuities withheld from him or her, for such time as the President may determine.

ARTICLE XIV.

The aforesaid nations and tribes of Indians, west of the Rocky mountains, parties to this treaty, do agree, in consideration of the provisions already made for them in existing treaties, to accept the guarantees of the peaceful occupation of their hunting grounds, and of the Rocky mountains, and of remuneration for depredations made by the other tribes, pledged to be secured to them, in this treaty out of the annuities of said tribes, in full compensation for the concessions which they, in common with the said tribes, have made in this treaty.

The Indians east of the mountains, parties to this treaty, likewise recognize and accept the guarantees of this treaty, in full compensation for the injuries or depredations which have been, or may be committed by the aforesaid tribes, west of the Rocky mountains.

ARTICLE XV.

The annuities of the aforesaid tribes shall not be taken to pay the debts of individuals.

ARTICLE XVI.

This treaty shall be obligatory upon the aforesaid nations and tribes of Indians, parties hereto, from the date hereof, and upon the United States as soon as the same shall be ratified by the President and Senate.

In testimony whereof the said A. Cumming and Isaac I. Stevens, commissioners on the part of the United States, and the undersigned chiefs, headmen, and delegates of the aforesaid nations and tribes of Indians, parties to this treaty, have hereunto set their hands and seals at the place and on the day and year hereinbefore written.

                         A. CUMMING. [L. S.]
                         ISAAC I. STEVENS. [L. S.]

Piegans.

Nee-ti-nee, or "the only chief," now called the Lame Bull	his x mark	[L. S.]
Mountain Chief,	his x mark.	[L. S.]
Low Horn,	his x mark.	[L. S.]
Little Grey Head,	his x mark.	[L. S.]
Little Dog,	his x mark.	[L. S.]
Big Snake,	his x mark.	[L. S.]
The Skunk,	his x mark.	[L. S.]
The Bad Head,	his x mark.	[L. S.]
Kitch-eepone-istah,	his x mark.	[L. S.]
Middle Sitter,	his x mark.	[L. S.]

Bloods.

Onis-tay-say-nah-que-im,	his x mark.	[L. S.]
The Father of all Children,	his x mark.	[L. S.]
The Bull's Back Fat,	his x mark.	[L. S.]
Heavy Shield,	his x mark.	[L. S.]
Nah-toos-onistah,	his x mark.	[L. S.]
The Calf Shirt,	his x mark.	[L. S.]

Gros Ventres.

Bear's Shirt,	his x mark.	[L. S.]
Little Soldier,	his x mark.	[L. S.]
Star Robe,	his x mark.	[L. S.]
Sitting Squaw,	his x mark.	[L. S.]
Weasel Horse,	his x mark.	[L. S.]
The Rider,	his x mark.	[L. S.]
Eagle Chief,	his x mark.	[L. S.]
Heap of Bears,	his x mark.	[L. S.]

Blackfeet.

The Three Bulls,	his x mark.	[L. S.]
The Old Kootonais,	his x mark.	[L. S.]
Pow-ah-que,	his x mark.	[L. S.]
Chief Rabbit Runner,	his x mark.	[L. S.]

Nez Percés.

Spotted Eagle,	his x mark.	[L. S.]
Looking Glass,	his x mark.	[L. S.]

8

The Three Feathers,	his x mark.	[L. S.]
Eagle from the Light,	his x mark.	[L. S.]
The Lone Bird,	his x mark.	[L. S.]
Ipshon-nee-wus,	his x mark.	[L. S.]
Jason,	his x mark.	[L. S.]
Wat-ti-wat-ti-wa-hinck,	his x mark.	[L. S.]
White Bird,	his x mark.	[L. S.]
Stabbing Man,	his x mark.	[L. S.]
Joon,	his x mark.	[L. S.]
Plenty Bears,	his x mark.	[L. S.]

Flathead Nation.

Victor,	his x mark.	[L. S.]
Alexander,	his x mark.	[L. S.]
Moose,	his x mark.	[L. S.]
Big Canoe,	his x mark.	[L. S.]
Ambrose,	his x mark.	[L. S.]
Konfle-rha,	his x mark.	[L. S.]
Michelle,	his x mark.	[L. S.]
Francis,	his x mark.	[L. S.]
Vincent,	his x mark.	[L. S.]
Andrew,	his x mark.	[L. S.]
Adolphe,	his x mark.	[L. S.]
Thunder,	his x mark.	[L. S.]

Piegans.

Running Rabbit,	his x mark.	[L. S.]
Chief Bear,	his x mark.	[L. S.]
The Little White Buffalo,	his x mark.	[L. S.]
The Big Straw,	his x mark.	[L. S.]

Flathead.

Bear Track,	his x mark.	[L. S.]
Little Michelle,	his x mark.	[L. S.]
Palchinah,	his x mark.	[L. S.]

Bloods.

The Feather,	his x mark.	[L. S.]
The White Eagle,	his x mark.	[L. S.]

Executed in presence of—

    JAMES DOTY, *Secretary.*
    ALFRED J. VAUGHAN, Jr.
    E. AM. HATCH, *Agent for Blackfeet.*
    THOMAS ADAMS, *Special Agent Flathead Nation.*
    R. H. LANSDALE, *Indian Agent Flathead Nation.*
    W. H. TAPPAN, *Sub-Agent for the Nez Percés.*

JAMES BIRD,
A. CULBERTSON, } Blackfeet Interpreters.
BENJ. DEROCHE,
BENJ. KIZER, his x mark,
  Witness, JAMES DOTY. } Flat Head Interpreters.
GUSTAVUS SOHON,
W. CRAIG,
DELAWARE JIM, his x mark, } Nez Percé Interpreters.
  Witness, JAMES DOTY,
A CREE CHIEF, (broken arm,) his mark,
  Witness, JAMES DOTY,
A. J. HOECKEN.
JAMES CROKE.
E. S. WILSON.
A. C. JACKSON.
CHARLES SCHUCETTE, his x mark.
CHIEF, P. HIGGINS.
A. H. ROBIE.
S. S. FORD, Jr.

And whereas, the said treaty having been submitted to the Senate of the United States for its constitutional action thereon, the Senate did, on the fifteenth day of April, eighteen hundred and fifty-six, advise and consent to the ratification of the same, by a resolution in the words and figures following, to wit:

IN EXECUTIVE SESSION,

SENATE OF THE UNITED STATES, *April 15, 1856.*

Resolved, (two thirds of the Senators present concurring,) That the Senate advise and consent to the ratification of the articles of agreement and convention made and concluded between the United States and the Blackfeet and other tribes of Indians, at the council ground on the Upper Missouri river, October seventeenth, eighteen hundred and fifty-five.

Attest: ASBURY DICKINS, *Secretary.*

Now, therefore, be it known, that I, Franklin Pierce, President of the United States of America, do, in pursuance of the advice and consent of the Senate as expressed in their resolution of the fifteenth day of April, one thousand eight hundred and fifty-six, accept, ratify, and confirm the said treaty.

In testimony whereof, I have caused the seal of the United States to be hereto affixed, having signed the same with my hand.

Done at the city of Washington, this twenty-fifth day of April, A. D. one thousand eight hundred and fifty-six, and of the Independence of the United States the eightieth.

[L. S.]

FRANKLIN PIERCE.

By the President:

W. L. MARCY, *Secretary of State.*

Census of the Blackfeet,

Montana, 1897

| 39876 | **OFFICE OF**
Indian Affairs,
Rec. SEP. 27 | **1897** |

Geo. B. McLaughlin
Blackfeet
Agency

Census of the -Piegan- Indians of Blackfeet Agency, Montana taken by Geo. B McLaughlin United States Indian Agent 1897

No.	English Name	Sex	Relation	Age
1.	Bear Chiefs Window No 2	F	----	31
2.	Maggie Bear Chief	F	Daughter	7
3.	Susie Bear Chief	F	Daughter	2
4.	Bear Chief Widow No 1	F	----	49
5.	Bead Woman	F	Mother	45
6.	Joseph Cayton	M	Son	21
7.	Isabella Cayton	F	Daughter	5
8.	Mary J. White	F	Mother	24
9.	Cora White	F	Daughter	4
10.	Lorenza White	M	Son	3
11.	Melvina White	F	Daughter	1
12.	David Riply	M	Brother	21
13.	Minnie Riply	F	Sister	16
14.	Big Snake	F	----	41
15.	Ellen Edwards	F	Mother	32
16.	Wm. Edwards	M	Son	8
17.	Thos. Edwards	M	Son	6
18.	Fanny Edwards	F	Daughter	4
19.	Elizabeth Edwards	F	Daughter	2
20.	John Edwards	M	Son	1
21.	Eagle Ribs	M	Father	43
23.	Susie Eagle Ribs	F	Daughter	3
24.	Cecil Eagle Ribs	F	Daughter	1
25.	Louie Trombly	M	Father	27
26.	Maggie Trombly	F	Wife	25
27.	Isaac Trombly	M	Son	2
28.	(Infant)	M	Son	
29.	Mad Plume	M	Father	44
30.	Kills In Night	F	Wife	29
31.	John Mad Plume	M	Son	12
32.	Geo. Mad Plume	M	Son	4
33.	Mad Plume No 2	F	Mother	75
34.	Mack M. Plume	M	Son	2
35.	John M. Plume	M	Son	1

Census of the -Piegan- Indians of Blackfeet Agency, Montana taken by Geo. B McLaughlin United States Indian Agent 1897

No.	English Name	Sex	Relation	Age
36.	Julia M. Plume	F	Daughter	8
37.	Annie Robinson	F	Mother	34
38.	Chas. Robinson	M	Son	9
39.	Jas. Robinson	M	Son	4
40.	Allen Robinson	M	Son	2
41.	Young Running Rabbit	M	Father	52
42.	Old Time Woman	F	Wife	31
43.	Strikes Good	F	Wife	50
44.	Julia R. Rabbitt	F	Daughter	10
45.	Mary R. Rabbitt	F	Daughter	5
46.	Kate R. Rabbitt	F	Daughter	6
47.	Alex Gardafree	M	Father	34
48.	Josephine Gardafree	F	Wife	20
49.	John Gardafree	M	Son	3
50.	(Infant)	M	Son	1
51.	Henry Heavy Gun	M	Husb'd	27
52.	Josephine H. Gun	F	Wife	16
53.	Thos. Two Stabs	M	Father	42
54.	Maggie Two Stabs	F	Wife	32
55.	Maggie 2 Stabs	F	Daughter	14
56.	Joe Two Stabs	M	Son	5
57.	Louie Two Stabs	M	Son	2
58.	Wild Gun	M	----	38
59.	Curley Bear	M	Father	46
60.	Minnie C. Bear	F	Wife	37
61.	Pays For Her Trouble	F	Wife	29
62.	Chas. C. Bear	M	Son	17
63.	Philip C. Bear	M	Son	4
64.	Willie C. Bear	M	Son	3
65.	Jennie C. Bear	F	Daughter	5
66.	Maggie C. Bear	F	Daughter	4
67.	Annie C. Bear	F	Daughter	1
68.	Spotted Eagle	M	Father	66

Census of the -Piegan- Indians of Blackfeet Agency, Montana taken by Geo. B McLaughlin United States Indian Agent 1897

No.	English Name	Sex	Relation	Age
69.	Going Back	F	Wife	48
70.	Two Guns S. Eagle	M	Son	19
71.	Jas. S. Eagle	M	Son	18
72.	Joe S. Eagle	M	Son	15
73.	John S. Eagle	M	Son	15
74.	Thos. Spotted Eagle	M	----	25
75.	Young Running Crane	M	Father	43
76.	Sun Woman	F	Wife	45
77.	John Running Crane	M	Son	11
78.	Lone Cut	F	----	80
79.	Poor Woman	F	----	75
80.	John Eagle Ribs	M	----	18
81.	Good Massacre	F	Mother	43
82.	Goes In Places	F	Daughter	3
83.	Bob Tail Horse	M	Father	46
84.	Old Time Woman	F	Wife	44
85.	John Bob Tail Horse	M	Son	19
86.	Joseph Bob Tail Horse	M	Son	10
87.	White Shirt	M	Son	23
88.	Takes Gun Both Sides	M	Father	30
89.	Strike Once	F	Wife	31
90.	Black Bird	M	Son	1
91.	Black Bull	M	Husb'd	30
92.	Jennie B. Bull	F	Wife	19
93.	Jas. Gambler	M	Husb'd	24
94.	Annie Gambler	F	Wife	20
95.	Louese Guardupin	F	Mother	52
96.	John Guardupin	M	Son	15
97.	Pete Guardupin	M	----	39
98.	War Bonnet	M	Father	32

Census of the -Piegan- Indians of Blackfeet Agency, Montana taken by Geo. B McLaughlin United States Indian Agent 1897

No.	English Name	Sex	Relation	Age
99.	Massacre Woman	F	Wife	25
100.	Jas. War Bonnet	M	Son	2
101.	Eagle Flag	M	Father	70
102.	Bounces Up	F	Wife	45
103.	Stella E. Flag	F	Daughter	14
104.	Annie E. Flag	F	Daughter	10
105.	Maggie Henault	F	Mother	45
106.	Stephen Henault	M	Son	20
107.	Nelson Henault	M	Son	18
108.	Moses Henault	M	Son	10
109.	Clara Henault	F	Daughter	7
110.	Mary Remsa	F	Mother	22
111.	Jesse Remsa	M	Son	2
112.	Michael Dayrider	M	Father	25
113.	Hellen Dayrider	F	Wife	22
114.	Oliver Dayrider	M	Son	2
115.	(Infant)	M	Son	1
116.	Geo. Four Horns	M	----	17
117.	Kills In Water	F	Mother	43
118.	Black Boy	M	Father	31
119.	Kills On Top	F	Mother	29
120.	Ruben Black Boy	M	Son	10
121.	Last Coyote	M	Father	45
122.	Every Body Looks At	F	Wife	37
123.	Fanny Coyote	F	Daughter	12
124.	Alice Coyote	F	Daughter	3
125.	Iron Eater	M	Father	42
126.	Long Time Rock	F	Wife	29
127.	Black Dress Woman	F	Wife	40
128.	Isabella Iron Eater	F	Daughter	8
129.	John Iron Eater	M	Son	2
130.	Susie Iron Eater	F	Daughter	9
131.	(Infant)	F	Daughter	1

Census of the -Piegan- Indians of Blackfeet Agency, Montana taken by Geo. B McLaughlin United States Indian Agent 1897

No.	English Name	Sex	Relation	Age
132.	Joe Calf Robe	M	Husb'd	22
133.	Emma Calf Robe	F	Wife	23
134.	Eagle Head	M	Father	58
135.	White Tail	F	Wife	45
136.	Straight Runner	M	Son	11
137.	Margaret E. Head	F	Daughter	7
138.	Bad Woman	F	Mother	50
139.	Albert Calf Robe	M	Son	16
140.	Calf Robe	F	Mother	61
141.	Richard Calf Robe	M	Son	18
142.	Lodge Pole Chief	M	Father	94
143.	Plume	F	Wife	55
144.	Ragged Man	M	Son	20
145.	Felix Marrorbones[sic]	M	Father	27
146.	Iron Woman	F	Wife	18
147.	Willie Marrowbones	M	Son	1
148.	After Buffalo	F	----	30
149.	New Crow	M	----	37
150.	Owl Chief	M	Father	42
151.	Mary O. Child	F	Wife	31
152.	Susie O. Child	F	Daughter	1
153.	John O. Child	M	Son	14
154.	Joe O. Child	M	Son	6
155.	Louie O. Child	M	Son	4
156.	Isabella O. Child	F	Daughter	10
157.	Annie O. Child	F	Daughter	3
158.	(Infant)	F	Daughter	1
159.	Crowning Owl Woman	F	----	66
160.	Under Otter	F	----	70
161.	Julia Rivis	F	Mother	39

Census of the -Piegan- Indians of Blackfeet Agency, Montana taken by Geo. B McLaughlin United States Indian Agent 1897

No.	English Name	Sex	Relation	Age
162.	August Rivis	M	Son	18
163.	Emet Rivis	M	Son	16
164.	Emma Rivis	F	Daughter	11
165.	Margaret Dechamp	F	----	55
166.	Young Bear Chief	M	Father	39
167.	Good Shield	F	Wife	36
168.	Howls In Water	F	Wife	31
169.	Issabella B. Chief	F	Daughter	19
170.	Edward B. Chief	M	Son	15
171.	John B. Chief	M	Son	7
172.	Geo. B. Chief	M	Son	2
173.	Maggie B. Chief	F	Daughter	10
174.	Mary B. Chief	F	Daughter	8
175.	Josephine B. Chief	F	Daughter	4
176.	Sabastian B. Chief	F	Daughter	2
177.	Big Plume	M	Father	65
178.	Catches On Top	F	Wife	41
179.	Jerry B. Plume	M	Son	20
180.	Comes Out of Brush	M	Son	7
181.	Louese H. Plume	F	Daughter	2
182.	Green Grass Bull	M	Father	35
183.	Medicine Tie	F	Wife	28
184.	Thos. G. Bull	M	Son	11
185.	Joseph G. Bull	M	Son	2
186.	Spotted Woman	F	Mother	57
187.	Many Guns	M	Father	35
188.	Mouse Woman	F	Wife	38
189.	Joe Many Guns	M	Son	5
190.	Thos. M. Guns	M	Son	2
191.	Blackfoot Woman	F	Mother	55
192.	John Blackfoot Woman	M	Son	16
193.	Flying Bear	M	Son	19
194.	Mary Blackfoot Woman	F	Daughter	3
195.	Susan Shultz	F	Mother	30

Census of the -Piegan- Indians of Blackfeet Agency, Montana taken by Geo. B McLaughlin United States Indian Agent 1897

No.	English Name	Sex	Relation	Age
196.	Hart Shultz	M	Son	13
197.	Louie Champin	M	Father	30
198.	Busy Woman	F	Wife	34
199.	George Champin	M	Son	6
200.	Peter Champin	M	Son	3
201.	Mary Champin	F	Daughter	1mo
202.	Chewing Back Bones	M	Father	30
203.	Jennie B. Bones	F	Daughter	6
204.	Issabella B. Bones	F	Daughter	8
205.	Maggie B. Bones	F	Daughter	3
206.	(Infant)	M	Son	4mo
207.	Goes in both Places	F	Mother	70
208.	Mary B. Bones	F	Wife	30
209.	Mountain Chief	M	Father	49
210.	Gun for Nothing	F	Wife	41
211.	Anthony M. Chief	M	Son	18
212.	John M. Chief	M	Son	14
213.	Thelsa M. Chief	F	Daughter	17
214.	Emma M. Chief	F	Daughter	2
215.	Crow Eyes	M	Father	36
216.	Running Rattler	F	Wife	23
217.	Takes Gun	M	Son	2
218.	Minnie Crawford	F	Mother	36
219.	Ellen Crawford	F	Daughter	3
220.	Joseph Crawford	M	Son	5mo
221.	Double Runner	M	Father	50
222.	Long Time Woman	F	Wife	40
223.	Edgar Double Runner	M	Son	20
224.	Edward D. Runner	M	Son	19
225.	Paul D. Runner	M	Son	5
226.	Louese Clark	F	Mother	28
227.	Jas. Clark	M	Son	13
228.	Geo. Clark	M	Son	11
229.	Robert Clark	M	Son	8

Census of the -Piegan- Indians of Blackfeet Agency, Montana taken by Geo. B McLaughlin United States Indian Agent 1897

No.	English Name	Sex	Relation	Age
230.	Old Chief	M	Father	46
231.	Morning Woman	F	Wife	38
232.	John Old Chief	M	Son	13
233.	Daniel O. Chief	M	Son	4
234.	Jas. O. Chief	M	Son	2
235.	Mary O. Chief	F	Daughter	5
236.	Calf Boss Ribs	M	Father	56
237.	Long Time Woman	F	Wife	40
238.	Iron Woman	F	Wife	24
239.	Joe Boss Woman	M	Son	2
240.	Minnie Boss Ribs	F	Daughter	4
241.	Barney Calf Ribs	M	----	24
242.	Tail Feathers Coming	M	Father	48
243.	Snake Woman	F	Wife	29
244.	Lots Massacree	F	Wife	70
245.	Cecil Feathers Coming	F	Daughter	9
246.	Susie Feathers Coming	F	Daughter	2
247.	Mary Feathers Coming	F	Daughter	5
248.	Paul	M	----	5
249.	Able Skunk Cap	M	Single	23
250.	Last Strike	F	Mother	50
251.	Young to go In	F	----	75
252.	Flat Tail	M	Father	46
253.	Medicine Pipe Woman	F	Wife	38
254.	John F. Tail	M	Son	5
255.	Jas. F. Tail	M	Son	1
256.	Sofa F. Tail	F	Daughter	4
257.	Takes Gun At Night	M	Single	24
258.	Strikes Edge Water	F	Mother	70
259.	Comes In Night	M	Father	43
260.	Elk Robe	F	Wife	30
261.	Double Rush	F	Wife	21

Census of the -Piegan- Indians of Blackfeet Agency, Montana taken by Geo. B McLaughlin United States Indian Agent 1897

No.	English Name	Sex	Relation	Age
262.	Fell Not Petrified	F	Daughter	4
263.	Pretty Woman	F	Daughter	3
264.	Chicken Shoe	M	Father	23
265.	Medicine Star	F	Wife	30
266.	Frank C. Shoe	M	Son	11
267.	Joseph C. Shoe	M	Son	4
268.	Mary C. Shoe	F	Daughter	1
269.	Drags Hir[sic] Robe	M	Father	35
270.	Sarsee Woman	F	Wife	42
271.	Susie D. Robe	F	Daughter	4
272.	Drags His Robe	M	Son	17
273.	Cold Feet	M	Father	49
274.	Dry Goods Woman	F	Wife	46
275.	Ugly Girl	F	Daughter	4
276.	(Infant)	M	Son	1mo
277.	Goes In All Lodges	F	----	6
278.	Mittens	M	Father	27
279.	Susie Strikes Close	F	Wife	22
280.	Jas. Mittens	M	Son	2
281.	John Mittens	M	Son	6mo
282.	Sophia Mittens	F	Daughter	4
283.	Chas. No Coat	M	Single	20
284.	Fell No Snake	F	Daughter	7
285.	Long Time Bird	F	Mother	31
286.	Bear Leggins	M	Father	54
287.	Big Woman	F	Wife	44
288.	Rushing Home	F	Wife	39
289.	Rachel B. Leggins	F	Daughter	12
290.	Mary B. Leggins	F	Daughter	10
291.	First Owl	M	Son	4
292.	Pete Cadotte	M	Father	26
293.	Lucy Cadotte	F	Wife	19
294.	Rhoda Cadotte	F	Daughter	1

Census of the -Piegan- Indians of Blackfeet Agency, Montana taken by Geo. B McLaughlin United States Indian Agent 1897

No.	English Name	Sex	Relation	Age
295.	Running Owl	M	Father	35
296.	Kills Two	F	Wife	39
297.	Agnes R. Owl	F	Daughter	13
298.	Susie R. Owl	F	Daughter	10
299.	Short Woman	F	Daughter	6
300.	Kills Close	F	----	80
301.	Arrow Maker	M	Father	35
302.	Takes Gun In The Morning	F	Wife	37
303.	Strikes Down	F	Daughter	3
304.	(Infant)	M	Son	4mo
305.	Annie Walley	F	----	12
306.	Pete Champin	M	Father	29
307.	Susie Champin	F	Wife	26
308.	George Champin	M	Son	5
309.	Maggie Champin	F	Daughter	3
310.	Annie Champin	F	Daughter	2mo
311.	Good Strike	F	----	90
312.	Frank Ville	M	Father	28
313.	Annie Ville	F	Wife	30
314.	John Ville	M	Son	2
315.	Day Rider	M	Father	25
316.	Crawling Away	F	Wife	30
317.	Joe Day Rider	M	Son	1
318.	Josephine D. Rider	F	Daughter	3
319.	Catches Edge Water	F	----	80
320.	White Man	M	Father	58
321.	Many Petrified	F	Wife	48
322.	Many Massacre	F	Wife	32
323.	Sweet Grass Woman	F	Wife	28
324.	Peter White Man	M	Son	15
325.	John White Man	M	Son	16
326.	George White Man	M	Son	1

Census of the -Piegan- Indians of Blackfeet Agency, Montana taken by Geo. B McLaughlin United States Indian Agent 1897

No.	English Name	Sex	Relation	Age
327.	Adam White Man	M	Father	22
328.	Annie White Man	F	Wife	20
329.	Duck Head	M	Father	31
330.	Fellow Horse Rider	F	Wife	25
331.	Peter Duck Head	M	Son	7
332.	Josephine D. Head	F	Daughter	9
333.	Mary D. Head	F	Daughter	1
334.	Bull Shoe	M	Father	49
335.	Small Woman	F	Wife	44
336.	Dirty Face	F	Wife	34
337.	Joseph Bull Shoe	M	Son	18
338.	Claud B. Shoe	M	Son	15
339.	Big Woman	F	Wife	42
340.	Patrick Bull Shoe	M	Son	10
341.	Chas. Iron Breast	M	Father	20
342.	Nancy Iron Breast	F	Wife	27
343.	Night Rider	M	Single	29
344.	Thunder Woman	F	Mother	80
345.	Weasel Head	M	Husb'd	34
346.	Mary Weasel Head	F	Wife	45
347.	Chas. Weasel Head	M	Son	12
348.	Mary Weasel Head	F	Daughter	13
349.	Peter Weasel Head	M	Son	11
350.	John Weasel Head	M	Son	9
351.	Lucy W. Head	F	Daughter	7
352.	John W. Head	M	Son	7
353.	Thos. W. Head	M	Son	1
354.	Isaac Wifer	M	Son	28
355.	Mary Wifer	F	Daughter	27
356.	The Bite	M	Husb'd	--
357.	Kills For Nothing	F	Wife	39
358.	Sheridan Bite	M	Son	20
359.	Howard Bite	M	Son	12
360.	Thos. Bite	M	Son	6
361.	Minnie Bite	F	Daughter	4

Census of the -Piegan- Indians of Blackfeet Agency, Montana taken by Geo. B McLaughlin United States Indian Agent 1897

No.	English Name	Sex	Relation	Age
362.	Joe Evans	M	Husb'd	22
363.	Mary Evans	F	Wife	17
364.	James Evans	M	Son	1
365.	Morning Gun	M	Husb'd	35
366.	Otter Woman	F	Wife	19
367.	John Morning Gun	M	Son	12
368.	Flying In Water	M	Son	5
369.	Emma Morning Gun	F	Daughter	3
370.	Briar	F	Daughter	2
371.	Little Otter	F	----	70
372.	Albert M. Plume	M	Husb'd	22
373.	Susie M. Plume	F	Wife	18
374.	Maggie M. Plume	F	Daughter	1
375.	Red Fox	M	Husb'd	24
376.	Good Massacre	F	Wife	20
377.	John Red Fox	M	Son	2
378.	Jas. Red Fox	M	Son	1
379.	Rattler	M	Husb'd	50
380.	Spear Woman	F	Wife	35
381.	Elmer Rattler	M	Son	22
382.	Old Man Chief	M	Husb'd	28
383.	Lucy Old Man Chief	F	Wife	22
384.	James Old Man Chief	M	Son	3
385.	Mary O. M. Chief	F	Daughter	2
386.	Old Running Crane	M	Husb'd	70
387.	White Woman	F	Wife	41
388.	Maggie R. Crane	F	Daughter	9
389.	Ed R. Crane	M	Husb'd	22
390.	Nellie R. Crane	F	Wife	17
391.	(Infant)	M	Son	1mo
392.	Small Petrified	F	Mother	48
393.	Jas. Running Crane	M	Son	9

Census of the -Piegan- Indians of Blackfeet Agency, Montana taken by Geo. B McLaughlin United States Indian Agent 1897

No.	English Name	Sex	Relation	Age
394.	Wades in Water	M	Husb'd	27
395.	Lucy W. in Water	F	Wife	24
396.	Rachel Neris	F	----	24
397.	Rosa Neris	F	Daughter	8
398.	Daniel Neris	M	Daughter[sic]	6
399.	(Infant)	F	Daughter	1mo
400.	Fine Bull	M	Husb'd	43
401.	Scattered Woman	F	Wife	39
402.	Rosa Fine Bull	F	Daughter	4
403.	Good Looking Girl	F	Daughter	6
404.	Chief	M	Son	10
405.	Jas. Fine Bull	M	Son	2
406.	(Infant)	M	Son	2mo
407.	Henry No Bear	M	Husb'd	30
408.	Jennie No Bear	F	Wife	25
409.	Thos. No Bear	M	Son	1
410.	Eddy Jack	M	Husb'd	28
411.	Snake Looking	F	Wife	36
412.	John Two Guns	M	Son	15
413.	Money Jack	F	Daughter	2
414.	Long Wolverine	F	----	65
415.	Jesse Pepion	F	----	23
416.	Thos. Pepion	M	Son	3
417.	L. Pepion	M	Son	3mo
418.	Cecil Pepion	F	----	22
419.	Lousese Pepion	F	----	19
420.	Frank Pepion	M	Brother	16
421.	Chester Pepion	M	Brother	13
422.	John Pepion	M	Husb'd	26
423.	Cecil Pepion	F	Wife	25
424.	Small Face	F	Mother	40
425.	Ground Snake	F	Daughter	8
426.	Lawrence Faber	M	Husb'd	23

Census of the -Piegan- Indians of Blackfeet Agency, Montana taken by Geo. B McLaughlin United States Indian Agent 1897

No.	English Name	Sex	Relation	Age
427.	Annie Faber	F	Wife	20
428.	Hellen Faber	F	Daughter	2
429.	(Infant)	F	Daughter	4mo
430.	Wolf Plume	M	Husb'd	37
431.	First Strike	F	Wife	30
432.	Wesley W. Plume	M	Son	10
433.	Harrison T. Lodge	M	Husb'd	52
434.	Good Woman	F	Wife	50
435.	Louese First One	F	----	23
436.	Smoking Flint	M	Husb'd	36
437.	Under Beaver	F	Wife	29
438.	Peter Smoking Flint	M	Son	13
439.	Jas. Smoking Flint	M	Son	5
440.	Louie S. Flint	M	Son	2
441.	Shoots at Another	M	Husb'd	32
442.	Tail Feathers	F	Wife	40
443.	Josephine Weatherwax	F	Daughter	18
444.	Mary Weatherwax	F	Daughter	14
445.	Joe Weatherwax	M	Son	11
446.	Iron Necklace	M	Husb'd	45
447.	Kills Inside	F	Wife	46
448.	Annie Iron Necklace	F	Daughter	5
449.	Minnie I. Necklace	F	Daughter	3
450.	Old Coyote	M	Husb'd	34
451.	Mary Old Coyote	F	Wife	41
452.	Philip Old Coyote	M	Son	15
453.	Double Blaze	M	Husb'd	36
454.	Medicine Beaver	F	Wife	33
455.	Joe Jackson	M	Son	16
456.	Oliver Jackson	M	Son	6
457.	Frank Jackson	M	Son	4
458.	Louie Jackson	M	Son	2
459.	(Infant)	M	Son	3mo

Census of the -Piegan- Indians of Blackfeet Agency, Montana taken by Geo. B McLaughlin United States Indian Agent 1897

No.	English Name	Sex	Relation	Age
460.	Singing	F	----	65
461.	Aims Back	M	Husb'd	23
462.	Emley A. Back	F	Wife	17
463.	John A. Back	M	Son	3
464.	Calf Looking	M	Husb'd	48
465.	Going Over	F	Wife	50
466.	Paul Calf Looking	M	Son	21
467.	Mary Big Head	F	Widow	32
468.	Morning Owl	M	Son	2
469.	Tail Feathers	M	Husb'd	48
470.	Jennie Tail Feathers	F	Wife	53
471.	Red Star	M	Son	8
472.	Shoots Close	M	Son	7
473.	Little Mink	M	Son	3
474.	Peter Tail Feathers	M	Son	21
475.	Long Time Rock	M	Husb'd	31
476.	Big Tiger	F	Wife	21
477.	(Infant)	M	Son	3mo
478.	Peter Old Rock	M	Brother	23
479.	Jennie Johnson	F	Mother	37
480.	Mary Johnson	F	Daughter	18
481.	Chas. Johnson	M	Son	16
482.	Willie Johnson	M	Son	14
483.	Belle Johnson	F	Daughter	12
484.	Jas. Johnson	M	Son	10
485.	Ida Johnson	F	Daughter	8
486.	Homer Johnson	F	Daughter[sic]	7
487.	Takes Gun Inside	F	----	55
488.	Chief All Over	M	Husb'd	45
489.	Small Rock	F	Wife	46
490.	Geo. Chief All Over	M	Son	7
491.	Thos. Kidd	M	Husb'd	36

Census of the -Piegan- Indians of Blackfeet Agency, Montana taken by Geo. B McLaughlin United States Indian Agent 1897

No.	English Name	Sex	Relation	Age
492.	Mary Kidd	F	Wife	28
493.	Willie Kidd	M	Son	2
494.	Alex Marcerd	M	Husb'd	33
495.	Theresa Marcerd	F	Wife	25
496.	Louise Marcerd	F	Daughter	4
497.	Peter Marcerd	M	Son	23
498.	Josephine Marcerd	F	Daughter	11
499.	Steady Woman	F	Mother	50
500.	Henry Larb	M	Brother	16
501.	Bessie Larb	F	Sister	14
502.	Running Wolf	F	Mother	43
503.	Miles R. Wolf	M	Son	17
504.	Herbert R. Wolf	M	Son	14
505.	Homer R. Wolf	M	Son	10
506.	Geo. R. Wolf	M	Son	5
507.	John R. Wolf	M	Son	3
508.	Fast Buffalo Horse	F	Widow	52
509.	Joseph F.B. Horse	M	Son	24
510.	Albert F.B. Horse	M	Son	22
511.	Deer	M	Son	13
512.	Owl Top Feathers	M	Husb'd	33
513.	Julia Owl Top Feathers	F	Wife	35
514.	Mary O.T. Feathers	F	Daughter	17
515.	John O.T. Feathers	M	Son	2
516.	Mary O.T. Feathers	F	Daughter	6
517.	Head Carrier	M	Husb'd	68
518.	Sitting On Top	F	Wife	50
519.	Catches	F	Wife	60
520.	John Head Carrier	M	Son	18
521.	Frank Calf Robe	M	Husb'd	26
522.	Jennie Calf Robe	F	Wife	18
523.	Jas. Fisher	M	----	10
524.	Mary Teasdale	F	Mother	47

Census of the -Piegan- Indians of Blackfeet Agency, Montana taken by Geo. B McLaughlin United States Indian Agent 1897

No.	English Name	Sex	Relation	Age
525.	Rose Teasdale	F	Daughter	17
526.	Josephine Teasdale	F	Daughter	14
527.	Nellie Teasdale	F	Daughter	11
528.	Red Head	M	Husb'd	39
529.	Two Strikes	F	Wife	50
530.	Daniel R. Head	M	Son	13
531.	Nick Green	M	----	24
532.	Dan Lone Chief	M	Husb'd	24
533.	Ellen Lone Chief	F	Wife	31
534.	Good Bear	F	Mother	50
535.	Many Stars	F	Mother	60
536.	Long Time Sleeping	M	Husb'd	26
537.	Calling One Other	F	Wife	31
538.	John L.T. Sleeping	M	Son	5
539.	Lizzie L.T. Sleeping	F	Daughter	2
540.	Beaver Eyes	F	Mother	27
541.	Dave Beaver Eyes	M	Son	1
542.	Patrick Beaver Eyes	M	Son	1
543.	Mary B. Eyes	F	Daughter	7

**Note: Next page in this census had roll numbers 522-543 repeated with different names. Also, he skipped roll number 544. The second page of repeat numbers are still included with the different names to maintain manuscript accuracy. New names pick up at number 545.

No.	English Name	Sex	Relation	Age
522.	Katie Pias	F	Sister	10
523.	Ruth Pias	F	Sister	6
524.	Daniel Pias	M	Brother	6
525.	(Infant)	F	Sister	1mo
526.	Calf Robe	F	Mother	45
527.	Richard Calf Robe	M	Son	16
528.	Carl Tail	M	Husb'd	37
529.	Takes Gun	F	Wife	40
530.	Charley C. Tail	M	Son	20
531.	Earnest C. Tail	M	Son	10

Census of the -Piegan- Indians of Blackfeet Agency, Montana taken by Geo. B McLaughlin United States Indian Agent 1897

No.	English Name	Sex	Relation	Age
532.	Mary C. Tail	F	Daughter	3
533.	Buffalo Growing	M	Husb'd	39
534.	Shield Woman	F	Wife	34
535.	Painted Wings	M	Husb'd	65
536.	Strikes On Top	F	Wife	50
537.	Double Strike	F	Wife	63
538.	Susie Painted Wings	F	Daughter	9
539.	John Painted Wings	M	Son	20
540.	Richard Sanderville	M	Husb'd	30
541.	Nancy Sanderville	F	Wife	22
542.	Agnes Sanderville	F	Daughter	8
543.	Irene Sanderville	F	Daughter	1
544.	**Missing, see note near bottom of page 19.			
545.	John Croft	M	Husb'd	22
546.	Louese Croft	F	Wife	25
547.	Lad Croft	M	Son	1
548.	Going to Move	M	Husb'd	43
549.	Scraper Woman	F	Wife	49
550.	Stabbing By Mistake	M	Husb'd	29
551.	Steals In Daytime	F	Wife	25
552.	Red Boy	M	Son	2
553.	(Infant)	M	Son	1mo
554.	Big Lodge Pole	M	Husband	34
555.	Mary L. Pole	F	Wife	46
556.	Sam'l Choat	M	Son	17
557.	Pete Choat	M	Son	12
558.	Geo. Choat	M	Husb'd	21
559.	Fanny Choat	F	Wife	18
560.	Frank Choat	M	Husb'd	24
561.	Josephine Choat	F	Wife	19

Census of the -Piegan- Indians of Blackfeet Agency, Montana taken by Geo. B McLaughlin United States Indian Agent 1897

No.	English Name	Sex	Relation	Age
562.	Black Face	F	Mother	45
563.	Roselia B. Face	F	Daughter	12
564.	Isabella Tromly	F	Mother	63
565.	Alfred Tromly	M	Son	19
566.	Medicine Weasel	M	Husb'd	53
567.	Good Cut	F	Wife	32
568.	Hits Down	F	Wife	45
569.	Eagle Face	F	Wife	36
570.	Talk Woman	F	----	62
571.	Young Man Chief	M	Husb'd	37
572.	Cecil Y.M. Chief	F	Wife	22
573.	Morgan Y.M. Chief	M	Son	1
574.	Joe Tatsey	M	Husb'd	33
575.	Anna Tatsey	F	Wife	25
576.	Josephine Tatsey	F	Daughter	7
577.	Hattie Tatsey	F	Daughter	5
578.	John Tatsey	M	Son	3
579.	Joe Tatsey	M	Son	1
580.	Susan Tatsey	F	Mother	81
581.	Fisher	M	Husb'd	22
582.	---- ----	F	Wife	23
583.	White Dog	M	Husb'd	42
584.	Medicine Pipe Woman	F	Wife	23
585.	Went to War	M	Son	2
586.	Weasel Woman	F	Daughter	3
587.	Blanket Woman	F	----	55
588.	Fell No Iron	M	Husb'd	40
589.	Middle Person	F	Wife	30
590.	Water Otter	F	Daughter	4
591.	(Infant)	M	Son	4mo
592.	Big Beaver	M	Husb'd	36
593.	Good Clean Up	F	Wife	27

Census of the -Piegan- Indians of Blackfeet Agency, Montana taken by Geo. B McLaughlin United States Indian Agent 1897

No.	English Name	Sex	Relation	Age
594.	Aaron B. Beaver	M	Son	11
595.	Eddy B. Beaver	M	Son	13
596.	Different Sugar	F	Daughter	3
597.	(Infant)	M	Son	6mo
598.	Belle Ripley	F	Mother	45
599.	Emma Ripley	F	Daughter	5
600.	White Quiver	M	Husb'd	38
601.	Wings	F	Wife	38
602.	Benj. W. Quiver	M	Son	12
603.	Maggie W. Quiver	F	Daughter	5
604.	Thos. W. Quiver	M	Son	2
605.	(Infant)	F	Daughter	5mo
606.	Red Bird Tail	----	----	50
607.	Four Horns	M	Husb'd	44
608.	Grove Ant Woman	F	Wife	30
609.	Benjamin Four Horns	M	Son	18
610.	Jas. Four Horns	M	Son	4
611.	Mary Steward	F	Mother	33
612.	Carrie Steward	F	Daughter	16
613.	Jennie Steward	F	Daughter	14
614.	Clara Steward	F	Daughter	12
615.	Mollie Steward	F	Daughter	9
616.	Cecil Steward	F	Daughter	4
617.	Maria Steward	F	Daughter	1
618.	Joe Trombly	M	Husb'd	40
619.	Julia Trombly	F	Wife	45
620.	Frank Racine	M	Son	19
621.	Oliver Racine	M	Son	18
622.	Louie Marcero	M	Husb'd	30
623.	Rosa Marcero	F	Wife	18
624.	Millie Labreech	F	Mother	48
625.	Lena Labreech	F	Daughter	17
626.	Millie Labreech	F	Daughter	15

Census of the -Piegan- Indians of Blackfeet Agency, Montana taken by Geo. B McLaughlin United States Indian Agent 1897

No.	English Name	Sex	Relation	Age
627.	Jessie Labreech	F	Daughter	13
628.	Chas. Labreech	M	Son	30
629.	Melvin Labreech	M	Son	20
630.	Phill Labreech	M	Son	10
631.	David Labreech	M	Husb'd	24
632.	Minnie Labreech	F	Wife	26
633.	Chas. Labreech	M	Son	1
634.	John White Calf	M	Husb'd	30
635.	Weasel Tail Woman	F	Wife	30
636.	Tall Head	F	Mother	60
637.	Annie W. Calf	F	Daughter	10
638.	Wakes Up Last	M	Husb'd	31
639.	Mollie Wakes Up Last	F	Wife	20
640.	(Infant)	F	Daughter	3mo
641.	Medicine	F	----	65
642.	No Coat	M	Husb'd	39
643.	Kills By Mistake	F	Wife	30
644.	Anna No Coat	F	Daughter	4
645.	Bear Shoe	M	Husb'd	39
646.	Mrs. Bear Shoe	F	Wife	19
647.	Eagle	M	Husb'd	30
648.	Medicine Beaver	F	Wife	25
649.	Calf Woman	F	----	80
650.	**Missing			
651.	**Missing			
652.	Big Moon	M	Husb'd	39
653.	Long Time Calf	F	Wife	30
654.	Jos. Casooth	M	Son	24
655.	Whips On Both Sides	F	Mother	80

Census of the -Piegan- Indians of Blackfeet Agency, Montana taken by Geo. B McLaughlin United States Indian Agent 1897

No.	English Name	Sex	Relation	Age
656.	Maggie Albertson	F	Mother	37
657.	Arthur Albertson	M	Son	17
658.	Geo. Albertson	M	Son	23
659.	Robert Albertson	M	Son	7
660.	Mary Albertson	F	Daughter	4
661.	Joe McKnight	M	Husb'd	24
662.	Lucy McKnight	F	Wife	22
663.	Irene McKnight	F	Daughter	8mo
664.	Anna McKnight	F	----	25
665.	Richard Rutherford	M	Husb'd	21
666.	Eliza Rutherford	F	Wife	20
667.	Mary Rutherford	F	Mother	47
668.	Wm. Rutherford	M	Son	14
669.	James Rutherford	M	Son	11
670.	Henry Rutherford	M	Son	8
671.	Alice Rutherford	F	Daughter	18
672.	Mary Davis	F	Mother	21
673.	Hattie Davis	F	Daughter	2
674.	Henry Chouquett[sic]	M	Husb'd	28
675.	Louise Choquett	F	Wife	24
676.	New Robe	M	Husb'd	40
677.	Short Face	F	Wife	45
678.	Tells In Night	F	Wife	30
679.	John New Robe	M	Son	13
680.	Joseph New Robe	M	Son	12
681.	(Infant)	F	Daughter	1mo
682.	Medicine Stab	M	Husb'd	45
683.	Slim Woman	F	Wife	35
684.	Gros-Ventre Woman	F	Wife	45
685.	George P. Chicken	M	Husb'd	24
686.	Jessie P. Chicken	F	Wife	18
687.	Cecil P. Chicken	F	Daughter	1

Census of the -Piegan- Indians of Blackfeet Agency, Montana taken by Geo. B McLaughlin United States Indian Agent 1897

No.	English Name	Sex	Relation	Age
688.	Gambler	M	Husb'd	42
689.	Annie Gambler	F	Wife	45
690.	---- Gambler	M	Son	18
691.	Jennie Gambler	F	Daughter	16
692.	Swims Under	M	Father	28
693.	Fell No Light	F	Daughter	----
694.	Iron Pipe	M	Husb'd	40
695.	Goes In Both Sides	F	----	----
696.	Joseph Iron Pipe	M	Son	9
697.	John Iron Pipe	M	Son	2
698.	Cecil Iron Pipe	F	Daughter	4
699.	(Infant)	M	Son	2mo
700.	Tells In Water	M	Husb'd	24
701.	Different Gun	F	Wife	22
702.	John In The Water	M	Son	3
703.	The Horn	M	Husb'd	50
704.	Good Looking Woman	F	Wife	60
705.	Under Chicken	F	Wife	35
706.	Maggie Horn	F	Daughter	6
707.	Harry Horn	M	Son	18
708.	Short Face	M	Husb'd	26
709.	Throws Gun	F	Wife	50
710.	Spotted Bear	M	Husb'd	65
711.	---- Bear	F	Wife	33
712.	Peter Spotted Bear	M	Son	17
713.	John Spotted Bear	M	Son	4
714.	Spotted Bear	F	Wife	42
715.	Jas. Spotted Bear	M	Son	6
716.	Minnie Spotted Bear	F	Daughter	8
717.	**Missing			
718.	Mary Spotted Bear	F	Mother	24
719.	Alice Spotted Bear	F	Daughter	2

Census of the -Piegan- Indians of Blackfeet Agency, Montana taken by Geo. B McLaughlin United States Indian Agent 1897

No.	English Name	Sex	Relation	Age
720.	Likes M. Bones	M	Husb'd	----
721.	Mrs. M. Bones	F	Wife	----
722.	Sure Chief	M	Husb'd	30
723.	Bird Wings Chief	F	Wife	20
724.	Phillip Sure Chief	M	Son	2
725.	Medicine Bull	M	Husb'd	34
726.	Sore Back	F	Wife	27
727.	Thos. Medicine Bull	M	Son	1
728.	Red Rock	F	Daughter	11
729.	Good Stabing	M	Husb'd	30
730.	Mary Good Stabing	F	Wife	34
731.	Annie Good Stabing	F	Daughter	2
732.	(Infant)	F	Daughter	1
733.	Kicking Woman	M	Husb'd	80
734.	Every Body Looks At	F	Wife	40
735.	Catches	F	Wife	75
736.	John Kicking Woman	M	Son	18
737.	After Buffalo	M	Husb'd	46
738.	Daisy Buffalo	F	Wife	22
739.	Chas. Buffalo	M	Son	2
740.	Sam'l. Randall	M	----	23
741.	Heavy Gun	M	Husb'd	40
742.	Mary Heavy Gun	F	Wife	30
743.	Goes In First	F	Wife	22
744.	Strikes Back	F	Mother	50
745.	Anna Strikes Back	F	Daughter	13
746.	Boy Chief	M	Husb'd	38
747.	Takes Last Gun	F	Wife	24
748.	Anthelia Boy Chief	F	Daughter	11
749.	Eagle Tail Feathers	M	Son	5
750.	Wm. B. Chief	M	Son	4
751.	(Infant)	F	Daughter	1

Census of the -Piegan- Indians of Blackfeet Agency, Montana taken by Geo. B McLaughlin United States Indian Agent 1897

No.	English Name	Sex	Relation	Age
752.	Stretches Out	M	----	32
753.	Little Plume	M	Husb'd	44
754.	Strange Cut	F	Wife	37
755.	Eagle Tail Feathers	F	Wife	34
756.	Irvin Little Plume	M	Son	19
757.	Jas. L. Plume	M	Son	16
758.	Louie L. Plume	M	Son	5
759.	(Infant)	M	Son	1
760.	Mary Little Plume	F	Daughter	5
761.	Josephine Little Plume	F	Daughter	3
762.	Susie Little Plume	F	Daughter	6mo
763.	Peter Little Plume	M	Son	2
764.	Cora Little Plume	F	Daughter	19
765.	Mary Little Plume	F	Daughter	4mo
766.	Fell No Kidney	M	Husb'd	26
767.	Minnie Kidney	F	Wife	20
768.	Mack Kidney	M	Son	4
769.	(Infant)	F	Daughter	1mo
770.	Catches In Side	F	----	60
771.	Little Plume Mother	F	----	----
772.	Wolf Head	M	Husb'd	49
773.	Sings High	F	Wife	40
774.	Pete Wolf Head	M	Son	7
775.	Wood Woman	F	Mother	56
776.	Kills Another	F	Daughter	3
777.	Red Plume	M	Husb'd	43
778.	Catches First	F	Wife	36
779.	Fell No Owl	M	Son	28
780.	Hungry	F	Mother	50
781.	Isaac Hungry	M	Son	11
782.	Henry Hungry	M	Son	18
783.	Little Bull	M	Husb'd	46
784.	Good Steel	F	Wife	30
785.	Two Guns	M	Son	3

Census of the -Piegan- Indians of Blackfeet Agency, Montana taken by Geo. B McLaughlin United States Indian Agent 1897

No.	English Name	Sex	Relation	Age
786.	Good Rush	F	Daughter	4
787.	Little Bull	F	Wife	39
788.	Cloth Woman	F	Daughter	13
789.	Found A Gun	M	----	19
790.	Michael Boy Child	M	Husb'd	24
791.	Strikes Back	F	Wife	26
792.	Annie B. Child	f	Daughter	1
793.	Spotted Calf	M	Husb'd	66
794.	Mink	F	Wife	60
795.	Medicine Pipe Woman	F	Wife	58
796.	Mike Little Dog	M	Husb'd	20
797.	Irene Little Dog	F	Wife	----
798.	Running Fisher	M	Husb'd	43
799.	Carrie R. Fisher	F	Wife	37
800.	First Prepared	M	Son	2
801.	Mary R. Fisher	F	Daughter	
802.	John Calf Ribs	M	Husb'd	33
803.	Sits In Front	F	Wife	30
804.	Joe Hits[sic] In Front	M	Son	18
805.	Austin Hits[sic] In Front	M	Son	10
806.	Berrie Carrier	M	Husb'd	42
807.	Jingles	F	Wife	34
808.	Rides In Front	M	Son	1
809.	Small Fox	F	Daughter	10
810.	Different Shield	F	Daughter	5
811.	Jim Blood	M	Husb'd	36
812.	Polly Blood	F	Wife	18
813.	Young Eagle	M	Husb'd	36
814.	Many Shells	F	Wife	25
815.	Jas. Eagle Child	M	Son	10

Census of the -Piegan- Indians of Blackfeet Agency, Montana taken by Geo. B McLaughlin United States Indian Agent 1897

No.	English Name	Sex	Relation	Age
816.	Strangled Wolf	M	Husb'd	50
817.	Short Woman	F	Wife	60
818.	No Chief	M	Husb'd	78
819.	Strikes In Front	F	Wife	50
820.	Jim No Chief	M	Son	13
821.	John Mountain Chief	M	Son	20
822.	Charges Both Sides	F	Wife	25
823.	Takes Good Gun	M	Husb'd	25
824.	Takes Gun For Nothing	M	Son	2
825.	Kills In Air	F	----	60
826.	Chas. Three Suns	M	----	79
827.	Cold Body	M	Husb'd	24
828.	Mary Cold Body	F	Wife	38
829.	Pete Grant	M	Son	10
830.	Maggie Grant	F	Daughter	6
831.	Cecil Grant	F	Daughter	3
832.	Old Person	M	Husb'd	27
833.	Grace Old Person	F	Wife	20
834.	Middle Rider	M	Son	4mo
835.	Rides In Middle	M	Husb'd	33
836.	Anna R.I. Middle	F	Wife	34
837.	Mary R.I. Middle	F	Daughter	3
838.	Levi R.I. Middle	M	Son	11
839.	Fred R.I. Middle	M	Son	14
840.	Jim No Chief	M	Husb'd	27
841.	Gertrude No Chief	F	Wife	17
842.	Grace No Chief	F	Daughter	2
843.	(Infant)	----	----	6mo
844.	Takes Gun Alone	M	Husb'd	40
845.	Night Cut	F	Wife	50
846.	Josephine Gun Alone	F	Daughter	3

Census of the -Piegan- Indians of Blackfeet Agency, Montana taken by Geo. B McLaughlin United States Indian Agent 1897

No.	English Name	Sex	Relation	Age
847.	Medicine Sugar	F	----	90
848.	Two Spears	M	Husb'd	24
849.	Small Woman	F	Wife	21
850.	Annie Two Spears	F	Daughter	3
851.	Big Chicken Hawk	F	Daughter	1
852.	Red Horn	M	----	65
853.	Womans Word	F	----	90
854.	New Breast	M	Husb'd	36
855.	Long Face	F	Wife	45
856.	Iron Woman	F	Daughter	3
857.	Morning Eagle	M	Husb'd	68
858.	Strikes On Top	F	Wife	47
859.	Catches On Ground	F	Wife	42
860.	Pittifull	M	Son	8
861.	Geo. Morning Eagle	M	Son	4
862.	(Infant)	M	Son	3mo
863.	Butterfly	M	Husb'd	48
864.	Medicine Pipe	F	Wife	43
865.	Mary Butterfly	F	Daughter	7
866.	Elmer Butterfly	M	Husb'd	24
867.	Saatal Butterfly	F	Wife	19
868.	Rushes Last	M	Son	2
869.	(Infant)	F	Daughter	1
870.	Big Wolf Medicine	M	Husb'd	33
871.	Good Massacre	F	Wife	37
872.	Head Woman	F	Daughter	4
873.	Lucy B.W. Medicine	F	Daughter	9
874.	Harry Face	M	Husb'd	36
875.	Dry Fox	F	Wife	30
876.	Glass Woman	F	Wife	25
877.	Rushes Home	M	Son	2
878.	Blind Girl	F	Daughter	11

Census of the -Piegan- Indians of Blackfeet Agency, Montana taken by Geo. B McLaughlin United States Indian Agent 1897

No.	English Name	Sex	Relation	Age
879.	Frank Denovan	M	Son	21
880.	Double Strike	F	Mother	50
881.	Under Bull	F	Mother	41
882.	Chas. Under Bull	M	Son	11
883.	Peter Under Bull	M	Son	3
884.	Under Bull	F	Mother	33
885.	Fine Young Man	M	Son	2
886.	Mary Under Bull	F	Daughter	5
887.	Almost Killed	F	----	75
888.	Little Dog	M	Husb'd	43
889.	Crossing Woman	F	Wife	16
890.	Oliver Little Dog	M	Son	14
891.	John Little Dog	M	Son	8
892.	Mary Little Dog	F	Daughter	1
893.	Big Crow	M	Husb'd	37
894.	Double Gun	F	Wife	28
895.	Cecil Big Crow	F	Daughter	9
896.	Under Mink	F	Daughter	11
897.	Wolf Eagle	M	Husb'd	47
898.	Blanket Woman	F	Wife	44
899.	Kills In Night	F	Wife	28
900.	Daniel Wolf Eagle	M	Son	7
901.	Geo. W. Eagle	M	Son	2
902.	Mummy	F	----	91
903.	Fisher	M	Husb'd	21
904.	Medicine Stone	F	Wife	20
905.	Little Owl	M	Husb'd	25
906.	Maggie Little Owl	F	Wife	17
907.	Good Killer	F	G Mother	80
908.	First Rider	M	Son	17
909.	Takes Iron Gun	F	G Mother	80
910.	John Iron Gun	M	Son	25
911.	Lucy Iron Gun	F	Daughter	17

Census of the -Piegan- Indians of Blackfeet Agency, Montana taken by Geo. B McLaughlin United States Indian Agent 1897

No.	English Name	Sex	Relation	Age
912.	No Runner	M	Husb'd	50
913.	White Woman	F	Wife	60
914.	Tim No Runner	M	Son	12
915.	Under Mink	M	----	25
916.	Old White Woman	F	----	75
917.	Many Guns	M	Husb'd	33
918.	Josephine M. Guns	F	Wife	16
919.	Buffalo Hide	M	Husb'd	32
920.	Cecil B. Hide	F	Wife	26
921.	Peter B. Hide	M	Son	4
922.	(Infant)	M	Son	1
923.	Buffalo Hide	F	Mother	90
924.	Turtle	M	Husb'd	28
925.	Mary Turtle	F	Wife	23
926.	Last Star	M	Husb'd	28
927.	White Arm Ride	F	Wife	20
928.	Philip Last Star	M	Son	8
929.	Tony Last Star	M	Son	4
930.	Takes Gun	M	Son	1
931.	Every Body Talks About	M	Husb'd	42
932.	Strikes Back	F	Wife	49
933.	Nut Woman	F	Wife	41
934.	Louie E.B. Talks	M	Son	7
935.	Geo. E.B. Talks	M	Son	6
936.	Susie E.B. Talks About	F	Daughter	2
937.	Paul E.B. Talks About	M	Son	4
938.	(Infant)	F	Daughter	2mo
939.	Kills In Brush	F	G Mother	74
940.	George Hazlett	M	Son	24
941.	Maggie Hazlett	F	Daughter	10
942.	Dog Taking Gun	M	Husb'd	30

Census of the -Piegan- Indians of Blackfeet Agency, Montana taken by Geo. B McLaughlin United States Indian Agent 1897

No.	English Name	Sex	Relation	Age
943.	Scissors Woman	F	Wife	22
944.	(Infant)	M	Son	8mo
945.	Spotted Head	M	----	80
946.	Philip Flat Tail	M	Husb'd	22
947.	Annie Flat Tail	F	Wife	15
948.	Emma Upham	F	Mother	35
949.	Rosa Upham	F	Daughter	18
950.	Katie Upham	F	Daughter	15
951.	Joseph Upham	M	Son	12
952.	John Upham	M	Son	8
953.	Murtie Upham	F	Daughter	5
954.	John Gobert	M	Husb'd	28
955.	Susie Gobert	F	Wife	20
956.	Alice Gobert	F	Daughter	2
957.	Wm. Russell	M	Husb'd	43
958.	Mary Russell	F	Wife	37
959.	Cecil Russell	F	Daughter	15
960.	Joseph Russell	M	Son	9
961.	Wm. Russell	M	Son	6
962.	Henry Russell	M	Son	1mo
963.	Petrified	F	G Mother	60
964.	Geo. Russell	M	Son	12
965.	First One Russell	M	----	24
966.	Small Woman	F	----	61
967.	Frank Rider	M	Husb'd	29
968.	Gretchen Rider	F	Wife	24
969.	Issabella Main	F	Mother	32
970.	Henry Main	M	Son	18
971.	Alice Main	F	Daughter	5
972.	Elizabeth Main	F	Daughter	2
973.	Rachel Norris	F	Mother	28
974.	Rose Norris	F	Daughter	9

Census of the -Piegan- Indians of Blackfeet Agency, Montana taken by Geo. B McLaughlin United States Indian Agent 1897

No.	English Name	Sex	Relation	Age
975.	Daniel Norris	M	Son	4
976.	Jas. Housman	M	Husb'd	30
977.	Susan Housman	F	Wife	31
978.	Thos. Housman	M	Son	9
979.	Joseph Housman	M	Son	7
980.	Mary Housman	F	Daughter	6
981.	Jenivene Housman	F	Daughter	3
982.	Josephine Housman	F	Daughter	1
983.	Caroline Hinkel	F	Mother	34
984.	Geo. Hinkel	M	Son	15
985.	William Hinkel	M	Son	13
986.	Lizzie Hinkel	F	Daughter	11
987.	Mamie Hinkel	F	Daughter	9
988.	William Lewis	M	Father	45
989.	Margaret Lewis	F	Mother	26
990.	Antone Lewis	M	Son	13
991.	Peter Lewis	M	Son	5
992.	Sarah Lewis	F	Daughter	4
993.	Geo. Lewis	M	Son	3
994.	Jesse Samples	M	----	23
995.	William Upham	M	Father	30
996.	Katie Upham	F	Wife	25
997.	Lazy Cut	F	M Law	60
998.	Mary Powell	F	Mother	45
999.	Chas. Powell	M	Son	21
1000.	Jenny Powell	F	Daughter	19
1001.	Jesse Powell	M	Son	15
1002.	Lucy Powell	F	Daughter	11
1003.	Eliza Galbraith	F	Mother	42
1004.	Phibe Galbraith	F	Daughter	4
1005.	Lizzy Galbraith	F	Daughter	13
1006.	John Galbraith	M	Son	13
1007.	Webster Galbraith	M	Son	15
1008.	Vine Samples	F	Mother	19

Census of the -Piegan- Indians of Blackfeet Agency, Montana taken by Geo. B McLaughlin United States Indian Agent 1897

No.	English Name	Sex	Relation	Age
1009.	Elsie Samples	F	Daughter	8mo
1010.	Joseph Howard	M	Son	21
1011.	Mary Howard	F	Mother	55
1012.	Walter Howard	M	Son	14
1013.	Ammie Howard	F	Daughter	10
1014.	Mary Stone	F	Mother	31
1015.	Robert Stone	M	Son	7
1016.	Henry Stone	M	Son	3
1017.	William Samples	M	Husb'd	29
1018.	Mary Samples	F	Mother	23
1019.	William Samples	M	Son	3
1020.	Florence Samples	F	Daughter	2
1021.	Mary Samples	F	Daughter	8mo
1022.	Chas. Delaney	M	Husb'd	23
1023.	Viola Delaney	F	Wife	18
1024.	Ben DeRoche	M	Husb'd	33
1025.	Sally DeRoche	F	Wife	35
1026.	Chas. DeRoche	M	Son	13
1027.	Geo. Horn	M	Single	27
1028.	Bear Child	M	Husb'd	44
1029.	Mattie Bear Child	F	Wife	30
1030.	William Bear Child	M	Son	14
1031.	Josepene Bear Child	F	Daughter	10
1032.	Lewis Bear Child	M	Son	8
1033.	Jas. Bear Child	F[sic]	Son	6
1034.	Ben Bear Child	M	Son	4
1035.	John Morgan	M	Husb'd	31
1036.	Lucy Morgan	F	Wife	22
1037.	Davis Morgan	M	Son	6
1038.	Joseph Morgan	M	Son	2
1039.	Amelia Fox	F	Mother	55
1040.	Elix Fox	M	Son	21

Census of the -Piegan- Indians of Blackfeet Agency, Montana taken by Geo. B McLaughlin United States Indian Agent 1897

No.	English Name	Sex	Relation	Age
1041.	Liza Fox	F	Daughter	14
1042.	Cream Antilope	M	Husb'd	40
1043.	Elk Woman	F	Wife	35
1044.	Old Person	M	Husb'd	32
1045.	Iron Woman	F	Wife	25
1046.	Mary Antilope	F	Daughter	22
1047.	Jas. Antilope	M	Son	12
1048.	Chas. Antilope	M	Son	20
1049.	Kills Alone	F	Daughter	7
1050.	Kills In Water	F	Daughter	3
1051.	Wallace Antilpoe[sic]	M	Brother	22
1052.	Louisa Paul	F	Wife	40
1053.	Solomon Paul	M	Son	19
1054.	Albert Paul	M	Son	17
1055.	Philip Paul	M	Son	14
1056.	Eddie Paul	M	Son	12
1057.	Rosena Paul	F	Daughter	9
1058.	Oliver Paul	M	Son	7
1059.	William Paul	M	Son	5
1060.	Selena Paul	F	Daughter	2
1061.	Mary Norman	F	Wife	21
1062.	Lena Norman	F	Daughter	2
1063.	Adolphas Norman	M	Son	1
1064.	Susan Arnoux	F	Mother	45
1065.	Frankie Arnoux	F	Daughter	20
1066.	Monroe Arnoux	M	Son	18
1067.	Marion Arnoux	M	Son	15
1068.	Geo. Arnoux	M	Son	13
1069.	Sarah Brown	F	Mother	45
1070.	William Brown	M	Son	25
1071.	Joseph Brown	M	Son	23
1072.	Jesse Brown	M	Son	14
1073.	Leo Brown	M	Son	1
1074.	Monnik Simons	F	Mother	64

Census of the -Piegan- Indians of Blackfeet Agency, Montana taken by Geo. B McLaughlin United States Indian Agent 1897

No.	English Name	Sex	Relation	Age
1075.	Jas. Parrine	M	Single	28
1076.	Amelia Galbraith	F	Adpd Sister	6
1077.	Pressly Houk	M	Single	20
1078.	Maggie Wetzel	F	Mother	40
1079.	William Wetzel	M	Son	16
1080.	Pearl Wetxel[sic]	F	Daughter	20
1081.	Daizy Wetzel	F	Daughter	18
1082.	Julia Thomas	F	Wife	25
1083.	Geo. Thomas	M	Son	3
1084.	Steven Bad Man	M	Brother	15
1085.	Sarah Thomas	F	Mother	42
1086.	Maggie Peterson	F	Mother	35
1087.	Oscar Peterson	M	Son	17
1088.	Walter Peterson	M	Son	15
1089.	Frank Peterson	M	Son	13
1090.	Melvin Peterson	M	Son	9
1091.	Eddie Beledeaux	M	Husb'd	33
1092.	Puss Beledeaux	F	Wife	28
1093.	Earl Beledeaux	M	Son	5
1094.	Genevive Beledeaux	F	Daughter	3
1095.	Xiver Beledeaux	M	Husb'd	38
1096.	Selena Beledeaux	F	Wife	31
1097.	William Beledeaux	M	Son	9
1098.	Chas. Beledeaux	M	Son	7
1099.	Warren Beledeaux	M	Son	5
1100.	Mable Beledeaux	F	Daughter	1
1101.	Joseph Livermore	M	Father	36
1102.	Clara Livermore	F	Daughter	6
1103.	Lilly Livermore	F	Daughter	3
1104.	Anthony Austin	M	Husb'd	27
1105.	Susan Austin	F	Wife	38
1106.	Levi Burd	M	Son	20

Census of the -Piegan- Indians of Blackfeet Agency, Montana taken by Geo. B McLaughlin United States Indian Agent 1897

No.	English Name	Sex	Relation	Age
1107.	Alice Burd	F	Daughter	17
1108.	Ire Burd	M	Son	11
1109.	Phebe Burd	F	Daughter	7
1110.	Mary Lehman	F	Wife	28
1111.	Jessie Lehman	F	Daughter	11
1112.	John Lehman	M	Son	10
1113.	Lewis Lehman	M	Son	7
1114.	Ammie Lehman	F	Daughter	3
1115.	Lee Lehman	M	Son	1
1116.	Sally Hagan	F	Wife	29
1117.	Maggie Hagan	F	Daughter	12
1118.	Nellie Hagan	F	Daughter	8
1119.	Iswell Hagan	M	Son	2
1120.	Thressa Pambrane	F	Wife	50
1121.	Perry Dennis	M	G Son	15
1122.	Elix Dubray	M	Cousin	35
1123.	Chief Elk	M	Husb'd	55
1124.	Elda Elk	F	Wife	45
1125.	Levi Ell[sic]	M	Husb'd	24
1126.	Elda Ell	F	Wife	18
1127.	Mary Murphy	F	Wife	40
1128.	William Murphy	M	Son	14
1129.	Hamlin Murphy	M	Son	8
1130.	Holond Murphy	M	Son	7
1131.	Albert Murphy	M	Son	5
1132.	Dick Croff	M	Husb'd	28
1133.	Maggie Croff	F	Wife	20
1134.	Auther Croff	M	Son	7mo
1135.	Louise Higgans	F	Wife	45
1136.	Geo. Croff	M	Son	19
1137.	Emma Croff	F	Daughter	17
1138.	Henry Higgans	M	Son	13
1139.	Alice Higgans	F	Daughter	10

Census of the -Piegan- Indians of Blackfeet Agency, Montana taken by Geo. B McLaughlin United States Indian Agent 1897

No.	English Name	Sex	Relation	Age
1140.	William Croff	M	Single	23
1141.	Jogn[sic] Tingly	M	Single	30
1142.	Henry Shoquette	M	Husb'd	32
1143.	Louisa Shoquette	F	Wife	25
1144.	Minnie DeMott	F	Daughter	14
1145.	Jenny DeMott	F	Daughter	13
1146.	Joseph Demott	M	Son	11
1147.	Geo. Wren	M	Husb'd	28
1148.	Susan Wren	F	Wife	28
1149.	Frank Marceau	M	B In Law	24
1150.	Chas. Marceau	M	B In Law	21
1151.	Milenda Wren	F	Mother	48
1152.	John Wren	M	Son	15
1153.	Robert ----	M	Son	12
1154.	Dora Wren	F	Daughter	10
1155.	William Wren	M	Son	7
1156.	Lilly Wren	F	Daughter	6
1157.	Ida Wren	F	Daughter	3
1158.	Baby Wren	F	Daughter	2
1159.	Liby Wren	F	Daughter	20
1160.	Kattie Wren	F	Daughter	18
1161.	Under Bear	M	Single	20
1162.	Last Strikes	F	Mother	78
1163.	Sally Allison	F	Wife	23
1164.	William Allison	M	Son	5
1165.	Maggie Allison	F	Daughter	11
1166.	Laffiatte Allison	M	Son	4
1167.	Wendle Allison	M	Son	2
1168.	Julia Pendergrass	F	Wife	27
1169.	Mellie Pendergrass	F	Daughter	2
1170.	Mary P. Higans	F	Wife	21
1171.	May Higans	F	Daughter	1

Census of the -Piegan- Indians of Blackfeet Agency, Montana taken by Geo. B McLaughlin United States Indian Agent 1897

No.	English Name	Sex	Relation	Age
1172.	Lucy King	F	Wife	30
1173.	Sady King	F	Daughter	12
1174.	Jas. King	M	Son	9
1175.	Chas. King	M	Son	6
1176.	William King	M	Son	4
1177.	Henry King	M	Son	5mo
1178.	Chas. Martin	M	Husb'd	30
1179.	Ross Martin	M	Son	3
1180.	Maud Martin	F	Wife	22
1181.	Mary Cobell	F	Mother	49
1182.	Julia Cobell	F	Daughter	22
1183.	Joseph Cobell	M	Son	20
1184.	Geo. Cobell	M	Son	18
1185.	Thos. Cobell	M	Son	17
1186.	Bessie Cobell	F	Daughter	15
1187.	John Cobell	M	Son	14
1188.	William Cobell	M	Son	8
1189.	Josephene Gilliam	M	Wife	27
1190.	Anthony Gilliam	M	Son	8
1191.	Julia Gilliam	F	Daughter	8
1192.	William Gilliam	M	Son	4
1193.	Jenette Coe	F	Daughter	12
1194.	Jas. Coe	M	Son	10
1195.	Agnes Coe	F	Daughter	7
1196.	Cut Bank John	M	Husb'd	34
1197.	Calf Woman	F	Wife	34
1198.	Jack B. John	M	Son	12
1199.	Josepg[sic] B. John	M	Son	9
1200.	William B. John	M	Son	4
1201.	Jerry B. John	M	Son	2
1202.	Mary Cuts	F	Mother	65
1203.	Chas. Guartipee	M	Husb'd	31
1204.	Kattie Guartipee	M[sic]	Wife	24
1205.	Mary Guartipee	F	Daughter	13
1206.	Bull Calf	M	Husb'd	43

Census of the -Piegan- Indians of Blackfeet Agency, Montana taken by Geo. B McLaughlin United States Indian Agent 1897

No.	English Name	Sex	Relation	Age
1207.	Blanket Woman	F	Wife	24
1208.	Chas. B. Calf	M	Son	8
1209.	Good Woman	F	Mother	40
1210.	Shoots Close	M	Husb'd	35
1211.	Tans Hides	F	Wife	20
1212.	Jas. S. Close	M	Son	8
1213.	Geo. S. Close	M	Son	3
1214.	Elli Guartipee	M	Husb'd	40
1215.	Saddie Guartipee	F	Wife	25
1216.	Thos. Guartipee	M	Son	17
1217.	Francie Guartipee	M	Son	12
1218.	Chas. Guartipee	M	Son	9
1219.	Josephene Guartipee	F	Daughter	7
1220.	Geo. Guartipee	M	Son	4
1221.	Maggie Guartipee	F	Daughter	1
1222.	Goes In Her Self	F	Mother	45
1223.	Tearing Lodge Pole	F	Daughter	17
1224.	Mary Devereaux	F	Wife	50
1225.	Henry Devereaux	M	Son	20
1226.	Chas. Devereaux	M	Son	17
1227.	Ammie Devereaux	F	Daughter	14
1228.	Abbie Devereaux	F	Daughter	5
1229.	Jason Devereaux	M	Son	19m
1230.	William Hazlett	M	Single	21
1231.	Chas. Buck	M	Husb'd	23
1232.	Spyna Buck	F	Wife	22
1233.	Kattie Stevenson	F	Wife	29
1234.	Henry Stevenson	M	Son	10
1235.	Ammie Stevenson	F	Daughter	7
1236.	Dora Stevenson	F	Daughter	14
1237.	Orcella Stevenson	F	Daughter	4
1238.	Phebe Stevenson	F	Daughter	1
1239.	Big Woman	F	Mother	51
1240.	Iron Woman	F	Mother	72

Census of the -Piegan- Indians of Blackfeet Agency, Montana taken by Geo. B McLaughlin United States Indian Agent 1897

No.	English Name	Sex	Relation	Age
1241.	Susan Sherman	F	Wife	50
1242.	Elix Sherman	M	Son	18
1243.	Robert Sherman	M	Son	16
1244.	Sophia Sherman	F	Daughter	14
1245.	Emma Sherman	F	Daughter	12
1246.	William Sherman	M	Husb'd	25
1247.	Geniveve Sherman	F	Wife	17
1248.	Mary Sherman	F	Daughter	8mo
1249.	Boy	M	Husb'd	50
1250.	Catches on Top	M	Husb'd	40
1251.	Oscar Boy	M	Son	18
1252.	Bad Boy	M	Son	8
1253.	Lame Bear	M	Husb'd	25
1254.	Mary Bear	F	Wife	19
1255.	Takes Alone	M	Son	1
1256.	Heavy Runner	M	Husb'd	39
1257.	Malat Rock	F	Wife	26
1258.	Blue Beeds	F	Wife	24
1259.	Rose H. Runner	F	Daughter	4
1260.	Wolf Girl	F	Daughter	2
1261.	Geo. H Runner	M	Son	7
1262.	Rides Yellow Horse	M	Son	5
1263.	Sweet Grass Girl	F	Daughter	1
1264.	Julia Mumburg	F	Wife	26
1265.	L.J. Mumburg	M	Son	2mo
1266.	Mary Kiser	F	Single	58
1267.	Jim Douglas	M	Husb'd	25
1268.	Jas. A. Douglas	M	Son	2
1269.	Lida Douglas	F	Daughter	11m
1270.	Lucy Hamilton	F	Wife	40
1271.	Robert Hamilton	M	Son	27
1272.	Ella Hamilton	F	Daughter	23

Census of the -Piegan- Indians of Blackfeet Agency, Montana taken by Geo. B McLaughlin United States Indian Agent 1897

No.	English Name	Sex	Relation	Age
1273.	Grace Hamilton	F	Daughter	17
1274.	Jack Miller	M	Husb'd	53
1275.	Julia Miller	F	Wife	40
1276.	John Kennedy	M	Adpd Son	20
1277.	Rose Sharp	F	Daughter	16
1278.	William Douglas	M	Single	23
1279.	Maggie Goss	F	Wife	45
1280.	William Goss	M	Son	20
1281.	Loamie Goss	M	Son	18
1282.	Nellie Goss	F	Daughter	17
1283.	Caroline Goss	F	Daughter	13
1284.	Susan Goss	F	Daughter	11
1285.	Maggie Goss	F	Daughter	----
1286.	Geo. Goss	M	Son	6
1287.	Albert Goss	M	Son	4
1288.	Francis Goss	M	Son	2
1289.	Albert Goss	M	Husb'd	23
1290.	Mary Goss	F	Wife	25
1291.	Albert Goss	M	Son	6mo
1292.	Cross Guns	M	Husb'd	30
1293.	Rider Cross Guns	F	Wife	45
1294.	Chas. Conway	M	Stepson	20
1295.	Frank Conway	M	Stepson	16
1296.	William Conway	M	Stepson	14
1297.	Percy Cross Guns	M	Son	1
1298.	Jas. Pambrane	M	Single	30
1299.	Boss Rib Hunter	M	Husb'd	45
1300.	Black Face Woman	F	Wife	40
1301.	Ammie B.R. Hunter	F	Daughter	12
1302.	Maggie B.R. Hunter	F	Daughter	2
1303.	Takes Gun	M	Husb'd	30
1304.	Woman Shape	F	Wife	25
1305.	Pipe Girl	F	Daughter	3

Census of the -Piegan- Indians of Blackfeet Agency, Montana taken by Geo. B McLaughlin United States Indian Agent 1897

No.	English Name	Sex	Relation	Age
1306.	William Jackson	M	Husb'd	39
1307.	Mary Jackson	F	Wife	25
1308.	Thos. Jackson	M	Son	11
1309.	Millie Jackson	F	Daughter	7
1310.	Hugh Jackson	M	Son	5
1311.	Maggie Jackson	F	Daughter	3
1312.	Mary Jackson	F	Daughter	1
1313.	Two Bear Woman	F	Single	50
1314.	Little Bear	M	Single	33
1315.	Calf Shield	M	Husb'd	51
1316.	Takes Short	F	Wife	65
1317.	Geo. Calf Shield	M	Son	5
1318.	Short Ribs	M	Husb'd	36
1319.	Charged All Arround[sic]	F	Wife	33
1320.	Ammie Short Ribs	F	Stepdaughter	40
1321.	Charged Alone	F	Daughter	28
1322.	Cicell S. Robe	F	Daughter	2
1323.	Emma S. Robe	F	Daughter	3
1324.	Rides Good Horse	M	Son	8mo
1325.	Young S. Robe	M	Son	20
1326.	Flying	F	Mother	65
1327.	Little Bear	M	Single	34
1328.	Lewis Matt	M	Husb'd	36
1329.	Adeline Matt	F	Wife	28
1330.	Francis Matt	M	Son	1
1331.	Alice Matt	F	Daughter	3
1332.	Chief Coward	M	Husb'd	40
1333.	Antilope Woman	F	Wife	27
1334.	Crow Girl	F	Daughter	6
1335.	Four Bulls	M	Son	17
1336.	Black Smoke	M	Husb'd	35
1337.	Medicine Grinder	F	Wife	27
1338.	Jim Black Looks	M	Son	6

Census of the -Piegan- Indians of Blackfeet Agency, Montana taken by Geo. B McLaughlin United States Indian Agent 1897

No.	English Name	Sex	Relation	Age
1339.	Puss Black Looks	F	Daughter	4
1340.	Bear Paw	M	Husb'd	40
1341.	Different Woman	F	Wife	30
1342.	Crane Woman	F	Daughter	7
1343.	John Bear Paw	M	Son	2
1344.	Jim Bear Paw	M	Son	11m
1345.	Old Person	M	Husb'd	26
1346.	Iron Woman	F	Wife	30
1347.	Jenny Old Person	F	Daughter	5
1348.	Addie Old Person	F	Daughter	3
1349.	John Old Person	M	Brother	26
1350.	Wolf Calf	M	Husb'd	80
1351.	Antilpoe[sic] Woman	F	Wife	75
1352.	Short Man	M	Husb'd	41
1353.	Victoria S. Man	F	Wife	28
1354.	Double Rider	M	Husb'd	39
1355.	Mary D. Rider	F	Wife	25
1356.	Addie D. Rider	F	Daughter	6
1357.	Minnie D. Rider	F	Daughter	1
1358.	Weasle Tail	M	Husb'd	37
1359.	Minnie Weasle Tail	F	Wife	32
1360.	Amie Weasle Tail	F	Daughter	11
1361.	Louize Weasle Tail	F	Daughter	4
1362.	Antoine Weasle Tail	M	Son	2
1363.	The Coat	M	Husb'd	30
1364.	Broken Leg	F	Wife	32
1365.	Mary Coat	F	Daughter	17
1366.	Jenny Coat	F	Daughter	3mo
1367.	Dry Goods Woman	F	Single	80
1368.	Many Tail Feathers	M	Husb'd	40
1369.	Old Bear	F	Wife	25
1370.	Broad Feet	F	Daughter	5
1371.	Mole Tail Feathers	M	Son	4

Census of the -Piegan- Indians of Blackfeet Agency, Montana taken by Geo. B McLaughlin United States Indian Agent 1897

No.	English Name	Sex	Relation	Age
1372.	Jenny Tail Feathers	F	Daughter	9
1373.	Jas. Tail Feathers	M	Son	20
1374.	Already Heard	M	Son	3
1375.	Lucy Tail Feathers	F	Daughter	14
1376.	Arrow Top Knott	M	Husb'd	35
1377.	Ground Squirrel	F	Wife	35
1378.	Philip A.T. Knott	M	Son	10
1379.	Silas A.T. Knott	M	Son	9
1380.	Louize A.T. Knott	F	Daughter	3
1381.	Geo. A.T. Knott	M	Son	1
1382.	John K. Way	M	Single	26
1383.	Kills Across Way	F	Mother	50
1384.	May Spotted Eagle	F	Daughter	16
1385.	Cries Medicine	M	Husb'd	30
1386.	Mary C. Medicine	F	Wife	34
1387.	Chas. C. Medicine	M	Son	14
1388.	Joseph C. Medicine	M	Son	21
1389.	Joseph C. Medicine	M	Son	3
1390.	Josephine C. Medicine	F	Daughter	10
1391.	John Middle Calf	M	Husb'd	48
1392.	Cradle Woman	F	Wife	48
1393.	Chas. M. Calf	M	Son	10
1394.	Mary M. Calf	F	Daughter	7
1395.	Sam M. Calf	M	Son	17
1396.	Bear Medicine	M	Husb'd	28
1397.	Far Away Woman	F	Wife	26

**Note: there are two 1398 roll numbers on the original film Peter and Maggie Bear Medicine.

No.	English Name	Sex	Relation	Age
1398.	Peter Bear Medicine	M	Son	5
1398.	Maggie Bear Medicine	F	Daughter	4
1399.	Robert Bear Medicine	M	Son	1
1400.	Joe W. Grass	M	Husb'd	28
1401.	Mary W. Grass	F	Wife	26
1402.	Sam W. Grass	M	Son	7
1403.	Susan W. Grass	F	Daughter	5

Census of the -Piegan- Indians of Blackfeet Agency, Montana taken by Geo. B McLaughlin United States Indian Agent 1897

No.	English Name	Sex	Relation	Age
1404.	Louis W. Grass	M	Son	4
1405.	Lucy W. Grass	F	Daughter	2
1406.	Makes Cold Weather	M	Husb'd	31
1407.	Spear Woman	F	Wife	24
1408.	Joe M.C. Weather	M	Son	4
1409.	Mary M.C. Weather	F	Daughter	1
1410.	Antoine	M	Husb'd	60
1411.	Sophia	F	Wife	55
1412.	Stingy	M	Husb'd	40
1413.	Kills First	F	Wife	55
1414.	White Hide	M	Son	5
1415.	Crow Head	F	Daughter	1
1416.	White Calf	M	Husb'd	65
1417.	Catches Together	F	Wife	60
1418.	Two Guns	M	Husb'd	27
1419.	Good Painter	F	Wife	20
1420.	Joseph Two Guns	M	Son	1
1421.	Catches White Calf	F	Wife	25
1422.	Thos. White Calf	M	Son	2
1423.	Mary White Calf	F	Daughter	6
1424.	Two Catches	F	Wife3	50
1425.	John White Calf	M	Son	11
1426.	Black Snake	F	Wife4	40
1427.	Hides Behind Blanket	F	Daughter	8
1428.	Minnie White Calf	F	Wife5	30
1429.	Jim White Calf	M	Son	23
1430.	Old Woman	F	Single	20
1431.	Wolf Tail	M	Husb'd	40
1432.	Paper Woman	F	Wife	35
1433.	Gilbert W. Tail	M	Son	11
1434.	Snow Flake Tail	F	Daughter	6
1435.	Paul W. Tail	M	Son	4
1436.	Thos. W. Tail	M	Son	1

Census of the -Piegan- Indians of Blackfeet Agency, Montana taken by Geo. B McLaughlin United States Indian Agent 1897

No.	English Name	Sex	Relation	Age
1437.	Catches First	F	Mother	60
1438.	Ear Rings	M	Husb'd	43
1439.	Suan[sic] Ear Rings	F	Wife	38
1440.	Burd Ear Rings	M	Sin[sic]	10
1441.	Jim Ear Rings	M	Son	14
1442.	Crane Woman	F	Single	73
1443.	Wolf Chief	M	Husb'd	25
1444.	Lone Woman	F	Wife	23
1445.	Iron	M	Husb'd	61
1446.	Fights In Front	F	Wife	57
1447.	Lazy Boy	M	Husb'd	56
1448.	Echo Woman	F	Wife	35
1449.	Steals Woman	F	Daughter	21
1450.	Steals Nothing	F	Daughter	8
1451.	Sam Lazy Boy	M	Son	2
1452.	Thos. Lazy Boy	M	Son	13
1453.	Goose Lazy Boy	M	Son	1
1454.	Fronr[sic] Rider	M	Husb'd	25
1455.	Rene Front Rider	F	Wife	19
1456.	Lazy Young Man	M	Husb'd	45
1457.	Spear Woman	F	Wife	57
1458.	John Ground	M	Husb'd	25
1459.	Minnie Ground	F	Wife	15
1460.	Ground	M	Husb'd	45
1461.	Jas. Ground	M	Son	22
1462.	John Shorty	M	Husb'd	37
1463.	Striped Stone	F	Wife	28
1464.	Annie Shorty	F	Daughter	11
1465.	Rides Behind	M	Husb'd	37
1466.	Shoots Weasle	F	Wife	35

Census of the -Piegan- Indians of Blackfeet Agency, Montana taken by Geo. B McLaughlin United States Indian Agent 1897

No.	English Name	Sex	Relation	Age
1467.	Weasle Fat	M	Husb'd	45
1468.	Good Shield	F	Wife	30
1469.	Souix[sic] Woman	F	Daughter	20
1470.	Ross White Grass	M	Husb'd	22
1471.	Already Had Teeth	F	Wife	15
1472.	Richard W. Grass	M	Son	4mo
1473.	Home Gun	M	Husb'd	32
1474.	Mary Pipe Stone	F	Wife	26
1475.	Mary H. Gun	F	Daughter	1
1476.	Paul H. Gun	M	Son	4
1477.	Three Chieves[sic]	M	Husb'd	30
1478.	Kills In The Night	F	Wife	43
1479.	Owl Squirel	M	Son	17
1480.	Good Killer	F	Mother	80
1481.	Goes In All Arround[sic]	F	Mother	40
1482.	Black Cloth Woman	F	Daughter	24
1483.	Lilly Round	F	Daughter	13
1484.	Good Chaser	M	Son	10
1485.	Nellie Shildt[sic]	F	Wife	33
1486.	Nettie Schildt	F	Daughter	15
1487.	Harry Schildt	M	Son	12

**Note: 1488 not on film, also there are two Harry's 1487 and 1489, different ages.

No.	English Name	Sex	Relation	Age
1489.	Harry Schildt	M	Son	7
1490.	Augusta Schildt	F	Daughter	5
1491.	Mary Schildt	F	Daughter	3
1492.	Irene Schildt	F	Daughter	7mo
1493.	Mad Wolf	M	Husb'd	65
1494.	Sits Away	F	Wife	80
1495.	Good Crane	M	Son	8
1496.	No Child	M	Son	18
1497.	Herman Dusty Bull	M	Husb'd	21
1498.	Louize D. Bull	F	Wife	16
1499.	Thos. D. Bull	M	Son	2

Census of the -Piegan- Indians of Blackfeet Agency, Montana taken by Geo. B McLaughlin United States Indian Agent 1897

No.	English Name	Sex	Relation	Age
1500.	Sam Little Dog	M	Husb'd	25
1501.	Face Together	F	Wife	23
1502.	Long Time Star	F	Mother	56
1503.	John Star	M	Son	13
1504.	Philip Star	M	Son	18
1505.	Heavy Breast	M	Husb'd	50
1506.	Laying Low	F	Wife	40
1507.	Kind Woman	F	Daughter	32
1508.	Small Head	F	Daughter	7mo
1509.	Young H. Breast	M	Son	18
1510.	Campbell Munro	M	Husb'd	28
1511.	Frezen Munro	F	Wife	22
1512.	Alfred Munro	M	Son	6
1513.	Ben Munro	M	Son	4
1514.	Henry Munro	M	Son	5mo
1515.	Geo. Star	M	Husb'd	29
1516.	Maggie Star	F	Wife	18
1517.	Christian Star	F	Daughter	2
1518.	Lora Star	F	Daughter	3mo
1519.	Double Cloth	F	Mother	52
1520.	Baptist W. Wolf	M	Son	22
1521.	Clement W. Wolf	M	Son	15
1522.	Barnett W. Wolf	M	Son	15
1523.	Geo. W. Wolf	M	Son	11
1524.	John W. Wolf	M	Son	3
1525.	Stabing Down	M	Husb'd	26
1526.	Cloth Woman	F	Wife	22
1527.	Peter S. Down	M	Son	1
1528.	White Grass	M	Husband	48
1529.	Night Kills	F	Wife	40
1530.	Two Catches	F	Wife	22
1531.	Little Rain	M	Son	5
1532.	Infent[sic]	M	Son	1
1533.	Bat Rondi	M	Husb'd	36

Census of the -Piegan- Indians of Blackfeet Agency, Montana taken by Geo. B McLaughlin United States Indian Agent 1897

No.	English Name	Sex	Relation	Age
1534.	Mary Rondi	F	Wife	36
1535.	Richard Rondi	M	Son	16
1536.	Sam Rondi	M	Son	14
1537.	Louize Rondi	F	Daughter	11
1538.	Mary Rondi	F	Daughter	8
1539.	Nancy Rondi	F	Daughter	2
1540.	Isabel Rondi	F	Daughter	5mo
1541.	Geneva Stewart	F	Wife	27
1542.	Earl Stewart	M	Son	6
1543.	Jas. Stewart	M	Son	1
1544.	Stink Tit	M	Husb'd	25
1545.	Ruth Stink Tit	F	Wife	17
1546.	Rose Stink Tit	F	Daughter	5mo
1547.	Bull Child	M	Husb'd	53
1548.	Good Catcher	F	Wife	40
1549.	Joe B. Child	M	Son	18
1550.	Stolen Fromm	F	Daughter	2
1551.	Flying Hen	F	Daughter	3
1552.	Puss Bull Child	M	Son	18
1553.	Catches Both Sides	F	Mother	60
1554.	Bull Child2	F	Mother	50
1555.	Geo. B. Child	M	Son	4
1556.	Mark B. Child	M	Son	2
1557.	Many White Horses	M	Husb'd	70
1558.	Jackrabbit Woman	F	Wife	52
1559.	Many Boys	M	Son	4
1560.	Spy Glass	M	Son	1
1561.	John M.W. Horses	M	Son	16
1562.	Hungry Woman	F	Daughter	6
1563.	Thos. M.W. Horses	M	Son	15
1564.	Many White Horses2	F	Wife	52
1565.	Gun M.W. Horses	M	Son	6
1566.	Crow M.W. Horses	M	Son	5
1567.	Joseph M.W. Horses	M	Son	7
1568.	Lone Girl M.W. Horses	F	Daughter	1

Census of the -Piegan- Indians of Blackfeet Agency, Montana taken by Geo. B McLaughlin United States Indian Agent 1897

No.	English Name	Sex	Relation	Age
1569.	Chicken Front	F	Mother	70
1570.	Young M.W. Horses	M	Son	23
1571.	Chief In Front	F	Mother	78
1572.	Long Time Owl	F	Daughter	18
1573.	Black Bear	M	Husb'd	50
1574.	Many Snakes	F	Wife	52
1575.	Makes[sic] Gun By Mistake	M	Son	25
1576.	Medicine Owl	M	Husb'd	30
1577.	Sheep Woman	F	Wife	50
1578.	Talaho Ashley	M	Husb'd	35
1579.	Singing Water	F	Wife	25
1580.	Lewis Ashley	M	Son	1
1581.	Nellie Ashley	F	Daughter	1
1582.	Doy Ears	M	Husb'd	25
1583.	Flat Face	F	Wife	20
1584.	Takes Gun On Top	M	Husb'd	28
1585.	Yellow Bird	F	Wife	30
1586.	Louize Top	F	Adu[sic] Dau	4
1587.	John Top	M	Son	16
1588.	Dives Long Ways	F	Mother	68
1589.	David Deval	M	Single	17
1590.	Little Young Man	M	Husb'd	40
1591.	Different Cut	F	Wife	56
1592.	Good Singer	F	Mother	80
1593.	Blackfoot Child	M	Husb'd	50
1594.	Buffalo Child	F	Wife	55
1595.	Grace B. Child	F	Daughter	17
1596.	Irene B. Child	F	Daughter	11m
1597.	Bad Married	M	Husb'd	39
1598.	Bear Leggings	F	Wife	27
1599.	Joseph B. Married	M	Son	10

Census of the -Piegan- Indians of Blackfeet Agency, Montana taken by Geo. B McLaughlin United States Indian Agent 1897

No.	English Name	Sex	Relation	Age
1600.	Morning Star	M	Son	7
1601.	Last Bear Woman	F	Daughter	5
1602.	Bear Skin	M	Husb'd	50
1603.	Three Cessors	F	Wife	35
1604.	Bad Boy	M	Son	21
1605.	All The Time Heard	F	Wife	16
1606.	Bear Head	F	Mother	37
1607.	Mary Bear Head	F	Daughter	9
1608.	Yellow Wolf	M	Husb'd	55
1609.	Two Irons	F	Wife	24
1610.	Yellow Grass	M	Son	1
1611.	Crow Girl	F	Daughter	4
1612.	Molley Yellow Wolf	F	Daughter	5
1613.	Agnes Y. Wolf	F	Daughter	21
1614.	Cicell Y. Wolf	F	Wife2	27
1615.	Emma Y. Wolf	F	Wife3	30
1616.	Runs Away	F	Mother	58
1617.	Mary R. Away	F	Daughter	15
1618.	Susan R. Away	F	Daughter	6
1619.	Sam Plume	M	Single	23
1620.	First Kills	F	Mother	35
1621.	Ben First Kills	M	Son	3
1622.	Agnes First Kills	F	Daughter	12
1623.	Curlew	F	Mother	70
1624.	Cut Finger	M	Husb'd	43
1625.	Strikes her self	F	Wife	30
1626.	Earnest Cut Finger	M	Son	14
1627.	Lewis Cut Finger	M	Son	12
1628.	Josephine Cut Finger	F	Daughter	11
1629.	Maggie Cut Finger	F	Daughter	4
1630.	Thos. Cut Finger	M	Son	3
1631.	Florence Cut Finger	F	Daughter	1
1632.	Jim Grant	M	Husb'd	25

Census of the -Piegan- Indians of Blackfeet Agency, Montana taken by Geo. B McLaughlin United States Indian Agent 1897

No.	English Name	Sex	Relation	Age
1633.	Josephene Grant	F	Wife	24
1634.	Richard Grant	M	Brother	20
1635.	Rides at Door	M	Husb'd	30
1636.	Mary R. at Door	F	Wife	28
1637.	Dick R. at Door	M	Son	7
1638.	Louize R. at Door	F	Daughter	5
1639.	Frank R. at Door	M	Son	2
1640.	Carry Munro	F	Wife	26
1641.	Mable Munro	F	Daughter	4
1642.	Jessie Munro	M	Son	2
1643.	Joseph Munro	M	Son	2mo
1644.	Jeo[sic] Kipp	M	Husb'd	47
1645.	Martha Kipp	F	Wife	37
1646.	William Kipp	M	Son	21
1647.	Jas. Kipp	M	Son	6
1648.	Mary Kippp[sic]	F	Daughter	9
1649.	Gro Kipp	M	Son	6mo
1650.	Mary Kipp	F	Mother	70
1651.	Dick Kipp	M	Husb'd	32
1652.	Chicken Woman	F	Wife	24
1653.	Lewis Kipp	M	Son	6
1654.	Geo. Kipp	M	Son	1
1655.	Cora Kipp	F	Daughter	8
1656.	Matt Litel	M	Single	23
1657.	Hits On Top	F	Single	46
1658.	Maggie Kennerly	F	Wife	45
1659.	Agnes Gobart	F	Daughter	13
1660.	Ammie Gobart	F	Daughter	9
1661.	Agnes Kennerly	F	Daughter	11
1662.	Jerome Kennerly	M	Son	9
1663.	Jas. Kennerly	M	Son	1
1664.	Molley Davis	F	Wife	24
1665.	Thos. Davis	M	Son	5

Census of the -Piegan- Indians of Blackfeet Agency, Montana taken by Geo. B McLaughlin United States Indian Agent 1897

No.	English Name	Sex	Relation	Age
1666.	Pearl Davis	F	Adu[sic]	3
1667.	Bryan Davis	M	Son	10m
1668.	Eddie Davis	M	Brother	18
1669.	Catherine Davis	F	Sister	14
1670.	Mary Lukins	F	Wife	50
1671.	Albert Lukins	M	Son	26
1672.	John Lukins	M	Son	16
1673.	Peter Lukins	M	Son	14
1674.	Dora Lukins	F	Daughter	20
1675.	Victoria Lukins	F	Daughter	19
1676.	Lou Paisley	F	Wife	36
1677.	Geo. Paisley	M	Son	12
1678.	Allen Paisley	M	Son	8
1679.	Mattie Paisley	F	Daughter	5
1680.	Chauncey Paisley	M	Son	11m
1681.	Lewis Pembrane	M	Husb'd	39
1682.	Ammie Pembrane	F	Wife	31
1683.	Eddie Pembrane	M	Son	11
1684.	Davis Pembrane	M	Son	9
1685.	Isabel Pembrane	F	Daughter	6
1686.	Geo. Pembrane	M	Son	4
1687.	Louize Aubery[sic]	F	Wife	40
1688.	Alice Aubary	F	Daughter	20
1689.	Rose Aubary	F	Daughter	19
1690.	Laura Aubary	F	Daughter	16
1691.	Thos. Aubary	M	Son	14
1692.	Lou Aubary	F	Daughter	11
1693.	Dora Aubary	F	Daughter	10
1694.	Philip Aubary	M	Son	5
1695.	May Aubary	F	Daughter	4
1696.	Janette Aubary	F	Daughter	2
1697.	Morning Plume	M	Husb'd	50
1698.	Snake Woman	F	Wife	47
1699.	Good Woman	F	Daughter	8mo
1700.	Pete After Buffalo	M	Husb'd	33

Census of the -Piegan- Indians of Blackfeet Agency, Montana taken by Geo. B McLaughlin United States Indian Agent 1897

No.	English Name	Sex	Relation	Age
1701.	Cut Nose	F	Wife	27
1702.	Two Owls	F	Wife	26
1703.	John A. Buffalo	M	Son	4
1704.	Joseph A. Buffalo	M	Son	3
1705.	Xzever A. Buffalo	M	Son	5
1706.	Susan A. Buffalo	F	Daughter	1
1707.	Ammie A. Buffalo	F	Daughter	2
1708.	Isabel A. Buffalo	F	Daughter	10
1709.	Strikes First	F	Mother	70
1710.	Crane Woman	F	Single	60
1711.	Makes Two Guns	----	----	----
1712.	Florence T. Guns	F	Wife	21
1713.	Joseph T. Guns	M	Son	1
1714.	Heading Off	M	Single	80
1715.	Elie Rider	M	Single	24
1716.	Julia Magee	F	Wife	30
1717.	Joseph Magee	M	Son	13
1718.	Mary Magee	F	Daughter	10
1719.	Thos. Magee	M	Son	7
1720.	Geo. Magee	M	Son	5
1721.	Walter Magee	M	Son	3
1722.	Henry Magee	M	Son	2
1723.	Bert Kennerly	M	Single	20
1724.	Perry Kennerly	M	Brother	18
1725.	Sophia Powell	F	Wife	25
1726.	Frank Powell	M	Son	1
1727.	Clara Powell	F	Daughter	6
1728.	Rose Ward	F	Wife	25
1729.	Jim Ward	M	Son	7
1730.	Geo. Ward	M	Son	5
1731.	Rose Ward	F	Daughter	2
1732.	Night Gun	M	Husb'd	39
1733.	Yellow Squirel	F	Wife	25

Census of the -Piegan- Indians of Blackfeet Agency, Montana taken by Geo. B McLaughlin United States Indian Agent 1897

No.	English Name	Sex	Relation	Age
1734.	Cloth Woman	F	Daughter	4
1735.	Susan N. Gun	F	Daughter	2
1736.	Samuel N. Gun	M	Daughter[sic]	11m
1737.	Strikes Back	F	Mother	70

**Note, 1738 missing.

No.	English Name	Sex	Relation	Age
1739.	Eagle Tail	M	Husb'd	40
1740.	Pretty Snake	F	Wife	44
1741.	Yellow Weasle	F	Daughter	6
1742.	Miner	F	Mother	82
1743.	Chas. Shoquette	M	Husb'd	33
1744.	Louize Shoquette	F	Wife	31
1745.	Josephene Shoquette	F	Daughter	21
1746.	Antoine Shoquette	M	Brother	44
1747.	Eagle Child	M	Husb'd	35
1748.	Spotted Woman	F	Wife	26
1749.	Jonh[sic] E. Child	M	Son	3
1750.	Geo. E. Child	M	Son	3da
1751.	Little Snake	F	Mother	70
1752.	Three Bear	M	Husb'd	45
1753.	Crow Head	F	Wife	58
1754.	Joseph Three Bear	M	Son	2
1755.	Cicell Tree Bear	F	Daughter	4
1756.	William Smith	M	Son	23
1757.	Lizza Smith	F	Mother	58
1758.	Peter Smith	M	Son	9
1759.	Harry No Chief	M	Single	24
1760.	Frank Munro	M	Husb'd	49
1761.	Mary Munro	F	Wife	44
1762.	Lewis Munro	M	Son	15
1763.	Antoine Munro	M	Son	9
1764.	Lucy Cook	F	Wife	25
1765.	Isabel Cook	F	Daughter	3

Census of the -Piegan- Indians of Blackfeet Agency, Montana taken by Geo. B McLaughlin United States Indian Agent 1897

No.	English Name	Sex	Relation	Age
1766.	Loratta[sic] Cook	F	Daughter	1
1767.	Frank Spearson	M	Husb'd	48
1768.	Mary Spearson	F	Wife	28
1769.	Got Gun in Side	M	Son	1
1770.	Clear Up	M	Husb'd	25
1771.	Owl Cry	F	Wife	28
1772.	Stays at Home	F	Daughter	10
1773.	Telling Stories	F	Daughter	3
1794.	Going Up Hill	F	Daughter	6mo
1795.	John Munro	M	Husb'd	76
1796.	Justine Munro	F	Wife	30
1797.	Guss Munro	M	Son	9
1798.	Lewis Munro	M	Son	8
1799.	Frank Munro Jr.	M	Stepson	16
1800.	Francis Munro	M	Son	22
1801.	Justine Munro	F	Daughter	28
1802.	John Dont Go Out	M	Husb'd	76
1803.	Cloth Woman	F	Wife	62
1804.	Mary Hazlett	F	Stepdaughter	14
1805.	Hary[sic] Coat	M	Husb'd	28
1806.	Mary Coat	F	Wife	25
1807.	Eli Rider	M	Single	25
1808.	Black Weasle	M	Husb'd	22
1809.	Two Horns	F	Wife	30
1810.	Lone Warrior	M	Son	1
1811.	Split Ears	M	Husb'd	27
1812.	Good Killer	F	Wife	40
1813.	Maggie S. Ears	F	Daughter	7
1814.	Susan S. Ears	F	Daughter	4
1815.	Wolverine	M	Husb'd	26
1816.	Walking Together	F	Daughter	19
1817.	Many Owls	M	Son	4

Census of the -Piegan- Indians of Blackfeet Agency, Montana taken by Geo. B McLaughlin United States Indian Agent 1897

No.	English Name	Sex	Relation	Age
1818.	Joseph Wolverine	M	Son	2
1819.	Hits In Water	F	Mother	70
1820.	Walking Smoke	M	Husb'd	40
1821.	Diver	F	Wife	38
1822.	Gather Wood	M	Son	19
1823.	Cicelia Huncbuger	F	Wife	57
1824.	John Huncbuger	M	Son	26
1825.	Thos. Huncbuger	M	Son	21
1826.	Clara Huncbuger	F	Daughter	18
1827.	Guss Huncbuger	M	Son	14
1828.	Gambler	M	Husb'd	33
1829.	Louize Gambler	F	Wife	34
1830.	John Vielle	M	Husb'd	32
1831.	Kills Away Off	F	Wife	28
1832.	William Vielle	M	Son	5
1833.	Mary Vielle	F	Daughter	4
1834.	Ben Vielle	M	Daughter[sic]	2
1835.	Joseph Vielle	M	Son	7
1836.	Tom Vielle	M	Brother	21
1837.	Oliver Sanderville	M	Husb'd	38
1838.	Mary Sanderville	F	Daughter[sic]	27
1839.	John Sanderville	M	Son	10
1840.	Black Sarcee	M	Husb'd	38
1841.	Kills Away Off	F	Wife	37
1842.	Chas. Rose	M	Husb'd	40
1843.	Breaks Good	F	Wife	22
1844.	Julia Rose	F	Daughter	10
1845.	Alice Rose	F	Daughter	7
1846.	Peter Rose	M	Son	6
1847.	Jim Rose	M	Son	2
1848.	Maggie Rose	F	Daughter	15
1849.	Joseph Evans	M	Husb'd	23
1850.	Mary C. Evans	F	Wife	18

Census of the -Piegan- Indians of Blackfeet Agency, Montana taken by Geo. B McLaughlin United States Indian Agent 1897

No.	English Name	Sex	Relation	Age
1851.	Jim Evans	M	Son	1
1852.	Victoria Robinson	F	Mother	36
1853.	Mary Robinson	F	Daughter	19
1854.	Geo. Robinson	M	Son	17
1855.	Joseph Robinson	M	Son	15
1856.	Louize Robinson	F	Daughter	9
1857.	Agnes Robinson	F	Daughter	6
1858.	Frank Bostwick	M	Husb'd	36
1859.	Louize Bostwick	F	Wife	24
1860.	Henry Bostwick	M	Son	4
1861.	Geo. Bostwick	M	Son	2
1862.	William Bostwick	M	Son	1
1863.	Doublr[sic] Wolf	F	Mother	47
1864.	Geo. Cook	M	Husb'd	33
1865.	Julia Cook	F	Wife	25
1866.	Chief Crow	M	Husb'd	39
1867.	Strikes Wit[sic] Gun	F	Wife	38
1868.	Jas. Crow	M	Son	17
1869.	Albert Crow	M	Son	12
1870.	Makes Noise	F	Daughter	5
1871.	Thos. Dawson	M	Husb'd	36
1871[sic]	Isabel Dawson	F	Wife	35
1872.	Lorena Dawson	F	Adpd Dau	13
1873.	Horace Clarke	M	Father	48
1874.	John Clarke	M	Son	16
1875.	Jas. Dawson	M	Husb'd	46
1876.	Erskins Dawson	M	Son	13
1877.	William Dawson	M	Son	10
1878.	Herald Dawson	M	Son	7
1879.	Malcolm Clarke	M	Single	21
1880.	Bird Rattle	M	Husb'd	37
1881.	Site Under	F	Wife	25

Census of the -Piegan- Indians of Blackfeet Agency, Montana taken by Geo. B McLaughlin United States Indian Agent 1897

No.	English Name	Sex	Relation	Age
1882.	Cloth Woman	F	Wife	30
1883.	Good Looking	M	Son	5
1884.	Bull Child	M	Son	20
1885.	Elmer B. Rattler	M	Son	15
1886.	Slim Tail	M	Husb'd	34
1887.	Kills In Water	F	Wife	48
1888.	Big Spring	M	Husb'd	31
1889.	No Owl Spring	F	Wife	30
1890.	Shoots Close	M	Son	23
1891.	Blanket	M	Son	20
1892.	Small Face	F	Wife2	22

Census of the Blackfeet,

Montana, 1898

38837　　　1898

Census of the Piegan Indians

by
Thomas P. Fuller
June 30, 1898

Census of the Piegan Indians of Blackfeet Agency, Montana taken by Thomas P. Fuller United States Indian Agent 1898

No.	English Name	Sex	Relation	Age
1.	Ellen Edwards	F	Mother	35
2.	Wm. Edwards	M	Son	9
3.	Thos. Edwards	M	Son	7
4.	Funny Edwards	F	Daughter	5
5.	Elisabeth Edwards	F	Daughter	3
6.	John Edwards	M	Son	1
7.	Mary Rutherford	F	Mother	45
8.	Alice Rutherford	F	Daughter	19
9.	Wm. Rutherford	M	Son	14
10.	Jas. Rutherford	M	Son	12
11.	Henry Rutherford	M	Son	10
12.	Mary Davis	F	Mother	23
13.	Hattie Davis	F	Daughter	2
14.	Maggie Heran	F	Mother	24
15.	Mary Heran	F	Daughter	8
16.	Able Skunk Cap	M	----	23
17.	Cree Medicine	M	S-Father	34
18.	Medicine Woman	F	Wife	31
19.	Maggie Bear Chief	F	Daughter	7
20.	Susie Bear Chief	F	Daughter	3
21.	Joe Bear Chief	M	Son	5
22.	Wild Gun	M	Father	39
23.	John W. Gun	M	Son	18
24.	Last Strike	F	----	50
25.	Young Running Rabbit	M	Father	52
26.	Long Time Woman	F	Wife	30
27.	Good Strike	F	Wife	50
28.	Julia Running Rabbit	F	Daughter	14
29.	Long Time Otter	F	Daughter	8
30.	Hester Running Rabbit	F	Daughter	15
31.	Alex Gardupin	M	Father	34
32.	Grass Snake	F	Wife	21

Census of the Piegan Indians of Blackfeet Agency, Montana taken by Thomas P. Fuller United States Indian Agent 1898

No.	English Name	Sex	Relation	Age
33.	John Gardupin	M	Son	4
34.	Curley Bear	M	Husb'd	45
35.	Minnie Curley Bear	F	Wife	33
36.	Mary Curley Bear	F	Wife	32
37.	Chas. Curley Bear	M	Son	17
38.	Wm. Curley Bear	M	Son	3
39.	Jennie Curley Bear	F	Daughter	6
40.	Annie Curley Bear	F	Daughter	2
41.	Small Woman	F	----	70
42.	Lane Trombly	M	Husb'd	28
43.	Maggie Trombley	F	Wife	25
44.	Isaac Trombley	M	Son	3
45.	Jos. Trombley	M	Son	2
46.	Frank Gardupin	M	Husb'd	28
47.	Mary Gardupin	F	Wife	20
48.	Frank Gardupin	M	Son	2
49.	Pete Gardupin	M	----	37
50.	Louise Gardupin	F	Mother	63
51.	John Gardupin	M	Son	16
52.	Eagle Flag	M	Husb'd	55
53.	Bounces Up	F	Wife	45
54.	Stella Eagle Flag	F	Daughter	14
55.	Anna Eagle Flag	F	Daughter	10
56.	Mrs. Eagle Ribs	F	Mother	34
57.	Susie Eagle Ribs	F	Daughter	5
58.	Ceeila Eagle Ribs	F	Daughter	2
59.	Black Bull	M	Husb'd	25
60.	Jennie Black Bull	F	Wife	19
61.	Mary Black Bull	F	Daughter	1
62.	War Bonnet	M	Husb'd	29
63.	First Clean Up	F	Wife	28

Census of the Piegan Indians of Blackfeet Agency, Montana taken by Thomas P. Fuller United States Indian Agent 1898

No.	English Name	Sex	Relation	Age
64.	Jas. War Bonnet	M	Son	3
65.	Anna War Bonnet	F	Daughter	65
66.	Young Running Crane	M	Husb'd	44
67.	Lead Woman	F	Wife	36
68.	John Running Crane	M	Son	14
69.	Maggie Henault	F	Mother	48
70.	Stephen Henault	F	Mother	21
71.	Nelson Henault	M	Son	19
72.	Clara Henault	F	Daughter	9
73.	Moses Henault	M	Son	12
74.	Rosa Roth	F	----	24
75.	Henry Heavy Gun	M	Husb'd	26
76.	Josephine Heavy Gun	F	Wife	17
77.	Strikes Last	F	----	55
78.	John Owl Child	M	Son	15
79.	Joseph Owl Child	M	Son	8
80.	Louis Owl Child	M	Son	6
81.	Under Otter	F	----	60
82.	Crowing Old Woman	F	----	60
83.	Calf Robe	F	----	55
84.	Bad Woman	F	Mother	40
85.	Richard Calf Robe	M	Son	19
86.	Joseph Calf Robe	M	Husb'd	20
87.	Emma Calf Robe	F	Wife	22
88.	Iron Eater	M	Husb'd	44
89.	Owl Face	F	Wife	34
90.	Blanket Woman	F	Wife	45
91.	Susie Iron Eater	F	Daughter	11
92.	Issabella Iron Eater	F	Daughter	12
93.	Maggie Iron Eater	F	Daughter	9

Census of the Piegan Indians of Blackfeet Agency, Montana taken by Thomas P. Fuller United States Indian Agent 1898

No.	English Name	Sex	Relation	Age
94.	Rosa Iron Eater	F	Daughter	2
95.	Red Head	M	Husb'd	40
96.	Two Strikes	F	Wife	40
97.	John Red Head	M	Son	1
98.	Spotted Bear	M	Husb'd	70
99.	Spotted Woman	F	Wif	34
100.	Joe Spotted Bear	M	Son	7
101.	Mike Spotted Bear	M	Son	1
102.	John Eagles Ribs	M	Son	19
103.	Good Clean Up	F	Mother	39
104.	Both Goes In	F	Daughter	3
105.	Thos. Two Stabs	M	Husb'd	40
106.	Mary Two Stabs	F	Wife	26
107.	Maggie Two Stabs	F	Daughter	16
108.	Joseph Two Stabs	M	Son	5
109.	Louis Two Stabs	M	Son	3
110.	Lawrence Two Stabs	M	Son	1
111.	Michael Day Rider	M	Husb'd	29
112.	Helen Day Rider	F	Wife	24
113.	Oliver Day Rider	M	Son	3
114.	Chas. Day Rider	M	Son	1
115.	Geo. Four Horns	M	Son	17
116.	Kills In Water	F	Mother	50
117.	Lone Cut	F	----	70
118.	Josephine Hall	F	Mother	28
119.	John Hall	M	Son	5
120.	David Hall	M	Son	3
121.	Wm. Hall	M	Son	1
122.	Black Boy	M	Husb'd	38
123.	Kills On Top	F	Wife	35
124.	Last Coyote	M	----	48
125.	Owl Child	M	Husb'd	43

Census of the Piegan Indians of Blackfeet Agency, Montana taken by Thomas P. Fuller United States Indian Agent 1898

No.	English Name	Sex	Relation	Age
126.	Mollie Owl Child	F	Wife	30
127.	Susie Owl Child	F	Daughter	17
128.	Issabella Owl Child	F	Daughter	11
129.	Anna Owl Child	F	Daughter	4
130.	Eagle Head	M	Husb'd	59
131.	White Tail	F	Wife	40
132.	Jas. Eagle Head	M	Son	12
133.	Margaret Eagle Head	F	Daughter	10
134.	Jackson Double Blaze	M	Husb'd	34
135.	Medicine Beaver	F	Wife	24
136.	Joe Double Blaze	M	Son	17
137.	Oliver Double Blaze	M	Son	9
138.	Frank Double Blaze	M	Son	6
139.	Louis Double Blaze	M	Son	3
140.	Dick Double Blaze	M	Son	1
141.	Singing	F	----	64
142.	New Crow	M	----	30
143.	Mamie Crawford	F	Mother	40
144.	Ellen Crawford	F	Daughter	4
145.	Joe Crawford	M	Son	1
146.	John Crawford	M	Son	8
147.	Belle Ripley	F	Mother	50
148.	Emma Ripley	F	Daughter	5
149.	Drives Long Way	F	----	70
150.	Big Beaver	M	Husb'd	38
151.	Minnie Big Beaver	F	Wife	29
152.	Hiram Big Beaver	M	Son	10
153.	Eddie Big Beaver	M	Son	12
154.	Jas. Big Beaver	M	Son	3
155.	Emma Big Beaver	F	Daughter	6
156.	Smoking Flint	M	Husb'd	38
157.	Under Beaver	F	Wife	41

Census of the Piegan Indians of Blackfeet Agency, Montana taken by Thomas P. Fuller United States Indian Agent 1898

No.	English Name	Sex	Relation	Age
158.	Peter Flint Smoker	M	Son	15
159.	Jas. Flint Smoker	M	Son	7
160.	Shoots At Another	M	Husb'd	35
161.	Martha Shoots At Another	F	Wife	43
162.	Josephine Weather Wax	F	Daughter	18
163.	Mary Weather Wax	F	Daughter	16
164.	Joe Weather Wax	M	Son	12
165.	Old Coyote	M	Husb'd	35
166.	Mary Old Coyote	F	Wife	40
167.	Philip Old Coyote	M	Son	17
168.	Calf Woman	F	----	66
169.	White Dog	M	Husb'd	40
170.	Medicine O. Woman	F	Wife	28
171.	Henry White Dog	M	Son	3
172.	Mollie Wite[sic] Dog	F	Daughter	4
173.	Wm. White Dog	M	Son	1
174.	Iron Necklace	M	Husb'd	36
175.	Minnie Iron Necklace	F	Wife	45
176.	Anna Iron Necklace	F	Daughter	6
177.	After Buffalo	F	Mother	39
178.	Joseph After Buffalo	M	Son	3
179.	Joe Kossuth	M	G-Son	25
180.	Cuts Both Sides	F	G-Mother	75
181.	Aims Back	M	Husb'd	30
182.	Emma Aims Back	F	Wife	20
183.	Thos. Aims Back	M	Son	4
184.	Sitting In The Road	F	G-Mother	70
185.	Shoots In The Night	M	G-Son	8
186.	Long Time Rock	M	Husb'd	34
187.	Nellie Long Time Rock	F	Wife	22
188.	Joe Long Time Rock	M	Son	1

Census of the Piegan Indians of Blackfeet Agency, Montana taken by Thomas P. Fuller United States Indian Agent 1898

No.	English Name	Sex	Relation	Age
189.	Peter Old Rock	M	----	22
190.	Tail Feathers	M	Husb'd	43
191.	Jane Tail Feathers	F	Wife	38
192.	Walter Tail Feathers	M	Son	9
193.	Thos. Tail Feathers	M	Son	7
194.	Peter Tail Feathers	M	Son	4
195.	Chas. Tail Feathers	M	Son	1
196.	Calf Looking	M	Husb'd	52
197.	Goes In Last	F	Wife	55
198.	Paul Calf Looking	M	Son	22
199.	Big Head	F	Mother	31
200.	Thos. Big Head	M	Son	3
201.	Stabbing By Mistake	M	Husb'd	28
202.	Anna Stabbing By Mistake	F`	Wife	25
203.	Peter Stabbing By Mistake	M	Son	3
204.	Mountain Chief	M	Husb'd	50
205.	Big Gun Woman	F	Wife	40
206.	Antoine Mountain Chief	M	Son	18
207.	Thakla Mountain Chief	F	Daughter	17
208.	Walter Mountain Chief	M	Son	15
209.	Anna Mountain Chief	F	Daughter	3
210.	Louis Mountain Chief	M	Son	1
211.	Chief All Over	M	Husb'd	46
212.	Little Peck	F	Wife	47
213.	Geo. Chief All Over	M	Son	6
214.	Frank Choat	M	----	25
215.	Geo. Choat	M	Husb'd	23
216.	Fannie Choat	F	Wife	19
217.	Minnie Choat	F	Mother	50
218.	Samuel Choat	M	Son	19
219.	Peter Lodge Pole	M	Son	13

Census of the Piegan Indians of Blackfeet Agency, Montana taken by Thomas P. Fuller United States Indian Agent 1898

No.	English Name	Sex	Relation	Age
220.	Jennie Johnson	F	Mother	35
221.	Mary Johnson	F	Daughter	18
222.	Wm. Johnson	M	Son	13
223.	Belle Johnson	F	Daughter	12
224.	Jas. Johnson	M	Son	11
225.	Ida Johnson	F	Daughter	9
226.	Big Lodge Pole	M	----	37
227.	Takes Gun	F	----	60
228.	Richard Sanderville	M	Husb'd	30
229.	Nancy Sanderville	F	Wife	24
230.	Agnes Sanderville	F	Daughter	9
231.	Irene Sanderville	F	Daughter	23
232.	Oliver Sanderville	M	Husb'd	39
233.	Mary Sanderville	F	Wife	29
234.	John Sanderville	M	Son	11
235.	Thos. Kyo	M	Husb'd	37
236.	Mary Kyo	F	Wife	24
237.	Wm. Kyo	M	Son	3
238.	Louis Marceau	M	Husb'd	32
239.	Rosa Marceau	F	Wife	19
240.	Alex Marceau	M	Husb'd	34
241.	Thereca Marceau	F	Wife	26
242.	Louise Marceau	F	Daughter	5
243.	Anna Marceau	F	Daughter	1
244.	Pete Mauceau #1	F[sic]	----	----
245.	Mrs. Running Wolf	F	Mother	42
246.	Miles Running Wolf	M	Son	19
247.	Geo. Running Wolf	M	Son	7
248.	John Running Wolf	M	Son	5
249.	Homer Running Wolf	M	Son	11
250.	Albert Running Wolf	M	Son	12

Census of the Piegan Indians of Blackfeet Agency, Montana taken by Thomas P. Fuller United States Indian Agent 1898

No.	English Name	Sex	Relation	Age
251.	Mrs. Fast Buffalo Horse	F	Mother	45
252.	Jos. Fast Buffalo Horse	M	Son	23
253.	Jas. Fast Buffalo Horse	M	Son	12
254.	Albert Fast Buffalo Horse	M	Son	21
255.	Poor Woman	F	----	70
256.	Owl Top Feathers	M	Husb'd	46
257.	Owl Woman	F	Wife	40
258.	John Owl Top Feathers	M	Son	20
259.	Jenny Owl Top Feathers	F	Daughter	17
260.	Fannie Owl Top Feathers	F	Daughter	6
261.	Good Looking Woman	F	Mother	30
262.	John Good Looking Woman	M	Son	7
263.	Day Rider	M	Husb'd	25
264.	Runs Away	F	Wife	26
265.	Jos. Day Rider	M	Son	2
266.	Head Carrier	M	Husb'd	68
267.	Mary Head Carrier	F	Wife	26
268.	John Head Carrier	M	Son	19
269.	Richard Rutherford	M	Husb'd	21
270.	Elizabetd[sic] Rutherford	F	Wife	20
271.	Edna Rutherford	F	Daughter	1
272.	Joe McKnight	M	Husb'd	24
273.	Lucy McKnight	F	Wife	23
274.	Irene McKnight	F	Daughter	2
275.	Anna Fisher	F	S-Mother	27
276.	Jas. Fisher	M	S-Son	12
277.	Maggie Albertson	F	Mother	37
278.	Julia Walters	F	Daughter	23
279.	Geo. Walters	M	Son	21
280.	Arthur Walters	M	Son	18
281.	Robert Albertson	M	Son	8
282.	Mary Albertson	F	Daughter	5
283.	Julia Albertson	F	Daughter	1

Census of the Piegan Indians of Blackfeet Agency, Montana taken by Thomas P. Fuller United States Indian Agent 1898

No.	English Name	Sex	Relation	Age
284.	Bob Tail Horse	M	Husb'd	46
285.	Long Time Woman	F	Wife	48
286.	Joe Bob Tail Horse	M	Son	16
287.	Jas. Gambler	M	Husb'd	23
288.	Anna Gambler	F	Wife	19
289.	John Gobert	M	Husb'd	30
290.	Susie Gobert	F	Wife	21
291.	Nellie Gobert	F	Daughter	1
292.	Millie La Breech	F	Mother	48
293.	Chas. La Breech	M	Son	30
294.	Medora La Breech	M	Son	21
295.	Leanora La Breech	F	Daughter	18
296.	Nellie La Breech	F	Daughter	16
297.	Jessie La Breech	F	Daughter	14
298.	Toxhiel La Breech	F	Daughter	11
299.	David La Breech	M	Husb'd	25
300.	Minnie La Breech	F	Wife	26
301.	Chas. La Breech	M	Son	2
302.	Clarence La Breech	M	Son	1
303.	Julia Pendergrast	F	Mother	27
304.	Emily Pendergrast	F	Daughter	3
305.	George Pendergrast	M	Son	1
306.	Mary Jean White	F	Mother	24
307.	David Ripley	M	Brother	21
308.	Minnie Ripley	F	Sister	16
309.	Cora White	F	Daughter	5
310.	Lorenzo White	M	Son	4
311.	Malinda White	F	Daughter	2
312.	Big Snake	F	----	39
313.	Dives Long Way	M	----	60
314.	Bead Woman	F	Mother	50
315.	Joe Cayton	M	Son	22

Census of the Piegan Indians of Blackfeet Agency, Montana taken by Thomas P. Fuller United States Indian Agent 1898

No.	English Name	Sex	Relation	Age
316.	Four Horns	M	Husb'd	44
317.	Gros-Ventre Woman	F	Wife	34
318.	Benjamin Four Horns	M	Son	18
319.	James Four Horns	M	Son	5
320.	Maggie Nichols	F	Mother	27
321.	Edith Inman	F	Daughter	17
322.	Ollie Inman	F	Daughter	9
323.	Cecil Nichols	M	Son	3
324.	Ellen McMullen	F	----	16
325.	Calf Tail	M	Husb'd	40
326.	Different Gun	F	Wife	40
327.	John Calf Tail	M	Son	20
328.	Ernest Calf Tail	M	Son	10
329.	Joe Evans	M	Husb'd	24
330.	Mary Evans	F	Wife	20
331.	Jas. Evans	M	Son	2
332.	Katie Pias	F	Sister	11
333.	Daniel Pias	M	Brother	8
334.	Ruben Pias	M	Brother	7
335.	Susie Pias	F	Sister	2
336.	Joe Tatsey	M	Husb'd	34
337.	Annie Tatsey	F	Wife	25
338.	Josephene Tatsey	F	Daughter	8
339.	Hattie Tatsey	F	Daughter	6
340.	John Tatsey	M	Son	4
341.	Joe Tatsey	M	Son	2
342.	Susan Tatsey	F	----	66
343.	Mary Teasdale	F	Mother	55
344.	Rose Teasdale	F	Daughter	21
345.	Josephene Teasdale	F	Daughter	16
346.	Nellie Teasdale	F	Daughter	10
347.	John Polite Pepion	M	Husb'd	27
348.	Cecil P. Pepion	F	Wife	27

Census of the Piegan Indians of Blackfeet Agency, Montana taken by Thomas P. Fuller United States Indian Agent 1898

No.	English Name	Sex	Relation	Age
349.	Jessie Pepion	F	S-Mother	24
350.	Frank Pepion	M	S-Son	18
351.	Chester Pepion	M	S-Son	14
352.	Louise Pepion	F	S-Daughter	19
353.	Cecil Pepion	F	S-Daughter	23
354.	Thos. Pepion	M	Son	3
355.	Joe Pepion	M	Son	1
356.	Pete Champine	M	Husb'd	33
357.	Susie Champine	F	Wife	28
358.	George Champine	M	Son	5
359.	Maggie Champine	F	Daughter	4
360.	Night Rider	F	----	30
361.	Thunder Woman	F	----	70
362.	Chas. Iron Breast	M	Husb'd	22
363.	Minnie Iron Breast	F	Wife	27
364.	Bull Shoe No. 1	M	Husb'd	51
365.	Small Woman	F	Wife	45
366.	Dirty Face	F	Wife	34
367.	Joe Bull Shoe	M	Son	19
368.	Pat Bull Shoe	M	Son	12
369.	Big Woman	F	Mother	44
370.	Three Guns	M	Son	15
371.	Many Necklass	F	----	80
372.	Catches First	F	----	70
373.	Painted Wings	M	Husb'd	72
374.	Hits On Top	F	Wife	48
375.	Elk	M	Son	20
376.	Lucy Painted Wings	F	Daughter	10
377.	Frank Donavon	M	Husb'd	21
378.	Jane Donavon	F	Wife	16

Census of the Piegan Indians of Blackfeet Agency, Montana taken by Thomas P. Fuller United States Indian Agent 1898

No.	English Name	Sex	Relation	Age
379.	Two Strikes	F	----	56
380.	Old Man Chief	M	Husb'd	28
381.	Lucy Old Man Chief	F	Wife	26
382.	Jas. Old Man Chief	M	Son	4
383.	John Old Man Choef[sic]	M	Son	1
384.	Rattler	M	Husb'd	70
385.	Spear Woman	F	Wife	40
386.	Elmer Rattler	M	Son	24
387.	Red Fox	M	Husb'd	26
388.	Good Clean Up	F	Wife	23
389.	John Red Fox	M	Son	3
390.	Jos. Red Fox	M	Son	2
391.	George Prarie Chicken	M	Husb'd	25
392.	Johanna Prarie Chicken	F	Wife	19
393.	Cecil Prarie Chicken	F	Daughter	2
394.	Morning Gun	M	Husb'd	36
395.	Otter Woman	F	Wife	25
396.	John Morming[sic] Gun	M	Son	11
397.	Flies In Water	F	Daughter	4
398.	Water Snake	F	Daughter	3
399.	Bryer	M	Son	2
400.	Many Morning Gun	F	Daughter	1
401.	Catches Edge Water	F	----	70
402.	Duck Head	M	Husb'd	32
403.	Buckskin Rider	F	Wife	26
404.	Peter Duck Head	M	Son	8
405.	Josephine Duck Head	F	Daughter	10
406.	Mary Duck Head	F	Daughter	2
407.	White Man	M	Husb'd	58
408.	Clean Up	F	Wife	3
409.	Sweet Grass Woman	F	Wife	36
410.	John White Man	M	Son	18
411.	George White Man	M	Son	2

Census of the Piegan Indians of Blackfeet Agency, Montana taken by Thomas P. Fuller United States Indian Agent 1898

No.	English Name	Sex	Relation	Age
412.	Peter White Man	M	Son	16
413.	White Quiver	M	Husb'd	38
414.	Minnie White Quiver	F	Wife	37
415.	Benjiman[sic] White Quiver	M	Son	13
416.	Thomas White Quiver	M	Son	3
417.	Maggie White Quiver	F	Daughter	6
418.	Mollie White Quiver	F	Daughter	1
419.	Long Wolverene	F	----	80
420.	After Buffalo	M	Husb'd	46
421.	Daisy After Buffalo	F	Wife	22
422.	John After Buffalo	M	Son	4
423.	Stabs	M	Son	1
424.	Red Horn	M	----	60
425.	Iron Pipe	M	Husb'd	40
426.	Both Goes In	F	Wife	32
427.	John Iron Pipe	M	Son	3
428.	Charles Iron Pipe	M	Son	1
429.	Maggie Iron Pipe	F	Daughter	6
430.	Joe Iron Pipe	M	Son	16
431.	Mittens	M	Husb'd	28
432.	Susie Mittens	F	Wife	22
433.	Jas. Mittens	M	Son	3
434.	Charles Mittens	M	Son	2
435.	Annie Mittens	F	Daughter	5
436.	Samuel Randel	M	----	21
437.	Felix Marrowbones	M	Husb'd	24
438.	Annie Marrow bones[sic]	F	Wife	19
439.	Comes In Night	M	Husb'd	40
440.	Elk Robe	F	Wife	32
441.	Charges	F	Wife	20
442.	Cecil Comes In Night	F	Daughter	5
443.	Minnie Comes In Night	F	Daughter	4

Census of the Piegan Indians of Blackfeet Agency, Montana taken by Thomas P. Fuller United States Indian Agent 1898

No.	English Name	Sex	Relation	Age
444.	Crow Eyes	M	Husb'd	39
445.	Running Rattler	F	Wife	26
446.	William Comes In Night	M	Son	3
447.	New Robe	M	Husb'd	44
448.	Sharp Nose	F	Wife	45
449.	Hewas In Night	F	Wife	34
450.	John New Robe	M	Son	17
451.	James New Robe	M	Son	11
452.	Annie New Robe	F	Daughter	1
453.	Henry Chouquette	M	Husb'd	26
454.	Louise Chouquette	F	Wife	29
455.	John Chouquette	M	Son	13
456.	Medicine Stab	M	Husb'd	45
457.	Grovent Woman	F	Wife	49
458.	Slim Woman	F	Wife	37
459.	Gambler	M	Husb'd	42
460.	Annie Gambler	F	Wife	45
461.	Richard Gambler	M	Son	19
462.	Jessie Gambler	F	Daughter	18
463.	Swims Under	F	Mother	30
464.	Josephene Swims Under	F	Daughter	2
465.	Lawrence Faber	M	Husb'd	25
466.	Annie Faber	F	Wife	21
467.	Ellen Faber	F	Daughter	3
468.	Nancy Faber	F	Daughter	1
469.	Small Face	M	----	40
470.	Mary Small Face	F	G-Daughter	8
471.	Spotted Bear No. 2	F	Mother	45
472.	Peter Spotted Bear	M	Son	18
473.	Minnie Spotted Bear	F	Daughter	5
474.	Eagle Child	F	Mother	37
475.	James Eagle Child	M	Son	11

Census of the Piegan Indians of Blackfeet Agency, Montana taken by Thomas P. Fuller United States Indian Agent 1898

No.	English Name	Sex	Relation	Age
476.	Young Man Chief	M	Husb'd	41
477.	Cecil Young Man Chief	F	Wife	26
478.	Hairy Face	M	Husb'd	37
479.	Blanket Woman	F	Wife	30
480.	Grass Woman	F	Wife	25
481.	Pete Hairy Face	M	Son	3
482.	James Hairy Face	M	Son	1
483.	Blind Woman	F	Daughter	12
484.	Under Bull Widow	F	Mother	34
485.	Joe Under Bull	M	Son	3
486.	Mollie Under Bull	F	Daughter	5
487.	Wolf Medicine	M	Husb'd	33
488.	Good Clean Up	F	Wife	34
489.	Chicken Woman	F	Daughter	6
490.	Head Woman	F	Daughter	5
491.	Hazlett Woman	F	Daughter	8
492.	Little Dog	M	Husb'd	44
493.	Wades In Water	F	Wife	17
494.	Harrison Little Dog	M	Son	12
495.	John Little Dog	M	Son	9
496.	Eliza Little Dog	F	Daughter	1
497.	Philomine St. Goddert	F	Mother	28
498.	Agnes St. Goddert	F	Daughter	8
499.	Almma St. Goddert	F	Daughter	3
500.	Elmer Butterfly	M	Husb'd	25
501.	Mary Butterfly	F	Wife	19
502.	Rides Behind	M	Son	3
503.	Snake Woman	F	Daughter	2
504.	Tearing Lodge	M	Husb'd	60
505.	Payes Plenty	F	Wife	50
506.	Louise First One	F	Mother	26
507.	Agnes Sanderville	F	Daughter	11
508.	Big Crow	M	Husb'd	39

Census of the Piegan Indians of Blackfeet Agency, Montana taken by Thomas P. Fuller United States Indian Agent 1898

No.	English Name	Sex	Relation	Age
509.	Two Guns	F	Wife	29
510.	Linx Woman	F	Daughter	12
511.	Cecil Big Crow	F	Daughter	10
512.	Under Bull No. 2	F	Mother	38
513.	John Under Bull	M	Son	12
514.	Peter Under Bull	M	Son	3
515.	Almost Killed	F	----	80
516.	Butter Fly	M	Husb'd	50
517.	Good Medicine	F	Wife	40
518.	Maryan Butter Fly	F	Daughter	6
519.	Longtime Sleeping	M	Husb'd	29
520.	Mary Longtime Sleeping	F	Wife	30
521.	John Longtime Sleeping	M	Son	8
522.	Julia Longtime Sleeping	F	Daughter	3
523.	Johnny Longtime Sleeping	M	Son	1
524.	Wolf Plume	M	Husb'd	38
525.	First Strike	F	Wife	29
526.	Wesley Wolf Plume	M	Son	11
527.	John White Calf	M	Husb'd	40
528.	Weasel Tail	F	Wife	30
529.	Annie White Calf	F	Daughter	14
530.	Going To Move	M	Husb'd	43
531.	Old Woman	F	Wife	60
532.	Morning Eagle	M	Husb'd	65
533.	Catches On Top	F	Wife	32
534.	Hits On Top	F	Wife	40
535.	John Morning Eagle	M	Son	7
536.	Geo. Morning Eagle	M	Son	4
537.	Two Rabbits	F	Daughter	2
538.	Kidney	M	Husb'd	28
539.	Mary Kidney	F	Wife	21

Census of the Piegan Indians of Blackfeet Agency, Montana taken by Thomas P. Fuller United States Indian Agent 1898

No.	English Name	Sex	Relation	Age
540.	Alice Kidney	F	Daughter	3
541.	Many Guns	M	Husb'd	35
542.	Josephene Many Guns	F	Wife	16
543.	No Runner	M	Husb'd	55
544.	White Woman	F	Wife	56
545.	Spotted Head	F	----	75
546.	Harry No Chief	M	----	27
547.	Wolf Eagle	M	Husb'd	46
548.	Blanket Woman	F	Wife	42
549.	Kills In Night	F	Wife	36
550.	Rufus Wolf Eagle	M	Son	9
551.	George Wolf Eagle	M	Son	2
552.	Little Owl	M	Husb'd	26
553.	Maggie Little Owl	F	Wife	17
554.	Mary Little Owl	F	Daughter	1
555.	Fish	M	Husb'd	25
556.	Lone Rock	F	Wife	24
557.	Josephene Fish	F	Daughter	1
558.	Takes Iron Gun	M	Father	29
559.	Gives Plenty	F	Mother	60
560.	Lucy Iron Gun	F	Daughter	17
561.	Turtle	M	Husb'd	28
562.	Minnie Turtle	F	Wife	19
563.	Everybody Talks About	M	Husb'd	46
564.	Strikes Back	F	Wife	47
565.	Hate Woman	F	Wife	39
566.	Lomie E.B.T. About	M	Son	8
567.	George E.B.T. About	M	Son	6
568.	Paul E.B.T. About	M	Son	5
569.	Susie E.B.T. About	F	Daughter	3
570.	Mollie E.B.T. About	F	Daughter	1

Census of the Piegan Indians of Blackfeet Agency, Montana taken by Thomas P. Fuller United States Indian Agent 1898

No.	English Name	Sex	Relation	Age
571.	Kills In Brush	F	----	65
572.	Drags Behind	M	Husb'd	39
573.	Last Goes In	F	Wife	43
574.	Yellow Head	M	Son	7
575.	Last Star	M	Husb'd	28
576.	Hellen Last Star	F	Wife	18
577.	Takes Gun Inside	F	Daughter	2
578.	Dog Taking Gun	M	Husb'd	32
579.	Cuts Herself	F	Wife	27
580.	Old Whiteman	M	----	80
581.	Big Mouth Spring	M	Husb'd	32
582.	No Owl	F	Wife	35
583.	Small Face	F	Wife	23
584.	Chas. Big Spring	M	Son	22 [sic]
585.	Anna Big Spring	F	Daughter	1
586.	John Big Spring	M	----	27
587.	Bird Rattler	M	Husb'd	37
588.	Blanket Woman	F	Wife	32
589.	Sits Under	F	Wife	25
590.	Daniel Big Plume	M	Son	19
591.	Cleans Up	F	Daughter	1
592.	Cow Hide Robe	M	Husb'd	21
593.	Grace Cow Hide Robe	F	Wife	21
594.	Rides In Middle	M	Son	21 [sic]
595.	Black Face Man	M	Husb'd	31
596.	Bead Woman	F	Wife	24
597.	Red Stone	F	Daughter	6
598.	John Black Face Man	M	Son	1
599.	Yellow Squirrel	M	Son	4
600.	Chas. Three Suns	M	----	25

Census of the Piegan Indians of Blackfeet Agency, Montana taken by Thomas P. Fuller United States Indian Agent 1898

No.	English Name	Sex	Relation	Age
601.	Old Woman	F	----	65
602.	Good Gun	M	Husb'd	25
603.	Charges Bothsides	F	Wife	35
604.	Last Gun	M	Son	3
605.	Rides In Middle	M	Husb'd	34
606.	Slim Woman	F	Wife	35
607.	Mary M. Rider	F	Daughter	4
608.	Levi M. Rider	M	Son	11
609.	Fred M. Rider	M	Son	16
610.	David Duval	M	----	23
611.	Strangle Wolf	M	Husb'd	55
612.	Lower Woman	F	Wife	65
613.	Jim Blood	M	Husb'd	38
614.	Fannie Blood	F	Wife	19
615.	Autern Blood	M	Son	13
616.	Berry Carrier	M	Husb'd	42
617.	Ratting	F	Wife	40
618.	Fox	M	Son	13
619.	Different Woman	F	Daughter	5
620.	Rides In Front	M	Son	2
621.	Kills In Air	F	----	55
622.	Don't Go Out	M	Husb'd	50
623.	Cloth Woman	F	Wife	60
624.	Mary Don't Go Out	F	Daughter	16
625.	Black Weasel	M	Husb'd	39
626.	Medicine Sheild	F	Wife	42
627.	Goes up Alone	F	Daughter	2
628.	Snow Girl	F	Daughter	11
629.	Eli Rider	M	----	25
630.	Clears Op[sic]	M	Husb'd	25

Census of the Piegan Indians of Blackfeet Agency, Montana taken by Thomas P. Fuller United States Indian Agent 1898

No.	English Name	Sex	Relation	Age
631.	Yells In Night	F	Wife	28
632.	Mabel Clears Up	F	Daughter	13
633.	Rosa Clears Up	F	Daughter	1
634.	Jim No Chief	M	Husb'd	26
635.	Rachel No Chief	F	Wife	18
636.	Grace No Chief	F	Daughter	3
637.	Mary No Chief	F	Daughter	2
638.	Takes Gun Alone	F	----	45
639.	Good Kills	F	----	80
640.	Medicine Singer	F	----	82
641.	Running Fisher	M	Husb'd	44
642.	Charging Woman	F	Wife	37
643.	Makes Cold Weather	M	Son	6
644.	George R. Fisher	M	Son	2
645.	Buffalo Hide	M	Husb'd	30
646.	Spotted Woman	F	Wife	25
647.	Wm. Buffalo Hide	M	Son	5
648.	Takes Gun	M	Son	2
649.	Buffalo Hide No. 2	F	----	80
650.	Chas. Reevis	M	Husb'd	22
651.	First Strikes	F	Wife	24
652.	Sam Reevis	M	Son	12
653.	Mary Reevis	F	Daughter	5
654.	Joe Reevis	M	Son	4
655.	Laureta Reevis	F	Daughter	1
656.	Beaver Woman	F	----	61
657.	Mud Head	M	Husb'd	36
658.	White Horse Rider	F	Wife	34
659.	Sits Against Wind	F	Daughter	12
660.	Joe Mud Head	M	Son	4
661.	Micheil Little Dog	M	Husb'd	22

Census of the Piegan Indians of Blackfeet Agency, Montana taken by Thomas P. Fuller United States Indian Agent 1898

No.	English Name	Sex	Relation	Age
662.	Irene L. Dog	F	Wife	16
663.	New Breast	M	Husb'd	36
664.	Long Fish	F	Wife	50
665.	Good L. Girl	F	Daughter	6
666.	Long T.M. Pipe	F	----	50
667.	Leggins	F	----	80
668.	Joe Calf Ribs	M	Husb'd	36
669.	Hits In Front	F	Wife	30
670.	Joe Calf Ribs	M	Son	19
671.	Austin Calf Ribs	M	Son	10
672.	No Chief	M	Husb'd	60
673.	Strikes Back	F	Wife	50
674.	Jim No Chief	M	Son	21
675.	John No Chief	M	Son	21
676.	Little Plume	M	Husb'd	45
677.	Cuts Different	F	Wife	33
678.	Tail F. Woman	F	Wife	31
679.	Jas. L. Plume	M	Son	13
680.	Louie L. Plume	M	Son	7
681.	Takes Gun	F	Daughter	4
682.	Joe L. Plume	M	Son	1
683.	Mollie L. Plume	F	Daughter	8
684.	Joe L. Plume	M	Son	5
685.	Susie L. Plume	F	Daughter	1
686.	Calf Woman No. 2	F	Mother	19
687.	Singing	F	Daughter	2
688.	Streched Out	F	----	39
689.	Wolf Head	M	Husb'd	52
690.	Sings On Top	F	Wife	41
691.	Pete Wolf Head	M	Son	8
692.	Red Plume	M	Husband	33

Census of the Piegan Indians of Blackfeet Agency, Montana taken by Thomas P. Fuller United States Indian Agent 1898

No.	English Name	Sex	Relation	Age
693.	One Strike	F	Wife	32
694.	John R. Plume	M	Son	2
695.	Pete R. Plume	M	Son	1
696.	Yellow Kidney	M	Husb'd	30
697.	Wolf Woman	F	Wife	19
698.	Mike Y. Kidney	M	Son	5
699.	Maggie Y. Kidney	F	Daughter	1
700.	Catches Inside	F	----	60
701.	Found A Gun	M	----	29
702.	Little Bull	M	Husb'd	57
703.	Good Strike	F	Wife	39
704.	Good Charging	F	Wife	18
705.	Two Guns	M	Son	2
706.	Kills In Brush	F	Mother	41
707.	Blanket Woman	F	Daughter	20
708.	Takes Gun Both Sides	M	Husb'd	33
709.	One Strike	F	Wife	32
710.	John G. Both Sides	M	Son	2
711.	Pete G. Both Sides	M	Son	1
712.	Irvin Little Plume	M	Husb'd	21
713.	Small Woman	F	Wife	21
714.	Jennie L. Plume	F	Daughter	4
715.	Mary L. Plume	F	Daughter	2
716.	Hungry	F	Mother	45
717.	Henry Hungry	M	Son	18
718.	Ezra Hungry	M	Son	5
719.	Cold Body	M	Husb'd	26
720.	Mary C. Body	F	Wife	38
721.	Pete C. Body	M	Son	10
722.	Maggie C. Body	F	Daughter	8
723.	Cecil C. Body	F	Daughter	4

Census of the Piegan Indians of Blackfeet Agency, Montana taken by Thomas P. Fuller United States Indian Agent 1898

No.	English Name	Sex	Relation	Age
724.	Running Owl	M	Husb'd	31
725.	Kills Fur	F	Wife	40
726.	Joe R. Owl	M	Son	6
727.	Agnes R. Owl	F	Daughter	15
728.	Rosa R. Owl	F	Daughter	7
729.	Mary R. Owl	F	Daughter	1
730.	Wakes Up Last	M	Husb'd	31
731.	Mollie W. Up Last	F	Wife	19
732.	Jennie W. Up Last	F	Daughter	1
733.	Arrow Maker	M	Husb'd	36
734.	Cuts Inside	F	Wife	38
735.	Maggie Arrow Maker	F	Daughter	7
736.	Chief Crow	M	Husb'd	40
737.	Strikes With Gun	F	Wife	44
738.	Jas. C. Crow	M	Son	17
739.	Alfred C. Crow	M	Son	12
740.	John C. Crow	M	Son	2
741.	Maggie C. Crow	F	Daughter	6
742.	Yellow Iron	M	Husb'd	35
743.	Cutting Woman	F	Wife	30
744.	Medicine	F	----	65
745.	Old Chief	M	Husb'd	47
746.	Winning Woman	F	Wife	38
747.	John O. Chief	M	Son	14
748.	Robert O. Chief	M	Son	5
749.	Paul O. Chief	M	Son	1
750.	Mary O. Chief	F	Daughter	9
751.	Drags His Robe	M	Husb'd	36
752.	Ekimo Woman	F	Wife	40
753.	Chas. D. His Robe	M	Son	20
754.	Scattered Girl	F	Daughter	4
755.	Bear Leggins	M	Husb'd	40
756.	War Bonnet	F	Wife	30

Census of the Piegan Indians of Blackfeet Agency, Montana taken by Thomas P. Fuller United States Indian Agent 1898

No.	English Name	Sex	Relation	Age
757.	Peter B. Leggins	M	Son	1
758.	Rachel B. Leggins	F	Daughter	14
759.	Mary B. Leggins	F	Daughter	11
760.	Old Woman	F	----	45
761.	Peter Cadott	M	Husb'd	27
762.	Lucy Cadott	F	Wife	22
763.	Rosa Cadott	F	Daughter	7
764.	Cold Feet	M	Husb'd	50
765.	Dry Goods Woman	F	Wife	47
766.	Spotted Horse Girl	F	Daughter	1
767.	Snake Girl	M	Son	10
768.	Flat Tail	M	Husb'd	55
769.	Medicine Pipe	F	Wife	43
770.	Jimmy F. Tail	M	Son	3
771.	Sofia F. Tail	F	Daughter	5
772.	Philip Flat Tail	M	Husb'd	22
773.	Anna F. Tail	F	Wife	18
774.	Chas. No Coat	M	Husb'd	21
775.	Long Time Chicken	F	Mother	43
776.	Jimmie No Coat	M	Son	7
777.	Takes Gun At Night	M	Son	23
778.	Strikes IN Air	F	Mother	57
779.	Chewing Black Bones	M	Husb'd	32
780.	Mary C.B. Bones	F	Wife	35
781.	Isabelle C.B. Bones	F	Daughter	8
782.	Henry Head Carrier	M	----	36
783.	Weasel Head	M	Husb'd	35
784.	Mary W. Head	F	Wife	46
785.	Issac Wipert	M	Son	21
786.	Joe W. Head	M	Son	11
787.	Pete W. Head	M	Son	9

Census of the Piegan Indians of Blackfeet Agency, Montana taken by Thomas P. Fuller United States Indian Agent 1898

No.	English Name	Sex	Relation	Age
788.	John W. Head	M	Son	8
789.	Mary W. Head	F	Daughter	13
790.	Lizzie W. Head	F	Daughter	7
791.	Thos. W. Head	M	Son	5
792.	Jennie W. Head	F	Daughter	4
793.	Tail Feathers Coming	M	Husb'd	53
794.	Snake Woman	F	Wife	30
795.	Cecil T.F. Coming	F	Daughter	12
796.	Mary T.F. Coming	F	Daughter	2
797.	Sicsie[sic] T.F. Coming	F	Daughter	3
798.	Wins Many Guns	F	Mother	50
799.	Mary T.F. Coming	F	Daughter	5
800.	Going To Go In	F	----	60
801.	Paul[sic]	F	----	5
802.	Blackfoot Woman	F	Mother	48
803.	Mike B.F. Woman	M	Son	20
804.	John B.F. Woman	M	Son	19
805.	Mary B.F. Woman	F	Daughter	6
806.	Young Bear Chief	M	Husb'd	39
807.	Good Shield	F	Wife	33
808.	Yells In Water	F	Wife	33
809.	Edward B. Chief	M	Son	16
810.	John B. Chief	M	Son	9
811.	Sebastin B. Chief	M	Son	4
812.	Isabella B. Chief	F	Daughter	18
813.	Maggie B. Chief	F	Daughter	12
814.	Joe B. Chief	M	Son	6
815.	Big Plume	M	Husb'd	70
816.	Catches In Water	F	Wife	45
817.	Jerry B. Plume	M	Son	19
818.	Thos. B. Plume	M	Son	9
819.	Louise B. Plume	F	Daughter	5
820.	Susan Shultz	F	Mother	34

Census of the Piegan Indians of Blackfeet Agency, Montana taken by Thomas P. Fuller United States Indian Agent 1898

No.	English Name	Sex	Relation	Age
821.	Hart Shultz	M	Son	15
822.	Margerete De Champs	F	----	59
823.	Julia Reevis	F	Mother	43
824.	August Reevis	M	Son	17
825.	Emet Reevis	M	Son	16
826.	Emma Reevis	F	Daughter	12
827.	Frank Reevis	M	Son	10
828.	Boy Chief	M	Husb'd	32
829.	Last Gun Woman	F	Wife	27
830.	Dennis B. Chief	M	Son	8
831.	Wm. B. Chief	M	Son	6
832.	Authelia B. Chief	F	Daughter	18
833.	Louie Champine	M	Husb'd	35
834.	Berry Woman	F	Wife	37
835.	George Champine	M	Son	6
836.	Pete Champine	M	Son	5
837.	Mary Champine	F	Daughter	1
838.	Eagle	M	Husb'd	30
839.	Medicine Beaver	F	Wife	25
840.	Dan Lone Chief	M	Husb'd	25
841.	Ellen L. Chief	F	Wife	23
842.	Good Bear Woman	F	----	50
843.	Sure Woman	F	----	80
844.	Hits On Top	F	----	46
845.	Mary Phemister	F	Mother	36
846.	George Phemister	M	Son	16
847.	William Russell	M	Husb'd	44
848.	Mary Russell	F	Wife	38
849.	Cecil Russell	F	Daughter	17
850.	Joe Russell	M	Son	10

Census of the Piegan Indians of Blackfeet Agency, Montana taken by Thomas P. Fuller United States Indian Agent 1898

No.	English Name	Sex	Relation	Age
851.	Wm. Russell	M	Son	8
852.	Henry Russell	M	Son	1
853.	First One Russell	M	----	27
854.	Petrified	F	G-Mother	57
855.	George Russell	M	G-Son	13
856.	Isabell Trombley	F	Mother	65
857.	Alfred Trombley	M	Son	20
858.	Many Guns	M	Husb'd	28
859.	Mouse Woman	F	Wife	42
860.	Joe M. Guns	M	Son	5
861.	Thos. M. Guns	M	Son	3
862.	The Bite	M	Husb'd	56
863.	Kills For Nothing	F	Wife	40
864.	Wolf Bite	M	Son	13
865.	Minnie Bite	F	Daughter	4
866.	John Bite	M	Son	1
867.	Mary Steward	F	Mother	33
868.	Carrie Steward	F	Daughter	18
869.	Jennie Steward	F	Daughter	16
870.	Clara Steward	F	Daughter	13
871.	Mollie Steward	F	Daughter	9
872.	Cecil Steward	F	Daughter	6
873.	Marion Steward	M	Son	2
874.	Double Runner	M	Husb'd	50
875.	Chip Munk	F	Wife	45
876.	Edward D. Runner	M	Son	20
877.	Edgar D. Runner	M	Son	19
878.	Paul D. Runner	M	Son	18
879.	Many Guns	M	Son	24
880.	Chicken Shoe	M	Husb'd	23
881.	Medicine Star	F	Wife	29
882.	Mary C. Shoe	F	Daughter	3

Census of the Piegan Indians of Blackfeet Agency, Montana taken by Thomas P. Fuller United States Indian Agent 1898

No.	English Name	Sex	Relation	Age
883.	Good Strike	F	----	90
884.	Chas. Rose	M	Husb'd	42
885.	Agnes Rose	F	Wife	24
886.	Maggie Rose	F	Daughter	18
887.	Jennie Rose	F	Daughter	9
888.	Alice Rose	F	Daughter	7
889.	Wm. Rose	M	Son	5
890.	Jas. Rose	M	Son	3
891.	Annie Rose	F	Daughter	1
892.	Bear Shoe	M	Husb'd	35
893.	Daisy B. Shoe	F	Wife	18
894.	Buffalo Growing	M	Husb'd	39
895.	Sheild Woman	F	Wife	37
896.	Mouse Girl	F	Daughter	3
897.	Barnet Calf Ribs	M	----	24
898.	Calf Boss Ribs	M	Husb'd	56
899.	Bad Eyes	F	Wife	53
900.	Iron Woman	F	Wife	25
901.	Minnie C. Ribs	F	Daughter	5
902.	Joe C. Ribs	M	Son	3
903.	Good Stabbing	M	Husb'd	32
904	Medicine Woman	F	Wife	30
905.	Anna G. Stabbing	F	Daughter	3
906.	Maggie G. Stabbing	F	Daughter	2
907.	Heavy Gun	M	Husb'd	41
908.	Good Woman	F	Wife	32
909.	First Goes In	F	Wife	27
910.	Kicking Woman	M	Husb'd	72
911.	Looks Plenty	F	Wife	60
912.	John K. Woman	M	Son	22
913.	Takes Gun On Top	M	Husb'd	30
914.	Yellow Bird	F	Wife	30
915.	John T.G. On Top	M	Son	19

Census of the Piegan Indians of Blackfeet Agency, Montana taken by Thomas P. Fuller United States Indian Agent 1898

No.	English Name	Sex	Relation	Age
916.	Louise T.G. On Top	F	Daughter	5
917.	Strikes Back	F	----	50
918.	Marrow Bones	M	Husb'd	60
919.	Good G. Woman	F	Wife	62
920.	Medicine Bull	M	Husb'd	34
921.	Sore Back	F	Wife	29
922.	Thos. M. Bull	M	Son	2
923.	Red Rock	F	Daughter	11
924.	Sure Chief	M	Husb'd	32
925.	Bird Woman	F	Wife	20
926.	Philip S. Chief	M	Son	3
927.	Gray Whiskers	M	Son	1
928.	Yells In Water	M	Husb'd	21
929.	Short Gun	F	Wife	19
930.	John Y. In Water	M	Son	5
931.	Short Face	M	Son	21
932.	Strikes Gun	F	Mother	60
933.	The Horn	M	Husb'd	60
934.	Good L. Woman	F	Wife	40
935.	Under Bird	F	Daughter	30
936.	Harry Horn	M	Son	15
937.	Albert Mad Plume	M	Husb'd	21
938.	Susie M. Plume	F	Wife	20
939.	Maggie M. Plume	F	Daughter	2
940.	Mad Plume	M	Husb'd	45
941.	Kills In Night	F	Wife	28
942.	John M. Plume	M	Son	13
943.	Geo. M. Plume	M	Son	8
944.	Mike M. Plume	M	Son	5
945.	Medicine M. Plume	F	Daughter	12
946.	Bad Old Man	M	Husb'd	64

Census of the Piegan Indians of Blackfeet Agency, Montana taken by Thomas P. Fuller United States Indian Agent 1898

No.	English Name	Sex	Relation	Age
947.	Sallie B.O. Man	F	Wife	53
948.	John B.O. Man	M	Son	16
949.	Jack Big Moon	M	Husb'd	39
950.	Annie B. Moon	F	Wife	35
951.	George Eats Alone	M	----	17
952.	Last Cayote No. 2	F	Mother	53
953.	Fanny L. Cayote	F	Daughter	14
954.	Two Guns	F	Daughter	2
955.	Eddie R. Crane	M	Husb'd	23
956.	Nellie R. Crane	F	Wife	19
957.	Medicine Hawk	F	Daughter	1
958.	Little Hawk	F	Mother	48
959.	Lazy Boy	M	Son	8
960.	No Coat	M	Husb'd	38
961.	Kills First	F	Wife	30
962.	Anna No Coat	F	Daughter	5
963.	Wades In Water	M	Husb'd	30
964.	Lucy W. In Water	F	Wife	20
965.	Little Otter	F	----	6
966.	Running Crane	M	Husb'd	68
967.	White Wiman[sic]	F	Wife	33
968.	Rachel Norris	F	Mother	27
969.	Rosa Norris	F	Daughter	9
970.	Dan Norris	M	Son	3
971.	Daisy Norris	F	Daughter	2
972.	Spotted Eagle	M	Husb'd	58
973.	Hands It Back	F	Wife	48
974.	Jas. S. Eagle	M	Son	23
975.	Begs Plenty	F	Daughter	7

Census of the Piegan Indians of Blackfeet Agency, Montana taken by Thomas P. Fuller United States Indian Agent 1898

No.	English Name	Sex	Relation	Age
976.	Thos. Spotted Eagle	M	----	24
977.	Green Grass Bull	M	Husb'd	38
978.	Mary G.G. Bull	F	Wife	40
979.	George G.G. Bull	M	Son	12
980.	Fine Bull	M	Husb'd	50
981.	Pretty Woman	F	Wife	40
982.	Stabs Down	M	Son	10
983.	Spider	F	Daughter	5
984.	Lucy F. Bull	F	Daughter	4
985.	Jas. F. Bull	M	Son	3
986.	Frank Rider	M	Husb'd	31
987.	Gretchen Rider	F	Wife	23
988.	Matilda I. Crow	F	Sister	14
989.	Elizabeth I. Crow	F	Sister	10
990.	Joe Trombley	M	Husb'd	40
991.	Julia Trombley	F	Wife	44
992.	Rheuben B. Boy	M	----	13
993.	Black Cayote	M	Husb'd	70
994.	Blue Woman	F	Wife	25
995.	Strikes On Top	F	----	60
996.	Tiger Woman	F	----	45
997.	Isabel Main	F	Mother	34
998.	Henry Main	M	Son	19
999.	Alice Main	F	Daughter	6
1000.	Lizzie Main	F	Daughter	3
1001.	Mary Powel	F	Mother	52
1002.	Chas. Powel	M	Son	21
1003.	Jennie Powel	F	Daughter	21
1004.	Jessie Powel	M	Son	16
1005.	Susie Powel	F	Daughter	11

Census of the Piegan Indians of Blackfeet Agency, Montana taken by Thomas P. Fuller United States Indian Agent 1898

No.	English Name	Sex	Relation	Age
1006.	Emma Upham	F	Mother	36
1007.	Johnson Upham	M	Son	13
1008.	Jack Upham	M	Son	9
1009.	Rose Upham	F	Daughter	19
1010.	Kutie Upham	F	Daughter	15
1011.	Mertie Upham	F	Daughter	6
1012.	Rosa Hinkle	F	Mother	38
1013.	George Hinkle	M	Son	18
1014.	William Hinkle	M	Son	16
1015.	Martha Hinkle	F	Daughter	14
1016.	Lizzie Hinkle	F	Daughter	12
1017.	Wm. Upham	M	Husb'd	32
1018.	Bell Coming	F	Wife	26
1019.	George Upham	M	Son	3
1020.	Lasy Cut	F	G-Mother	50
1021.	Old Person	M	Husb'd	32
1022.	Iron Eater	F	Wife	23
1023.	Sipota	M	Ad-Son	23
1024.	Woman Chief	M	Ad-Son	17
1025.	Eliza Galbraith	F	St-Mother	44
1026.	Lizzie Galbraith	F	St-Daughter	14
1027.	John Galbraith	M	St-Son	15
1028.	Webster Galbraith	m	St-Son	17
1029.	Mollie Galbraith	F	St-Daughter	7
1030.	Annie Galbraith	F	St-Daughter	6
1031.	Phoebie Galbraith	F	Gd-Daughter	5
1032.	Wm. Samples	M	Husb'd	30
1033.	Mary Samples	F	Wife	23
1034.	Willie Samples	M	Son	4
1035.	Florence Samples	F	Daughter	3
1036.	Annie Samples	F	Daughter	2
1037.	Jessie Samples	M	----	24
1038.	Vina Hall	F	Mother	20
1039.	Elsie Hall	F	Daughter	2

Census of the Piegan Indians of Blackfeet Agency, Montana taken by Thomas P. Fuller United States Indian Agent 1898

No.	English Name	Sex	Relation	Age
1040.	John Wagner	M	Husb'd	22
1041.	Mary Wagner	F	Wife	28
1042.	Lilly Wagner	F	Daughter	2
1043.	Mary Stone	F	Mother	33
1044.	Robert Stone	M	Son	8
1045.	Henry Stone	M	Son	4
1046.	Joseph Stone	M	Son	1
1047.	Mary Howard	F	Mother	57
1048.	Joseph Howard	M	Son	23
1049.	Walter Howard	M	Son	16
1050.	Annie Howard	F	Ad-Daughter	11
1051.	Louise Higgins	F	Mother	52
1052.	George Croff	M	Son	20
1053.	Emma Croff	F	Daughter	18
1054.	Henry Higgins	M	Son	15
1055.	Alice Higgins	F	Daughter	10
1056.	Willie Croff	M	Son	23
1057.	Minnie Lamott	F	Ad-Daughter	15
1058.	Jennie La Mott	F	Ad-Daughter	13
1059.	Joe Lamott	M	Ad-Son	11
1060.	Theresa Pambrun	F	Gd-Mother	56
1061.	Persy Dennis	M	Gd-Son	16
1062.	Louis Pambrun	M	Husb'd	39
1063.	Annie Pambrun	F	Wife	28
1064.	Eddie Pambrun	M	Son	12
1065.	David Pambrun	M	Son	10
1066.	Isabel Pambrun	F	Daughter	7
1067.	Geo. Pambrun	M	Son	5
1068.	May Pambrun	F	Daughter	1
1069.	Alex Du Brell	M	Husb'd	41
1070.	Lillie Dubrell	F	Wife	20
1071.	George Wren	M	Husb'd	29
1072.	Susie Wren	F	Wife	29

Census of the Piegan Indians of Blackfeet Agency, Montana taken by Thomas P. Fuller United States Indian Agent 1898

No.	English Name	Sex	Relation	Age
1073.	Melinda Wren	F	Mother	50
1074.	Katie Wren	F	Daughter	20
1075.	John Wren	M	Son	16
1076.	Robert Wren	M	Son	11
1077.	Dora Wren	F	Daughter	16
1078.	William Wren	M	Son	8
1079.	Lillie Wren	F	Daughter	6
1080.	Ida Wren	F	Daughter	4
1081.	Melinda Wren	F	Daughter	2
1082.	Frank Marcero	M	Brother	24
1083.	Chas. Marcero	M	Brother	22
1084.	Mary Murphy	F	Mother	50
1085.	Willie Murphy	M	Son	15
1086.	Hamlin Murphy	M	Son	10
1087.	Holland Murphy	M	Son	8
1088.	Albert Murphy	M	Son	6
1089.	Louis Ell[sic]	M	Husb'd	25
1090.	Aldah Ell	F	Wife	19
1091.	Chas. Ell	M	Son	1
1092.	Chief Elk	M	Husb'd	65
1093.	Last Star	F	Wife	55
1094.	Mary Lemon	F	Mother	32
1095.	Jessie Lemon	F	Daughter	11
1096.	Louise Lemon	F	Daughter	7
1097.	Emma Lemon	F	Daughter	3
1098.	John Lemon	M	Son	10
1099.	Lee Lemon	M	Son	2
1100.	Levi Burd	M	Husb'd	21
1101.	Daisy Burd	F	Wife	19
1102.	Ira Burd	M	Brother	11
1103.	Phoebe Burd	F	Sister	7
1104.	Sallie Hagan	F	Mother	32
1105.	Maggie Hagan	F	Daughter	13
1106.	Nellie Hagan	F	Daughter	8
1107.	Esturill Hagan	F	Daughter	3

Census of the Piegan Indians of Blackfeet Agency, Montana taken by Thomas P. Fuller United States Indian Agent 1898

No.	English Name	Sex	Relation	Age
1108.	Sadie Hagan	F	Daughter	1
1109.	Maggie Peterson	F	Mother	37
1110.	Oscar Peterson	M	Son	18
1111.	Walter Peterson	M	Son	16
1112.	Frank Peterson	M	Son	14
1113.	Melvin Peterson	M	Son	12
1114.	Mitchel Peterson	M	Son	10
1115.	Julia Thomas	F	Mother	28
1116.	George Thomas	M	Son	3
1117.	Nora Thomas	F	Daughter	1
1118.	Maggie Wetzil[sic]	F	Mother	40
1119.	Pearl Wetzel	F	Daughter	21
1120.	Willie Wetzel	M	Son	17
1121.	Tom Bogy	M	----	19
1122.	Eddie Bull Plume	M	----	17
1123.	Sarah Brown	F	Mother	44
1124.	Jesse Brown	M	Son	16
1125.	Leo Brown	M	Son	2
1126.	Sarah Brown	F	----	50
1127.	Wm. Brown	M	----	26
1128.	Susan Arnoux	F	Mother	46
1129.	Monroe Arnoux	M	Son	19
1130.	Marion Arnoux	M	Son	16
1131.	George Arnoux	M	Son	14
1132.	Mary Norman	F	Mother	22
1133.	Valina Norman	F	Daughter	4
1134.	Adolphus Norman	M	Son	2
1135.	Louise Paul	F	Mother	41
1136.	Solomon Paul	M	Son	20
1137.	Albert Paul	M	Son	17

Census of the Piegan Indians of Blackfeet Agency, Montana taken by Thomas P. Fuller United States Indian Agent 1898

No.	English Name	Sex	Relation	Age
1138.	Philip Paul	M	Son	15
1139.	Eddie Paul	M	Son	12
1140.	Rosina Paul	F	Daughter	10
1141.	Oliver Paul	M	Son	8
1142.	Willie Paul	M	Son	5
1143.	Selina Paul	F	Daughter	2
1144.	Amelia Fox	F	Mother	62
1145.	Andrew Jackson	M	Gd-Son	19
1146.	John Jackson	M	Gd-Son	17
1147.	Eliza Jackson	F	Gd-Daughter	15
1148.	Milly Jackson	F	Gd-Daughter	13
1149.	Lizzie Jackson	F	Gd-Daughter	11
1150.	Aleic Fox	M	Son	21
1151.	Campbell Munroe	M	Husb'd	30
1152.	Frezine Munroe	F	Wife	23
1153.	Henry Munroe	M	Son	1
1154.	Small Leggins	M	Husb'd	55
1155.	Comes To Make Dust	F	Wife	60
1156.	Turns Back	M	Son	5
1157.	Many White Horses	M	Husb'd	77
1158.	Long Time Good	F	Wife	60
1159.	Thunder Nest Woman	F	Wife	34
1160.	Last Wolf	M	Son	17
1161.	Joe W. Horses	M	Son	8
1162.	Gives Gun Away	M	Son	5
1163.	Crow W. Horses	M	Son	3
1164.	Only Girl	F	Daughter	2
1165.	Gun Fringe	M	Son	1
1166.	Rabbit Old Woman	F	Wife	36
1167.	Hungry Woman	F	Daughter	5
1168.	Telescope	M	Son	2
1169.	Ben De Roche	M	Husb'd	35
1170.	Sallie De Roche	F	Wife	36
1171.	Chas. De Roche	M	Son	14
1172.	Cream Antelope	M	Husb'd	37

Census of the Piegan Indians of Blackfeet Agency, Montana taken by Thomas P. Fuller United States Indian Agent 1898

No.	English Name	Sex	Relation	Age
1173.	Gives To The Sun	F	Wife	37
1174.	Jas. C. Antelope	M	Son	11
1175.	Mule Rider	M	Son	1
1176.	Striped Elk	F	Aunt	70
1177.	Susan Sherman	F	Mother	56
1178.	Alex Sherman	M	Son	19
1179.	Robert Sherman	M	Son	17
1180.	Sophia Sherman	F	Daughter	15
1181.	Emma Sherman	F	Daughter	13
1182.	Mary Gardipee[sic]	F	Ad-Daughter	15
1183.	Annie Clark	F	Ad-Daughter	10
1184.	William Sherman	M	Husb'd	26
1185.	Genevieva Sherman	F	Wife	19
1186.	Mary Sherman	F	Daughter	2
1187.	Louisa Clarke	F	Mother	30
1188.	Jas. Clarke	M	Son	15
1189.	Geo. Clarke	M	Son	12
1190.	Robert Clarke	M	Son	8
1191.	Kate Guardipee	F	----	25
1192.	John Kipp	M	Husb'd	36
1193.	Calf Woman	F	Wife	36
1194.	Julia Kipp	F	Daughter	3
1195.	Willie Kipp	M	Son	5
1196.	Joe Kipp	M	Son	10
1197.	Jack Kipp	M	Son	13
1198.	Many Cats	F	----	65
1199.	Katie Stevenson	F	Mother	29
1200.	Laura Stevenson	F	Daughter	15
1201.	Annie Stevenson	F	Daughter	8
1202.	Henry Stevenson	M	Son	11
1203.	Cecil Stevenson	F	Daughter	5
1204.	Phoebe Stevenson	F	Daughter	2
1205.	Big Woman	F	Gd-Mother	60
1206.	Mary Cobell	F	Mother	50

Census of the Piegan Indians of Blackfeet Agency, Montana taken by Thomas P. Fuller United States Indian Agent 1898

No.	English Name	Sex	Relation	Age
1207.	Jos. Cobell	M	Son	21
1208.	Geo. Cobell	M	Son	19
1209.	Tommy Cobell	M	Son	17
1210.	John Cobell	M	Son	13
1211.	Willie Cobell	M	Son	9
1212.	Bessie Cobell	F	Daughter	15
1213.	Louis Cobell	M	Husb'd	41
1214.	Mary R. Cobell	F	Wife	38
1215.	Peter Cobell	M	Son	15
1216.	Jule Cobell	M	Son	4
1217.	Dewey Cobell	M	Son	1
1218.	Maggie Cobell	F	Daughter	18
1219.	Clara Cobell	F	Daughter	12
1220.	Louise Cobell	F	Daughter	2
1221.	Angeline Connolly	F	Mother	31
1222.	Boyan Connolly	M	Son	11
1223.	Victor Connolly	M	Son	10
1224.	John Connolly	M	Son	9
1225.	Mary Connolly	F	Daughter	14
1226.	Rose Connolly	F	Daughter	13
1227.	Mary Higgins	F	Mother	23
1228.	May Higgins	F	Daughter	3
1229.	Charles Higgins	M	Son	1
1230.	Josephene Gilham	F	Mother	26
1231.	Wm. Gilham	M	Son	5
1232.	Anthony Gilham	M	Son	7
1233.	Bull Calf	M	Husb'd	42
1234.	Blanket Woman	F	Wife	54
1235.	Good Killer	F	Mother	80
1236.	John B. Calf	M	Son	10
1237.	Iron Woman	F	----	90
1238.	Heavy Runner	M	Husb'd	37
1239.	Different Rock	F	Wife	29
1240.	Geo. H. Runner	M	Son	8
1241.	Buck Skin Rider	M	Son	6
1242.	Close Gun	M	Son	1

Census of the Piegan Indians of Blackfeet Agency, Montana taken by Thomas P. Fuller United States Indian Agent 1898

No.	English Name	Sex	Relation	Age
1243.	Sweet Grass	F	Daughter	3
1244.	Blue Beads	F	Wife	27
1245.	Rosa H. Runner	F	Daughter	5
1246.	Work Woman	F	Daughter	2
1247.	Bear Skin	M	Husb'd	23
1248.	Geneva B. Skin	F	Wife	21
1249.	Medicine Boss Ribs	M	Husb'd	45
1250.	Black Face Woman	F	Wife	38
1251.	Emma M.B. Ribs	F	Daughter	13
1252.	Maggie M.B. Ribs	F	Daughter	2
1253.	Takes Gun	M	Husb'd	36
1254.	Katie T. Guns	F	Wife	26
1255.	Bear Leader	M	Son	1
1256.	Lucy Hamilton	F	Mother	46
1257.	Ella Hamilton	F	Daughter	24
1258.	Gracie Hamilton	F	Daughter	17
1259.	Jack Miller	M	Husb'd	54
1260.	Julia Miller	F	Wife	55
1261.	Rosa Sharp	F	Mother	17
1262.	Julia Sharp	F	Daughter	1
1263.	Night Shoot	M	Husb'd	34
1264.	Oktiya	F	Wife	21
1265.	Jos. N. Shoot	M	Son	9
1266.	Geo. N. Shoot	M	Son	3
1267.	Small Eyes	F	Daughter	1
1268.	Maggie Goss	F	Daughter[sic]	42
1269.	Willie Goss	M	Son	21
1270.	Lomie Goss	M	Son	19
1271.	Nathan Goss	M	Son	11
1272.	George Goss	M	Son	7
1273.	Albert Goss	M	Son	5
1274.	Francis Goss	F	Daughter	3
1275.	Nellie Goss	F	Daughter	17

Census of the Piegan Indians of Blackfeet Agency, Montana taken by Thomas P. Fuller United States Indian Agent 1898

No.	English Name	Sex	Relation	Age
1276.	Carrie Goss	F	Daughter	14
1277.	Susie Goss	F	Daughter	11
1278.	Maggie Goss	F	Daughter	9
1279.	Albert Goss	M	Husb'd	24
1280.	Mary J. Goss	F	Wife	24
1281.	Albert R. Goss	M	Son	1
1282.	Mary Keiser	F	----	70
1283.	Julie Mumberg	F	Mother	27
1284.	Louis J. Mumberg	M	Son	1
1285.	Two Bears	F	Mother	45
1286.	Ora Sherrif	M	Son	18
1287.	Cross Gun	M	Husb'd	30
1288.	Kate C. Gun	F	Wife	46
1289.	Presly C. Gun	M	Son	2
1290.	Fred Girard	M	Son	25
1291.	Chas. Conway	M	Son	21
1292.	Frank Coway[sic]	M	Son	17
1293.	Willie Conway	M	Son	15
1294.	Wm. Jackson	M	Husb'd	39
1295.	Mary Jackson	F	Wife	28
1296.	Thos. Jackson	M	Son	12
1297.	Millie Jackson	F	Daughter	8
1298.	Hugh Jackson	M	Son	6
1299.	Maggie Jackson	F	Daughter	5
1300.	Annie Jackson	F	Daughter	2
1301.	Frank Bostwick	M	Husb'd	36
1302.	Mary Bostwick	F	Wife	25
1303.	Henry Bostwick	M	Son	6
1304.	Geo. Bostwick	M	Son	4
1305.	Wm. Bostwick	M	Son	2
1306.	John Bostwick	M	----	24
1307.	Double Wolf	F	----	52

Census of the Piegan Indians of Blackfeet Agency, Montana taken by Thomas P. Fuller United States Indian Agent 1898

No.	English Name	Sex	Relation	Age
1308.	Black Weasel	M	Husb'd	30
1309.	Striking Fire	F	Daughter	29
1310.	Steals Horse Alone	M	Son	2
1311.	Black Looks	M	Husb'd	34
1312.	Medicine Top	F	Wife	21
1313.	Double Gun	M	Son	9
1314.	Puss	F	Daughter	6
1315.	Bob Tail Mouse	F	Daughter	1
1316.	George Pablo	M	Husb'd	36
1317.	Maggie Pablo	F	Wife	24
1318.	Mary Pablo	F	Daughter	3
1319.	Susan Pablo	F	Daughter	1
1320.	Mike Berry Child	M	Husb'd	25
1321.	Strikes Back	F	Wife	27
1322.	Double Steal	F	Daughter	2
1323.	Boy	M	Husb'd	50
1324.	Catches On Top	F	Wife	57
1325.	Oscar	M	Son	11
1326.	Bad Boy	M	Son	9
1327.	Charles Buck	M	Son	24
1328.	Spina Buck	F	Wife	23
1329.	Lame Bear	M	Husb'd	25
1330.	Mary L. Bear	F	Wife	22
1331.	James L. Bear	M	Son	2
1332.	Good Rider	M	Son	1
1333.	Mary Devereux	F	Mother	50
1334.	Henry Devereux	M	Son	21
1335.	Chas. Devereux	M	Son	18
1336.	Annie Devereux	F	Daughter	14
1337.	Abby Devereux	F	Daughter	6
1338.	Jason Devereux	M	Son	2
1339.	Eli Guardipee	M	Husb'd	41
1340.	Sadie Guardipee	F	Wife	28
1341.	Tom Guardipee	M	Son	18

Census of the Piegan Indians of Blackfeet Agency, Montana taken by Thomas P. Fuller United States Indian Agent 1898

No.	English Name	Sex	Relation	Age
1342.	Frank Guardipee	M	Son	13
1343.	Chas. Guardipee	M	Son	10
1344.	Josephene Guardipee	F	Daughter	8
1345.	Mary Guardipee	F	Daughter	5
1346.	Agnes Guardipee	F	Daughter	2
1347.	Lodge Pole Chief	F	Mother	50
1348.	Ragged Clothes	M	Son	18
1349.	Went In Herself	F	Mother	55
1350.	Lousia Lodgepole	F	Daughter	18
1351.	Elmer Rattler	M	----	23
1352.	Chas. Guardipee	M	----	32
1353.	John Merchant	M	----	23
1354.	Chief Coward	M	Husb'd	46
1355.	Little Antelope	F	Wife	56
1356.	Victor C. Coward	M	Son	20
1357.	Good Looking Crow Woman	F	Daughter	6
1358.	Bull Child	M	Husb'd	53
1359.	Joseph B. Child	M	Son	19
1360.	Percy B. Child	M	Son	18
1361.	Poor Toung[sic] Man	M	Son	5
1362.	Maggie B. Child	F	Daughter	4
1363.	Active Bird	F	Daughter	5
1364.	Driving Back	F	Daughter	3
1365.	Catches Last	F	----	45
1366.	Good Catch	F	----	35
1367.	Flying	F	----	70
1368.	Tom Little Bear	M	----	25
1369.	Bear Paw	M	Husb'd	55
1370.	Different Person Killed	F	Mother	30
1371.	Minnie B. Paw	F	Daughter	8

Census of the Piegan Indians of Blackfeet Agency, Montana taken by Thomas P. Fuller United States Indian Agent 1898

No.	English Name	Sex	Relation	Age
1372.	John B. Paw	M	Son	3
1373.	Jim B. Paw	M	Son	1
1374.	Short Robe	M	Husb'd	39
1375.	Approched From All Sides	F	Wife	30
1376.	Water Carrier	F	Wife	28
1377.	Annie S. Robe	F	Daughter	4
1378.	Already Killed	F	Daughter	1
1379.	Emma S. Robe	F	Daughter	3
1380.	Long Time Owl	F	----	17
1381.	First Chief	F	----	65
1382.	Coat	M	Husb'd	32
1383.	Broken Leg	F	Wife	31
1384.	Day Old Woman	F	Daughter	20
1385.	Little Diver	F	Daughter	1
1386.	Dry Goods Woman	F	G-Mother	70
1387.	Mike Shortman	M	Husb'd	35
1388.	Killed & Got Away	F	Wife	29
1389.	Many Tail Feathers	M	Husb'd	49
1390.	Long Bear	F	Wife	30
1391.	Jas. M.T. Feathers	M	Son	18
1392.	Elk Necklace	M	Son	3
1393.	Under Bear	F	Daughter	10
1394.	Bad Foot	F	Daughter	8
1395.	Heard It Before	F	Daughter	3
1396.	Hits In Front	F	Daughter	1
1397.	Double Rider	M	Husb'd	35
1398.	Annie D. Rider	F	Wife	24
1399.	Draws Rations	F	Daughter	6
1400.	Minnie D. Rider	F	Daughter	2
1401.	Stingy	M	Husb'd	50
1402.	Died First	F	Wife	50
1403.	White Hide	M	Son	8
1404.	Money	F	Daughter	2

Census of the Piegan Indians of Blackfeet Agency, Montana taken by Thomas P. Fuller United States Indian Agent 1898

No.	English Name	Sex	Relation	Age
1405.	Morning Plume	M	Husb'd	50
1406.	Snake Woman	F	Wife	30
1407.	Nice Looking Woman	F	Daughter	1
1408.	Herman Dusty Bull	M	Husb'd	27
1409.	Louise D. Bull	F	Wife	16
1410.	Tom D. Bull	M	Son	3
1411.	Mad Wolf	M	Husb'd	60
1412.	Gives To The Sun	F	Wife	70
1413.	Charley M. Wolf	M	Son	19
1414.	Henry M. Wolf	M	Son	11
1415.	Medicine Weasel	M	Husb'd	60
1416.	Eagle Face	F	Wife	30
1417.	The Crow	F	Daughter	4
1418.	Plenty Hair	F	Daughter	7
1419.	Hirs[sic] In Same Place	F	Wife	30
1420.	Cutting	F	Wife	40
1421.	Goes In All Lodges	F	Mother	50
1422.	Black Blanket	F	Daughter	16
1423.	Went In Herself	F	Daughter	14
1424.	Something Good	M	Son	8
1425.	Baptiste Rondin	M	Husb'd	37
1426.	Mary Rondin	F	Wife	40
1427.	Richard Rondin	M	Son	16
1428.	Sam Rondin	M	Son	13
1429.	Louisa Rondin	F	Daughter	9
1430.	Mary Rondin	F	Daughter	7
1431.	Nancy Rondin	F	Daughter	3
1432.	Isabel Rondin	F	Daughter	1
1433.	John Thomas	M	Ad-Son	21
1434.	Ida Thomas	F	Ad-Daughter	23
1435.	Mary Neuquette[sic]	F	Mother	44
1436.	Joe Nequette	M	Son	20
1437.	Chas. Nequette	M	Son	12
1438.	Josephene Nequette	F	Daughter	11

Census of the Piegan Indians of Blackfeet Agency, Montana taken by Thomas P. Fuller United States Indian Agent 1898

No.	English Name	Sex	Relation	Age
1439.	Arrow Top Knot	M	Husb'd	32
1440.	Flying Squirrel	F	Wife	27
1441.	Philip A.T. Knot	M	Son	11
1442.	Stink A.T. Knot	M	Son	10
1443.	Antoine A.T. Knot	M	Son	3
1444.	Louise A.T. Knot	F	Daughter	4
1445.	Yellow Bird	F	Daughter	1
1446.	Lazy Boy	M	Husb'd	45
1447.	Annie L. Boy	F	Wife	35
1448.	Tom L. Boy	M	Son	18
1449.	Sam L. Boy	M	Son	3
1450.	Swan L. Boy	M	Son	1
1451.	Rebecca L. Boy	F	Daughter	16
1452.	Annie L. Boy	F	Daughter	5
1453.	White Grass	M	Husb'd	57
1454.	Kills At Night	F	Wife	44
1455.	Little Rain	M	Son	6
1456.	Eneas W. Grass	M	Son	2
1457.	Catches Two	F	Wife	34
1458.	Ross W. Grass	M	Son	22
1459.	John Shorty	M	Husb'd	58
1460.	Mary Shorty	F	Wife	27
1461.	Annie Shorty	F	Daughter	10
1462.	Shoots First	M	Husb'd	24
1463.	Calf S. First	F	Wife	37
1464.	Cecil S. First	F	Daughter	2
1465.	Henry S. First	M	St-Son	17
1466.	Louise S. First	F	St-Daughter	16
1467.	Makes Cold Weather	M	Husb'd	37
1468.	Julia M.C. Weather	F	Wife	30
1469.	Joe M.C. Weather	M	Son	3
1470.	Lazy Young Man	M	Husb'd	45
1471.	Bayonet	F	Wife	50
1472.	First Rider	M	Son	23
1473.	Reney F. Rider	F	Wife	20

Census of the Piegan Indians of Blackfeet Agency, Montana taken by Thomas P. Fuller United States Indian Agent 1898

No.	English Name	Sex	Relation	Age
1474.	John Middle Calf	M	Husb'd	53
1475.	Acowas	F	Wife	70
1476.	John M. Calf	M	Son	20
1477.	Crow Woman	F	Daughter	8
1478.	Iron	M	Husb'd	65
1479.	Woman In The Center	F	Wife	47
1480.	Bear Medicine	M	Husb'd	30
1481.	Raggid Woman	F	Wife	30
1482.	Willie B. Medicine	M	Son	7
1483.	Maggie B. Medicine	F	Daughter	5
1484.	Joseph B. Medicine	M	Son	2
1485.	Joe Shorty	M	Husb'd	31
1486.	Mary Shorty	F	Wife	26
1487.	Sam Shorty	M	Son	7
1488.	Susan Shorty	F	Daughter	4
1489.	Louis Shorty	M	Son	3
1490.	Dick Shorty	M	Son	1
1491.	Lizzie Shorty	F	Daughter	2
1492.	Two Guns	M	Husb'd	28
1493.	Breaks Good	F	Wife	22
1494.	Wolf Tail	M	Husb'd	45
1495.	Gilbert W. Tail	M	Son	11
1496.	Found Herself	F	Daughter	6
1497.	Wolf Getting Up	M	Son	4
1498.	Grass Hopper	M	Son	2
1499.	James White Calf	M	Husb'd	32
1500.	Minnie W. Calf	F	Wife	30
1501.	Stink Teat	M	Husb'd	28
1502.	Sleeping Woman	F	Wife	18
1503.	Stabs Down	M	----	29
1504.	Cloth Woman	F	----	23
1505.	Edward S. Teat	M	Son	1
1506.	White Calf	M	Husb'd	80

Census of the Piegan Indians of Blackfeet Agency, Montana taken by Thomas P. Fuller United States Indian Agent 1898

No.	English Name	Sex	Relation	Age
1507.	Catches Two	F	Wife	50
1508.	Black Snake	F	Wife	55
1509.	Diving Around	F	Daughter	6
1510.	Catches Both Sides	F	Wife	20
1511.	Stole Inside	F	Daughter	6
1512.	Old Man Beaver	M	Son	1
1513.	Jas. Pambrun	M	----	32
1514.	Peter After Buffalo	M	Husb'd	34
1515.	Cut Nose	F	Wife	26
1516.	Isabel A. Buffalo	F	Daughter	11
1517.	Joe A. Buffalo	M	Son	3
1518.	Annie A. Buffalo	F	Daughter	2
1519.	Double Owl	F	Wife	25
1520.	Blue Owl	M	Son	6
1521.	Ignace	F	Daughter	3
1522.	Fanny A. Buffalo	F	Daughter	1
1523.	Double Cloth	F	Mother	50
1524.	Baptiste West Wolf	M	Son	24
1525.	Bernard W. Wolf	M	Son	24
1526.	George W. Wolf	M	Son	12
1527.	John W. Wolf	M	Son	4
1528.	Crane Woman	F	----	60
1529.	Strikes First	F	----	55
1530.	Many Hides	M	Husb'd	25
1531.	Maggie M. Hides	F	Wife	17
1532.	Louis Matt	M	Husb'd	38
1533.	Adaline Matt	F	Wife	31
1534.	Julia Matt	F	Daughter	4
1535.	Francis Matt	F	Daughter	2
1536.	Ada Matt	F	Daughter	1
1537.	Frank Munroe	M	Husb'd	52
1538.	Mary Munroe	F	Wife	45
1539.	Louis Munroe	M	Son	17
1540.	Antoine Munroe	M	Son	10

Census of the Piegan Indians of Blackfeet Agency, Montana taken by Thomas P. Fuller United States Indian Agent 1898

No.	English Name	Sex	Relation	Age
1541.	Slim Tail	M	Husb'd	35
1542.	Kills Water	F	Wife	45
1543.	Flint Smoker	M	Husb'd	30
1544.	Diver	F	Wife	47
1545.	Alekis	M	Son	18
1546.	Louis F. Smoker	M	Son	5
1547.	Eagle Child	M	Husb'd	36
1548.	Fawn	F	Wife	32
1549.	Bark	M	Son	2
1550.	Cecil Child	F	Daughter	9
1551.	Clears Up	M	Husb'd	29
1552.	Calls At Night	F	Wife	29
1553.	Rose Clears Up	F	Daughter	2
1554.	Mabel Clears Up	F	Daughter	10
1555.	Chas. Chouquette	M	Husb'd	33
1556.	Louise Chouquette	F	Wife	34
1557.	Josephene Vhouquette[sic]	F	Daughter	20
1558.	Frank Racine	M	----	20
1559.	Antoine Chouquette	M	----	38
1560.	Looking For Smoke	M	Husb'd	37
1561.	Rising From The Water	F	Wife	46
1562.	Louis L.F. Smoke	M	Son	6
1563.	Double Clean Up	M	----	19
1564.	Fine Kills	F	Mother	70
1565.	Big Top	M	Son	16
1566.	Wood Woman	F	Mother	40
1567.	Kills Forward	F	Daughter	5
1568.	Hits In Water	F	Gd-Mother	60
1569.	Hungry	F	Mother	50
1570.	Jos. Hungry	M	Son	18

Census of the Piegan Indians of Blackfeet Agency, Montana taken by Thomas P. Fuller United States Indian Agent 1898

No.	English Name	Sex	Relation	Age
1571.	Austin Hungry	M	Son	11
1572.	Two Spears	F	Mother	22
1573.	Woman Alone	F	Daughter	4
1574.	Big Eagle	F	Daughter	2
1575.	Womans Word	F	Gd-Mother	70
1576.	Frank Spearson	M	Husb'd	42
1577.	Yellow Beaver	F	Wife	30
1578.	Alfred Spearson	M	Son	2
1579.	Mary Cobell	F	Mother	25
1580.	Norah Cobell	F	Daughter	7
1581.	Josie Cobell	F	Daughter	5
1582.	Weasel Tail	M	Husb'd	38
1583.	Hateing Woman	F	Wife	34
1584.	Annie W. Tail	F	Daughter	12
1585.	Louisa W. Tail	F	Daughter	5
1586.	Fred W. Tail	M	Son	1
1587.	Three Bears	M	Husb'd	45
1588.	Mary Bears	F	Wife	48
1589.	Cecil T. Bears	F	Daughter	8
1590.	Jos. T. Bears	M	Son	4
1591.	Julia Magee	F	Mother	31
1592.	Joe Magee	M	Son	14
1593.	Tom Magee	M	Son	8
1594.	Geo. Magee	M	Son	6
1595.	Walter Magee	M	Son	4
1596.	Henry Magee	M	Son	2
1597.	Dewey Magee	M	Son	1
1598.	Mary Magee	F	Daughter	10
1599.	Ed Billedeaux	M	Husb'd	33
1600.	Virginia Billedeaux	F	Wife	29
1601.	Carl Billedeaux	M	Son	6
1602.	Geneviein Billedeaux	F	Daughter	4
1603.	Martha Billedeaux	F	Daughter	3
1604.	Eddie Billedeaux	M	Son	1

Census of the Piegan Indians of Blackfeet Agency, Montana taken by Thomas P. Fuller United States Indian Agent 1898

No.	English Name	Sex	Relation	Age
1605.	Geneva Stewart	F	Mother	28
1606.	Earl Stewart	M	Son	7
1607.	Jas. Stewart	M	Son	2
1608.	Vera Stewart	F	Daughter	1
1609.	Xavier Billedeaux	M	Husb'd	38
1610.	Selena Billedeaux	F	Wife	30
1611.	Willie Billedeaux	M	Son	10
1612.	Chas. Billedeaux	M	Son	8
1613.	Wearen Billedeaux	M	Son	6
1614.	Greeley Billedeaux	M	Son	4
1615.	Mabel Billedeaux	F	Daughter	2
1616.	Oliver Sanderville	M	Husb'd	39
1617.	Mary Sanderville	F	Wife	29
1618.	John Sanderville	M	Son	11
1619.	Joe Kipp	M	Husb'd	48
1620.	Martha Kipp	F	Wife	40
1621.	Jas. Kipp	M	Son	7
1622.	Mary Kipp	F	Daughter	9
1623.	Geo. Kipp	M	Son	1
1624.	Wm. Kipp	M	Ad-Son	22
1625.	Matt Fitzpatrick	M	Ad-Son	20
1626.	Dick Lucero	M	----	19
1627.	Oliver Racine	M	----	20
1628.	Black Sarcee	M	Husb'd	36
1629.	Kills Far	F	Wife	37
1630.	Little Young Man	M	Husb'd	39
1631.	Iyockatopsis	F	Wife	50
1632.	Good Singer	F	G-Mother	90
1633.	Blackfoot Child	M	Husb'd	53
1634.	Buffalo Road	F	Wife	70
1635.	Grace B. Child	F	Daughter	17
1636.	Irene B. Child	F	Daughter	2

Census of the Piegan Indians of Blackfeet Agency, Montana taken by Thomas P. Fuller United States Indian Agent 1898

No.	English Name	Sex	Relation	Age
1637.	Anthony Austin	M	Husb'd	28
1638.	Susin Austin	F	Wife	36
1639.	Black Bear	M	Husb'd	56
1640.	Many Snakes	F	Wife	40
1641.	John B. Bear	M	Son	26
1642.	Tallow Ashley	M	Husb'd	35
1643.	Small Beads	F	Wife	35
1644.	Louis Ashley	M	Son	2
1645.	Mary Ashley	F	Ad-Son[sic]	2
1646.	Dog Ears	M	Husb'd	23
1647.	Mary D. Ears	F	Wife	20
1648.	Medicine Owl	M	Husb'd	32
1649.	Elk Woman	F	Wife	50
1650.	Runs Away	F	Mother	38
1651.	Mary R. Away	F	Daughter	16
1652.	Susie R. Away	F	Daughter	5
1653.	Bear Head	M	Father	42
1654.	Mary B. Head	F	Daughter	10
1655.	Sam Yellow Wolf	M	----	27
1656.	Gambler	M	Husb'd	35
1657.	Louise Gambler	F	Wife	36
1658.	Round Butte	M	Son	1
1659.	Yellow Wolf	M	Husb'd	51
1660.	Annie Y. Wolf	F	Daughter	4
1661.	Double Iron Woman	F	Wife	25
1662.	John Y. Wolf	M	Son	2
1663.	Mollie Y. Wolf	F	Daughter	5
1664.	Cecil Sanderville	F	Mother	28
1665.	Agnes Sanderville	F	Daughter	12
1666.	Edward Sanderville	M	Son	1
1667.	Curlew	F	----	65

Census of the Piegan Indians of Blackfeet Agency, Montana taken by Thomas P. Fuller United States Indian Agent 1898

No.	English Name	Sex	Relation	Age
1668.	Joe Spanish	M	Husb'd	29
1669.	Kills First	F	Wife	37
1670.	Wm. Clark	M	Son	5
1671.	Agnes Clark	F	Daughter	14
1672.	Mary Hazlett	F	Ad-Daughter	18
1673.	Geo. Hazlett	M	Ad-Son	20
1674.	Rides At The Door	M	Husb'd	32
1675.	Mary R.A.T. Door	F	Wife	28
1676.	Dick R.A.T. Door	M	Son	8
1677.	Louise R.A.T. Door	F	Daughter	6
1678.	Frank R.A.T. Door	m	Son	3
1679.	Jas. R.A.T. Door	M	Son	1
1680.	Richard Grant	M	----	21
1681.	Alice Burd	F	----	18
1682.	Mary Rumsy	F	Mother	22
1683.	Jessie Rumsey	M	Son	2
1684.	Mollie Davis	F	Mother	24
1685.	Thos. Davis	M	Son	7
1686.	Pearl Davis	F	Daughter	4
1687.	Bryan Davis	M	Son	2
1688.	Ed Gobert	M	Ad-Son	18
1689.	Catherine Gobert	F	Ad-Daughter	16
1690.	Cecil Hunsberger	F	Mother	58
1691.	John Hunsberger	M	Son	27
1692.	Thos. Hunsberger	M	Son	21
1693.	Isaac Hunsberger	M	Son	25
1694.	Clara Hunsburger	F	Daughter	19
1695.	Augustus Hunsburger	M	Son	15
1696.	Maggie Kennerley	F	Mother	45
1697.	Agnes Kennerley	F	Daughter	11
1698.	Agnes Gobert	F	Daughter	12
1699.	Annie Gobert	F	Daughter	10
1700.	Jerome Kennerley	M	Son	9
1701.	Jas. Kennerley	M	Son	3

Census of the Piegan Indians of Blackfeet Agency, Montana taken by Thomas P. Fuller United States Indian Agent 1898

No.	English Name	Sex	Relation	Age
1702.	Mary Smith	F	----	23
1703.	John Douglas	M	----	21
1704.	John Vielle	M	Husb'd	31
1705.	Annie Vielle	F	Wife	26
1706.	Mary Vielle	F	Daughter	5
1707.	Willie Vielle	M	Son	7
1708.	Joe Vielle	M	Son	4
1709.	Tom Vielle	M	----	19
1710.	Janet Coe	F	----	13
1711.	James Coe	M	Brother	12
1712.	Agnes Coe	F	Sister	8
1713.	Geo. W. Cook	M	Husb'd	35
1714.	Julie Cook	F	Wife	26
1715.	Chas. Martin	M	Father	31
1716.	Ross Martin	M	Son	4
1717.	Mary Johnson	F	----	18
1718.	Mary Lukin	F	Mother	50
1719.	John Lukin	M	Son	19
1720.	Peter Lukin	M	Son	17
1721.	Dora Lukin	F	Daughter	22
1722.	Victoria Lukin	F	Daughter	20
1723.	Louise Aubrey	F	Mother	42
1724.	Alice Aubrey	F	Daughter	21
1725.	Rosa Aubrey	F	Daughter	19
1726.	Laura Aubrey	F	Daughter	16
1727.	Lucy Aubrey	F	Daughter	11
1728.	Dora Aubrey	F	Daughter	10
1729.	May Aubrey	F	Daughter	6
1730.	Jeanette Aubrey	F	Daughter	3
1731.	Thos. Aubrey	M	Son	14
1732.	Philip Aubrey	M	Son	7
1733.	Weasel Fat	M	Husb'd	46

Census of the Piegan Indians of Blackfeet Agency, Montana taken by Thomas P. Fuller United States Indian Agent 1898

No.	English Name	Sex	Relation	Age
1734.	Good Sheild[sic]	F	Wife	30
1735.	Cree Woman	F	Sister	24
1736.	Bad Married	M	Husb'd	38
1737.	Little Fox	F	Wife	35
1738.	Last Shoot	M	Son	9
1739.	Lost Her Finger	F	Daughter	7
1740.	Last Bear	F	Daughter	6
1741.	Last Hollow	F	Daughter	1
1742.	Wolf Chief	M	Husb'd	30
1743.	Lone Woman	F	Wife	30
1744.	Bear Child	M	Husb'd	46
1745.	Oars	F	Wife	36
1746.	William B. Child	M	Son	15
1747.	Josephene B. Child	F	Daughter	11
1748.	Louis B. Child	M	Son	6
1749.	Jas. B. Child	M	Son	7
1750.	Ben B. Child	M	Son	4
1751.	Earrings	M	Husb'd	40
1752.	Susan	F	Wife	55
1753.	Three Riders	M	Son	19
1754.	Takes-Meat	M	Son	12
1755.	Talking Woman	M	----	70
1756.	Bear Skin	M	Husb'd	80
1757.	Three Scissors	F	Wife	70
1758.	Chas. DeLaney	M	Husb'd	24
1759.	Viola DeLaney	F	Wife	16
1760.	Root Digger	F	----	70
1761.	John Night Gun	M	Husb'd	37
1762.	Blanket Woman	F	Daughter	6
1763.	Short Woman	F	Daughter	5
1764.	Yellow Squirrel	F	Wife	25

Census of the Piegan Indians of Blackfeet Agency, Montana taken by Thomas P. Fuller United States Indian Agent 1898

No.	English Name	Sex	Relation	Age
1765.	Big Old Woman	F	----	40
1766.	Mary Dunbar	F	Mother	27
1767.	Jane Dunbar	F	Daughter	11
1768.	Andrew Dunbar	M	Son	8
1769.	Frank Dunbar	M	Son	6
1770.	Carrie Dunbar	F	Daughter	4
1771.	Esther Dunbar	F	Daughter	3
1772.	Jas. Dunbar	M	Son	1
1773.	Carrie Monroe	F	Mother	30
1774.	Mabel Monroe	F	Daughter	6
1775.	Jessie Monroe	M	Son	4
1776.	Jos. Monroe	M	Son	1
1777.	Sallie Allison	F	Mother	26
1778.	Willie Allison	M	Son	6
1779.	Allen Allison	M	Son	4
1780.	Wendell Allison	M	Son	2
1781.	Infant	M	Son	1
1782.	Jas. Dawson	M	Father	44
1783.	Jas. Dawson	M	Son	11
1784.	Wm. Dawson	M	Son	8
1785.	Harrold Dawson	M	Son	6
1786.	Tom Dawson	M	Husb'd	37
1787.	Isabel Dawson	F	Wife	37
1788.	Fanny Dawson	F	Ad-Daughter	12
1789.	Split Ears	M	Husb'd	30
1790.	Good Kill	F	Wife	40
1791.	Maggie S. Ears	F	Daughter	8
1792.	Susie S. Ears	F	Daughter	5
1793.	Wolverine	M	Husb'd	27
1794.	Walks Backwards	F	Wife	20
1795.	William Wolverine	M	Son	5
1796.	Joe Wolverine	M	Son	3
1797.	Monic Simon	F	Mother	66

Census of the Piegan Indians of Blackfeet Agency, Montana taken by Thomas P. Fuller United States Indian Agent 1898

No.	English Name	Sex	Relation	Age
1798.	Jas. Perrin	M	Son	29
1799.	Presley Hawk	M	Son	1
1800.	Eddie Jack	M	Husb'd	33
1801.	Mary Jack	F	Wife	37
1802.	Maggie Jack	F	Daughter	13
1803.	John Two Guns	M	Son	16
1804.	Moonic	F	Daughter	3
1805.	Sarah Jack	F	Daughter	1
1806.	Ground	M	Father	48
1807.	John Ground	M	Son	23
1808.	Jas. Ground	M	Son	22
1809.	Puts Face Front	F	----	21
1810.	Vic Robinson	F	Mother	38
1811.	Geo. Robinson	M	Son	18
1812.	Mary Robinson	F	Daughter	19
1813.	Joe Robinson	M	Son	16
1814.	Louise Robinson	F	Daughter	8
1815.	Ad Robinson	F	Daughter	6
1816.	Henry Larb	M	----	19
1817.	East Woman	F	----	67
1818.	Hunter Powell	M	Husb'd	37
1819.	Sophia Powell	F	Wife	26
1820.	Frank Powell	M	Son	3
1821.	Clara Powell	F	Daughter	7
1822.	Wm. Powell	M	Son	6
1823.	Francis Monroe	M	----	25
1824.	Rosa Ward	F	Mother	26
1825.	Jas. Ward	M	Son	8
1826.	Geo. Ward	M	Son	7
1827.	Mary Ward	F	Daughter	3
1828.	Emma Ward	F	Daughter	1
1829.	Nellie Schildt	F	Mother	37
1830.	Joe Schildt	M	Son	17

Census of the Piegan Indians of Blackfeet Agency, Montana taken by Thomas P. Fuller United States Indian Agent 1898

No.	English Name	Sex	Relation	Age
1831.	Harry Schildt	M	Son	13
1832.	Nellie Schildt	F	Daughter	14
1833.	Andrew Schildt	M	Son	8
1834.	Augusta Schildt	F	Daughter	6
1835.	Mary Schildt	F	Daughter	4
1836.	Irene Schildt	F	Daughter	3
1837.	Sam Smith	M	----	19
1838.	Poor Woman	F	----	60
1839.	John Morgan	M	Husb'd	32
1840.	Lucy Morgan	F	Wife	23
1841.	Davis Morgan	M	Son	7
1842.	Ire Morgan	M	Son	3
1843.	Infant	M	Son	1
1844.	Under Mink	M	----	26
1845.	Making Signs	F	Mother	35
1846.	Blood Woman	F	Daughter	5
1847.	Skunk Cap	F	Mother	50
1848.	Good Chases	F	Daughter	5
1849.	Black Blanket Woman	F	Daughter	10
1850.	Maggie S. Cap	F	Daughter	11
1851.	Talk Woman	F	----	68
1852.	Under Bear	M	----	21
1853.	Libby Kipp	F	----	18
1854.	Young Eagle	M	Husb'd	37
1855.	Many Sheilds	F	Wife	26
1856.	Jas. Eagle Child	M	Son	11
1857.	Home Gun	M	Husb'd	33
1858.	Mary Pipe Stone	F	Wife	27
1859.	Mary H. Gun	F	Daughter	2
1860.	Paul H. Gun	M	Son	5

Census of the Piegan Indians of Blackfeet Agency, Montana taken by Thomas P. Fuller United States Indian Agent 1898

No.	English Name	Sex	Relation	Age
1861.	Heavy Breast	M	Husb'd	51
1862.	Laying Low	F	Wife	40
1863.	Kind Woman	F	Daughter	33
1864.	Young H. Breast	M	Son	18
1865.	Small Head	F	Daughter	1
1866.	Heading Off	F	----	61
1867.	Lucy Cook	F	Mother	26
1868.	Isabel Cook	F	Daughter	4
1869.	Loratta Cook	F	Daughter	2
1870.	Hairy Coat	M	Husb'd	29
1871.	Mary H. Coat	F	Wife	26
1872.	Three Guns	M	Husb'd	31
1873.	Kills At Night	F	Wife	43
1874.	Owl Squirrel	M	Son	17
1875.	Good Killer	F	Gd-Mother	80
1876.	John Croff	M	Husb'd	23
1877.	Louise Croff	F	Wife	26
1878.	Lad Croff	M	Son	2
1879.	Jas. Housman	M	Son	31
1880.	Susan Housman	F	Wife	32
1881.	Thos. Housman	M	Son	10
1882.	Jas. Housman	M	Son	8
1883.	Mary Housman	F	Daughter	7
1884.	Geneva Housman	F	Daughter	4
1885.	Josephene Housman	F	Daughter	2
1886.	Wm. Lewis	M	Husb'd	46
1887.	Margarete Lewis	F	Wife	27
1888.	Antoine Lewis	M	Son	14
1889.	Piler Lewis	M	Son	6
1890.	Sarah Lewis	F	Daughter	5
1891.	Geo. Lewis	M	Son	4
1892.	Geo. Horn	M	----	28
1893.	Jos. Livinmore	M	Father	37

Census of the Piegan Indians of Blackfeet Agency, Montana taken by Thomas P. Fuller United States Indian Agent 1898

No.	English Name	Sex	Relation	Age
1894.	Clara Livinmore	F	Daughter	7
1895.	Lilly Livinmore	F	Daughter	4
1896.	John Tingley	M	----	31
1897.	Cut Finger	M	Husb'd	35
1898.	Strikes Back	F	Wife	23
1899.	Ernest C. Finger	M	Son	17
1900.	Paul C. Finger	M	Son	14
1901.	Josephene C. Finger	F	Daughter	12
1902.	Maggie C. Finger	F	Daughter	9
1903.	Thos. C. Finger	M	Son	4
1904.	Cut Finger	M	Son	1
1905.	John Monroe	M	Husb'd	76
1906.	Christina Monroe	F	Wife	41
1907.	Louis Monroe	M	Son	16
1908.	Angus Monroe	M	Son	10
1909.	Wm. Hazlett	M	----	23
1910.	Martha Kipp	F	----	80
1911.	Mary Lippincott	F	Mother	34
1912.	Ray Lippincott	M	Son	12
1913.	Arthur Lippincott	M	Son	11
1914.	Chas. Juneau	M	----	20
1915.	John Mestas	m	----	26
1916.	Mary Douglas	F	Mother	46
1917.	Wm. Douglas	M	Son	24
1918.	Henry Merchant	M	----	25
1919.	Eliza Carney	F	----	22
1920.	Chas. Simon	M	----	38
1921.	Josephene Miller	F	----	20
1922.	John Kennedy	M	Husb'd	23
1923.	Mary Kennedy	F	Wife	22

Census of the Piegan Indians of Blackfeet Agency, Montana taken by Thomas P. Fuller United States Indian Agent 1898

No.	English Name	Sex	Relation	Age
1924.	John Kennedy	M	Son	7
1925.	Emily Eldridge	F	----	45
1926.	Julia Cobell	F	----	23
1927.	Mary Big Road	F	----	18
1928.	Garret White Horses	M	----	23
1929.	Frank Calf Robe	M	Husb'd	26
1930.	Jeanette Robe	F	Wife	22
1931.	Louise Paisley	F	Mother	26
1932.	Geo. Paisley	M	Son	13
1933.	Allen Paisley	M	Son	9
1934.	Walter Paisley	M	Son	6
1935.	Chauncey Paisley	M	Son	20[sic]
1936.	Horace J. Clark[sic]	M	Father	51
1937.	Malcomn Clarke	M	Son	22
1938.	John Clarke	M	Son	18
1939.	Dick Kipp	M	Husb'd	33
1940.	Mary Kipp	F	Wife	28
1941.	Cora Kipp	F	Daughter	10
1942.	Louis Kipp	M	Son	6
1943.	Geo. Kipp	M	Son	2
1944.	Hannah Kipp	F	Daughter	1
1945.	Frank Vielle	M	Husb'd	29
1946.	Annie Vielle	F	Wife	30
1947.	Annie Vielle	F	Ad-Daughter	16
1948.	Jack Vielle	M	Son	3
1949.	Andy Vielle	M	Son	1
1950.	Jas. Douglas	M	Father	27
1951.	Jas. A. Douglas	M	Son	4
1952.	Lida Douglas	F	Daughter	2
1953.	Lucy King	F	Mother	31

Census of the Piegan Indians of Blackfeet Agency, Montana taken by Thomas P. Fuller United States Indian Agent 1898

No.	English Name	Sex	Relation	Age
1954.	Sadie King	F	Daughter	13
1955.	Jas. King	M	Son	10
1956.	Chas. King	M	Son	7
1957.	William King	M	Son	5
1958.	Henry King	M	Son	1
1959.	Robert Hamilton	M	----	28
1960.	Dick Croff	M	Husb'd	29
1961.	Maggie Croff	F	Wife	21
1962.	Arthur Croff	M	Son	2
1963.	Infant	M	Son	1
1964.	Calf Shield	M	Husb'd	52
1965.	Takes Short	F	Wife	65
1966.	Geo. C. Shield	M	Son	6
1967.	Wolf Calf	M	Husb'd	80
1968.	Antelope Woman	F	Wife	75
1969.	Rides Behind	M	Husb'd	38
1970.	Shoots Weasel	F	Wife	36
1971.	Chief In Front	M	Husb'd	26
1972.	Irene F. Rider	F	Wife	20
1973.	Yellow Iron	F	Mother	70
1974.	Mary Y. Iron	F	Daughter	4[sic]
1975.	Sand Y. Iron	F	Daughter	2[sic]
1976.	Louise Tingley	F	Mother	45
1977.	Oliver Tingley	M	Son	29
1978.	Robert Tingley	M	Son	27
1979.	Lizzie Tingley	F	Daughter	21
1980.	Moses Tingley	M	Son	17
1981.	David Tingley	M	Son	12
1982.	Rosa Luvero	F	----	17
1983.	Isabel Thomas	F	----	45
1984.	Matilda Buckley	F	Mother	22

Census of the Piegan Indians of Blackfeet Agency, Montana taken by Thomas P. Fuller United States Indian Agent 1898

No.	English Name	Sex	Relation	Age
1985.	Infant	M	Son	1
1986.	Paul Austin	M	Husb'd	40
1987.	Louise Austin	F	Wife	30
1988.	Mabel Austin	F	Daughter	13
1989.	Fanny Austin	F	Daughter	5
1990.	Mattie Burd	F	Mother	32
1991.	Martha Burd	F	Daughter	16
1992.	Sam Burd	M	Son	14
1993.	Chas. Burd	M	Son	12
1994.	Johnson Burd	M	Son	10
1995.	Henry Burd	M	Son	2
1996.	Infant	M	Son	1
1997.	Mary Morgan	F	Mother	36
1998.	Jessie Morgan	M	Son	15
1999.	Geo. Morgan	M	Son	17
2000.	Lizzie Morgan	F	Daughter	12
2001.	Nellie Morgan	F	Daughter	8
2002.	Fanny Morgan	F	Daughter	6
2003.	Albert Morgan	M	Son	4
2004.	Alice Morgan	F	Daughter	2
2005.	Katie Morgan	F	Daughter	1
2006.	Mollie Davlin	F	----	30
2007.	Susan Williamson	F	----	40
2008.	Pipe Woman	F	Mother	40
2009.	Annie Wagner	F	Daughter	18
2010.	Mary Wagner	F	Daughter	14
2011.	Wm. Wagner	M	Son	12
2012.	Jennie Harrison	F	Daughter	6
2013.	Frank Harrison	M	Son	2
2014.	Strikes Two	F	Mother	----
2015.	Red Head	M	Husb'd	----
2016.	Skip Jack	M	Son	----
2017.	Nick Green	M	Son	27

Census of the Piegan Indians of Blackfeet Agency, Montana taken by Thomas P. Fuller United States Indian Agent 1898

No.	English Name	Sex	Relation	Age
2018.	Annie Magee	F	----	32
2019.	Wipes His Eyes	M	Husb'd	30
2020.	Takes Gun	F	Wife	40
2021.	Kills Another	F	Daughter	4
2022.	Morning Star	F	Daughter	1

-Census-

-Recapitulation-
-o0o-

Males above eighteen years of age,-----556

Females above fourteen years of age,--577

School children between six & sixteen,

        Males,-----------------------------201

        Females--------------------------152

Males between sixteen & eighteen,------44

Males under six years of age,------------148

Females under six years of age,---------<u>214</u>
        Total, all ages,---------1,892

Census of the Blackfeet,

Montana, 1899

	OFFICE OF	
44048	Indian Affairs, Rec. SEP. 16	**1899**

W. R. Logan
    Blackfeet A.
        Sept. 1, 1899

    Census of Indians

-RECAPITULATION-
June 30, 1899.

Males--- 966
Females--- 991
                                Total   1957
Males above 18 years of age----------------------------- 483
Females above 14 years of age-------------------------- 610
School children 6 to 16 years---------------------------- 431
Male School children--------------------------------------- 215
Female School children------------------------------------ 216

Census of the Piegan tribe of Indians of Blackfeet Agency, Montana taken by W. R. Logan United States Indian Agent, September 1st, 1899

No.	English Name	Sex	Relation	Age
1	Abel Skunk Cap	M	Son	24
2	Hits Last	F	Moth.	56
3	Aims Back	M	Hus.	31
4	Emma Aims Back	F	Wife	21
5	Thomas Aims Back	M	Son	5
6	Joseph Aims Back	M	Son	1
7	Adam White Man	M	Hus.	25
8	Anna White Man	F	Wife	-
9	Maggie Albertson	F	Moth.	
10	Julia Walters	F	Dau.	24
11	George Walters	M	Son	22
12	Arthur Walters	M	Son	19
13	Robert Albertson	M	Son	9
14	Mary Albertson	F	Dau.	6
15	Julia Albertson	F	Dau.	2
16	May Albertson	F	Dau.	1
17	After Buffalo	M	Hus.	47
18	Daisy Buffalo	F	Wife	23
19	John Buffalo	M	Son	5
20	Stabs Buffalo	M	Son	2
21	Almost Killed	F	Wid.	81
22	After Buffalo #2	F	Moth.	40
23	James After Buffalo	M	Son	4
24	Bead Woman	F	Mother	50
25	Joe Cayton	M	Son	24
26	Bobtail Horse	M	Husband	46
27	Old Woman	F	Wife	35
28	Joe Bobtail Horse	M	Son	12
29	Black Boy	M	Father	39
30	Reuben Black Boy	M	Son	12
31	Boy Chief	M	Husband	33
32	Last Gun Woman	F	Wife	28

Census of the Piegan tribe of Indians of Blackfeet Agency, Montana taken by W. R. Logan United States Indian Agent, September 1st, 1899

No.	English Name	Sex	Relation	Age
33	Big Beaver	M	Husband	39
34	Minnie Big Beaver	F	Wife	30
35	Horace Big Beaver	M	Son	11
36	Eddie Big Beaver	M	Son	13
37	James Big Beaver	M	Son	14
38	Bad Woman	F	Mother	41
39	Richard Calf Robe	M	Son	20
41	Bull Shoe	M	Husband	52
42	Small Woman	F	Wife	46
43	Dirty Face	F	Wife	35
44	Joe Bull Shoe	M	Son	20
45	Pat Bull Shoe	M	Son	13
46	Bull Shoe #2	F	Mother	45
47	Three Guns	M	Son	16
48	Barney Calf Ribs	M	Husband	25
49	Good Charge	F	Wife	17
50	Black Bull	M	-----	32
51	Big Smoke	M	Husband	55
52	Black Bird	F	Wife	48
53	Joe Big Smoke	M	Son	2
54	Big Lodge Pole	M	Father	38
55	Peter Lodge Pole	M	Son	14
56	Big Tiger Woman	F	Mother	46
57	Minnie Spotted Bear	F	Dau.	6
58	Agnes Big Road	F	Sister	16
59	Minnie Big Road	F	Sister	5
60	Bear Leggins	M	Husband	47
61	War Woman	F	Wife	31
62	Old Woman	F	Wife	47
63	Peter Bear Leggins	M	Son	2
64	Rachel Bear Leggins	F	Dau.	14
65	Mary Bear Leggins	F	Dau.	12

Census of the Piegan tribe of Indians of Blackfeet Agency, Montana taken by W. R. Logan United States Indian Agent, September 1st, 1899

No.	English Name	Sex	Relation	Age
66	Bad Old Man	M	Husband	65
67	Sallie Bad Old Man	F	Wife	54
68	John Bad Old Man	M	Son	17
69	The Bite	M	Husband	57
70	Kills For Nothing	F	Wife	41
71	Wolf Bite	M	Son	14
72	Minnie Bite	F	Dau.	5
73	John Bite	M	Son	2
74	Mrs. Butterfly	F	Mother	41
75	Mary Butterfly	F	Dau.	7
76	Bear Shoe	M	Husband	36
77	Daisy Bear Shoe	F	Wife	19
78	Minnie Bear Shoe	F	Dau.	1
79	Buffalo Growing	M	Husband	40
80	Shield Woman	F	Wife	38
81	Big Crow	M	Husband	40
82	Two Guns	F	Wife	30
83	Lynx Woman	F	Dau.	13
84	Cecil Big Crow	F[sic]	Dau.	11
85	Buffalo Hide	M	Father	40
86	Mary Buffalo Hide	F	Mother	26
87	James Buffalo Hide	M	Son	3
88	Billy B. Hide	M	Son	6
89	Jennie B. Hide	F	Dau.	5m.
90	Elmer Butterfly	M	Husband	26
91	Mary Butterfly	F	Wife	2
92	Runs Behind	M	Son	4
93	Buffalo Hide	F	G. Mother	81
94	Louise Clarke	F	Mother	30
95	Geo. Clarke	M	Son	14
96	James Clarke	M	Son	12
97	Robert Clarke	M	Son	10

Census of the Piegan tribe of Indians of Blackfeet Agency, Montana taken by W. R. Logan United States Indian Agent, September 1st, 1899

No.	English Name	Sex	Relation	Age
98	Croning[sic] Old Woman	F	Widow	66
99	Cree Medicine	M	Husband	35
100	Medicine Woman	F	Wife	32
101	Maggie Bear Chief	F	Dau.	8
102	Susie Bear Chief	F	Dau.	3
103	Joe Cree Medicine	M	Son	6
104	Curley Bear	M	Husband	46
105	Minnie Curley Bear	F	Wife	34
106	Mary Curley Bear	F	Wife	33
107	Charles Curley Bear	M	Son	18
108	William Curley Bear	M	Son	4
109	Jennie Curley Bear	F	Dau.	7
110	Anna Curley Bear	F	Dau.	3
111	Calf Looking	M	Husband	53
112	Goes In Last	F	Wife	56
113	Paul Calf Looking	M	Son	23
114	Calf Tail	M	Husband	41
115	Different Woman	F	Wife	43
116	John Calf Tail	M	Son	21
117	Earnest Calf Tail	M	Son	11
118	Mamie Crawford	F	Mother	41
119	Ellen Crawford	F	Dau.	5
120	Joe Crawford	M	Son	2
121	John Crawford	M	Son	9
122	Chas. No Coat	M	Son	22
123	Long Time Chicken	F	Mother	44
124	Jennie No Coat	F	Dau.	8
125	Calf Robe	F	----	56
126	Joe Calf Robe	M	Husband	21
127	Emma Calf Robe	F	Wife	23
128	Calf Woman	F	----	67
129	Mrs. Pete Champine	F	Mother	34
130	George Champine	M	Son	6

Census of the Piegan tribe of Indians of Blackfeet Agency, Montana taken by W. R. Logan United States Indian Agent, September 1st, 1899

No.	English Name	Sex	Relation	Age
131	Maggie Champine	F	Dau.	5
132	Pete Champine	M	Son	1
133	Catches Edge Water	F	-----	79
134	Chicken Shoe	M	Husband	24
135	Medicine Star	F	Wife	30
136	Mary Chicken Shoe	F	Dau.	4
137	John Chicken Shoe	M	Son	1
138	Peter Chicken Shoe	M	Son	16
139	Chas. Iron Breast	M	Husband	23
140	Minnie Iron Breast	F	Wife	28
141	Catches First	F	-----	70
142	Crow Eyes	M	Husband	40
143	Running[sic] Rattler	F	Wife	27
144	William Crow Eyes	M	Son	4
145	Mary Crow Eyes	F	Dau.	1
146	Calf Boss Ribs	M	Husband	57
147	Bad Eyes	F	Wife	54
148	Plenty Iron Woman	F	Wife	25
149	Minnie Boss Ribs	F	Dau.	6
150	Joseph Boss Ribs	M	Son	4
151	Chief All Over	M	Husband	47
152	Medicine Woman	F	Wife	48
153	George Chief All Over	M	Son	9
154	Minnie Choate	F	Mother	51
155	Samuel Choate	M	Son	20
156	George Choate	M	Husband	24
157	Fanny Choate	F	Wife	20
158	Cold Feet	M	Husband	51
159	Dry Goods Woman	F	Wife	48
160	Snake Girl	F	Dau.	11
161	Comes In Night	M	Husband	41

Census of the Piegan tribe of Indians of Blackfeet Agency, Montana taken by W. R. Logan United States Indian Agent, September 1st, 1899

No.	English Name	Sex	Relation	Age
162	Elk Robe	F	Wife	33
163	Charges	F	Wife	21
164	Cecil C. I. Night	F	Dau.	6
165	Minnie C. I. Night	F	Dau.	5
166	James C. I. Night	M	Son	1
167	Louie Champine	M	Husband	36
168	Busy Woman	F	Wife	38
169	George Champine	M	Son	7
170	Pete Champine	M	Son	6
171	Mary Champine	F	Dau.	2
172	Frank Calf Robe	M	Husband	24
173	Minnie Calf Robe	F	Wife	20
174	Frank Choate	M	Husband	26
175	Big Head	F	Wife	32
176	Chas. Big Head	M	Son	4
177	James Choate	M	Son	1
178	Mary Davis	F	Mother	24
179	Hattie Davis	F	Dau.	3
180	Michael Day Rider	M	Husband	30
181	Helen Day Rider	F	Wife	25
182	Oliver Day Rider	M	Son	4
183	Chas. Day Rider	M	Son	2
184	John Day Rider	M	Son	1
185	Dives Long Way	F	----	71
186	Duck Head	M	Husband	33
187	Buckskin Rider	F	Wife	27
188	Peter Duck Head	M	Son	9
189	Josephine Duck Head	F	Dau.	11
190	Mary Duck Head	F	Dau.	3
191	Louie Duck Head	M	Son	1
192	Day Rider	M	Husband	26
193	Runs Away	F	Wife	27
194	Joe Day Rider	M	Son	3
195	George Day Rider	M	Son	9

Census of the Piegan tribe of Indians of Blackfeet Agency, Montana taken by W. R. Logan United States Indian Agent, September 1st, 1899

No.	English Name	Sex	Relation	Age
196	Mary Day Rider	F	Dau.	1
197	Frank Donivan	M	Husband	22
198	Jennie Donivan	F	Wife	17
199	Two Strikes	F	Mother	57
200	Drags His Robe	M	Husband	37
201	Esquimo Woman	F	Wife	41
202	Minnie D. H. Robe	F	Dau.	5
203	Chas. White Swan	M	Son	20
204	Dan Lone Chief	M	Husband	26
205	Ellen Lone Chief	F	Wife	24
206	Double Runner	M	Husband	51
207	Good Woman	F	Wife	46
208	Edgar Double Runner	M	Son	20
209	Paul Double Runner	M	Son	19
210	Many Guns	M	Son	25
211	Margaret DeChamp	F	----	60
212	Drags His Blanket	M	Husband	29
213	Last Goes In	F	Wife	19
214	Yellow Head	M	Son	3
215	Dog Taking Gun	M	Husband	33
216	Cuts Herself	F	Wife	28
217	Ellen Edwards	F	Mother	40
218	William Edwards	M	Son	10
219	Thomas Edwards	M	Son	8
220	Fanny Edwards	F	Dau.	6
221	Elizabeth Edwards	F	Dau.	4
222	John Edwards	M	Son	2
223	Rosa Edwards	F	Dau.	1
224	Eagle Flag	M	Husband	56
225	Bounces Up	F	Wife	46
226	Emma E. Flag	F	Dau.	11
227	Mrs. Eagle Ribs	F	Mother	35

Census of the Piegan tribe of Indians of Blackfeet Agency, Montana taken by W. R. Logan United States Indian Agent, September 1st, 1899

No.	English Name	Sex	Relation	Age
228	Cecil Eagle Ribs	F	Dau.	3
229	Everybody Looks At	F	Mother	45
230	Fanny Double Fox	F	Dau.	14
231	Mary Double Fox	F	Dau.	5
232	Eagle Head	M	Husband	60
233	White Tail	F	Wife	41
234	James Eagle Head	M	Son	13
235	Margaret Eagle Head	F	Dau.	11
236	Eagle	M	Husband	32
237	Mary Eagle	F	Wife	28
238	Catches On Top	F	Mother	50
239	John Eagle Ribs	M	Husband	24
240	Louisa Eagle Ribs	F	Wife	27
241	Agnes Eagle Ribs	F	Dau.	11
242	Everybody Talks	M	Husband	47
243	Strikes Back	F	Wife	48
244	Hates Woman	F	Wife	40
245	Louie Everybody Talks	M	Son	9
246	Paul Everybody Talks	M	Son	6
247	Susie Everybody Talks	F	Dau.	4
248	Mollie Everybody Talks	F	Dau.	2
249	Joe Evans	M	Husband	25
250	Mary Evans	F	Wife	21
251	James Evans	M	Son	3
252	Irene Evans	F	Dau.	1
253	Anna Fisher	F	Mother	27
254	James Fisher	M	Son	12
255	Jesse Fisher	M	Son	1
256	Four Horns	M	Husband	48
257	Gros Ventres Woman	F	Wife	31
258	Benj. Four Horns	M	Son	20
259	James Four Horns	M	Son	6
260	Flint Smoker	M	Husband	39

Census of the Piegan tribe of Indians of Blackfeet Agency, Montana taken by W. R. Logan United States Indian Agent, September 1st, 1899

No.	English Name	Sex	Relation	Age
261	Under Beaver	F	Wife	42
262	Peter Flint Smoker	M	Son	16
263	James Flint Smoker	M	Son	7
264	Frank Rider	M	---	32
265	First One Russell	M	Husband	28
266	Isabella Russell	F	Wife	18
267	Mrs. Fast Buffalo Horse	F	Mother	46
268	James Buffalo Horse	M	Son	24
269	Albert Buffalo Horse	M	Son	22
270	Joe Buffalo Horse	M	Son	13
271	Felix Marrow Bones	M	Husband	25
272	Anna Marrow Bones	F	Wife	20
273	Lawrence Faber	M	Husband	26
274	Anna Faber	F	Wife	21
275	Mary Faber	f	Dau	4
276	Flat Tail	M	Husband	56
277	Medicine Pipe Woman	F	Wife	44
278	Sophia Flat Tail	F	Dau.	6
279	Philip Flat Tail	M	Husband	23
280	Anna Flat Tail	F	Wife	19
281	Fine Bull	M	Husband	51
282	Pretty Star	F	Wife	41
283	Stabs Down	F	Dau.	11
284	Spider	F	Dau.	6
285	Lucy Fine Bull	F	Dau.	5
286	James Fine Bull	M	Son	4
287	Fisher	F	-----	90
288	Fish	M	Husband	26
289	Lone Rock	F	Wife	25
290	Found A Gun	F	-----	30

Census of the Piegan tribe of Indians of Blackfeet Agency, Montana taken by W. R. Logan United States Indian Agent, September 1st, 1899

No.	English Name	Sex	Relation	Age
291	George Four Horns	M	Son	18
292	Kills In Water	F	Mother	51
293	Gambler	M	Husband	43
294	Anna Gambler	F	Wife	46
295	Richard Gambler	M	Son	19
296	James Gambler	M	Husband	26
297	Anna Gambler	F	Wife	23
298	Mary Gambler	F	Dau.	1
299	Good Clear Up	F	Mother	40
300	Double Go In	F	Dau.	4
301	Alex Guardipee	M	Husband	36
302	Louisa Guardipee	F	Wife	22
303	John Guardipee	M	Son	5
304	Maggie Guardipee	F	Dau.	1
305	Kittie Guardipee	F	Dau.	9
306	Louisa Guardipee	F	Mother	64
307	John Guardipee	M	Son	17
308	Pete Guardipee	M	----	38
309	Geo. Prairie Chicken	M	Husband	26
310	Johannah P. Chicken	F	Wife	20
311	Cecil P. Chicken	F	Dau.	3
312	Thomas P. Chicken	M	Son	1
313	Good Strike	F	-----	80
314	John Gobert	M	Husband	31
315	Susie Gobert	F	Wife	22
316	Nellie Gobert	F	Dau.	2
317	Good Stab	M	Husband	33
318	Medicine Woman	F	Wife	31
319	Maggie Good Stab	F	Dau.	3
320	Goes In All Lodges	F	----	50

Census of the Piegan tribe of Indians of Blackfeet Agency, Montana taken by W. R. Logan United States Indian Agent, September 1st, 1899

No.	English Name	Sex	Relation	Age
321	Good Bear Woman	F	----	51
322	Green Grass Bull	M	Husband	39
323	Mary G. Bull	F	Wife	41
324	George G. Bull	M	Son	13
325	Cecil G. Bull	F	Dau.	1
326	Going To Move	M	Husband	44
327	Owl Woman	F	Wife	61
328	Richard Grant	M	Husband	23
329	Rosa Grant	F	Wife	22
330	Josephine Hall	F	Mother	28
331	John P. Hall	M	Son	6
332	David Hall	M	Son	4
333	W. H. Hall	M	Son	2
334	Mary Hall	F	Dau.	9
335	Maggie Henault	F	Mother	49
336	Steve Henault	M	Son	22
337	Moses Henault	M	Son	11
338	Clara Henault	F	Dau.	9
339	Nelson Henault	M	Husband	20
340	Hesler[sic] Henault	F	Wife	18
341	Head Carrier	M	Husband	69
342	Mary Head Carrier	F	Wife	66
343	John Head Carrier	M	Son	20
344	Henry No Bear	M	Husband	27
345	No Snake	F	Wife	27
346	Thomas No Bear	M	Son	3
347	Mary No Bear	F	Dau.	1
348	The Horn	M	Husband	61
349	Good Looking Woman	F	Wife	41
350	Under Bird	F	Wife	31
351	Harry Horn	M	Son	16
352	Heavy Gun	M	Husband	42

Census of the Piegan tribe of Indians of Blackfeet Agency, Montana taken by W. R. Logan United States Indian Agent, September 1st, 1899

No.	English Name	Sex	Relation	Age
353	Good Woman	F	Wife	33
354	First Go In	F	Wife	28
355	Henry Heavy Gun	M	Husband	25
356	Good Looking Woman	F	Wife	31
357	Hits On Top	F	-----	47
358	Harry Face	M	Husband	38
359	Blanket Woman	F	Wife	31
360	Glass Woman	F	Wife	26
361	Peter Harry Face	S	Son	4
362	James Harry Face	M	Son	2
363	Blood Woman	F	Dau.	13
364	Hits In Water	F	Wid.	78
365	Iron Necklace	M	Husband	37
366	Minnie Iron Necklace	F	Wife	46
367	Anna Iron Necklace	F	Dau.	7
368	Iron Pipe	M	Husband	41
369	Both Go In	F	Wife	33
370	John Iron Pipe	M	Son	4
371	Charles Iron Pipe	M	Son	2
372	Maggie Iron Pipe	F	Dau.	7
373	Joe Iron Pipe	M	Son	11
374	Jack Big Moon	M	Husband	40
375	Anna Big Moon	F	Wife	36
376	George Eats Alone	M	Son	19
377	Joe Kossuth	M	G. Son	26
378	Cuts Both Sides	F	G. Mother	78
379	Jackson Double Blaze	M	Husband	35
380	Medicine Beaver	F	Wife	25
381	Joe Double Blaze	M	Son	18
382	Oliver Double Blaze	M	Son	10
383	Louie Double Blaze	M	Son	3
384	Dick Double Blaze	M	Son	2
385	Jennie Johnson	F	Mother	36

Census of the Piegan tribe of Indians of Blackfeet Agency, Montana taken by W. R. Logan United States Indian Agent, September 1st, 1899

No.	English Name	Sex	Relation	Age
386	Mary Johnson	F	Dau.	19
387	William Johnson	M	Son	14
388	Joe Johnson	M	Son	12
389	Ida Johnson	F	Dau.	10
390	Eddie Jack	M	Husband	33
391	Snake Looking	F	Wife	36
392	John Two Guns	M	Son	19
393	Maggie Two Guns	F	Dau.	13
394	Monic Jack	F	Dau.	4
395	Cecil Jack	F	Dau.	2
396	Kidney	M	Husband	29
397	Mary Kidney	F	Wife	22
398	John Kidney	M	Son	1
399	Kills In Brush	F	----	66
400	Thomas Kyo	M	Husband	38
401	Mary Kyo	F	Wife	25
402	William Kyo	M	Son	4
403	Mary Kyo	F	Dau	1
404	Kicking Woman	M	Husband	73
405	Looks Plenty	F	Wife	61
406	John Kicking Woman	M	Son	23
407	Millie LaBreeche	F	Mother	48
408	Chas. LaBreeche	M	Son	30
409	Leanor LaBreeche	M	Son	18
410	Millie LaBreeche	F	Dau.	16
411	Jessie LaBreeche	F	Dau.	14
412	Joseph LaBreeche	M	Son	11
413	David LaBreeche	M	Husband	26
414	Minnie LaBreeche	F	Wife	25
415	Chas. LaBreeche	M	Son	4
416	Clarrisia[sic] LaBreeche	M[sic]	Son	2
417	Medor LaBreeche	M	Single	22
418	Last Strike	F	-----	56

Census of the Piegan tribe of Indians of Blackfeet Agency, Montana taken by W. R. Logan United States Indian Agent, September 1st, 1899

No.	English Name	Sex	Relation	Age
419	Last Coyote	M	-----	49
420	Long Time Rock	M	Husband	35
421	Nellie L. T. Rock	F	Wife	24
422	Joe L. T. Rock	M	Son	2
423	Little Rock	F	Mother	49
424	James R. Crane	M	Son	9
425	Little Otter	F	-----	61
426	Long Wolverine	F	-----	81
427	Long Time Sleeping	M	Husband	30
428	Catches Another	F	Wife	31
429	John L. T. Sleeping	M	Son	7
430	James L. T. Sleeping	M	Son	2
431	Good Catch	F	Daughter	1
432	Lone Cut	F	Widow	81
433	Little Owl	M	Husband	27
434	Maggie Little Owl	F	Wife	18
435	Mary Little Owl	F	Daughter	2
436	Little Dog	M	Husband	45
437	Water Snake	F	Wife	18
438	Harrison Little Dog	M	Son	13
439	Eliza Little Dog	F	Daughter	2
440	Mary Little Dog	F	Daughter	1
441	Little Plume	M	Husband	46
442	Cuts Different	F	Wife	34
443	Tail Feathers Woman	F	Wife	32
444	James Little Plume	M	Son	14
445	Louis Little Plume	M	Son	8
446	Takes Gun	F	Daughter	5
447	Joe Little Plume	M	Son	2
448	Mollie Little Plume	F	Daughter	9
449	Joe Little Plume	M	Son	6
450	Susie Little Plume	M	Daughter	2

Census of the Piegan tribe of Indians of Blackfeet Agency, Montana taken by W. R. Logan United States Indian Agent, September 1st, 1899

No.	English Name	Sex	Relation	Age
451	Little Bull	M	Husband	58
452	Good Strike	F	Wife	40
453	Good Charging	F	Wife	19
454	Two Guns	M	Son	3
455	Kills In Brush	F	Mother	42
456	Blanket Woman	F	Daughter	21
457	Joe McKnight	M	Husband	25
458	Lucy McKnight	F	Wife	23
459	Irene McKnight	F	Daughter	3
460	James McKnight	m	Son	3m.
461	Matildo[sic] Iron Crow	F	Sister	15
462	Elizabeth Iron Crow	F	Sister	11
463	Ellen McMullen	F	Single	17
464	Louie Marceau	M	Husband	33
465	Rosa Marceau	F	Wife	20
466	Alex Marceau	M	Husband	35
467	Theresa Marceau	F	Wife	27
468	Louise Marceau	F	Daughter	6
469	Anna Marceau	F	Daughter	1
470	Pete Marceau	M	Son	24
471	Josephine Marceau	F	Daughter	12
472	Mrs. Marceau	F	Mother	53
473	Many Necklace	F	-----	80
474	Medicine Bull	M	Husband	35
475	Sore Back	F	Wife	30
476	Thomas Medicine Bull	M	Son	3
477	Red Rock	F	Daughter	16
478	Mary Medicine Bull	F	Daughter	1
479	Mittens	M	Husband	29
480	Susie Mittens	F	Wife	23
481	Joseph Mittens	M	Son	4
482	Chas. Mittens	M	Son	3
483	Anna Mittens	F	Daughter	6

Census of the Piegan tribe of Indians of Blackfeet Agency, Montana taken by W. R. Logan United States Indian Agent, September 1st, 1899

No.	English Name	Sex	Relation	Age
484	Medicine Stab	M	Husband	46
485	Sure Woman	F	Wife	38
486	Marrow Bones	M	Husband	61
487	Good Gun Woman	F	Wife	63
488	Mountain Chief	M	Husband	51
489	Big Gun Woman	F	Wife	41
490	Arthur Mountain Chief	M	Son	19
491	Walter Mountain Chief	M	Son	16
492	Amy Mountain Chief	F	Daughter	4
493	Louie Mountain Chief	M	Son	2
494	Anna Mountain Chief	F	Daughter	1
495	Thekla Mountain Chief	F	Daughter	18
496	John Mountain Chief	M	G. Son	1
497	Morning Gun	M	Husband	37
498	Otter Woman	F	Wife	26
499	John Morning Gun	M	Son	12
500	Flys In Water	M	Son	5
501	Water Snake	F	Daughter	4
502	Brier	F	Daughter	3
503	Mary Morning Gun	F	Daughter	2
504	Mad Plume	M	Husband	46
505	Kills In Night	F	Wife	29
506	John Mad Plume	M	Son	14
507	George Mad Plume	M	Son	9
508	Michael Mad Plume	M	Son	6
509	Medicine Mad Plume	F	Daughter	13
510	James Mad Plume	M	Son	2
511	Albert Mad Plume	M	Husband	22
512	Susie Mad Plume	F	Wife	21
513	Maggie Mad Plume	F	Daughter	3
514	George Mad Plume	M	Son	1
515	Many Guns	M	Husband	36
516	Josephine Many Guns	F	Wife	17
517	Many Guns	M	Husband	57
518	Mouse Woman	F	Wife	41

Census of the Piegan tribe of Indians of Blackfeet Agency, Montana taken by W. R. Logan United States Indian Agent, September 1st, 1899

No.	English Name	Sex	Relation	Age
519	John Many Guns	M	Son	5
520	Thomas Many Guns	M	Son	2
521	Morning Eagle	M	Husband	66
522	Catches On Top	F	Wife	33
523	Hits On Top	F	Wife	41
524	John Morning Eagle	M	Son	8
525	George Morning Eagle	M	Son	5
526	Two Rabbits	F	Daughter	3
527	Maggie Nichols	F	Mother	28
528	Edith Nichols	F	Daughter	12
529	Olive Nichols	F	Daughter	10
530	Cecil Nichols	M	Son	4
531	No Coat	M	Husband	39
532	Kills First	F	Wife	31
533	Anna No Coat	F	Daughter	6
534	Night Rider	M	Son	31
535	Thunder Woman	F	Mother	71
536	New Robe	M	Husband	44
537	Sharp Nose	F	Wife	46
538	Hide In Night	F	Wife	35
539	Joseph New Robe	M	Son	12
540	Night Gun	M	Husband	28
541	Stella Night Gun	F	Wife	16
542	No Runner	M	Husband	56
543	White Woman	F	Wife	57
544	Old Coyote	M	Husband	36
545	Mary Old Coyote	F	Wife	41
546	Philip Old Coyote	M	Son	18
547	Owl Child	M	Husband	44
548	Mollie Owl Child	F	Wife	31
549	Susie Owl Child	F	Daughter	18
550	Isabella Owl Child	F	Daughter	12
551	Annie Owl Child	F	Daughter	5

Census of the Piegan tribe of Indians of Blackfeet Agency, Montana taken by W. R. Logan United States Indian Agent, September 1st, 1899

No.	English Name	Sex	Relation	Age
552	John Owl Child	M	Son	16
553	Joseph Owl Child	M	Son	9
554	Louie Owl Child	SM	Son	7
555	William Owl Child	M	Son	1
556	Owl Top Feathers	M	Husband	47
557	Owl Woman	F	Wife	41
558	Jennie Owl Top Feathers	F	Daughter	18
559	Fanny Owl Top Feathers	F	Daughter	7
560	Old Man Chief	M	Husband	29
561	Lucy O. M. Chief	F	Wife	27
562	James O. M. Chief	M	Son	5
563	John O. M. Chief	M	Son	2
564	Old White Woman	F	-----	80
565	Old Chief	M	Husband	48
566	Morning Woman	F	Wife	39
567	John Old Chief	M	Son	15
568	Robt. Old Chief	M	Son	6
569	Paul Old Chief	M	Son	2
570	Mary Old Chief	F	Daughter	10
571	Katie Pias	F	Sister	13
572	Dan Pias	M	Brother	10
573	Reuben Pias	M	Brother	8
574	Susie Pias	F	Sister	3
575	Peter Old Rock	M	Single	23
576	Painted Wings	M	Husband	73
577	Hits On Top	F	Wife	49
578	Elk	F	Daughter	21
579	Lucy Painted Wings	F	Daughter	11
580	Petrified	F	------	58
581	John Peppion	M	Husband	28
582	Cecil Peppion	F	Wife	28
583	Jessie Peppion	F	Mother	25

Census of the Piegan tribe of Indians of Blackfeet Agency, Montana taken by W. R. Logan United States Indian Agent, September 1st, 1899

No.	English Name	Sex	Relation	Age
584	Frank Peppion	M	Brother	19
585	Chester Peppion	M	Brother	15
586	Louise Peppion	F	Sister	20
587	Cecil Peppion	F	Sister	24
588	Thomas Peppion	M	Son	4
589	Joe Peppion	M	Son	2
590	Michael Peppion	M	Son	1
591	Peter Spotted Bear	M	Husband	20
592	Anna Spotted Bear	F	Wife	18
593	Annie Spotted Bear	F	Daughter	1
594	Mary Phemister	F	Mother	37
595	George Phemister	M	Son	11
596	Poor Woman	F	Widow	76
597	Mary Ramsey	F	Mother	24
598	Jessie Ramsey	F	Daughter	3
599	Melvin Ramsey	M	Son	1
600	Alice Rutherford	F	Sister	20
601	William Rutherford	M	Brother	15
602	James Rutherford	M	Brother	13
603	Henry Rutherford	M	Brother	11
604	Richard Rutherford	M	Husband	22
605	Eliza Rutherford	F	Wife	22
606	Edna Rutherford	F	Daughter	1
607	Minnie Ripley	F	Mother	17
608	James Ripley	M	Son	3m.
609	Belle Ripley	F	Mother	51
610	Emma Ripley	F	Daughter	6
611	Red Head	M	Husband	41
612	Two Strikes	F	Wife	41
613	Eddie Running Crane	M	Husband	25
614	Nellie Running Crane	F	Wife	20
615	Medicine Hawk	M	Son	2

Census of the Piegan tribe of Indians of Blackfeet Agency, Montana taken by W. R. Logan United States Indian Agent, September 1st, 1899

No.	English Name	Sex	Relation	Age
616	Chas. Rose	M	Husband	43
617	Agnes Rose	F	Wife	25
618	Maggie Rose	F	Daughter	19
619	Julia Rose	F	Daughter	10
620	Alice Rose	F	Daughter	8
621	William Rose	M	Son	6
622	James Rose	M	Son	4
623	Annie Rose	F	Daughter	2
624	Running Crane	M	Husband	69
625	White Woman	F	Wife	34
626	Red Fox	M	Husband	27
627	Good Clear Up	F	Wife	24
628	John Red Fox	M	Son	4
629	James Red Fox	M	Son	3
630	Rattler	M	Husband	70
631	Spear Woman	F	Wife	41
632	Elmer Rattler	M	Son	25
633	William Russell	M	Husband	45
634	Mary Russell	F	Wife	39
635	Cecil Russell	F	Daughter	18
636	Joe Russell	M	Son	11
637	William Russell	M	Son	9
638	Henry Russell	M	Son	2
639	George Russell	M	Son	14
640	Red Horn	M	-----	61
641	Mrs. Running Wolf	F	Mother	43
642	Mile Running Wolf	M	Son	20
643	Herbert Running Wolf	M	Son	8
644	Homer Running Wolf	M	Son	6
645	Albert Running Wolf	M	Son	13
646	George Running Wolf	M	Son	12
647	Oliver Racine	M	Husband	20
648	Belle Racine	F	Wife	18
649	Julia Revis	F	Mother	44

Census of the Piegan tribe of Indians of Blackfeet Agency, Montana taken by W. R. Logan United States Indian Agent, September 1st, 1899

No.	English Name	Sex	Relation	Age
650	August Augers	M	Son	18
651	Emmet Augers	M	Son	17
652	Emma Augers	F	Daughter	13
653	Frances Augers	F	Daughter	11
654	Small Woman	F	----	70
655	Shoots At Another	M	Husband	36
656	Martha S. A. Another	F	Wife	44
657	Josephine Weatherwax	F	Daughter	19
658	Joe Weatherwax	M	Son	13
659	Mary Weatherwax	F	Daughter	17
660	Susie Shoots At Another	F	Daughter	1
661	Singing	F	-----	65
662	Sitting In Road	F	G. Moth.	70
663	Shoots In Night	M	G. Son	9
664	Richard Sanderville	M	Husband	31
665	Mary Sanderville	F	Wife	25
666	Agnes Sanderville	F	Daughter	10
667	Mary Sanderville	F	Daughter	1
668	Strikes Back	F	------	50
669	Sam Randall	M	-----	26
670	Stabs By Mistake	M	Husband	29
671	Anna S. B. Mistake	F	Wife	26
672	Peter S. B. Mistake	M	Son	4
673	Sure Chief	M	Husband	33
674	Bird Woman	F	Wife	21
675	Philip Sure Chief	M	Son	4
676	Gray Whiskers	M	Son	2
677	Swims Under	M	Father	31
678	Josephine Swims Under	F	Daughter	3
679	Spotted Eagle	M	Husband	59
680	Hands It Back	F	Wife	49

Census of the Piegan tribe of Indians of Blackfeet Agency, Montana taken by W. R. Logan United States Indian Agent, September 1st, 1899

No.	English Name	Sex	Relation	Age
681	James Spotted Eagle	M	Son	23
682	Begs Plenty	F	Daughter	8
683	John Spotted Eagle	M	Son	19
684	Spotted Bear	M	Husband	71
685	Spotted Woman	F	Wife	35
686	Joe Spotted Bear	M	Son	8
687	Mike Spotted Bear	M	Son	2
688	Small Face	F	Mother	41
689	Mary Small Face	F	Daughter	9
690	Spotted Calf	M	Husband	67
691	Mink Woman	F	Wife	60
692	Long Time Woman	F	Wife	50
693	Sure Woman	F	-----	80
694	Susan Schultz	F	Mother	35
695	Hart Schultz	M	Son	16
696	Spotted Head	M	-----	78
697	Mary Stewart	F	Mother	34
698	Carrie Stewart	F	Daughter	19
699	Jennie Stewart	F	Daughter	17
700	Clara Stewart	F	Daughter	14
701	Mollie Stewart	F	Daughter	10
702	Cecil Stewart	F	Daughter	7
703	Marion Stewart	F	Daughter	3
704	Thomas Spotted Eagle	M	Single	25
705	Short Face	M	Son	22
706	Strikes Gun	F	Mother	61
707	Joe Tatsey	M	Husband	36
708	Anna Tatsey	F	Wife	27
709	Josephine Tatsey	F	Daughter	11
710	Hattie Tatsey	F	Daughter	8
711	John Tatsey	M	Son	6
712	Joe Tatsey	M	Son	4

Census of the Piegan tribe of Indians of Blackfeet Agency, Montana taken by W. R. Logan United States Indian Agent, September 1st, 1899

No.	English Name	Sex	Relation	Age
713	Mary Tatsey	F	Daughter	1
714	Susan Tatsey	F	------	70
715	Thomas Two Stabs	M	Husband	40
716	Comes Singing	F	Wife	38
717	Maggie Two Stabs	F	Daughter	20
718	Joe Two Stabs	M	Son	7
719	Louie Two Stabs	M	Son	3
720	Louise Two Stabs	F	Daughter	1
721	Joseph Trombley	M	Husband	41
722	Julia Trombley	F	Wife	45
723	Louie Trombley	M	Husband	29
724	Maggie Trombley	F	Wife	26
725	Isaac Trombley	M	Son	4
726	Joe Trombley	M	Son	2
727	John Trombley	M	Son	1
728	Mary Teasdale	F	Mother	56
729	Josephine Teasdale	F	Daughter	17
730	Nellie Teasdale	F	Daughter	11
731	Tail Feathers	M	Husband	44
732	Jennie Tail Feathers	F	Wife	39
733	Walter Tail Feathers	M	Son	10
734	Chas. Tail Feathers	M	Son	8
735	Peter Tail Feathers	M	Son	5
736	Charley Tail Feathers	M	Son	2
737	Takes Gun Both Sides	F	-----	61
738	Lone Cut	F	-----	71
739	Dives Long Way	F	-----	61
740	Tearing Lodge	M	Husband	61
741	Pays Plenty	F	Wife	51
742	Takes Gun At Night	M	Son	24
743	Agnes T. G. A. Night	F	Daughter	16
744	Hits Last	F	Mother	58

Census of the Piegan tribe of Indians of Blackfeet Agency, Montana taken by W. R. Logan United States Indian Agent, September 1st, 1899

No.	English Name	Sex	Relation	Age
745	Isabella Trombley	F	Mother	66
746	Alfred Trombley	M	Son	21
747	Takes Iron Gun	M	Son	30
748	Lucy Takes Iron Gun	F	Daughter	18
749	Gives Plenty	F	Mother	61
750	Turtle	M	Husband	29
751	Minnie Turtle	F	Wife	20
752	Takes Gun Both Sides	M	Husband	34
753	One Strike	F	Wife	33
754	John T. G. B. Sides	M	Son	3
755	Pete T. G. B. Sides	M	Son	2
756	Under Otter	F	----	61
757	Under Bull #2 (Strikes Back)	F	Mother	39
758	John Under Bull	M	Son	13
759	Peter Under Bull	M	Son	4
760	Frank Vielle	M	Husband	31
761	Anna Vielle	F	Wife	32
762	Jack Vielle	M	Son	4
763	Andrew Vielle	M	Son	1
764	Mary J. White	F	Mother	25
765	David Ripley	M	Brother	22
766	Cora White	F	Daughter	6
767	Lorenzo White	M	Son	5
768	Melvina White	F	Daughter	3
769	Wild Gun	M	Husband	40
770	Big Tiger Woman	F	Wife	88
771	Arthur Wild Gun	M	Brother	19
772	War Bonnet	M	Husband	30
773	First Clear Up	F	Wife	29
774	James War Bonnet	M	Son	4
775	White Quiver	M	Husband	39
776	Minnie White Quiver	F	Wife	38

Census of the Piegan tribe of Indians of Blackfeet Agency, Montana taken by W. R. Logan United States Indian Agent, September 1st, 1899

No.	English Name	Sex	Relation	Age
777	Ben White Quiver	M	Son	14
778	Thomas White Quiver	M	Son	4
779	Maggie White Quiver	F	Daughter	7
780	Mollie White Quiver	F	Daughter	2
781	White Dog	M	Husband	41
782	Medicine Pine Woman	F	Wife	29
783	Henry White Dog	M	Son	4
784	Mollie White Dog	F	Daughter	5
785	William White Dog	M	Son	2
786	Wades In Water	M	Husband	30
787	Lucy Wades in Water	F	Wife	21
788	White Man	M	Husband	59
789	Clean Up	F	Wife	38
790	Sweet Grass Woman	F	Wife	31
791	John White Man	M	Son	19
792	Peter White Man	M	Son	17
793	Louie White Man	M	Son	1
794	Wakes Up Last	M	Husband	32
795	Mollie Wakes Up Last	F	Wife	20
796	Jennie Wakes Up Last	F	Daughter	2
797	Wolf Plume	M	Husband	39
798	First Strike	F	Wife	30
799	Wesley Wolf Plume	M	Son	12
800	Weasel Head	M	Husband	36
801	Mary Weasel Head	F	Wife	47
802	Isaac Wipert	M	Son	22
803	Peter Weasel Head	M	Son	10
804	John Weasel Head	M	Son	9
805	Mary Weasel Head	F	Daughter	14
806	Lizzie Weasel Head	F	Daughter	8
807	Thomas Weasel Head	M	Son	6
808	James Weasel Head	M	Son	5
809	John White Calf	M	Husband	41
810	Weasel Tail	F	Wife	31
811	Anna White Calf	F	Daughter	15

Census of the Piegan tribe of Indians of Blackfeet Agency, Montana taken by W. R. Logan United States Indian Agent, September 1st, 1899

No.	English Name	Sex	Relation	Age
812	Susie White Calf	F	Daughter	1
813	Wolf Eagle	M	Husband	47
814	Blanket Woman	F	Wife	43
815	Kills In Night	F	Wife	37
816	Wolf Medicine	M	Husband	34
817	Good Clean Up	F	Wife	36
818	Chicken Woman	F	Daughter	6
819	Hazlet Wolf Medicine	F	Daughter	8
820	Wolf Head	M	Husband	53
821	Sings On Top	F	Wife	42
822	Pete Wolf Head	M	Son	9
823	Young Running Rabbit	M	Husband	53
824	Good Strike	F	Wife	51
825	Long Time Woman	F	Wife	31
826	Julia Running Rabbit	F	Daughter	15
827	Long Time Otter	F	Daughter	9
828	Mary Running Rabbit	F	Daughter	1
829	Young Running Crane	M	Husband	45
830	Lead Woman	F	Wife	37
831	John Running Crane	M	Son	15
832	Yells In Water	M	Husband	24
833	Short Gun	F	Wife	20
834	John Yells In Water	M	Son	6
835	Thomas Yells In Water	M	Son	1
836	Yellow Iron	F	Mother	34
837	John Chief Crow	M	Son	2
838	Yellow Kidney	M	Father	31
839	Maggie Kidney	F	Mother	29
840	Mike Kidney	Male	Son	5
841	Maggie Kidney	F	Daughter	2
842	Mary Kidney	F	Daughter	5
843	Yellow Owl	M	Husband	26
844	Margaret Yellow Owl	F	Wife	20

Census of the Piegan tribe of Indians of Blackfeet Agency, Montana taken by W. R. Logan United States Indian Agent, September 1st, 1899

No.	English Name	Sex	Relation	Age
845	Young Bear Chief	M	Husband	40
846	Good Shield	F	Wife	34
847	Yells In Water	F	Wife	34
848	Edward Bear Chief	M	Son	17
849	John Bear Chief	M	Son	10
850	Sebastian Bear Chief	M	Son	5
851	Isabel Bear Chief	F	Daughter	19
852	Maggie Bear Chief	F	Daughter	13
853	Joe Bear Chief	M	Son	7
854	Young Man Chief	M	Husband	42
855	Cecil Young Man Chief	F	Wife	27
856	Blackfoot Woman	F	Mother	49
857	John Big Lake	M	Son	20
858	Mike Blackfoot Woman	M	Son	21
859	Mary Blackfoot Woman	F	Daughter	7
860	Big Plume	M	Husband	70
861	Catches Inside	F	Wife	46
862	Jerry Big Plume	M	Son	20
863	Thomas Big Plume	M	Son	10
864	Louise Big Plume	F	Daughter	6
865	Chewing B. Bones	M	Husband	33
866	Mary C. B. Bones	F	Wife	36
867	Isabella C. B. Bones	F	Daughter	9
868	Maggie C. B. Bones	F	Daughter	1
869	Julia C. B. Bones	F	Daughter	3
870	John C. B. Bones	M	Son	4
871	John Chouquette	M	Son	13
872	Kills Close	F	Mother	56
873	Susie Kills Close	F	Daughter	14
874	Paul	F	- -----	6
875	Running Owl	M	Husband	38
876	Kills Two	F	Wife	41
877	Agnes Running Owl	F	Daughter	16
878	Rosa Running Owl	F	Daughter	8
879	Mary Running Owl	F	Daughter	2

Census of the Piegan tribe of Indians of Blackfeet Agency, Montana taken by W. R. Logan United States Indian Agent, September 1st, 1899

No.	English Name	Sex	Relation	Age
880	Wins Many Guns	F	Mother	50
881	Mary Tail Feathers Coming	F	Daughter	6
882	Tail Feathers Coming	M	Husband	54
883	Snake Woman	F	Wife	31
884	Cecil T. F. Coming	F	Daughter	13
885	Susie Tail F. Coming	F	Daughter	4
886	Mary T. Feathers Coming	F	Daughter	3
887	Susan Arnoux	F	Mother	47
888	Monroe Arnoux	M	Son	22
889	Marion Arnoux	M	Son	17
890	George Arnoux	M	Son	15
891	Sallie Allison	F	Mother	27
892	Willie Allison	M	Son	7
893	Allen Allison	M	Son	5
894	Wendell Allison	M	Son	3
895	Infant Allison	M	Son	2
896	Louise Aubrey	F	Mother	43
897	Alice Aubrey	F	Daughter	22
898	Rosa Aubrey	F	Daughter	20
899	Laura Aubrey	F	Daughter	17
900	Lucy Aubrey	F	Daughter	12
901	Dora Aubrey	F	Daughter	11
902	May Aubrey	F	Daughter	7
903	Janette Aubrey	F	Daughter	4
904	Thomas Aubrey	M	Son	16
905	Philip Aubrey	M	Son	8
906	Carrol Aubrey	M	Son	6m.
907	Tallow Ashley	M	Father	36
908	Small Beads	F	Mother	24
909	Louis Ashley	M	Son	3
910	Mary Ashley	F	Daughter	3
911	Arrow Topknot	M	Father	33
912	Flying Squirrel	F	Mother	28
913	Philip Topknot	M	Son	12
914	Stink Topknot	M	Son	11
915	Antoine Topknot	M	Son	6

Census of the Piegan tribe of Indians of Blackfeet Agency, Montana taken by W. R. Logan United States Indian Agent, September 1st, 1899

No.	English Name	Sex	Relation	Age
916	Yellow Bird	F	Daughter	3
917	Anthony Austin	M	Husband	29
918	Susan Austin	F	Wife	37
919	Paul Austin	M	Father	33
920	Louise Austin	F	Mother	32
921	Mabel Austin	F	Daughter	14
922	Maude Austin	F	Daughter	10
923	Agnes Austin	F	Daughter	5
924	Willie Austin	M	Son	6m.
925	Maggie Abbot	F	Single	15
926	Antoine	M	Husband	62
927	Sophia	F	Wife	57
928	Levi Burd	M	Father	22
929	Daisy Burd	F	Mother	20
930	Daisy D. Burd	F	Daughter	1
931	Ira Burd	M	Brother	12
932	Phoebe Burd	F	Sister	8
933	Thomas Bogy	M	Single	20
934	Sarah Brown	F	Mother	45
935	Jesse Brown	M	Son	17
936	Leo Brown	M	Son	3
937	William Brown	M	Father	27
938	Victoria Brown	F	Mother	21
939	Sarah Adele Brown	F	Daughter	2m.
940	Frank Bostwick	M	Father	38
941	Mary Bostwick	F	Mother	24
942	Henry Bostwick	M	Son	6
943	George Bostwick	M	Son	4
944	Billy Bostwick	M	Son	2
945	Annie Bostwick	F	Daughter	2m.
946	John Bostwick	M	Single	24

Census of the Piegan tribe of Indians of Blackfeet Agency, Montana taken by W. R. Logan United States Indian Agent, September 1st, 1899

No.	English Name	Sex	Relation	Age
947	Boy	M	Father	51
948	Oscar Boy	M	Son	12
949	Bad Boy	M	Son	10
950	Bear Child	M	Father	47
951	Oats Bear Child	F	Mother	37
952	William Bear Child	M	Son	16
953	Josephine Bear Child	F	Daughter	12
954	Louis Bear Child	M	Son	7
955	James Bear Child	M	Son	8
956	Ben Bear Child	M	Son	5
957	Bear Paw	M	Father	54
958	Different Persons Killed	F	Mother	31
959	Minnie Bear Paw	F	Daughter	9
960	John Bear Paw	M	Son	4
961	James Bear Paw	M	Son	2
962	Bear Skin	M	Father	24
963	Geneva Bear Skin	F	Mother	22
964	Mary Bear Skin	F	Daughter	1m.
965	Chas. Buck	M	Husband	25
966	Spyna Buck	F	Wife	24
967	Bull Calf	M	Father	43
968	Blanket Woman	F	Mother	55
969	Chas. Bull Calf	M	Son	11
970	Iron Woman	F	Widow	91
971	Bear Head	M	Father	43
972	Julia Bear Head	F	Mother	23
973	Albert Bear Head	M	Son	5
974	Mattie Burd	F	Mother	32
975	Martha Burd	F	Daughter	16
976	Samson Burd	M	Son	13
977	Charley Burd	M	Son	11
978	Johnson Burd	M	Son	9
979	Nellie Burd	F	Daughter	6
980	Henry Burd	M	Son	4
981	George Burd	M	Son	2

Census of the Piegan tribe of Indians of Blackfeet Agency, Montana taken by W. R. Logan United States Indian Agent, September 1st, 1899

No.	English Name	Sex	Relation	Age
982	Bad Marriage	M	Father	39
983	Little Fox	F	Mother	36
984	Last Shoot	M	Son	10
985	Lost Her Finger	F	Daughter	8
986	Last Bear	F	Daughter	7
987	Last Hollow	F	Daughter	2
988	Bear Skin	M	-----	50
989	Blackfoot Child	M	Father	54
990	Buffalo Road	F	Wife	71
991	Grace B. Child	F	Mother	18
992	Irene B. Child	F	Daughter	3
993	Black Sarcee	M	Husband	37
994	Kills Far	F	Wife	38
995	Black Bear	M	Husband	57
996	Many Snakes	F	Wife	41
997	Bear Medicine	M	Father	31
998	Ragged Woman	F	Mother	31
999	Willie Bear Medicine	M	Son	8
1000	Maggie Bear Medicine	F	Daughter	6
1001	Joseph Bear Medicine	M	Son	3
1002	Xavier Billedeaux	M	Father	39
1003	Salina Billedeaux	F	Mother	31
1004	Willie Billedeaux	M	Son	11
1005	Chas. Billedeaux	M	Son	9
1006	Wern[sic] Billedeaux	M	Son	7
1007	Greely Billedeaux	M	Son	5
1008	Mabel Billedeaux	F	Daughter	3
1009	Salina Billedeaux	F	Daughter	1
1010	Blacksnake Woman	F	Mother	42
1011	Hides Behind Blanket	F	Daughter	10
1012	Black Looks	M	Father	35
1013	Medicine Top	F	Mother	28
1014	Double Gun	M	Son	10
1015	Puss B. Looks	F	Daughter	7

Census of the Piegan tribe of Indians of Blackfeet Agency, Montana taken by W. R. Logan United States Indian Agent, September 1st, 1899

No.	English Name	Sex	Relation	Age
1016	Bobtail Mouse	F	Daughter	2
1017	Black Weasel	M	Father	35
1018	Medicine Stone	F	Mother	42
1019	James B. Weasel	M	Son	3
1020	Big Old Woman	F	-----	41
1021	Bull Child	M	Father	53
1022	Joseph Bull Child	M	Son	20
1023	Percy Bull Child	M	Son	19
1024	Poor Young Man	M	Son	6
1025	Maggie Bull Child	F	Daughter	5
1026	Active Bird	F	Daughter	6
1027	Driving Back	F	Daughter	4
1028	Ed Billedeaux	M	Father	35
1029	Puss Billedeaux	F	Mother	29
1030	Carrol Billedeaux	M	Son	7
1031	Jeniveve Billedeaux	F	Daughter	5
1032	Martha Billedeaux	F	Daughter	3
1033	Eddie Billedeaux	M	Son	1
1034	Bird Rattler	M	Father	39
1035	May Sits Under	F	Wife	27
1036	Bull Plume	M	Son	22
1037	Big Spring	M	Husband	33
1038	No Owl Spring	F	Wife	32
1039	Shoots Close	M	Son	25
1040	Blanket	M	Son	22
1041	Berry Carrier	M	Husband	43
1042	Rattling	F	Wife	41
1043	Fox	M	Son	14
1044	Different Woman	F	Daughter	6
1045	Rides In Front	M	Son	3
1046	Alice Burd	F	Single	19
1047	Black Face Man	M	Husband	36
1048	Bead Woman	F	Wife	25

Census of the Piegan tribe of Indians of Blackfeet Agency, Montana taken by W. R. Logan United States Indian Agent, September 1st, 1899

No.	English Name	Sex	Relation	Age
1049	Red Stone	F	Daughter	7
1050	John B. F. Man	M	Son	2
1051	Yellow Squirrel	M	Son	5
1052	Beaver Woman	F	-----	61
1053	Black Coyote	M	Husband	71
1054	Blue Woman	F	Wife	26
1055	John Black Bear	M	Husband	27
1056	Birdie Spotted Eagle	F	Wife	20
1057	Joe Brown	M	Husband	25
1058	Frances Brown	F	Wife	22
1059	Wesley Brown	M	Son	1
1060	Chas. Old Wood	M	Husband	21
1061	Blanket Woman	F	Wife	19
1062	Chief Elk	M	Husband	65
1063	Last Star	F	Wife	56
1064	Chief Coward	M	Father	47
1065	Little Antelope	F	Mother	57
1066	Victor Chief Coward	M	Son	21
1067	Good Looking Crow Woman	F	Daughter	7
1068	Antoine Chouquette	M	Single	39
1069	John Croff	M	Husband	27
1070	Louise Croff	F	Wife	27
1071	Cross Guns	M	Father	31
1072	Katie Cross Guns	F	Mother	47
1073	Presley C. Guns	M	Son	3
1074	Fred Gerard	M	Son	26
1075	Chas. Conway	M	Son	22
1076	Frank Conway	M	Son	18
1077	Willie Conway	M	Son	16
1078	Esther Carney	F	Wife	28

Census of the Piegan tribe of Indians of Blackfeet Agency, Montana taken by W. R. Logan United States Indian Agent, September 1st, 1899

No.	English Name	Sex	Relation	Age
1079	Mary Cobell	F	Mother	51
1080	Joseph Cobell	M	Son	22
1081	George Cobell	M	Son	20
1082	Tom Cobell	M	Son	18
1083	John Cobell	M	Son	14
1084	Willie Cobell	M	Son	10
1085	Bessie Cobell	F	Daughter	16
1086	Angeline Connelly	F	Mother	32
1087	Victor Connelly	M	Son	11
1088	John Connelly	M	Son	10
1089	Mary Connelly	F	Daughter	15
1090	Rose Connelly	F	Daughter	14
1091	George W. Cook	M	Husband	36
1092	Julia Cook	F	Wife	27
1093	Louis Cobell	M	Father	42
1094	Mary Rose Cobell	F	Mother	39
1095	Peter Cobell	M	Son	16
1096	Jule Cobell	M	Son	5
1097	Dewey Cobell	M	Son	2
1098	Maggie Cobell	F	Daughter	19
1099	Clara Cobell	F	Daughter	13
1100	Louise Cobell	F	Daughter	3
1101	Richard Croff	M	Father	28
1102	Maggie Croff	F	Mother	22
1103	Arthur Croff	M	Son	3
1104	Eva Croff	F	Daughter	1
1105	Janet Coe	F	Sister	14
1106	James Coe	M	Brother	13
1107	Agnes Coe	F	Sister	9
1108	Chas. Chouquette	M	Husband	34
1109	Louise Chouquette	F	Mother	35
1110	Josephine Chouquette	F	Daughter	21
1111	Curlew	F	Widow	66
1112	Clears Up	M	Father	30

Census of the Piegan tribe of Indians of Blackfeet Agency, Montana taken by W. R. Logan United States Indian Agent, September 1st, 1899

No.	English Name	Sex	Relation	Age
1113	Calls At Night	F	Mother	30
1114	Mabel Clears Up	F	Daughter	11
1115	Cold Body	M	Father	27
1116	Mary Cold Body	F	Mother	36
1117	Maggie Cold Body	F	Daughter	9
1118	Cecil Cold Body	F	Daughter	5
1119	Pete Cold Body	M	Son	11
1120	Cut Finger	M	Father	46
1121	Strikes Herself	F	Mother	37
1122	Earnest Cut Finger	M	Son	18
1123	Thomas Cut Finger	M	Son	3
1124	Maggie Cut Finger	F	Daughter	6
1125	Josephine Cut Finger	F	Daughter	10
1126	Catches On Top	F	-----	41
1127	Cream Antelope	M	Father	37
1128	Gives To the Sun	F	Mother	37
1129	James C. Antelope	M	Son	11
1130	Mule Rider	M	Son	1
1131	Striped Elk	F	Aunt	71
1132	Horace Clarke	M	Father	50
1133	Malcolm Clarke	M	Son	23
1134	John Clarke	M	Son	18
1135	Chief Crow	M	Father	41
1136	Strikes With Gun	F	Mother	40
1137	James Chief Crow	M	Son	19
1138	Albert Chief Crow	M	Son	14
1139	Makes Noise	F	Daughter	7
1140	Coat	M	Father	32
1141	Broken Leg	F	Wife	35
1142	Mary Coat	F	Daughter	19
1143	Pete Cadotte	M	Husband	28
1144	Lucy Cadotte	F	Wife	23
1145	Rosa Cadotte	F	Daughter	8
1146	Jennie Cadotte	F	Daughter	1

Census of the Piegan tribe of Indians of Blackfeet Agency, Montana taken by W. R. Logan United States Indian Agent, September 1st, 1899

No.	English Name	Sex	Relation	Age
1147	Cowhide Robe	M	Husband	30
1148	Grace Cowhide Robe	F	Wife	22
1149	Rides In Middle	M	Son	2
1150	Calf Shield	M	Husband	57
1151	Comes To Make Dust	F	Wife	61
1152	Turns Back	M	Son	6
1153	Crow Woman	F	Widow	68
1154	Catches Last	F	Widow	62
1155	Under Bear	M	Son	22
1156	Chas. DeLaney	M	Father	25
1157	Viola DeLaney	F	Mother	17
1158	Margaret DeLaney	F	Daughter	1
1159	Double Rider	M	Father	36
1160	Anna Double Rider	F	Mother	25
1161	Draws Rations	F	Daughter	7
1162	Minnie Double Rider	F	Daughter	3
1163	Mary Devereaux	F	Mother	51
1164	Henry Devereaux	M	Son	22
1165	Chas. Devereaux	M	Son	19
1166	Annie Devereaux	F	Daughter	15
1167	Abby Devereaux	F	Daughter	7
1168	Geo. Devereaux	M	Son	3
1169	Mollie Davis	F	Mother	25
1170	Thomas Davis	M	Son	8
1171	Pearl Davis	F	Daughter	6
1172	Bryan Davis	M	Son	3
1173	Ed Gobert	M	Ad. Son	19
1174	Catherine Gobert	F	Ad. Dau.	16
1175	Double Owl	F	Mother	26
1176	Blue Owl	M	Son	7
1177	Ignace Owl	F	Daughter	4
1178	Fanny Owl	F	Daughter	2
1179	Double Clear Up	M	Single	20

Census of the Piegan tribe of Indians of Blackfeet Agency, Montana taken by W. R. Logan United States Indian Agent, September 1st, 1899

No.	English Name	Sex	Relation	Age
1180	Double Cloth	F	Mother	51
1181	Baptist West Wolf	M	Son	25
1182	Bernard West Wolf	M	Son	15
1183	George West Wolf	M	Son	13
1184	John West Wolf	M	Son	5
1185	Mary Dunbar	F	Mother	29
1186	Jane Dunbar	F	Daughter	12
1187	Andrew Dunbar	M	Son	9
1188	Frankie Dunbar	F	Daughter	7
1189	Carrie Dunbar	F	Daughter	5
1190	Esther Dunbar	F	Daughter	4
1191	James Dunbar	M	Son	2
1192	James Dawson	M	Father	45
1193	James Dawson, Jr.	M	Son	12
1194	William Dawson	M	Son	9
1195	Harold Dawson	M	Son	7
1196	Tom Dawson	M	Father	38
1197	Isabella Dawson	F	Mother	38
1198	Fanny Dawson	F	Ad. Dau.	13
1199	Drags Behind	M	Father	40
1200	Last Go In	F	Mother	41
1201	Geo. D. Behind	M	Son	12
1202	Don't Go Out	M	Husband	46
1203	Blanket Woman	F	Wife	35
1204	William Douglas	M	Husband	25
1205	Florence Douglas	F	Wife	19
1206	Annie C. Douglas	F	Daughter	1m.
1207	David Duvall	M	Single	20
1208	Alex. Dubrey	M	Husband	28
1209	Lily Dubrey	F	Wife	21
1210	Joseph Dubrey	M	Son	1
1211	James Douglas	M	Father	28
1213[sic]	James Douglas, Jr.	M	Son	5

Census of the Piegan tribe of Indians of Blackfeet Agency, Montana taken by W. R. Logan United States Indian Agent, September 1st, 1899

No.	English Name	Sex	Relation	Age
1214	Lydia Douglas	F	Daughter	3
1215	Arthur Douglas	M	Son	1
1216	Ben DeRoche	M	Father	36
1217	Sallie DeRoche	F	Mother	37
1218	Charley DeRoche	M	Son	15
1219	Dry Goods Woman	F	Widow	82
1220	Dog Ear	M	Father	23
1221	Mary Dog Ear	F	Mother	20
1222	Billy Dog Ear	M	Son	6m.
1223	Dry Wood	M	Single	21
1224	Louis Ell	M	Father	26
1225	Adah Ell	F	Mother	20
1226	Chas. Ell	M	Son	2
1227	Emma Eldridge	F	Mother	46
1228	Ear-rings	M	Father	41
1229	Susan Ear-rings	F	Mother	51
1230	Three Riders	M	Son	20
1231	Takes Meat	M	Son	13
1232	East Woman	F	Widow	68
1233	Eagle Child	M	Father	37
1234	Fawn E. Child	F	Mother	33
1235	Bark E. Child	M	Son	3
1236	Cecil E. Child	F	Daughter	10
1237	Eagle Tail Feathers	M	Father	54
1238	Nice Snake	F	Mother	67
1239	Weasel Woman	F	Daughter	7
1240	Ely Rider	M	Single	26
1241	Amelia Fox	F	Mother	63
1242	Eliza Fox	F	G. Dau.	16
1243	John Jackson	M	G. Son	18

Census of the Piegan tribe of Indians of Blackfeet Agency, Montana taken by W. R. Logan United States Indian Agent, September 1st, 1899

No.	English Name	Sex	Relation	Age
1244	Alex. Fox	M	Husband	22
1245	Anna Fox	F	Wife	19
1246	Rena First Rider	F	Widow	21
1247	Matt Fitzpatrick	M	Husband	21
1248	Kate Fitzpatrick	F	Wife	21
1249	Chas. Fitzpatrick	M	Son	1m.
1250	Fine Kill	F	Widow	71
1251	Fred Bigtop	M	Son	17
1252	Flying	F	Widow	71
1253	Josephine Gilham	F	Mother	27
1254	William Gilham	M	Son	6
1255	Anthony Gilham	M	Son	8
1256	Eliza Galbreath	F	S. Moth.	45
1257	Lizzie Galbreath	F	S. Dau.	15
1258	John Galbreath	M	S. Son	15
1259	Webster Galbreath	M	S. Son	17
1260	Mollie Galbreath	F	S. Dau.	10
1261	Anna Galbreath	F	S. Dau.	7
1262	Phoebe Galbreath	F	S. Dau.	6
1263	Maggie Goss	F	Mother	42
1264	William Goss	M	Son	22
1265	Lome Goss	M	Son	20
1266	Nathan Goss	M	Son	12
1267	George Goss	M	Son	8
1268	Abbot Goss	M	Son	6
1269	Francis Goss	M	Son	4
1270	Nellie Goss	F	Daughter	18
1271	Caroline Goss	F	Daughter	15
1272	Susie Goss	F	Daughter	12
1273	Maggie Goss	F	Daughter	10
1274	Albert Goss	M	Father	25
1275	Mary Goss	F	Mother	25
1276	Albert Goss, Jr.	M	Son	2
1277	Mamie Goss	F	Daughter	1

Census of the Piegan tribe of Indians of Blackfeet Agency, Montana taken by W. R. Logan United States Indian Agent, September 1st, 1899

No.	English Name	Sex	Relation	Age
1278	Ely Guardipee	M	Father	42
1279	Sadie Guardipee	F	Mother	29
1280	Tom Guardipee	M	Son	19
1281	Frank Guardipee	M	Son	14
1282	Chas. Guardipee	M	Son	11
1283	Josephine Guardipee	F	Daughter	9
1284	Mary Guardipee	F	Daughter	6
1285	Agnes Guardipee	F	Daughter	3
1286	Joe Guardipee	M	Son	2m.
1287	James Grant	M	Husband	26
1288	Josephine Grant	F	Wife	24
1289	Ground	M	Father	49
1290	James Ground	M	Son	23
1291	Puts Face In Front	F	Widow	22
1292	John Ground	M	Husband	24
1293	Mary Ground	F	Wife	16
1294	Frank Guardipee	M	Husband	29
1295	Mary Guardipee	F	Wife	24
1296	Frank Guardipee, Jr.	M	Son	4
1297	Chas. Guardipee	M	Single	33
1298	Gambler	M	Father	36
1299	Louise Gambler	F	Wife	37
1300	Round Butte	M	Son	2
1301	Good Kill	F	Widow	81
1302	Gretchen Rider	F	----	26
1303	Good Medicine Pipe	M	Father	39
1304	Sallie Medicine Pipe	F	Daughter	4
1305	James Housman	M	Father	32
1306	Thomas Housman	M	Son	10
1307	Mary Housman	F	Daughter	8
1308	Josephine Housman	F	Daughter	2

Census of the Piegan tribe of Indians of Blackfeet Agency, Montana taken by W. R. Logan United States Indian Agent, September 1st, 1899

No.	English Name	Sex	Relation	Age
1309	Rosa Hinkle	F	Mother	35
1310	Geo. Hinkle	M	Son	19
1311	Willie Hinkle	M	Son	17
1312	Mamie Hinkle	F	Daughter	11
1313	Lizzie Hinkle	F	Daughter	13
1314	Vina Hall	F	Mother	21
1315	Elsie Hall	F	Daughter	3
1316	Abner Hall	M	Son	3m.
1317	Mary Howard	F	Mother	58
1318	Joe Howard	M	Son	24
1319	Walter Howard	M	Son	17
1320	Anna Howard	F	Ad. Dau.	12
1321	Sallie Hagan	F	Mother	33
1322	Maggie Hagan	F	Daughter	14
1323	Nellie Hagan	F	Daughter	9
1324	Esther Hagan	F	Daughter	4
1325	Sadie Hagan	F	Daughter	2
1326	Robert Hamilton	M	Husband	28
1327	Rosa Hamilton	F	Wife	24
1328	Ella J. Hamilton	F	Single	25
1329	Herman Dusty Bull	M	Father	28
1330	Louise D. Bull	F	Mother	17
1331	Ralph D. Bull	M	Son	1
1332	Heavy Runner	M	Father	38
1333	Different Rock	F	Mother	30
1334	Geo. Heavy Runner	M	Son	9
1335	Mary Higgins	F	Mother	24
1336	May Higgins	F	Daughter	3
1337	Chas. Higgins	M	Son	1
1338	John E. Higgins	M	Son	2m.
1339	John Hunsberger	M	Father	28
1340	Mary Hunsberger	F	Mother	24
1341	Willie Hunsberger	M	Son	1m.

Census of the Piegan tribe of Indians of Blackfeet Agency, Montana taken by W. R. Logan United States Indian Agent, September 1st, 1899

No.	English Name	Sex	Relation	Age
1342	Cecil Hunsberger	F	Mother	59
1343	Tom Hunsberger	M	Son	22
1344	Isaac Hunsberger	M	Son	26
1345	Clara Hunsberger	F	Daughter	20
1346	Augustus Hunsberger	M	Son	16
1347	Hairy Coat	M	Husband	43
1348	Mary H. Coat	F	Wife	23
1349	Hungry	F	Mother	51
1350	Joseph Hungry	M	Son	19
1351	Austin Hungry	M	Son	12
1352	Heading Off	F	-----	82
1353	Home Gun	M	Husband	34
1354	Mary Pipe Stone	F	Wife	28
1355	Mary Home Gun	F	Daughter	3
1356	Paul Home Gun	M	Son	7
1357	Harry No Chief	M	Single	26
1358	Heavy Breast	M	Husband	51
1359	First Woman	F	Wife	42
1360	Owen Heavy Breast	M	Son	20
1361	Quiet Woman	F	Wife	37
1362	George Horn	M	Single	33
1363	Mary Hazlett	F	Mother	19
1364	Baby Hazlett	M	Son	4m.
1365	Iron	M	Father	56
1366	Woman In Center	F	Wife	47
1367	Iron Woman	F	Widow	74
1368	Irwin Little Plume	M	Husband	22
1369	Small Woman	F	Wife	20
1370	Jessie Little Plume	F	Daughter	5
1371	Mary Little Plume	F	Daughter	3

Census of the Piegan tribe of Indians of Blackfeet Agency, Montana taken by W. R. Logan United States Indian Agent, September 1st, 1899

No.	English Name	Sex	Relation	Age
1372	William Jackson	M	Father	40
1373	Mary Jackson	F	Mother	29
1374	Thomas Jackson	M	Son	13
1375	Billie Jackson	F	Daughter	9
1376	Hugh Jackson	M	Son	7
1377	Maggie Jackson	F	Daughter	6
1378	Anna Jackson	F	Daughter	3
1379	Julia Jackson	F	Daughter	1
1380	Mary Johnson	F	-----	19
1381	John Big Springs	M	Single	28
1382	Jim No Chief	M	Father	28
1383	Gertrude No Chief	F	Mother	19
1384	Grace No Chief	F	Daughter	4
1385	Good Grass Woman	F	Daughter	4m.
1386	John Night Gun	M	Father	33
1387	Yellow Squitrel[sic]	F	Mother	23
1388	Short Woman	F	Daughter	5
1389	Blanket Woman	F	Daughter	7
1390	Buckskin Woman	F	Daughter	1
1391	Jim Blood	M	Husband	39
1392	Fanny Blood	F	Wife	20
1393	Austin Blood	M	Son	14
1394	Herman Blood	M	Son	3m.
1395	John Middle Calf	M	Father	54
1396	Cradle Woman	F	Mother	50
1397	John Middle Calf, Jr.	M	Son	21
1398	Crow Woman	F	Daughter	9
1399	Joe Still Smoking	M	Husband	17
1400	Minnie Still Smoking	F	Wife	15
1401	John Calf Ribs	M	Husband	35
1402	Sits In Front	F	Wife	32
1403	Joe Hits In Front	M	Son	20
1404	Austin Hits In Front	M	Son	12

Census of the Piegan tribe of Indians of Blackfeet Agency, Montana taken by W. R. Logan United States Indian Agent, September 1st, 1899

No.	English Name	Sex	Relation	Age
1405	Jim Bigtop	M	Single	20
1406	John Mountain Chief	M	Single	20
1407	John Kipp	M	Father	37
1408	Calf Woman	F	Mother	37
1409	Julia Kipp	F	Daughter	4
1410	Willie Kipp	M	Son	6
1411	Joe Kippp[sic]	M	Son	11
1412	Jack Kipp	M	Son	14
1413	Lucy King	F	Mother	32
1414	Sadie King	F	Daughter	14
1415	Chas. Carson	M	Son	19
1416	Jane King	F	Daughter	10
1417	Charley King	M	Son	8
1418	Willie King	M	Son	5
1419	Henry King	M	Son	2
1420	Dewey King	M	Son	1
1421	Joe Kipp	M	Father	49
1422	James Kipp	M	Son	8
1423	Mary Kipp	F	Daughter	10
1424	Geo. Kipp	M	Son	2
1425	William Kipp	M	Father	24
1426	Libby Kipp	F	Mother	22
1427	Ursula Kipp	F	Daughter	1
1428	Mary Keiser	F	Widow	71
1429	Kills Across Way	F	Mother	52
1430	May Spotted Eagle	F	Daughter	18
1431	Kills In Air	F	------	55
1432	John Kills Across Way	M	Single	27
1433	Maggie Kennerly	F	Mother	46
1434	Agnes Gobert	F	Daughter	14
1435	Agnes Kennerly	F	Daughter	13
1436	Annie Gobert	F	Daughter	12

Census of the Piegan tribe of Indians of Blackfeet Agency, Montana taken by W. R. Logan United States Indian Agent, September 1st, 1899

No.	English Name	Sex	Relation	Age
1437	Jerome Kennerly	M	Son	11
1438	James Kennerly	M	Son	4
1439	Leo Kennerly	M	Son	2m.
1440	Bert Kennerly	M	Single	22
1441	Perry Kennerly	M	Single	20
1442	Dick Kipp	M	Husband	36
1443	Yellow Bird	F	Wife	27
1444	Cora Kipp	F	Daughter	11
1445	Louis Kipp	M	Son	9
1446	Geo. Kipp	M	Son	3
1447	Cecil Kipp	F	Daughter	1
1448	William Lewis	M	Father	46
1449	Wesley Mellegan	M	Nephew	18
1450	Antoine Lewis	M	Son	17
1451	Pete Lewis	M	Son	7
1452	Sarah Lewis	F	Daughter	6
1453	Bessie Lewis	F	Daughter	1
1454	Lee Lemon	M	Son	3
1455	Mary Lemon	F	Mother	33
1456	Julian Lemon	M	Son	1
1457	Louise Lemon	F	Daughter	8
1458	Emma Lemon	F	Daughter	4
1459	John Lemon	M	Son	11
1460	Lazy Young Man	M	Husband	46
1461	Bayonet	F	Wife	51
1462	Lame Bear	M	Father	29
1463	Mary Lame Bear	F	Mother	23
1464	James Lame Bear	M	Son	3
1465	Good Rider	M	Son	2
1466	Lodge Pole Chief	F	Mother	51
1467	Ragged Clothes	M	Son	19
1468	Mary Lukens	F	Mother	51
1469	John Lukens	M	Son	20
1470	Peter Lukens	M	Son	18
1471	Dora Lukens	F	Daughter	23

Census of the Piegan tribe of Indians of Blackfeet Agency, Montana taken by W. R. Logan United States Indian Agent, September 1st, 1899

No.	English Name	Sex	Relation	Age
1472	Little Young Man	M	Father	40
1473	Ivockatopsis	F	Wife	51
1474	Good Singer	F	G. Mother	91
1475	Dick Lucero	M	Single	20
1476	Henry larb[sic]	M	Single	20
1477	Looking For Smoke	M	Father	39
1478	Rising From Water	F	Mother	46
1479	Louis L. F. Smoke	M	Son	7
1480	Lucy Cook	F	Mother	27
1481	Isabel Cook	F	Daughter	5
1482	Laura Cook	F	Daughter	3
1483	Joseph Cook	M	Son	4m.
1484	Little Owl	M	Husband	27
1485	Maggie Little Owl	F	Wife	18
1486	Mary Little Owl	F	Daughter	2
1487	Longtime Owl	F	Single	18
1488	Last Star	M	Husband	29
1489	Helen Last Star	F	Wife	19
1490	Takes Gun Inside	F	Daughter	3
1491	Lazy Boy	M	Husband	45
1492	Mary Lazy Boy	F	Wife	35
1493	Annie Lazy Boy	F	Daughter	11
1494	Sam Lazy Boy	M	Son	4
1495	Mike Lazy Boy	M	Son	2
1496	Tom Lazy Boy	M	Son	17
1497	Joe Livermore	M	Father	38
1498	Clara Livermore	F	Daughter	8
1499	Lily Livermore	F	Daughter	5
1500	Leggins	F	Widow	81
1501	Chas. Martin	M	Father	32
1502	Ross Martin	M	Son	5

Census of the Piegan tribe of Indians of Blackfeet Agency, Montana taken by W. R. Logan United States Indian Agent, September 1st, 1899

No.	English Name	Sex	Relation	Age
1503	Rena Martin	F	Daughter	1
1504	Isabel Main	F	Mother	35
1505	Alice Main	F	Daughter	7
1506	Lizzie Main	F	Daughter	4
1507	Henry Main	M	Husband	20
1508	Mary Main	F	Wife	20
1509	John Mestas	M	Single	29
1510	Mike Short Man	M	Husband	36
1511	Killed & Got Away	F	Wife	30
1512	Mary Murphy	F	Mother	51
1513	Willie Murphy	M	Son	16
1514	Hamlin Murphy	M	Son	11
1515	Holland Murphy	M	Son	9
1516	Albert Murphy	M	Son	7
1517	Makes Cold Weather	M	Father	38
1518	Julia M. C. Weather	F	Mother	30
1519	Joe M. C. Weather	M	Son	4
1520	Many Tail Feathers	M	Father	50
1521	Long Bear	F	Mother	31
1522	James M. T. Feathers	M	Son	19
1523	Elk Necklace	M	Son	4
1524	Under Bear	F	Daughter	11
1524[sic]	Broad Foot	F	Daughter	9
1525	Heard It Before	F	Daughter	4
1526	Hits In Front	F	Daughter	2
1527	Morning Plume	M	Father	51
1528	Snake Woman	F	Mother	31
1529	Nice Looking Girl	F	Daughter	2
1530	John Merchant	M	Single	24
1531	Mad Wolf	M	Father	61
1532	Gives To Sun	F	Mother	71
1533	Chas. Mad Wolf	M	Son	20

Census of the Piegan tribe of Indians of Blackfeet Agency, Montana taken by W. R. Logan United States Indian Agent, September 1st, 1899

No.	English Name	Sex	Relation	Age
1534	Henry Mad Wolf	M	Son	12
1535	Medicine Boss Ribs	M	Father	46
1536	Blackface Woman	F	Mother	39
1537	Emma Boss Ribs	F	Daughter	14
1538	Maggie Boss Ribs	F	Daughter	3
1539	Jack Miller	M	Husband	55
1540	Julia Miller	F	Wife	56
1541	Julia Momberg	F	Mother	28
1542	Jacob Momberg	M	Son	2
1543	Mabel Momberg	F	Daughter	1
1544	Carrie Monroe	F	Mother	31
1545	Mabel Monroe	F	Daughter	7
1546	Jessie Monroe	M	Son	4
1547	Joseph Monroe	M	Son	2
1548	Frank Monroe	M	Father	53
1549	Mary Monroe	F	Mother	46
1550	Louis Monroe	M	Son	18
1551	Antoine Monroe	M	Son	11
1552	Many Hides	M	Husband	26
1553	Maggie Many Hides	F	Wife	18
1554	Louis Matt	M	Father	39
1555	Adaline Matt	F	Mother	32
1556	Julia Matt	F	Daughter	5
1557	Frances Matt	F	Daughter	3
1558	Ada Matt	F	Daughter	2
1559	Michael Matt	M	Son	18
1560	Mud Head	M	Husband	37
1561	White H. Rider	F	Wife	35
1562	Sits Against Wind	F	Daughter	13
1563	Joe Mud Head	M	Son	5
1564	Frank Monroe	M	Single	26
1565	Julia Magee	F	Mother	32

Census of the Piegan tribe of Indians of Blackfeet Agency, Montana taken by W. R. Logan United States Indian Agent, September 1st, 1899

No.	English Name	Sex	Relation	Age
1566	Joe Magee	M	Son	15
1567	Tom Magee	M	Son	9
1568	George Magee	M	Son	7
1569	Walter Magee	M	Son	5
1570	Henry Magee	M	Son	3
1571	Dewey Magee	M	Son	2
1572	Mary Magee	F	Daughter	11
1573	Medicine Singer	F	Mother	90
1574	Takes Gun Alone	F	Daughter	28
1575	Mike Little Dog	M	Husband	27
1576	Irene Little Dog	F	Wife	18
1577	William Monroe	M	Father	45
1578	John Monroe	M	Son	8
1579	Isabel Monroe	F	Daughter	6
1580	Donald Monroe	M	Son	3
1581	Henry Monroe	M	Son	1
1582	Many Cuts	F	Widow	66
1583	Henry Merchant	M	Single	26
1584	John Morgan	M	Husband	33
1585	Lucy Morgan	F	Mother	24
1586	Davis Morgan	M	Son	8
1587	Joseph Morgan	M	Son	4
1588	Mary Morgan	F	Daughter	1
1589	John Monroe	M	Father	76
1590	Louis Monroe	M	Son	18
1591	Hanks Monroe	M	Son	11
1592	Frank Marcereau	M	Single	26
1593	Chas. Marcereau	M	Brother	21
1594	Mike Berry Child	M	Father	26
1595	Hits Back	F	Mother	27
1596	Anna Berry Child	F	Daughter	2
1597	Many Necklace	F	Widow	81

Census of the Piegan tribe of Indians of Blackfeet Agency, Montana taken by W. R. Logan United States Indian Agent, September 1st, 1899

No.	English Name	Sex	Relation	Age
1598	Medicine Weasel	M	Husband	61
1599	Eagle Face	F	Wife	31
1600	She Crow	F	Daughter	5
1601	Plenty Hair	F	Daughter	8
1602	Hits In Same Place	F	Wife	31
1603	Cutting	F	Wife	41
1604	Medicine Owl	M	Husband	33
1605	Elk Woman	F	Wife	51
1606	Campbell Monroe	M	Husband	31
1607	Frezoni Monroe	F	Wife	24
1608	Henry C. Monroe	M	Son	2
1609	Makes Signs	F	Mother	43
1610	Louise M. Signs	F	Daughter	12
1611	Mary Norman	F	Mother	22
1612	Lena Norman	F	Daughter	4
1613	Alfred Norman	M	Son	11
1614	Adolph Norman	M	Son	3
1615	No Chief	M	Husband	57
1616	Hits First	F	Wife	46
1617	Rachel Norris	F	Mother	29
1618	Rosa Norris	F	Daughter	11
1619	Dan Norris	M	Son	6
1620	Mary D. Norris	F	Daughter	2
1621	Mary Niequette	F	Mother	35
1622	Joe Niequette	M	Son	20
1623	Chas. Niequette	M	Son	13
1624	Josephine Niequette	F	Daughter	12
1625	Night Shoot	M	Father	35
1626	Oktiga	F	Mother	22
1627	Joseph Night Shoot	M	Son	10
1628	George Night Shoot	M	Son	4
1629	Maggie Night Shoot	F	Daughter	1
1630	New Breast	M	Father	32

Census of the Piegan tribe of Indians of Blackfeet Agency, Montana taken by W. R. Logan United States Indian Agent, September 1st, 1899

No.	English Name	Sex	Relation	Age
1631	Long Face	F	Mother	41
1632	Mary New Breast	F	Daughter	5
1633	Nick Green	M	Single	26
1634	Peter Oscar	M	Single	26
1635	Old Person	M	Husband	28
1636	Iron Woman	F	Wife	32
1637	Jennie Old Person	F	Daughter	8
1638	John Old Person	M	Brother	28
1639	James A. Perrine	M	Son	30
1640	Monic Simons	F	Mother	67
1641	Presley Houke	M	Son	22
[sic]	Mary Powell	F	Mother	53
1642	Chas. Powell	M	Son	22
1643	Jessie Powell	M	Son	17
1644	Susie Powell	F	Daughter	12
1645	Jennie Powell	F	Mother	20
1646	Maggie Powell	F	Daughter	4m.
1647	Maggie Peterson	F	Mother	38
1648	Walter Peterson	M	Son	18
1649	Oscar Peterson	M	Son	19
1650	Frank Peterson	M	Son	16
1651	Melvin Peterson	M	Son	13
1652	Michael Peterson	M	Son	11
1653	Louise Paul	F	Mother	44
1654	Solomon Paul	M	Son	21
1655	Albert Paul	M	Son	19
1656	Philip Paul	M	Son	16
1657	Eddie Paul	M	Son	13
1658	Rosa Paul	F	Daughter	11
1659	Oliver Paul	M	Son	8
1660	Willie Paul	M	Son	6
1661	Salina Paul	F	Daughter	3
1662	James Pambrun	M	Single	33

Census of the Piegan tribe of Indians of Blackfeet Agency, Montana taken by W. R. Logan United States Indian Agent, September 1st, 1899

No.	English Name	Sex	Relation	Age
1663	Peter After Buffalo	M	Husband	35
1664	Cut Nose	F	Wife	27
1665	Isabel P. A. Buffalo	F	Daughter	12
1666	Joe P. A. Buffalo	M	Son	4
1667	Annie P. A. Buffalo	F	Daughter	3
1668	George Pablo	M	Husband	30
1669	Maggie Pablo	F	Wife	21
1670	Christina Pablo	F	Daughter	4
1671	Agnes Pablo	F	Daughter	3
1672	Nellie Pablo	F	Daughter	4m.
1673	Hunter Powell	M	Husband	38
1674	Sophia Powell	F	Wife	27
1675	William Powell	M	Son	7
1676	Theresa Pambrun	F	G. Moth.	57
1677	Percy Dennis	M	G. Son	17
1678	Julia Pendergrest	F	Mother	28
1679	Emily Pendergrest	F	Daughter	4
1680	George Pendergrest	M	Son	2
1681	Lou Paisly[sic]	F	Mother	38
1682	George Paisley	M	Son	14
1683	Allen Paisley	M	Son	10
1684	Mattie Paisley	F	Daughter	7
1685	Chauncey Paisley	M	Son	3
1686	Frank Racine	M	Husband	21
1687	Nettie Racine	F	Wife	16
1688	Rides At Door	M	Husband	33
1689	Mary R. A. Door	F	Wife	29
1690	Dick R. A. Door	M	Son	9
1691	Louise R. A. Door	F	Daughter	7
1692	Frank R. A. Door	M	Son	4
1693	James R. A. Door	M	Son	2
1694	Root Digger	F	Widow	84
1695	Runs Away	F	Mother	53

Census of the Piegan tribe of Indians of Blackfeet Agency, Montana taken by W. R. Logan United States Indian Agent, September 1st, 1899

No.	English Name	Sex	Relation	Age
1696	Mary Runs Away	F	Daughter	17
1697	Susie Runs Away	F	Daughter	7
1698	Sam Yellow Wolf	M	Son	30
1699	Vic. Robinson	F	Mother	39
1700	George Robinson	M	Son	19
1701	Joe Robinson	M	Son	17
1702	Louise Robinson	F	Daughter	9
1703	Agnes Robinson	F	Daughter	7
1704	Baptist Rondan	M	Father	38
1705	Mary Rondan	F	Mother	41
1706	Richard Rondan	M	Son	17
1707	Sam Rondan	M	Son	14
1708	Louisa Rondan	F	Daughter	10
1709	Mary Rondan	F	Daughter	8
1710	Nancy Rondan	F	Daughter	3
1711	Isabel Rondan	F	Daughter	2
1712	John Thomas	M	S. Son	22
1713	Ida Thomas	F	S. Dau.	24
1714	Rubert Under Bear	M	Husband	28
1715	Maggie Under Bear	F	Wife	17
1716	Philip Under Bear	M	Son	1
1717	Running Fisher	M	Husband	34
1718	Grace Running Fisher	F	Wife	24
1719	First Runner	M	Son	3
1720	Rides Behind	M	Husband	39
1721	Shoots Weasel	F	Wife	37
1722	Rides In Middle	M	Husband	35
1723	Slim Woman	F	Wife	36
1724	Mary R. I. Middle	F	Daughter	5
1725	Levi R. I. Middle	M	Son	12
1726	Fred R. I. Middle	M	Son	17
1727	Chas. Revis	M	Father	25
1728	First Strike	F	Mother	28
1729	Sam Revis	M	Son	14

Census of the Piegan tribe of Indians of Blackfeet Agency, Montana taken by W. R. Logan United States Indian Agent, September 1st, 1899

No.	English Name	Sex	Relation	Age
1730	Many Guns	M	Son	7
1731	Good Gun	F	Daughter	1
1732	Joe Revis	M	Son	5
1733	Mrs. Big Nose	F	G. Moth.	75
1734	Nellie Scheldt	F	Mother	35
1735	Harry Scheldt	M	Son	14
1736	Andrew Scheldt	M	Son	10
1737	Augusta Scheldt	F	Daughter	8
1738	Mary Scheldt	F	Daughter	6
1739	Irene Scheldt	F	Daughter	3
1740	Stillman Scheldt	F	Daughter	3m.
1741	Mary Stone	F	Mother	34
1742	Henry Stone	M	Son	4
1743	Joseph Stone	M	Son	2
1744	Frank Stone	M	Son	3m.
1745	Slim Tail	M	Husband	36
1746	Kills In Water	F	Wife	46
1747	Joe Shorty	M	Father	32
1748	Mary Shorty	F	Mother	37
1749	Sam Shorty	M	Son	8
1750	Susan Shorty	F	Daughter	5
1751	Louis Shorty	M	Son	4
1752	Lizzie Shorty	F	Daughter	3
1753	Kate Stephenson	F	Mother	30
1754	Laura Stephenson	F	Daughter	16
1755	Cecil Stephenson	F	Daughter	6
1756	Phoebe Stephenson	F	Daughter	3
1757	Stink Teat	M	Father	29
1758	One Girl	F	Mother	28
1759	Little Stink Teat	M	Son	2
1760	Short Robe	M	Father	40
1761	Approach From All Sides	F	Mother	31
1762	Water Carrier	F	Mother	28
1763	Annie Short Robe	F	Daughter	4
1764	Already Killed	F	Daughter	2

Census of the Piegan tribe of Indians of Blackfeet Agency, Montana taken by W. R. Logan United States Indian Agent, September 1st, 1899

No.	English Name	Sex	Relation	Age
1765	Emma Short Robe	F	Daughter	5
1766	Rosa Sharp	F	Mother	18
1767	Julia Sharp	F	Daughter	2
1768	Susan Sherman	F	Mother	57
1769	Alexander Sherman	M	Son	20
1770	Robert Sherman	M	Son	18
1771	Sophia Sherman	F	Daughter	16
1772	Emma Sherman	F	Daughter	14
1773	Anna Clarke	F	Ad. Dau.	11
1774	Wm. Samples	M	Father	31
1775	Mary Samples	F	Mother	24
1776	Willie Samples	M	Son	5
1777	Florence Samples	F	Daughter	4
1778	Annie Samples	F	Daughter	3
1779	Baby Samples	F	Daughter	3m.
1780	Shoots First	M	Father	25
1781	Calf S. First	F	Mother	38
1782	Cecil S. First	F	Daughter	2
1783	Henry S. First	M	S. Son	18
1784	Louise S. First	F	S. Dau.	17
1785	Geneva Stewart	F	Mother	29
1786	Earl Stewart	M	Son	10
1787	James Stewart	M	Son	3
1787[sic]	Vera Stewart	F	Daughter	2
1788	Virginia Stewart	F	Daughter	1
1789	Oliver Sanderville	M	Father	39
1790	Mary Sanderville	F	Mother	30
1791	John Sanderville	M	Son	12
1792	Joe Spanish	M	S. Father	29
1793	Kills First	F	Mother	38
1794	William Clarke	M	Son	6
1795	Agnes Clarke	F	Daughter	15
1796	Split Ears	M	Father	31
1797	Good Kill	F	Mother	41

Census of the Piegan tribe of Indians of Blackfeet Agency, Montana taken by W. R. Logan United States Indian Agent, September 1st, 1899

No.	English Name	Sex	Relation	Age
1798	Maggie Split Ears	F	Daughter	9
1799	Susie Split Ears	F	Daughter	6
1800	Strangles Wolf	M	Husband	50
1801	Short Woman	F	Wife	57
1802	John Shorty	M	Father	59
1803	Mary Shorty	F	Mother	28
1804	Anna Shorty	F	Daughter	11
1805	Frank Spearson	M	Father	43
1806	Yellow Beaver	F	Mother	31
1807	Alfred Beaver	M	Son	3
1808	William Smith	M	Son	25
1809	Lizzie Smith	F	Mother	60
1810	Peter Smith	M	Son	14
1811	Stabs Down	M	Father	30
1812	Cloth Woman	F	Mother	24
1813	Edward S. Down	M	Son	2
1814	William Sherman	M	Husband	26
1815	Geneva Sherman	F	Wife	20
1816	Mary Sherman	F	Daughter	3
1817	Charley Sherman	M	Son	1
1818	Cecil Sanderville	F	Mother	29
1819	Agnes Sanderville	F	Daughter	13
1820	Edward Sanderville	M	Son	1
1821	Jess Samples	M	Single	25
1822	Strikes Back	F	Widow	64
1823	Stingy	M	Husband	51
1824	Died First	F	Wife	51
1825	White Hide	M	Son	9
1826	Money	F	Daughter	3
1827	Julia Thomas	F	Mother	29
1828	George Thomas	M	Son	4

Census of the Piegan tribe of Indians of Blackfeet Agency, Montana taken by W. R. Logan United States Indian Agent, September 1st, 1899

No.	English Name	Sex	Relation	Age
1829	Nora Thomas	F	Daughter	2
1830	Two Bears	F	Widow	46
1831	Ira Sheriff	N	Son	19
1832	Takes Gun	M	Father	37
1833	Katie Takes Gun	F	Mother	27
1834	Bear Leader	M	Son	2
1835	Sarah Thomas	F	Mother	51
1836	Tom Little Bear	M	Single	26
1837	Two Guns	M	Husband	29
1838	Breaks Good	F	Wife	23
1839	Three Bears	M	Father	46
1840	Mary Three Bears	F	Mother	49
1841	Cecil T. Bears	F	Daughter	9
1842	Joseph T. Bears	M	Son	5
1843	Talking Woman	F	Widow	71
1844	Two Strikes	F	-----	57
1845	Takes Gun On Top	M	Husband	31
1846	Yellow Bird	F	Wife	31
1847	John T. G. O. Top	M	Son	20
1848	Louise T. G. O Top	F	Daughter	6
1849	Takes Gun Alone	F	-----	46
1850	Chas. Three Guns	M	Single	26
1851	Three Guns	M	Husband	32
1852	Kills In Night	F	Wife	45
1853	Owl Squirrel	M	Son	19
1854	Emma Upham	F	Mother	37
1855	Jack Upham	M	Son	10
1856	Rose Upham	F	Daughter	20
1857	Katie Upham	F	Daughter	16

Census of the Piegan tribe of Indians of Blackfeet Agency, Montana taken by W. R. Logan United States Indian Agent, September 1st, 1899

No.	English Name	Sex	Relation	Age
1858	Myrtie Upham	F	Daughter	7
1859	William Upham	M	Father	33
1860	Bell Coming	F	Mother	27
1861	Geo. Upham	M	Son	4
1862	Lazy Cut	F	G. Moth.	51
1863	John Vielle	M	Father	32
1864	Anna Vielle	F	Mother	27
1865	Mary Vielle	F	Daughter	6
1866	Willie Vielle	M	Son	8
1867	Joe Vielle	M	Son	1
1868	Tom Vielle	M	Single	20
1869	Maggie Wetzel	F	Mother	41
1870	Pearl Wetzel	F	Daughter	22
1871	William Wetzel	M	Son	18
1872	Rosa Ward	F	Mother	32
1873	Jim Ward	M	Son	8
1874	Geo. Ward	M	Son	6
1875	Mary Ward	F	Daughter	4
1876	Emma Ward	F	Daughter	2
1877	Melinda Wren	F	Mother	51
1878	John Wren	M	Son	17
1879	Robert Wren	M	Son	12
1880	Dora Wren	F	Daughter	11
1881	William Wren	M	Son	9
1882	Lillie Wren	F	Daughter	7
1883	Ida Wren	F	Daughter	5
1884	Melinda Wren	F	Daughter	3
1885	Geo. Wren	M	Husband	29
1886	Susie Wren	F	Wife	29
1887	Shorty White Grass	M	Father	59
1888	Kills At Night	F	Mother	45
1889	Little Ram	M	Son	7
1890	Eneas White Grass	M	Son	3
1891	Catches Two W. Grass	F	Mother	35

Census of the Piegan tribe of Indians of Blackfeet Agency, Montana taken by W. R. Logan United States Indian Agent, September 1st, 1899

No.	English Name	Sex	Relation	Age
1892	Ross White Grass	M	Son	23
1893	Wolf Tail	M	Father	46
1894	Gilbert Wolf Tail	M	Son	12
1895	Found Herself	F	Daughter	7
1896	Wolf Sitting Up	M	Son	5
1897	Jim White Calf	M	Husband	33
1898	Minnie White Calf	F	Wife	31
1899	White Calf	M	Father	81
1900	Catches Two	F	Mother	51
1901	Black Smoke	F	Mother	56
1902	Diving Around	F	Daughter	7
1903	Catches Both Sides	F	Daughter	7
1904	Stole Inside	F	Daughter	7
1905	Blanche White Calf	F	Daughter	9
1906	Went In Herself	F	Mother	56
1907	Louisa Lodge Pole	F	Daughter	19
1908	Weasel Fat	M	Husband	47
1909	Good Shield	F	Mother	31
1910	Cree Woman	F	Single	25
1911	Wolverine	M	Father	28
1912	Walks Backward	F	Mother	21
1913	William Wolverine	M	Son	6
1914	Joe Wolverine	M	Son	4
1915	Good Woman	F	Mother	41
1916	Kill Forward	F	Daughter	6
1917	Woman's Word	F	G. Moth.	71
1918	Two Spear	F	Mother	23
1919	Woman Alone	F	Daughter	5
1920	Big Eagle	F	Daughter	3
1921	John Wagner	M	Father	23
1921[sic]	Mary Wagner	F	Mother	29
1922	Lily Wagner	F	Daughter	3

Census of the Piegan tribe of Indians of Blackfeet Agency, Montana taken by W. R. Logan United States Indian Agent, September 1st, 1899

No.	English Name	Sex	Relation	Age
1923	Wolf Chief	M	Husband	31
1924	Lone Woman	F	Wife	31
1925	Garret White	M	Husband	25
1926	Many White Horses	M	Father	77
1927	Long Time Good	F	Mother	60
1928	Thunder Nest Woman	F	Mother	34
1929	Last Wolf	M	Son	17
1930	Joe White Horses	M	Son	8
1931	Gives Gun Away	M	Son	5
1932	Crow White Horses	M	Son	3
1933	Only Girl	F	Daughter	2
1934	Gun Fringe	M	Son	1
1935	Rabbit Old Woman	F	Mother	36
1936	Hungry Woman	F	Daughter	5
1937	Telescope	M	Son	2
1938	Weasel Tail	M	Husband	39
1939	Minnie Weasel Tail	F	Wife	34
1940	Amy Weasel Tail	F	Daughter	13
1941	Antoine Weasel Tail	M	Son	4
1942	Wolf Calf	M	Husband	81
1943	Antelope Woman	F	Wife	77
1944	Wipes His Eyes	M	Husband	31
1945	Takes Gun	F	Wife	41
1946	Kills Another	F	Daughter	5
1947	Wallace Night Gun	M	Husband	22
1948	Mary Night Gun	F	Wife	21
1949	Yellow Wolf	M	Father	52
1950	Double Iron Woman	F	Mother	26
1951	Annie Yellow Wolf	F	Daughter	[sic]
1952	John Yellow Wolf	M	Son	3
1953	Mollie Yellow Wolf	F	Daughter	6
1954	Mary Yellow Wolf	F	Daughter	4m.

Census of the Blackfeet,

Montana, 1900

BLACK Feet

43648	Indian Office, Incl. No. X	1900

Census of the [Piegan] Indians of [Blackfeet] Agency, [Montana] taken by United States Indian Agent, , 18

No.	English Name	Sex	Relation	Age
#1	Chief Coward	M	Father	48
2	Antelope Woman	F	Wife	49
3	Four Bulls	M	Son	23
4	Crow Good Looking	F	Dau.	7
#5	Black Bear	M	Father	59
6	Many Snakes	F	Wife	50
#7	Medicine Owl	M	Father	34
8	Sheep Woman	F	Wife	45
#9	Gambler	M	Father	43
10	Yellow Spotted Woman	F	Wife	33
#11	John Black Bear	M	Father	31
12	Pretty Bird Woman	F	Wife	20
#13	Wm. Lewis	M	Father	45
14	Joe Kossuth	M	Son	6
15	Sarah Lewis	F	Dau	8
16	Baby Lewis	F	Dau	2
#17	Many Tail Feathers	M	Father	45
18	Long Time Bear Woman	F	Wife	31
19	Under Bear	F	Dau	10
20	Double Stealing Woman	F	Dau	9
21	Strikes In Front	F	Dau	3
22	Heard First	F	Dau	5
#23	Cecil Sanderville	F	Moth	30
24	Agnes Yellow Wolf	F	Dau	15
25	Mary Yellow Wolf	F	Dau	8
26	Samuel Yellow Wolf	M	Son	2
#27	Bear Skin #2	M	Father	46
#28	Yellow Wolf	M	Father	45
29	Two Iron Woman	F	Wife	29
30	Anna Yellow Wolf	F	Dau	1
#31	Sam Yellow Wolf	M	Neph	30
32	Runs Away	F	Mother	40
#33	John Shorty	M	Father	37
34	White Petrified Woman	F	Wife	22
35	Cecil Shorty	F	Dau	4
#36	Shoots First	M	Father	26
37	Calf Woman	F	Wife	30
38	Maggie Shoots First	F	Dau	1
39	Henry Marceau	M	Step-son	18
#40	Eagle Child	M	Father	38
41	Rushing On Both Sides	F	Wife	36
42	James Eagle Child	M	Son	11

Census of the [Piegan] Indians of [Blackfeet] Agency, [Montana] taken by United States Indian Agent, , 18

No.	English Name	Sex	Relation	Age
43	Takes Gun For Nothing	M	Son	5
44	New Comer Eagle Child	M	Son	1mo
#45	Strangled Wolf	M	Father	50
46	Small Woman	F	Wife	60
#47	Wm Sherman	M	Father	29
48	Genevieve Sherman	F	Wife	20
49	Charles Sherman	M	Son	2
50	Mary Sherman	F	Dau	3
51	James Clark	M	Neph	18
#52	Iron	M	Father	60
53	Taking In The Brush	F	Wife	50
#54	Frank Guardipee	M	Father	29
55	Mary Guardipee	F	Wife	22
56	Frank Guardipee	M	Son	4
57	Eli Guardipee	M	Son	1
#58	Stephen Henault	M	Husb'd	24
59	Caroline Henault	F	Wife	19
#60	Grounds	M	Wdr	45
#61	James Grounds	M	Father	24
62	Double Face	F	Wife	21
63	Black Rider	M	Son	2
#64	Mary Davis	F	Moth	24
65	Hattie Davis	F	Dau	4
#66	Mattie Bird	F	Moth	30
67	Sam Bird	M	Son	15
68	Martha Bird	F	Dau	18
69	Charles Bird	M	Son	13
70	John Bird	M	Son	10
71	Henry Bird	M	Son	4
72	George Bird	M	Son	3
73	Millie Bird	F	Dau	7
74	Infant	M	Son	1
#75	Emily Eldridge	F	Wife	35
#76	John Dont[sic] Go Out	M	Husb'd	49
77	Blanket Woman	F	Wife	50
#78	Good Medicine Ripe	F	Wid	40
79	Good Bird Woman	F	Dau	9
#80	James Many Tail Feathers	M	Single	34
#81	Heading Off	F	Wid	70
#82	Goes In All Around	F	Moth	45
83	Black Cloth Woman	F	Dau	25
84	Lays Fine	M	Son	10

Census of the   [Piegan]   Indians of [Blackfeet] Agency, [Montana]
taken by   United States Indian Agent,   , 18

No.	English Name	Sex	Relation	Age
85	Minnie Skunk Cap	F	Dau	14
#86	Little Young Man	M	Husb'd	45
87	Slashes On Both Sides	F	Wife	70
#88	Dog Ears	M	Father	26
89	High Forhead[sic]	F	Wife	23
90	Red Mouse	M	Son	1
#91	Wallace Night Gun	M	Father	24
92	Mary Night Gun	F	Wife	21
93	Infant	F	Dau	1
#94	Black Sarcee	M	Husb'd	33
95	Kils[sic] Long Way	F	Wife	35
#96	Catches Both Sides	M	Wdr	70
97	Dry Goods Woman	F	Widow	60
98	Lizzie Marceau	F	Ad. Dau	14
#99	Coat	M	Father	30
100	Broken Leg	F	Wife	32
101	Medicine	F	Dau	5
#102	James Blood	M	Father	40
103	Good Looking Owl	F	Wife	25
104	Antoine Blood	M	Son	15
105	John Blood	M	Son	1
#106	Charles Couuquette[sic]	M	Father	38
107	Louise Chouquette	F	Wife	45
108	Josephine Chouquette	F	Dau	23
#109	Running Fisher	M	Father	43
110	Rushing Alone	F	Wife	35
111	Stops First	M	Son	3
112	Dont Care	F	Dau	11
#113	Mike Little Dog	M	Father	23
114	Good Tied Woman	F	Wife	18
115	Good Stealing Woman	F	Dau	1
#116	Leggins	F	Wid	60
#117	James Grant	M	Hus	26
118	Josephine Grant	F	Wife	25
#119	Blackfoot Child	M	Father	52
120	Buffalo Trail	F	Wife	50
121	Blanket Woman	F	Dau	3
#122	Baptiste West Wolf	M	Hus	23
123	Anna Shorty West Wolf	F	Wife	16
#124	Double Cloth	F	Wid	45
125	Lone Mouse	M	Son	28
126	Shooting Close	M	Son	15

Census of the [Piegan] Indians of [Blackfeet] Agency, [Montana] taken by United States Indian Agent, , 18

No.	English Name	Sex	Relation	Age
127	Taking Gun In the Middle	M	Son	13
128	John West Wolf	M	Son	5
#129	Frank Spearson	M	Father	44
130	Yellow Beaver	F	Wife	26
131	Albert Spearson	M	Son	4
#132	Stabs Down	M	Father	30
133	Blanket Woman	F	Wife	29
134	Short Face	M	Son	2
135	Infant	M	Son	1
#136	Joseph Bull Child	M	Father	22
137	Catching	F	Wife	19
138	Thos Bull Child	M	Son	2
#139	Bull Child	M	Father	60
140	Fine Catching	F	Wife	40
141	Driving Backward	F	Dau	4
#142	Morning Plume	M	Father	62
143	Snake People	F	Wife	40
144	Fine War Woman	F	Dau	4
#145	Many White Horses	M	Father	67
146	Thunder Nest	F	Wife	35
147	Joseph White Horses	M	Son	11
148	Giving War Club	M	Son	9
149	Last Life	M	Son	6
150	French Gun Cover	M	Son	2
151	Medicine Child	F	Dau	4
#152	Rabbit Woman	F	2nd Wife	39
153	Glass In Front	M	Son	4
#154	Kills By Mistake	F	Wid	70
155	Long Time Owl Woman	F	Wid	24
#156	Jack Miller	M	Hus	52
157	Julia Miller	F	Wife	49
#158	Rosa Sharp	F	Moth	22
159	Julia Sharp	F	Dau	2
#160	Mary Keiser	F	Wid	78
#161	Jim No Chief	M	Fath	26
162	Fetching Her Back	F	Wife	18
163	Drives Back Fine	F	Dau	5
164	Long Time Singing	F	Dau	1
#165	Medicine Singer	F	Wid	80
#166	Takes Gun Alone	F	Wid	50
#167	Clears Up	M	Father	28
168	Howls At Night	F	Wife	30

Census of the [Piegan] Indians of [Blackfeet] Agency, [Montana] taken by United States Indian Agent, , 18

No.	English Name	Sex	Relation	Age
169	George Clears Up	M	Son	2
#170	Night Shoot	M	Father	34
171	Scraping Hide	F	Wife	25
172	Joe Night Shoot	M	Son	11
173	Geo. Night Shoot	M	Son	2
174	Maggie Night Shoots[sic]	F	Dau	3
175	Infant	F	Dau	1
#176	Susan Sherman	F	Moth	60
177	Alexander Sherman	M	Son	21
178	Robert Sherman	M	Son	19
179	Sophia Sherman	F	Dau	17
180	Emma Sherman	F	Dau	16
181	Geo. Clark	M	Gd Son	14
182	Robert Clark	M	Gd Son	10
183	Anna Clark	F	Gd Dau	12
184	Louise Clark	F	Dau	28
#185	Thos. Lone Bear	M	Wdr	38
#186	Antoine	M	Hus	62
187	Sophia Antoine	F	Wife	62
#188	Joe Shorty	M	Father	30
189	Mary Shorty	F	Wife	28
190	Susan Shorty	F	Dau	6
191	Lucy Shorty	F	Dau	3
192	Rosalie Shorty	F	Dau	1
193	Samuel Shorth[sic]	M	Son	11
#194	Julia Pendergrass	F	Moth	28
195	Millie Pendergrass	F	Dau	4
196	George Pendergrass	M	Son	3
197	Philip Pendergrass	M	Son	1
#198	Wm Morgan	M	Father	30
199	Millie Morgan	F	Dau	13
200	Lizzie Morgan	F	Dau	12
201	Alice Morgan	F	Dau	8
202	Wilber Morgan	M	Son	7
203	Robert Morgan	M	Son	2
204	Claude Morgan	M	Son	1
#205	Medicine Boss Ribs	M	Father	45
206	Black Face Woman	F	Wife	40
207	Maggie Boss Ribs	F	Dau	4
#208	Cut Finger	M	Father	40
209	Strikes Her-self	F	Wife	39
210	Ernest Cut Finger	M	Son	20

Census of the [Piegan] Indians of [Blackfeet] Agency, [Montana] taken by United States Indian Agent, , 18

No.	English Name	Sex	Relation	Age
211	Josephine Cut Finger	F	Dau	13
212	Thos. Cut Finger	M	Son	5
213	Maggie Cut Finger	F	Dau	7
214	Annie Cut Finger	F	Dau	3
#215	Root Digger	F	Wd⌐	80
#216	Bad Marriage	M	Father	40
217	Little Fox	F	Wife	30
218	Yelling Last	M	Son	13
219	Thunder Star	M	Son	10
220	Last Bear Woman	F	Dau	6
221	Last Yelling Woman	F	Dau	3
222	Infant	M	Son	1
[sic]				
[sic]				
#225	Nick Green	M	Father	29
226	Long Time Chicken	F	Wife	44
227	Mary Green	F	Dau	10
#226[sic]	Cow Hide Robe	M	Father	33
227[sic]	Grace Cowhide Robe	F	Wife	29
228	Black Young Man	M	Son	3
#229	John Morgan	M	Father	34
230	Lucy Morgan	F	Wife	24
231	David Morgan	M	Son	8
232	Joe Morgan	M	Son	5
232[sic]	Mary Morgan	F	Dau	2
#233[sic]	John Ground	M	Hus	25
235	Mary Ground	F	Wife	18
#236	Tallow Ashley	M	Father	35
237	Rosa Ashley	F	Wife	28
238	Louis Ashley	M	Son	4
239	John Ashley	M	Son	1
240	Mary Ashley	F	Dau	3
#241	Catches Last	F	Moth	40
242	Poor Young Man	M	Son	7
#243	Lazy Boy	M	Father	40
244	Shatter	F	Wife	30
245	Steals for Nothing	F	Dau	7
246	Thos Lazy Boy	M	Son	17
247	Samuel Lazy Boy	M	Son	4
248	Mack Lacy[sic] Boy	M	Son	3
#249	Henry Merchant	M	Hus	33
250	Emma Merchant	F	Wife	16

Census of the [Piegan] Indians of [Blackfeet] Agency, [Montana] taken by United States Indian Agent, , 18

No.	English Name	Sex	Relation	Age
#251	John Merchant	M	Single	26
#252	Takes Gun Up	M	Father	34
253	Strikes In Front	F	Wife	39
254	John Mountain Chief	M	S-son	23
255	Jim Big Top	M	S-son	26
#256	First One Russell	M	Fath	29
257	Isabel Russell	F	Wife	19
258	Joseph Russel	M	Son	1
#259	Black Face Man	M	Father	45
260	Bead Woman	F	Wife	20
261	Red Petrified Rock	F	Dau	5
262	Long Time Red Squirrel	F	Dau	4
#263	Blanket Woman	F	Moth	40
264	Dan Bull Plume	M	Son	22
265	Infant	F	Dau	1
#266	Bird Rattler	M	Father	39
267	Sitting Under	F	Wife	29
268	Cleans Up at Night	F	Dau	3
#269	Lizzie Smith	F	Wid	48
270	Smithy Smith	M	Son	14
#271	Sam Smith	M	Son	23
#272	Wm Smith	M	Son	27
#273	Mattie Buckley	F	Wid	30
274	Lone Young Man	M	Son	3
275	Bow Legs	M	Son	2
#276	Womans Word	F	Wid	80
#277	Irvin Little Plume	M	Father	23
278	Small Woman	F	Wife	27
279	John Cross Guns	M	Son	2
280	Widow Woman	F	Dau	3
#281	Mud Head	M	Father	31
282	White Horse Rider	F	Wife	36
283	Setting West	M	Son	11
284	Tarlow Mud Head	M	Son	5
#285	Chief In the Middle	M	Hus	27
286	Makes First Treaty	F	Wife	21
287	Long Time Medicine Pipe	F	Moth	50
288	Wipes His Eyes	M	Father	37
289	Takes the Man	F	Wife	40
290	Evening Star	F	Dau	3
291	Infant	M	Son	1
#292	Eagle Tail Feathers	M	Father	50

Census of the [Piegan] Indians of [Blackfeet] Agency, [Montana] taken by United States Indian Agent, , 18

No.	English Name	Sex	Relation	Age
293	Pretty Snake	F	Wife	60
294	Weasel Woman	F	Ad Dau	10
295	Blanket Woman	F	Ad Dau	7
#296	John Night Gun	M	Father	30
297	Red Squirrel	F	Wife	20
298	Short Woman	F	Dau	6
299	Antelope Woman	F	Dau	2
#300	Looking For Smoke	M	Father	46
301	Diving At Shore	F	Wife	42
302	Louis Looking For Smoke	M	S-son	8
#303	Dry Limb	M	Hus	27
304	Blanket Woman	F	Wife	15
305	Wood Chief Woman	F	Wid	45
306	Kills One Another	F	Dau	5
#307	George Horn	M	Single	36
#308	Bear Child	N	Father	47
309	Grain Woman	F	Wife	47
310	Wm Bear Child	M	Son	14
311	Louis Bear Child	M	Son	9
312	Benj. Bear Child	M	Son	5
313	James Bear Child	M	Son	7
314	Josephine Bear Child	F	Dau	12
#315	Mike Berry Child	M	Father	27
316	Strikes One Another	F	Wife	28
317	Small Mouth	F	Dau	4
318	Henry Berry Child	M	Son	1
#319	Kills Across the Way	F	Wid	50
#320	John Kill Across the Way	M	Single	28
#321	Morning Eagle	M	Father	66
322	Strikes On Top	F	Wife	49
323	Catching	F	Wife	36
324	Many Yells	M	Son	13
325	Rattles Running On Top	M	Son	7
326	Two Rabbits	M	Son	2m
#327	Takes Gun	M	Father	38
328	Minnie Takes Gun	F	Wife	17
329	James Takes Gun	M	Son	3
#330	Charles Reevis	M	Father	26
331	Strikes First	F	Wife	33
332	Many Guns	M	Son	6
333	Joseph Reevis	M	Son	5
334	Fine Gun Woman	F	Dau	2

Census of the   [Piegan]   Indians of [Blackfeet] Agency, [Montana]
taken by   United States Indian Agent,   , 18

No.	English Name	Sex	Relation	Age
#335	Beaver Woman	F	Wid	50
336	Takes Fine Gun	M	Gd-son	16
#337	Makes Signs at One Another	F	Wid	50
338	Blood Woman	F	Dau	11
#339	Pete After Buffalo	M	Father	37
340	Cut Nose	F	Wife	29
341	Jos. After Buffalo	M	Son	8
342	Anna After Buffalo	F	Dau	4
343	Cecil After Buffalo	F	Dau	2
#344	Double Rider	M	Father	45
345	Dont Care for Nothing	F	Wife	25
346	Minnie Double Rider	F	Dau	5
347	Infant	F	Dau	1
348	Ration Woman	F	Dau	10
#349	Rachel Norris	F	Moth	28
350	Daniel Norris	M	Son	6
351	Rosa Norris	F	Dau	11
352	Daisy Norris	F	Dau	3
#353	East Woman	F	Wid	80
#354	Charles DeLaney	M	Father	29
355	Viola Delaney	F	Wife	19
356	Infant	F	Dau	1
#357	Benj. DeRoche	M	Father	38
358	Big Pine Tree	F	Wife	40
359	Chas. DeRoche	M	Son	15
#360	Robert Hamilton	M	Father	31
361	Rosa Hamilton	F	Wife	28
362	Infant	F	Dau	1
#363	Edward Billideaux[sic]	M	Father	35
364	Virginia Billideaux	F	Wife	31
365	Carl Billedeaux	M	Son	8
366	Genevieve Billedeaux	F	Dau	6
367	Martha Billedeaux	F	Dau	4
368	Edward Billedeaux	M	Son	2
369	Mitchell Joseph Billedeaux	M	Son	1
#370	Strikes Back	F	Wid	45
371	Fine Slaughter	F	Dau	12
#372	Mary Howard	F	Wid	50
373	Joseph Howard	M	Son	23
374	Walter Howard	M	Son	18
#375	Mary Stone	F	Mother	35
376	Henry Stone	M	Son	5

Census of the [Piegan] Indians of [Blackfeet] Agency, [Montana] taken by United States Indian Agent, , 18

No.	English Name	Sex	Relation	Age
377	Joseph Stone	F[sic]	Son	3
378	Frank Stone	M	Son	1
379	Anna Howard	F	Dau-ad	15
#380	Shorty White Grass	M	Father	60
381	Kills at Night	F	Wife	45
384[sic]	Catches Twice	F	Wife	19
385	Small Rain	M	Son	7
386	Long Time Standing Rock Sioux	M	Son	2
#387	Ross White Grass	M	Hus	22
388	Minnie White Grass	F	Wife	30
#389	Chief Elk	M	Hus	60
390	Last Star	F	Wife	45
#391	Rided[sic] at Door	M	Fath	34
392	Mary Rided at Door	F	Wife	30
393	Richard Rides at Door	M	Son	11
394	Louis Rides at Door	M	Son	7
395	Round Face	M	Son	5
396	Rides at Door	M	Son	3
#382	Black Coyote	M	Hus	50
383	Blue Woman	F	Wife	27
#397	Geo. W. Cook	M	Hus.	36
398	Julis[sic] Cook	F	Wife	26
399	Mary Higgins	F	Moth	25
400	Charles Higgins	M	Son	3
401	John Higgins	M	Son	1
402	Mary Higgins	F	Dau	4
#403	Wolf Calf	F	Wid	90
#404	Old Person	M	Father	34
405	Iron Woman	F	Wife	24
406	Kills On the Middle	F	Dau	8
407	Kills In Front	F	Dau	8
408	Jumper	M	Br-Law	20
409	Last Boy	M	Son	1
#410	Wm Upham	M	Father	35
411	Coming Rattling	F	Wife	25
412	Infant	M	Son	1
#413	Mike Short Man	M	Hus	40
414	Sophronia Short Man	F	Wife	32
#415	Mary Powell	F	Wife	45
416	Chas. Powell	M	Son	24
417	Jennie Powell	F	Dau	22
418	Jessee Powell	M	Son	19

Census of the [Piegan] Indians of [Blackfeet] Agency, [Montana]
taken by United States Indian Agent, , 18

No.	English Name	Sex	Relation	Age
419	Susie Powell	F	Dau	14
420	Hattie Powell	F	Dau	1
#421	Rosa Hinkel	F	Moth	35
422	Geo. Hinkel	M	Son	16
423	Wm. Hinkel	M	Son	14
424	Elizzie Hinkel	F	Dau	12
425	Mamie Hinkel	F	Dau	10
#426	Pearl Wetzel	F	Moth	23
427	Infant	M	Son	1
#428	Maggie Wetzel	F	Wid	45
429	Wm Wetzel	M	Son	18
#430	Makes Cold Weather	M	Father	34
431	Spear Woman	F	Wife	29
432	Jos. Makes Cold Weather	M	Son	5
#433	Arrow Top Knot	M	Father	34
434	Squirrel Woman	F	Wife	30
435	Antoine Top Knot	M	Son	4
436	Big Top	M	Son	12
437	Stinks	M	Son	10
#438	Joseph Livermore	M	Wdr	37
439	Clara Livermore	F	Dau	9
440	Lillie Livermore	F	Dau	6
#441	Bear Paw	M	Father	46
442	Kills Different	F	Wife	30
443	John Bear Paw	M	Son	5
444	Baptiste Bear Paw	M	Son	3
445	Otto Bear Paw	M	Son	1
446	Called From the Other Side	F	Dau	12
#447	Heavy Runner	M	Father	38
448	Petrified Rock	F	Wife	32
449	Blue Bead	F	Wife	22
450	Geo. Heavy Runner	M	Son	11
451	Yellow Horse Rider	M	Son	7
452	Squirrell Woman	F	Dau	10
453	Coyote Woman	F	Dau	5
454	Jack Heavy Runner	M	Son	1
455	Sweet Grass Hills	F	Dau	4
#456	Plume Woman	F	Wid	50
457	Yells at Night	M	Son	23
#458	George Pablo	M	Father	31
459	Maggie Pablo	F	Wife	22
460	Christina Pablo	F	Dau	6

Census of the [Piegan] Indians of [Blackfeet] Agency, [Montana]
taken by United States Indian Agent, , 18

No.	English Name	Sex	Relation	Age
461	Agnes Pablo	F	Dau	14
462	Eva Pablo	F	Dau	1
463	Emma Pablo	F	Dau	9
#464	Joseph Kipp	M	Wdr	52
465	James Kipp	M	Son	10
466	Mary Kipp	F	Dau	12
467	Geo. Kipp	M	Son	3
#468	Eliza McGowen	F	Moth	25
469	Jocie McGowen	F	Dau	4
470	Georgia McGowen	F	Dau	1
#471	Sophia McGovern	F	Moth	26
472	Jas McGovern	M	Son	7
473	John McGovern	M	Son	4
#474	Mary Camp	F	Moth	22
475	John Camp	M	Son	2
476	Susie Camp	F	Dau	1
#477	Collins Anderson	M	Hus	25
478	Phena M Anderson	F	Wife	24
#479	Wm Hazlett	M	Sing	21
#480	Mary Sample	F	Wid	24
481	Wm A. Sample	M	Son	6
482	Florence E Sample	F	Dau	5
483	Annie J. Sample	F	Dau	3
484	Stella M Sample	F	Dau	1
#485	Cecil Hunsberger	F	Wid	60
486	Gussie Hunsberger	M	Son	17
487	Clara Hunsberger	F	Dau	20
488	Thomas Hunsberger	M	Son	19
#489	John Hunsberger	M	Father	27
490	Mary Hunsberger	F	Wife	24
491	Wm Hunsberger	M	Son	1
#492	Maggie Peterson	F	Moth	35
493	Oscar Peterson	M	Son	19
494	Walter Peterson	M	Son	18
495	Frank Peterson	M	Son	16
496	Melvin Peterson	M	Son	14
497	Mitchell Peterson	M	Son	12
#498	Sarah Thomas	F	Wid	46
#499	Iron Woman	F	Wid	70
#500	Bill Calf	M	Father	37
501	Blanket Woman	F	Wife	37
502	John Bull Calf	M	Son	10

Census of the   [Piegan]   Indians of [Blackfeet] Agency, [Montana]
taken by   United States Indian Agent,   , 18

No.	English Name	Sex	Relation	Age
#503	Good Killing	F	Wid	80
#504	Bear Skin	M	Father	26
505	Geneva Bear Skin	F	Wife	19
506	Come With the Wind	F	Dau	1
#507	Antoine Chouquette	M	Sing	40
#508	Perry Kennerly	M	Single	24
509	Bert Kennerly	M	Brother	23
#510	Split Ears	M	Hus	33
511	Good Killer	F	Wife	40
512	Susie Split Ear	F	Dau	7
513	Maggie Split Ear	F	Dau	10
514	Agnes Split Ear	F	Step-Dau	14
#515	Mollie Davlin	F	Mother	28
#516	Wolverine	M	Father	29
517	Walks Back	F	Wife	23
518	Many Owls	M	Son	7
519	Joe Wolverine	M	Son	5
520	Red Howling	F	Dau	3
521	Big Rump	M	Son	1
#522	Hits in the Middle	F	Wid	80
#523	Kills In the Air	R	Moth	80
524	Good Gun	M	Son	32
#525	Berry Carrier	M	Father	45
526	Rattling	F	Wife	50
527	Little Fox	F	Dau	20
528	Different Shield	F	Dau	5
#529	Rides In the Middle	M	Father	33
530	Slim Woman	F	Wife	34
531	Sweet Grass Hills	M	Son	20
532	Otter	M	Son	13
533	Joe Rides In the Middle	M	Son	1
534	Squirrel Girl	F	Dau	6
#535	Last Star	M	Father	33
536	White Horse Rider	F	Wife	22
537	Takes Gun Inside	M	Son	6
538	Yellow Head	M	Son	10
#539	Drags Behind	M	Father	40
540	Goes In Last	F	Wife	40
541	Red Head	M	Son	12
#542	Rushes On Both Sides	F	Wife	60
#543	Richard Grant	M	Father	24
544	Rosa Grant	F	Wife	20

Census of the [Piegan] Indians of [Blackfeet] Agency, [Montana] taken by United States Indian Agent, , 18

No.	English Name	Sex	Relation	Age
545	Dick Grant	M	Son	1
546	Mad Wolf	M	Father	59
547	Going to the Sun	F	Wife	46
548	Chas. Mad Wolf	M	Son	20
549	Joseph Mad Wolf	M	Son	10
#550	Joseph Niequette	M	Son	22
#551	New Breast	M	Hus	33
552	Long Face	F	Wife	40
#553	Anthony Austin	M	Hus	32
554	Susan Austin	F	Wife	40
555	Ira Burd	M	S-Son	12
556	Phoebe Burd	F	S-Dau	9
557	Alice Burd	F	S-Dau	20
#558	John Mestas	M	Sing	36
#559	Mrs Pete After Buffalo	F	Moth	28
560	John After Buffalo	M	Son	8
561	Agnes After Buffalo	F	Dau	5
562	Short Face	F	Dau	3
563	Infant	M	Son	1
#564	Cold Body	M	Father	38
565	Mrs Cold Body	F	Wife	40
566	Peter Cold Body	M	Son	13
567	Maggie Cold Body	F	Dau	10
568	Cecelia Cold Body	F	Dau	5
#569	Lama Bear	M	Father	29
570	Skunk Woman	F	Dau	22
571	Takes Gun	M	Son	4
572	Good Rider	M	Son	3
573	Good Stealing	F	Dau	2
#574	Boy	M	Father	50
575	Medicine Child	M	Son	13
576	Good For Nothing	M	Son	10
#577	Eli Rider	M	Father	27
578	Already Had Teeth	F	Wife	20
579	Henry Rider	M	Son	3
#580	Louis Ell	M	Father	27
581	Alda Ell	F	Wife	20
582	Chas Ell	M	Son	3
583	Louis Ell	M	Son	3mo
584	Willie Murphy	M	H-Brother	18
585	Hamlin Murphy	M	H-Brother	15
586	Nellie Hagen	F	Cous	8

Census of the   [Piegan]   Indians of [Blackfeet] Agency, [Montana]
taken by   United States Indian Agent,   , 18

No.	English Name	Sex	Relation	Age
587	Mary Hagen	F	Cous	5
#588	Flying	F	Wid	80
#589	Strikes #3	F	Wid	70
590	Wild Gun	M	G-son	3
#591	Baptiste Rondin	M	Father	37
592	Mary Rondin	F	Wife	46
593	Louise Rondin	F	Dau	13
594	Mary Rondin	F	Dau	10
595	Nancy Rondin	F	Dau	5
596	Isabella Rondin	F	Dau	3
597	Philip Rondin	M	Son	1-5[sic]
598	Richard Rondin	M	Son	20
599	Smuel[sic] Rondin	M	Son	15
#600	Rides Behind	M	Hus	44
601	Kills In the Brush	F	Wife	35
#602	Sophia Powell	F	Wife	28
603	Lorenza Powell	M	Son	2
604	Maggie Powell	F	Dau	15
#605	John Munroe	M	Father	75
606	August Munroe	M	Son	12
607	Louis Munroe	M	Son	20
#608	John Vielle	M	Father	32
609	Kills Long Way	F	Wife	24
610	Francis Vielle	M	Son	8
611	Jennie Vielle	F	Dau	6
612	Infant	M	Son	1
613	Bad Growth	M	Son	5
#614	Short Robe	M	Father	41
615	Runs on both Sides	F	Wife	38
616	Lone Rusher	F	Wife	27
617	Wm Short Robe	M	Son	1
618	Anna Short Robe	F	Dau	8
619	Emma Short Robe	F	Dau	7
620	Cecil Short Robe	F	Dau	5
#621	Black Weasel	M	Hus	34
622	Sparks	F	Wife	40
623	Going Alone	M	Son	3
#624	Carrie Monroe	F	Wife	30
625	Jessie Monroe	M	Son	6
626	Mabel Monroe	F	Dau	7
627	Jos Monroe	M	Son	4
628	Grinnell Monroe	M	Son	1

Census of the [Piegan] Indians of [Blackfeet] Agency, [Montana] taken by United States Indian Agent, , 18

No.	English Name	Sex	Relation	Age
#629	Frank Munroe	M	Father	52
630	Mary Munroe	F	Wife	44
631	Louis Munroe	M	Son	21
632	Antone Munroe	M	Son	11
#633	Lucy Cook	F	Wife	25
634	Isabella Cook	F	Dau	6
635	Mountain W Cook	M	Son	5
#636	Bad Woman	F	Wid	80
[#]637	Medicine Weasel	M	Father	45
638	Fine Cutter	F	Wife	38
639	Eagle Face	F	Wife	40
640	Heavy Set of Hair	F	Dau	4
641	Owl Woman	F	Dau	3
642	Goes in last	F	Dau	1
#643	Slim Tail	M	Hus	38
644	Kills In Water	F	Wife	45
#645	Three Bears	M	Father	49
646	Crow Head	F	Wife	53
647	Many Different Petrified Woman[sic]	F	Dau	10
648	Nobody Likes	M	Son	6
#649	Dog Takes Gun	M	Hus	34
650	Cuts for Herself	F	Wife	25
651	Medicine Road	F	Dau	1
#652	Spotted Head	M	Wid	79
#653	Louize Paisley	F	Wife	38
654	George Paisley	M	Son	15
655	Allen Paisley	M	Son	11
656	Mattie Paisley	F	Dau	8
657	Chauncy Paisley	M	Son	3
#658	Ear Rings	M	Father	45
659	Susan Ear Rings	F	Wife	50
660	James Ear Rings	M	Son	17
661	Bert Ear Rings	M	Son	14
#662	Wolf Chief	M	Hus	22
663	Mrs Wolf Chief	F	Wife	24
#664	Strikes Back	F	Wid	80
#665	Crane Woman	F	Wid	78
#666	Jos. Still Smoking	M	Hus	25
667	Rocking Owner	F	Wife	16
668	Infant	F	Dau	4mo
#669	Young Eagle	M	Father	40
670	Spotted Back	F	Wife	29

Census of the [Piegan] Indians of [Blackfeet] Agency, [Montana]
taken by United States Indian Agent, , 18

No.	English Name	Sex	Relation	Age
671	Joseph Young Eagle	M	Son	3
672	Infant	M	Son	1
#673	Bear Head	M	Hus	44
674	Cree Bear Head	M	Son	8
#675	Sharp	M	Hus	40
676	Bayonet	F	Wife	60
677	Peter Smith	M	Adptd-S	19
#678	Home Gun	M	Father	36
679	Many Pipes	F	Wife	25
680	Paul Home Gun	M	Son	5
681	Minnie Home Gun	F	Dau	3
682	Infant	M	Son	1
#683	Calf Shield	M	Hus	50
684	Only Smokes	M	Son	16
#685	Weasel Fat	M	Hus	49
686	Mrs Weasel; Fat	F	Wife	38
#687	Many Tail Feathers	M	Hus	70
688	Cree Woman	F	Dau	28
#689	Takes Gun On Top	M	Father	38
690	Yellow Bird	F	Wife	49
691	Maggie Takes Gun On Top	F	Dau	20
692	Louise Takes Gun On Top	F	Dau	1
#693	Dives Long Woman	F	Wid	80
#694	David Duvall	M	Hus	36
695	Gretchen Duvall	F	Wife	28
696	Mary Iron Crow	F	S-Dau	18
#697	John Middle Calf	M	Father	56
698	Mrs John Middle Calf	F	Wife	60
699	Sam Middle Calf	M	Son	28
#700	Bear Medicine	M	Father	36
701	Ragged Woman	F	Wife	32
702	Wm Bear Medicine	M	Son	9
703	John Bear Medicine	M	Son	4
704	Infant	F	Dau	1
705	Maggie Bear Medicine	F	Dau	8
706	Mollie Middle Calf	F	Dau	11
#707	Stretched Out	M	Sing	38
#708	Little Plume	M	Father	46
709	Tail Feathers Woman	F	Wife	35
710	Cuts In Different Places	F	Wife	39
711	James Little Plume	M	Son	20

Census of the [Piegan] Indians of [Blackfeet] Agency, [Montana] taken by United States Indian Agent, , 18

No.	English Name	Sex	Relation	Age
712	Louis Little Plume	M	Son	9
713	Mary Little Plume	F	Dau	9
714	Josephine Little Plume	F	Dau	5
715	Susie Little Plume	F	Dau	3
716	Peter Little Plume	M	Son	4
717	Little Person	M	Son	3
#718	Yellow Kidney	M	Father	28
719	Minnie Kidney	F	Wife	22
720	Mack Kidney	M	Son	8
721	Mad Been Yelling	F	Dau	3
#722	White Calf	M	Hus	67
723	Catches Together	F	Wife	60
#724	James White Calf	M	Hus	34
725	Mary White Calf	F	Wife	17
#726	White Calf #2	F	Wid	50
727	Diving Around Behind	F	Dau	12
#728	Cream Antelope	M	Father	39
729	Mrs Cream Antelope	F	Wife	39
730	James Cream Antelope	M	Son	13
731	Joe Cream Antelope	M	Son	3
#732	Red Plume	M	Father	38
733	Catches First	F	Wife	47
734	Got Many Different Things	M	Son	2
#735	Little Owl	M	Father	26
736	Runs Back	F	Wife	19
737	Swift Girl	F	Dau	3
#738	Good Killer	F	Wid	80
#739	Hairy Coat	M	Hus	33
740	Mary Hairy Coat	F	Wife	35
#741	Heavy Breast	M	Hus	50
742	Swift Woman	F	Wife	38
743	Way Laying	F	Wife	40
#744	Little Bull	M	Father	56
745	Pretty Stealing Woman	F	Wife	34
746	Kills In the Brush	F	Wife	49
747	Two Guns	M	Son	3
#748	Found A Gun	M	Single	26
#749	Buffalo Hide	M	Father	38
750	Spotted Woman	F	Wife	26
751	Dog Medicine	M	Son	6
752	Crow Pittier[sic]	M	Son	3
753	Yellow Buffalo Rock	F	Dau	1

Census of the [Piegan] Indians of [Blackfeet] Agency, [Montana] taken by United States Indian Agent, , 18

No.	English Name	Sex	Relation	Age
#754	Good Looking Woman	F	Wid	80
#755	Owen Heavy Breast	M	Hus	22
756	Lone Woman	F	Wife	28
#757	Wolf Horn	M	Hus	52
758	Sings On Top	F	Wife	37
759	Takes Good Gun	M	Son	12
#760	Catches On Top	F	Sing	90
#761	Frank Munroe	M	Hus	31
762	Louize Munroe	F	Wife	28
763	Weasel Tail	M	Father	40
764	Dont[sic] Like To Be A Woman	F	Wife	36
765	Louize Weasel Tail	F	Dau	6
766	Lights At Night	M	Son	2
767	John Weasel Tail	M	Son	3mo
768	Anna Weasel Tail	F	Dau	16
#769	Many Hides	M	Hus	26
770	Mary Many Hides	F	Wife	19
771	Under Bear	M	Son	3
#772	Catches In Side	F	Wid	60
#773	Takes Gun Both Sides	M	Hus	30
774	Strikes First	F	Wife	30
775	Medicine Black Bird	M	Son	4
776	Cat	M	Son	2
777	Infant	F	Dau	4mo
#778	Talking Woman	F	Wid	50
#779	Chief Crow	M	Hus	48
780	Hits With A Gun	F	Wife	45
781	Hollowing Last	F	Dau	14
782	James Chief Crow	M	Son	20
783	Chicken	M	Son	17
#784	Yellow Iron	F	Wid	30
#785	Bear Leggins	M	Father	30
786	Big Woman	F	Wife	40
787	Home Rushing	F	Wife	30
788	Round Head	F	Dau	14
789	Black Face	F	Dau	13
790	Hungry Woman	F	Dau	4
791	Little Chip Munk[sic]	F	Dau	4
#792	Pete Cadotte	M	Father	34
793	Good Slaughter	F	Wife	25
794	Yellow Otter	F	Dau	5
796[sic]	Short Man	M	Son	3

Census of the [Piegan] Indians of [Blackfeet] Agency, [Montana] taken by United States Indian Agent, , 18

No.	English Name	Sex	Relation	Age
#795	Joseph Bull Child	M	Sing	18
#797	Henry Under Bear	M	Father	35
798	Mary Nequette	F	Wife	37
799	Chas Nequette	M	Son	14
800	John Nequette	M	Son	16
801	Josephine Nequette	F	Dau	13
#802	Geneva Stewart	F	Wife	30
803	Earl Stewart	M	Son	9
804	James Stewart	M	Son	5
805	Vera Stewart	F	Dau	2
806	Virginia Stewart	F	Dau	1
#807	Big Spring	M	Father	34
808	No Home	F	Wife	40
809	Small Face	F	Wife	27
#810	Two Strikes	F	Wid	70
#811	Many Necklace	F	Wid	70
#812	Frank Racine	M	Hus	24
813	Nettie Racine	F	Wife	20
#814	First Catcher	F	Wid	54
815	Henry Hungry	M	Son	24
816	Ezra Piegan	M	Son	13
#817	Yellow Owl	M	Father	27
818	Margaret Yellow Owl	F	Wife	17
819	Infant	M	Son	1
#820	Chas. Buck	M	Hus	26
821	Spyna Buck	F	Wife	35
#822	Mary Deveraux	F	Wife	45
823	Charles Deveraux	M	Son	20
824	Jason Devereaux	M	Son	4
825	Anna Devereaux	F	Dau	17
826	Abbie Devereaux	F	Dau	8
#827	Henry Bird	M	Sing	22
#828	Henry Devereaux	M	Sing	23
#829	Nellie Schildt	F	Wife	35
830	Joseph Schildt	M	Son	17
831	Harry Schildt	M	Son	16
832	Henry Schildt	M	Son	8
833	Augusta Schildt	F	Dau	7
834	Mary Schildt	F	Dau	6
835	Irene Schildt	F	Dau	4
836	Infant	M	Son	3mo
#839[sic]	Mollie Davlin	F	Wife	28

Census of the [Piegan] Indians of [Blackfeet] Agency, [Montana] taken by United States Indian Agent, , 18

No.	English Name	Sex	Relation	Age
#837	Dick Kipp	M	Father	38
838	Rosa Kipp	F	Wife	29
840	Louis Kipp	M	Son	9
841	George Kipp	M	Son	4
842	Cora Kipp	F	Dau	12
843	Cecelia Kipp	F	Dau	3
844	Infant	F	Dau	3mo
#845	Wm Kipp	M	Father	30
846	Susan Kipp	F	Wife	28
847	Infant	F	Dau	4mo
#838	Bessie Lahr	F	Sing	16
849	Henry Lahr	M	Sing	19
#850	Three Guns	M	Father	32
851	Night Kills	F	Wife	44
852	Agnes Three Guns	F	Dau	3
#853	Fine Kills	F	Wid	80
854	Fred Big Tip	M	Son	20
#855	Two Bears	F	Sing	50
856	Ora Shears	M	Son	28
#857	Wold[sic] Tail	M	Father	43
858	Ivory Woman	F	Wife	30
859	Finding	F	Dau	14
860	Cecile Wolf Tail	F	Dau	7
861	Wolf Speaking	M	Son	5
862	Small Face	F	Dau	5
#863	Two Guns	M	Father	22
864	Taking Good	F	Wife	20
865	Joseph Two Guns	M	Son	2
#866	Xavier Billedeaux	M	Father	41
867	Salina Billedeaux	F	Wife	34
868	Wm Billedeaux	M	Son	12
869	Chas Billedeaux	M	Son	10
870	Weren[sic] Billedeaux	M	Son	8
871	Greely Billedeaux	M	Son	6
872	Mable Catharine Billedeaux	F	Dau	4
873	Salina Billedeaux	F	Dau	2
#874	Dick Lucero	M	Sing	22
#875	James Douglas	M	Father	30
876	Archibald Douglas	M	Son	5
877	Lydia Douglas	F	Dau	3
878	Arthur W Douglas	M	Son	2
#879	Peter Douglas	M	Father	31

Census of the [Piegan] Indians of [Blackfeet] Agency, [Montana] taken by United States Indian Agent, , 18

No.	English Name	Sex	Relation	Age
880	Mollie Douglas	F	Wife	23
881	Edward Douglas	M	Son	2
882	Henry Douglas	M	Son	1
#883	Maggie Goss	F	Wife	45
884	Nellie Goss	F	Dau	19
885	Nathan Goss	M	Son	14
886	George Goss	M	Son	10
887	Albert Goss	M	Son	6
888	Francis Goss	M	Son	4
889	Carrie Goss	F	Dau	16
890	Susa[sic] Goss	F	Dau	14
891	Maggie Goss	F	Dau	11
892	Vina Goss	F	Dau	5mo
#893	Albert Goss	M	Father	27
894	Mary J Goss	F	Wife	25
895	Albert Goss	M	Son	3
896	Mammie Goss	F	Dau	1
#897	Wm Goss	M	Hus	23
898	Maggie Goss	F	Wife	20
#899	Loammie[sic] Goss	M	Sing	21
#900	Frank Bostwick	M	Father	40
901	Louize Bostwick	F	Wife	27
902	Henry Bostwick	M	Son	7
903	George Bostwick	M	Son	5
904	Wm Bostwick	M	Son	3
905	Anna Bostwick	F	Dau	1
#906	John Bostwick	M	Brother	22
#907	Louis Matt	M	Father	22
908	Matchell[sic] Matt	M	Son	18
909	Francis Bostwick	M	Son	4
910	Infant	M	Son	3mo
911	Alice Bostwick	F	Dau	6
912	Lena Bostwick	F	Dau	3
#913	Louize Aubrey	F	Wife	42
914	Alice Aubrey	F	Dau	22
915	Rosa Aubrey	F	Dau	20
916	Laura Aubrey	F	Dau	18
917	Lucy Aubrey	F	Dau	14
918	Dora Aubrey	F	Dau	12
919	May Aubrey	F	Dau	10
920	Janette Aubrey	F	Dau	5
921	Karl Aubrey	M	Son	1

Census of the   [Piegan]   Indians of [Blackfeet] Agency, [Montana]
taken by   United States Indian Agent,   , 18

No.	English Name	Sex	Relation	Age
922	Thos Aubrey	M	Son	17
923	Philip Aubrey	M	Son	8
#924	~~Chas Marceau~~	~~M~~	~~Single~~	~~23~~
#924	Julia Momberg	F	Wife	27
925	L. J. Momberg	M	Son	3
926	Mable Momberg	F	Dau	2
927	Bessie Momberg	F	Dau	4mo
928	Maud Momberg	F	Dau	4mo
#929	Susan Arnoux	F	Wife	48
930	Marian Arnoux	M	Son	18
931	George Arnoux	M	Son	16
932	Monroe Arnoux	M	Son	21
#933	Eliza Galbreath	F	Wife	54
934	Phoebe La Page	F	G Dau	8
935	Webster Galbreath	M	Son	18
~~935~~	~~Jesse Samples~~	~~M~~	~~Son~~	~~26~~
936	Jack Galbreath	M	Son	14
937	Lizzie Galbreath	F	Dau	14
938	Mollie Galbreath	F	Dau	10
#939	Julia Thomas	F	Wife	25
940	George Thomas	M	Son	5
941	Nora Thomas	F	Dau	3
#942	Mollie Davis	F	Wife	26
943	Thos Davis	M	Son	8
944	Bryan Davis	M	Son	4
945	Pearl Davis	F	Dau	6
#946	Eddie Gobert	M	Sing	21
947	Catharine Gobert	F	Sister	17
#948	Josephine Gilham	F	Wife	30
#949	Chas Marceau	M	Sing	23
950	Anthony Gilham	M	Son	10
951	Wm Gilham	M	Son	7
#952	Sallie Allison	F	Wife	27
953	Wm Allison	M	Son	7
954	Lafayette Allison	M	Son	5
956	Winslow Allison	M	Son	4
957	Jas Allison	M	Son	2
958	Anna Allison	F	Dau	6mo
959	Zella Allison	F	Dau	6mo
960	Maggie Allison	F	Dau	13
#961	Mary Cobell	F	Wid	50
962	George Cobell	M	Son	20

Census of the [Piegan] Indians of [Blackfeet] Agency, [Montana]
taken by United States Indian Agent, , 18

No.	English Name	Sex	Relation	Age
963	Joseph Cobell	M	Son	22
964	Thomas Cobell	M	Son	19
964[sic]	John Cobell	M	Son	13
965	Wm Cobell	M	Son	11
966	Bessie Cobell	F	Dau	16
967	Julia Cobell	F	Dau	26
968	Jas Cobell	M	Son	29
#969	Isabelle Stewart	F	Wife	32
970	Agnes Stewart	F	Dau	8
#971	Angelline Connelly	F	Wid	33
972	Mary Connelly	F	Dau	16
973	Rosa Connelly	F	Dau	15
974	Brina Connelly	F	Dau	14
975	Victor Connelly	M	Son	13
976	Johnny Connelly	M	Son	11
#977	Louis Cobell	M	Hus	45
978	Peter Cobell	M	Son	17
979	Clara Cobell	F	Dau	15
980	Jule Cobell	M	Son	6
981	Louize Cobell	F	Dau	4
982	Dewey Cobell	M	Son	2
#983	Stingy	M	Father	56
984	Kills First	F	Wife	54
985	White Skin	M	Son	5
986	Moniac Stingy	M	Son	4
#987	Joseph Brown	M	Father	26
988	Franky Brown	F	Wife	23
989	Wesley Brown	M	Son	2
990	Joseph Brown	M	Son	6mo
#993[sic]	Jesse Samples	M	Sing	26
#991	Henry Main	M	Hus	21
992	Mary Main	F	Wife	20
#994[sic]	Isabelle Main	F	Wife	34
995	Alice Main	F	Dau	7
996	Elizabeth	F	Dau	5
#997	Horrace Clark	M	Single	50
998	John Clark	M	Son	20
#999	Malcolm Clark	M	Hus	23
1000	Ella J. Clark	F	Wife	25
#1001	Thomas Dawson	M	Hus	38
1002	Isabelle Dawson	F	Wife	37
1003	Irene Dawson	F	Adptd Dau	15

Census of the   [Piegan]   Indians of [Blackfeet] Agency, [Montana]
taken by   United States Indian Agent,   , 18

No.	English Name	Sex	Relation	Age
1004	Fred Patterson	M	Neph	7
1005	Oscar Patterson	M	Neph	5
1006	James Dawson	M	Bro	48
#1007	Mary Dunbar	F	Wife	30
1008	Jane Dunbar	F	Dau	12
1009	Andrew Dunbar	M	Son	10
1010	Frankie Dunbar	F	Dau	8
1011	Carrie Dunbar	F	Dau	7
1012	Esther Dunbar	F	Dau	5
1013	James Dunbar	M	Son	2
#1014	Louize Paul	F	Wife	42
1015	Solomon Paul	M	Son	22
1016	Albert Paul	M	Son	20
1017	Philip Paul	M	Son	16
1018	Eddie Paul	M	Son	14
#1019	Oliver Paul	M	Son	10
1020	Wm Paul	M	Son	7
1021	Rosa Paul	F	Dau	12
1022	Salina Paul	F	Dau	5
#1023	Mary Norman	F	Wife	23
1024	Adolph Norman	M	Son	4
1025	Alfred Norman	M	Son	2
1026	Lena Norman	F	Dau	6
#1027	Wm Brown	M	Hus	28
1028	Victoria Brown	F	Wife	22
1029	Sarah A Brown	F	Dau	1
#1030	Sarah Brown	F	Wife	48
1031	Jesse Brown	M	Son	17
1032	Leo Brown	M	Son	3
#1033	Dick Croff	M	Father	30
1034	Maggie Croff	F	Wife	23
1035	Arthur Croff	M	Son	3
1036	Eva Croff	F	Dau	2
#1037	Fred Girard	M	Sing	25
#1038	Chas. Conway	M	Hus	22
1039	Laura Conway	F	Wife	18
#1040	Mrs Cross Guns	F	Wid	45
1041	Willie Conway	M	Son	18
1042	Pressey[sic] Cross Guns	M	Son	3
1043	James Cross Guns	M	Son	2
1044	John Stink Teat	M	Ad-Son	2
#1045	Margaret Schmidt	F	Wife	57

Census of the [Piegan] Indians of [Blackfeet] Agency, [Montana] taken by United States Indian Agent, , 18

No.	English Name	Sex	Relation	Age
1046	Alex Schmidt	M	Son	38
1047	Geo Schmidt	M	Son	22
1048	Karl Schmidt	M	Son	24
1049	Stewart Hazlett	M	Gd-son	17
#1050	George Wren	M	Hus	31
1051	Susie Wren	F	Wife	31
#1052	Frank Marceau	M	Hus	25
1053	Mable Marceau	F	Wife	17
#1054	Mary Lemmon	F	Wife	30
1055	John Lemmon	M	Son	11
1056	Louise Lemmon	F	Dau	8
1057	Emma Lemmon	F	Dau	5
1058	Lee Lemmon	M	Son	3
1059	Maggie Hagen	F	Ad-Dau	15
1060	Sadie Hagen	F	Ad-Dau	2
1061	Albert Murphy	M	Ad-Son	7
1062	Harlem Murphy	M	Ad-Son	10
#1063	Campbell Munroe	M	Hus	33
1064	Frizini Monroe	F	Wife	25
1065	Campbell Munroe	M	Son	3
1066	Isabelle Munroe	F	Dau	2
#1067	Francis Munroe	M	Hus	32
1068	John Munroe	M	Son	2
#1069	James Pambrun	M	Hus	33
1070	Catches On Both Sides	F	Wife	22
1071	Blanche White Calf	[sic]	Ad-Dau	1
#1072	Mary Luken	F	Wife	50
1073	John Luken	M	Son	20
1074	Peter Luken	M	Son	19
#1075	Dora Luken	F	Dau	23
#1076	Mandan Woman	F	Wid	85
#1077	Rosa Upham	F	Single	22
#1078	Emma Upham	F	Wife	38
1079	Katie Upham	F	Dau	17
1080	John Upham	M	Son	10
1081	Myrtle Upham	F	Dau	8
1082	Winifred Upham	F	Dau	1
#1083	Maggie Kennerly	F	Wife	42
1084	Jerome Kennerly	M	Son	11
1085	James Kennerly	M	Son	4
1086	Leo Kennerly	M	Son	1
1087	Annie Kennerly	F	Dau	13

Census of the [Piegan] Indians of [Blackfeet] Agency, [Montana] taken by United States Indian Agent, , 18

No.	English Name	Sex	Relation	Age
1088	Agnes Gobert	F	Dau	14
#1089	Many Cuts	F	Wid	80
#1090	John Kipp	M	Father	39
1091	Calf W. Kipp	F	Wife	39
1092	John Kipp	M	Son	15
1093	Joseph Kipp	M	Son	12
1094	Wm Kipp	M	Son	9
1095	Julia Kipp	F	Dau	5
1096	Sadie Kipp	F	Dau	1
#1097	Malinda Wren	F	Wid	40
1098	John Wren	M	Son	18
1099	Robert Wren	M	Son	15
1100	Wm Wren	M	Son	10
1101	John Chouquette	M	Ad-son	15
1102	Dora Wren	F	Dau	13
1103	Nellie Wren	F	Dau	8
1104	Ida Wren	F	Dau	6
1105	Salina Wren	F	Dau	5
#1106	Matt Lytle	M	Father	27
1107	Katie Lytle	F	Wife	21
1108	Matt Lytle	M	Son	1
#1109	Herman Dusty Bull	M	Father	28
1110	Louise Dusty Bull	F	Wife	18
1111	James Dusty Bull	M	Son	2
#1112	Wm Munroe	M	Father	45
1113	Jennie Munroe	F	Wife	29
1114	Wm Wallace Munroe	M	Son	9
1115	Donald Munroe	M	Son	6
1116	Henry Munroe	M	Son	2
1117	Isabel Munroe	F	Dau	7
#1118	Rosa Ward	F	Wife	36
1119	James Ward	M	Son	8
1120	George Ward	M	Son	7
1121	Wm Ward	M	Son	1
1122	Mary Ward	F	Dau	4
1123	Emma Ward	F	Dau	3
1124	Kate Pias	F	Sing	14
#1125	Eli Guardipee	M	Father	41
1126	Sadie Guardipee	F	Wife	30
1127	Frank Guardipee	M	Son	15
1128	Thos Guardipee	M	Son	20
1129	Chas Guardipee	M	Son	12

Census of the [Piegan] Indians of [Blackfeet] Agency, [Montana] taken by United States Indian Agent, , 18

No.	English Name	Sex	Relation	Age
1130	George Guardipee	M	Son	7
1131	Josephine Guardipee	F	Dau	9
1132	Maggie Guardipee	F	Dau	3
#1133	Went In Herself	F	Wife	40
1134	Louise Rattler	F	Dau	20
#1135	Chas Guardipee	M	Sing	35
#1136	Mary Jackson	F	Wid	26
1137	Thos Jackson	M	Son	14
1138	Minnie Jackson	F	Dau	10
1139	Michael Jackson	M	Son	9
1140	Maggie Jackson	F	Dau	6
1141	Julia Jackson	F	Dau	4
1142	Annie Jackson	F	Dau	2
#1143	Sallie Hagen	F	Wife	30
1144	Infant	F	Dau	1
#1145	Thos Vielle	M	Sing	22
#1146	Emily Fox	F	Wife	64
1147	Eliza Fox	F	Dau	17
#1148	Levi Burd	F	Wife	22
1150	Dorthy Burd	F	Dau	2
1151	Infant	F	Dau	6mo
#1152	Victoria Robinson	F	Wife	40
1153	Joe Robinson	M	Son	18
1154	Louise Robinson	F	Dau	12
1155	Agnes Robinson	F	Dau	1
#1156	Jas Parrine	M	Sing	29
1157	Moniac	F	Mother	65
#1158	Pressley Houk	M	Hus	23
1159	Margaret Houk	F	Wife	17
#1160	Henry Ford	M	Father	40
1161	Adell Ford	F	Dau	16
1162	Florestine Ford	F	Dau	13
1163	Ellen Ford	F	Dau	11
1164	Daniel Ford	M	Son	9
1165	Joseph Ford	M	Son	7
1166	Samuel Ford	M	Son	5
1167	Corbett Ford	M	Son	4
1168	James Ford	M	Son	2
1169	Nelson Ford	M	Son	8mo
#1170	Joseph Ford	M	Father	33
1171	Anna Ford	F	Wife	27
1172	Emiline Ford	F	Dau	7

Census of the   [Piegan]   Indians of [Blackfeet] Agency, [Montana]
taken by   United States Indian Agent,   , 18

No.	English Name	Sex	Relation	Age
1173	Arthur Frd[sic]	M	Son	5
1174	Dewey Ford	M	Son	2
1175	Rosa Ford	F	Dau	1mo
#1176	John Kennedy	M	Father	23
1177	Mary Kennedy	F	Wife	37
1178	Chas Potts	M	Son	9
1179	Willie Kennedy	M	Son	1
#1180	Theresa Pambrun	F	Wife	50
1181	Percy Pambrun	M	Son	19
#1182	Louis Pambrun	M	Father	38
1183	Annie Pambrun	F	Wife	30
1184	Eddie Pambrun	M	Son	14
1185	David Pambrun	M	Son	11
1186	George Pambrun	M	Son	6
1187	Isabella Pambrun	F	Dau	8
1188	Dora Pambrun	F	Dau	2
#1189	Alex Dubrey	M	Father	34
1190	Joseph Dubrey	M	Son	1
1191	George Dubrey	M	Son	4mo
#1192	Augustine Auger	M	Sing	22
#1193	Alex Fox	M	Father	22
1194	Infant Fox	F	Dau	1
#1195	Peter Oscar	M	Sing	32
#1196	Chas Martin	M	Father	35
1197	Ross Martin	M	Son	7
1198	Maud Martin	F	Dau	1
#1199	Joseph Munroe	M	Father	38
1200	Joseph H Munroe	M	Son	2
1201	Mary Munroe	F	Dau	15
1202	Jennie Munroe	F	Dau	12
1203	Eliza Munroe	F	Dau	10
1204	Amelia Munroe	F	Dau	8
1205	Alice Munroe	F	Dau	6
1206	Sarah Munroe	F	Dau	4
#1207	Joe Tatsey	M	Father	37
1208	Annie Tatsey	F	Wife	29
1209	Josephine Tatsey	F	Dau	11
1210	Hattie Tatsey	F	Dau	8
1211	John Tatsey	M	Son	6
1212	Joseph Tatsey	M	Son	4
1213	Elizabeth Tatsey	F	Dau	1
#1214	Susan Tatsey	F	Wid	80

Census of the [Piegan] Indians of [Blackfeet] Agency, [Montana]
taken by United States Indian Agent, , 18

No.	English Name	Sex	Relation	Age
#1215	Martha Kuka	F	Wid	27
1216	Fred Hill	M	Son	9
1217	Daniel Hill	M	Son	6
#1218	Alice Rutherford	F	Sing	20
1219	Wm Rutherford	M	Bro	16
1220	Jas Rutherford	M	Bro	14
1221	Henry Rutherford	M	Bro	12
#1222	Richard Rutherford	M	Father	24
1223	Eliza Rutherford	F	Wife	22
1224	Edna Rutherford	F	Dau	3
1225	George Rutherford	M	Son	1
#1226	Wm Russell	M	Father	46
1227	Mary Russell	F	Wife	41
1228	Geo. Russell	M	Son	15
1229	Joe Russell	M	Son	12
1230	Wm Russell	M	Son	10
1231	Henry Russell	M	Son	3
#1232	Petrified	F	Wid	58
#1233	John Gobert	M	Father	31
1234	Susie Gobert	F	Wife	23
1235	Nellie Gobert	F	Dau	3
1236	Mary Gobert	F	Dau	1
#1237	Green Grass Bull	M	Father	36
1238	Medicine Tie	F	Wife	30
1239	Thos Bull	M	Son	14
#1240	Alfred Trombly	M	Hus	22
1241	Cecelia Trombly	F	Wife	18
#1242	Anna Fisher	F	Wife	28
1243	James Fisher	M	Son	13
1244	Eugine[sic] Fishere[sic]	M	Son	1
#1245	Joe McKnight	M	Father	26
1246	Lucy McKnight	F	Wife	23
1247	Irene McKnight	F	Dau	4
1248	Aaron McKnight	M	Son	1
#1249	Last Coyote	M	Sing	45
#1250	Likes Marrow Bones	M	Hus	50
1251	Maggie Marrow Bones	F	Wife	60
#1252	Yells In The Water	M	Father	26
1253	Mary Yells In the Water	F	Wife	25
1254	John Yells In the Water	M	Son	5
1255	George Yells In the Water	M	Son	2
#1256	The Bite	M	Father	45

Census of the [Piegan] Indians of [Blackfeet] Agency, [Montana]
taken by United States Indian Agent, , 18

No.	English Name	Sex	Relation	Age
1257	Kills for Nothing	F	Wife	42
1258	Wolf Bite	M	Son	15
1259	Minnie Bite	F	Dau	7
1260	John Bite	M	Son	3
1261	Lucy Bite	F	Dau	1
#1262	Curley Bear	M	Father	48
1263	Minnie Bear	F	Wife	35
1264	Mary Bear	F	Wife	33
1265	Chas Bear	M	Son	19
1266	Wm Bear	M	Son	5
1267	Jennie Bear	F	Dau	8
1268	Annie Bear	F	Dau	4
1269	Frank Bear	M	Son	3
#1270	David La Breeche[sic]	M	Father	26
1271	Minnie La Breech	F	Wife	26
1272	Chas La Breech	M	Son	5
~~1273~~	~~Viola La Breech~~	~~F~~	~~Dau~~	~~1~~
1274	Clarence La Breech	M	Son	3
#1275	Millie La Breech	F	Wife	52
1276	Chas La Breech	M	Son	30
1277	Philip La Breech	M	Son	14
1278	Laura La Breech	F	Dau	20
1279	Millie La Breech	F	Dau	18
1280	Jessie La Breech	F	Dau	16
#1281	Madore La Breech	M	Sing	23
#1282	Buffalo Growing	M	Hus	40
1283	Seal Woman	F	Wife	38
#1284	Frank Calf Robe	M	Hus	28
1285	Minnie Calf Robe	F	Wife	32
#1286	Mary Teasdale	F	Moth	64
1287	Annie Teasdale	F	Dau	10
#1288	Old Coyote	M	Father	33
1289	Mary Coyote	F	Wife	47
1290	Philip Coyote	M	Son	19
#1291	Calf Woman	F	Wid	86
#1292	Eagle	M	Hus	33
1293	Medicine Beaver	F	Wife	28
1294	Wm Eagle	F[sic]	Ad-Dau	4
#1295	Black Face	F	Wid	51
1296	Chas. Weasel Head	M	Ad-son	14
#1297	Under Otter	F	Wid	65
#1298	Craning Woman	F	Wid	68

Census of the [Piegan] Indians of [Blackfeet] Agency, [Montana] taken by United States Indian Agent, , 18

No.	English Name	Sex	Relation	Age
#1299	Black Face	F	Wid	64
1300	Henry Black Face	M	Son	11
#1301	White Dog	M	Hus	49
1302	Medicine Ripe Woman	F	Wife	26
#1303	Boy Chief	M	Father	38
1304	Last Gun	F	Wife	25
1305	Dennie Boy Chief	M	Son	11
1306	Wm Boy Chief	M	Son	8
1307	Annie Boy Chief	F	Dau	14
1308	Emma Boy Chief	F	Dau	5
1309	Susie Boy Chief	F	Dau	1
#1310	Calf Looking	M	Father	56
1311	Rising Sun	F	Wife	65
1312	Paul Calf Looking	M	Son	22
#1313	Charges Both Sides	F	Wid	70
1314	Savage Wolf	M	Ad-son	11
#1315	Flint Smoke	M	Father	39
1316	Minnie Flint Smoke	F	Wife	35
1317	Peter Flint Smokes	M	Son	20
1318	Jas Flint Smoker	M	Son	9
#1319	Matilda Iron Crow	F	Sing	16
1320	Isabella Iron Crow	F	Sis	13
#1321	Iron Eater	M	Father	46
1322	Blanket Woman	F	Wife	37
1323	Owl Face	F	Wife	35
1324	Susie Iron Eater	F	Dau	14
1325	Rosa Iron Eater	F	Dau	4
1326	Maggie Iron Eater	F	Dau	8
1327	Jennie Iron Eater	F	Dau	1
#1328	Medicine Bull	M	Father	38
1329	Sore Back	F	Wife	32
1330	Thos M. Bull	M	Son	4
1331	Josephine Bull	F	Dau	1
#1332	Morning Gun	M	Father	46
1333	Otter Woman	F	Wife	20
1334	Joe M Gun	M	Son	8
1335	Thos M Gun	M	Son	12
1336	Minnie M Gun	F	Dau	5
1337	Chas M Gun	M	Son	1
1338	Brier	F	Dau	4
#1339	Ellen Edwards	F	Wife	30
1340	Wm Edwards	M	Son	11

Census of the [Piegan] Indians of [Blackfeet] Agency, [Montana]
taken by United States Indian Agent, , 18

No.	English Name	Sex	Relation	Age
1341	Thos Edwards	M	Son	9
1342	Fanny Edwards	F	Dau	7
1343	Elizabeth Edwards	F	Dau	5
1344	John Edwards	M	Son	3
1345	Rosa Edwards	F	Dau	2
#1346	John Croff	M	Hus	27
1347	Louize Croff	F	Wife	27
1348	Edward Croff	M	Neph	8
#1349	Wm Croff	M	Sing	26
#1350	Night Gun	M	Father	28
1351	Stella Night Gun	F	Wife	17
1352	John Night Gun	N	Son	1
1353	Strikes Edge	F	Moth	60
#1354	Eagle Flag	M	Father	65
1355	Bounces Up	F	Wife	63
1356	Anna Eagle Flag	F	Dau	12
1357	Percy Eagle Flag	M	Son	13
#1358	Henry No Bear	M	Father	33
1359	Sure Woman	F	Wife	27
1360	Thos No Bear	M	Son	4
1361	Rosa No Bear	F	Dau	2
#1362	Maggie Henault	F	Wife	49
1363	Nelson Henault	M	Son	21
1364	Moses Henault	M	Son	13
1365	Clara Henault	F	Dau	11
#1366	Thos Two Stabs	M	Father	42
1367	Maggie Two Stabs	F	Wife	34
1368	Joseph Two Stabs	M	Son	8
1369	Louis Two Stabs	M	Son	4
1370	Louize Two Stabs	F	Dau	3
#1371	Richard Sanderville	M	Father	33
1372	Nancy Sanderville	F	Wife	25
1373	Bridges Sanderville	F	Dau	2
1374	Agnes Sanderville	F	Dau	11
#1375	Oliver Sanderville	M	Father	41
1376	Mary Sanderville	F	Wife	32
1377	John Sanderville	M	Son	13
#1378	Louis Trombly	M	Father	30
1379	Maggie Trombly	F	Wife	28
1380	Isaac Trombly	M	Son	5
1381	Joseph Trombly	M	Son	3
1382	George Trombly	M	Son	2

Census of the [Piegan] Indians of [Blackfeet] Agency, [Montana] taken by United States Indian Agent, , 18

No.	English Name	Sex	Relation	Age
#1383	Thos Kyo	M	Father	40
1384	Mary Kyo	F	Wife	36
1385	Wm Kyo	M	Son	5
1386	Nellie Kyo	F	Dau	1
#1387	Isabella Trombly	F	Wid	67
#1388	Eddie Running Crane	M	Father	26
1389	Nellie Running Crane	F	Wife	21
1390	Peter Running Crane	M	Son	3
1391	Paul Running Crane	M	Son	1
#1392	Running Crane	F	Wid	50
1393	Jas Running Crane	M	Son	10
#1394	Little Otter	F	Wid	75
#1395	Running Crane #1	M	Hus	80
1396	White Woman	F	Wife	60
#1397	Wades In the Water	M	Hus	30
1398	Lucy Wades In the Water	F	Wife	23
#1399	Spotted Eagle	M	Father	55
1400	Gives Back	F	Wife	23
1401	Jas Spotted Eagle	M	Son	22
1402	John Spotted Eagle	M	Son	13
1403	George Spotted Eagle	M	Son	7
#1404	Thos Spotted Eagle	M	Sing	24
#1405	Sure Chief	M	Father	32
1406	Bird Wing	F	Wife	29
1407	Willie Sure Chief	M	Son	5
1408	Gray Whiskers	M	Son	3
1409	Geo. Sure Chief	M	Son	1
#1410	The Horn	M	Father	70
1411	Good Looking	F	Wife	60
1412	Under Chicken	F	Wife	50
#1413	Louise Tingley	F	Moth	49
1414	John Tingley	M	Son	33
1415	Oliver Tingley	M	Son	31
1416	Robert Tingley	M	Son	29
1417	Elizabeth Tingley	F	Dau	25
1418	Mose Tingley	M	Son	20
1419	Daniel Tingley	M	Son	15
1420	Harry Horn	M	Son	16
#1421	Albert Mad Plume	M	Father	26
1422	Susie Mad Plume	F	Wife	24
1423	Joseph Mad Plume	M	Son	3
1424	Maggie Mad Plume	F	Dau	4

Census of the   [Piegan]   Indians of [Blackfeet] Agency, [Montana]
taken by   United States Indian Agent,   , 18

No.	English Name	Sex	Relation	Age
1425	Mollie Mad Plume	F	Dau	1
#1426	Red Fox	M	Father	28
1427	Good Kill	F	Wife	22
1428	Chas Fox	M	Son	4
1429	Jas Fox	M	Son	3
1430	Peter Fox	M	Son	1
#1431	No Coat	M	Father	39
1432	Kills for Nothing	F	Wife	32
1433	Annie No Coat	F	Dau	7
#1434	Chas No Coat	M	Sing	22
#1435	Good Strikes	F	Wife	50
1436	Esther Running Rabbit	M[sic]	Son	19
1437	Katie Running Rabbit	M[sic]	Son	7
1438	Mary Running Rabbit	F	Dau	1
#1439	Chas Under Bull	M	Sing	15
1440	Strikes Back	F	Moth	30
#1441	Almost Killed	F	Wid	70
#1442	Spotted Head	F	Wid	65
#1443	War Bonnet	M	Father	40
1444	Susie War Bonnet	F	Wife	30
1445	Jas War Bonnet	M	Son	4
1446	Thos War Bonnet	M	Son	1
#1447	Frank Rider	M	Hus	34
1448	Maggie Rider	F	Wife	17
#1449	Going to Move	M	Hus	48
1450	Jas G.T. Move	M	Son	22
#1451	Felix Marroe[sic] Bones	M	Father	29
1452	Fannie Marrow Bones	F	Wife	18
1453	Lucy Marrow Bones	F	Dau	1
#1454	Every Body Looks At	F	Moth	50
1455	Annie Looks At	F	Dau	7
#1456	Peter Spotted Bear	M	Father	20
1457	Annie Spotted Bera[sic]	F	Wife	17
1458	Rosa Spotted Bera	F	Dau	2
#1459	Spotted Bear	M	Father	80
1460	Tooth Woman	F	Wife	40
1461	John Spotted Bear	M	Son	6
#1462	Takes Iron Gun	F	Moth	75
1463	Lucy Takes Iron Gun	F	Dau	16
#1464	Mittens	M	Father	30
1465	Strikes Close	F	Wife	27
1466	Jas Mittens	M	Son	6

Census of the [Piegan] Indians of [Blackfeet] Agency, [Montana]
taken by   United States Indian Agent,   , 18

No.	English Name	Sex	Relation	Age
1467	John Mittens	M	Son	4
1468	Anna Mittens	F	Dau	8
1469	Minnie Mittens	F	Dau	2
#1470	Frank Dunovon	M	Hus	22
1471	Jennie Dunovon	F	Wife	16
1472	Double Hid	F	G-moth	50
#1473	Geo Eats Alone	M	Sing	21
#1474	Jack Big Moon	M	Hus	40
1475	Long Time Calf	F	Wife	39
#1476	Paul Austin	M	Father	33
1477	Jennie Austin	F	Wife	30
1478	Jas Austin	M	Son	1
1479	Agnes Austin	F	Dau	5
1480	Annie Austin	F	Dau	4
#1481	Pete Guardipee	M	Sing	40
#1482	Louize Guardipee	F	Moth	60
1483	John Guardipee	M	Son	19
#1484	Painted Wings	M	Father	78
1485	Hits On Top	F	Wife	54
1486	Little Star	M	Son	21
1487	Susie P Wings	F	Dau	11
#1488	Elmer Butter Fly	M	Father	26
1489	Long Time Chicken	F	Wife	20
1490	Joe Butter Fly	M	Son	5
1491	John Butter Fly	M	Son	1
1492	Snake Woman	F	Dau	4
#1493	Medicine Stab	M	Hus	40
1494	Slim Woman	F	Wife	35
#1495	Cree Medicine	M	Father	38
1496	Medicine Woman	F	Wife	36
1497	Maggie Bear Chief	F	Dau	10
#1498	Wild Gun	M	Hus	39
1499	Big Tiger	F	Wife	45
1500	Julia Wild Gun	F	Ad-dau	1
#1501	Calf Tail	M	Father	43
1502	Different Gun	F	Wife	46
1503	Ernest Calf Tail	M	Son	13
1504	John Calf Tail	M	Son	22
#1505	Swims Under	M	Hus	30
1506	Maggie Swims Under	F	Wife	17
#1507	Owl Child	M	Father	45
1508	Mollie Owl Child	F	Wife	33

Census of the [Piegan] Indians of [Blackfeet] Agency, [Montana] taken by United States Indian Agent, , 18

No.	English Name	Sex	Relation	Age
1509	John Owl Child	M	Son	17
1510	Joe Owl Child	M	Son	10
1511	Louis Owl Child	M	Son	6
1512	Wm Owl Child	M	Son	2
1513	Susie Owl Child	F	Dau	19
1514	Isabella Owl Child	F	Dau	11
1515	Anna Owl Child	F	Dau	5
#1516	Gambler	M	Father	45
1517	Annie Gambler	F	Wife	58
1518	Jennie Gambler	F	Dau	3
#1519	Geo Choat	N	Hus	24
1520	Fannie Choat	F	Wife	21
#1521	Fine Bull	M	Father	45
1522	Scattered Woman	F	Wife	32
1523	Stabbing	M	Son	12
1524	Jas Fine Bull	M	Son	4
1525	Yellow Spider	F	Dau	8
1526	Lucy Fine Bull	F	Dau	5
1527	Maggie Fine Bull	F	Dau	1
#1528	John White Calf	M	Father	36
1529	Weasel Tail Woman	F	Wife	30
1530	Anna White Calf	F	Dau	14
1531	Josephine White Calf	F	Dau	1
#1532	Alex Guardipee	M	Father	38
1533	Grass Snake	F	Wife	25
1534	John Guardipee	M	Son	5
#1535	Young Running Rabbit	M	Father	52
1536	Long Time Woman	F	Wife	30
1537	Julia Running Rabbit	F	Dau	14
#1538	Young Running Crane	M	Father	46
1539	Petrified Stone	F	Wife	48
#1540	John Running Crane	M	Son	16
1541	Josephine Running Crane	F	Dau	4
#1542	Lone Cut	F	Wid	80
#1543	Jas Gambler	M	Father	26
1544	Annie Gambler	F	Wife	23
1545	Mary Gambler	F	Dau	2
#1546	Mrs Bob Tail Horse	F	Wid	43
1547	Joe Bob Tail Horse	M	Son	19
#1548	Henry Head Carrier	M	Father	36
1549	Good Kill	F	Wife	46
1550	Goes In Both	F	Dau	5

Census of the [Piegan] Indians of [Blackfeet] Agency, [Montana] taken by United States Indian Agent, , 18

No.	English Name	Sex	Relation	Age
#1551	Last Strikes	F	Wid	55
#1552	Four Horns	M	Father	42
1553	Short Woman	F	Wife	40
1554	Benjamin Four Horns	M	Son	20
1555	Jas Four Horns	M	Son	7
#1556	George Four Horns	M	Son	21
1557	Kills Close	F	Moth	60
#1558	Eagle Head	M	Father	67
1559	White Tail	F	Wife	54
1560	Margaret Eagle Head	F	Dau	10
1561	Jas Eagle Head	M	Son	14
#1562	Singing	F	Wid	76
1563	Frank Jackson	M	Ad-son	7
#1564	Bouble[sic] B Jackson	M	Father	40
1565	Lucy Jackson	F	Wife	38
1566	Joseph Jackson	M	Son	19
1567	Louis Jackson	M	Son	4
1568	Dick Jackson	M	Son	3
#1569	Big Beaver	M	Father	39
1570	Annie Beaver	F	Wife	31
1571	Eddie Beaver	M	Son	16
1572	Aaron Beaver	M	Son	14
1573	George Beaver	M	Son	1
1574	Rosa Beaver	F	Dau	5
#1575	Oliver Racine	M	Father	21
1576	Belle Racine	F	Wife	19
1577	Joseph Racine	M	Son	1
#1578	Owl Top	M	Father	42
1579	Buckskin Horse	F	Wife	35
1580	Mary Snow	F	Ad-dau	18
1581	Mable Owl Top	F	Dau	11
#1582	Poor Woman	F	Wid	70
#1583	Old Lone Cut	F	Wid	65
#1584	Catches First	F	Wid	70
#1585	Bull Shoe	M	Father	55
1586	Small Woman	F	Wife	42
1587	Dirty Face	F	Wife	31
1588	Pat Bull Shoe	M	Son	13
1589	Different Woman	F	Ad-dau	6
#1590	Joe Bull Shoe	M	Sin	21
#1591	Chewing Black Bones	M	Father	34
1592	Mary Chewing Black Bones	F	Wife	31

Census of the   [Piegan]   Indians of [Blackfeet] Agency, [Montana]
taken by   United States Indian Agent,   , 18

No.	English Name	Sex	Relation	Age
1593	John Chewing Black Bones	M	Son	13
1594	Isabelle Chewing Black Bones	F	Dau	11
1595	Agnes Chewing Black Bones	F	Dau	9
1596	Mary Chewing Black Bones	F	Dau	7
1597	Maggie Chewing Black Bones	F	Dau	6
#1598	Chewing Black Bones	F	G-moth	60
1599	Isabelle Black Bones	F	G-dau	12
1600	Cecil Black Bones	D	G-dau	8
#1601	White Man	M	Father	59
1602	Kills Plenty	F	Wife	35
1603	Sweet Grass	F	Wife	30
1604	Peter White Man	M	Son	15
1605	John White Man	M	Son	20
1606	Jas White Man	M	Son	2
#1607	Catches Edge Water	F	Wid	80
#1608	Long Time Rock	M	Father	33
1609	Nellie Time Rock	F	Wife	24
1610	George Time Rock	M	Son	3
1611	Jas Time Rock	M	Son	1
#1612	Comes In Night	M	Father	40
1613	Elk Robe	F	Wife	31
1614	Charges	F	Wife	21
1615	James Comes In Night	M	Son	1
1616	Cecil Comes In Night	F	Dau	8
1617	Minnie Comes In Night	F	Dau	6
1618	Julia Comes In Night	F	Dau	2
#1619	Kills In the Brush	F	Wid	67
#1620	Iron Necklace	M	Father	42
1621	Kills Inside	F	Wife	35
1622	Anna Iron Necklace	F	Dau	8
#1623	Big Snake	M	Father	70
1624	Black Bird	F	Wife	46
1625	Petrified Stone	M	Son	1
1626	Briar Woman	F	Dau	3
#1637	Strikes Back	F	Wid	50
#1628	Cold Feet	M	Hus	52
1629	Goods Woman	F	Wife	40
#1630	John Pepion	F	Hus	30
1631	Cecil Pepion	F	Wife	29
#1632	Cecil Pepion	F	Sing	26
#1633	Big Wolf Medicine	M	Father	33
1634	Good Clean Up	F	Wife	37

Census of the   [Piegan]   Indians of [Blackfeet] Agency, [Montana]
taken by   United States Indian Agent,   , 18

No.	English Name	Sex	Relation	Age
1635	Ellen Big Wolf Medicine	F	Dau	10
#1636	Jessie Pepion	F	Moth	28
1637	Thos Pepion	M	Son	5
1638	Louis Pepion	M	Son	3
1639	Victor Pepion	M	Son	1
#1640	Frank Pepion	M	Sing	20
1641	Chester Pepion	M	Bro	17
1642	Louise Pepion	F	Sis	23
#1643	Flat Tail	M	Father	50
1644	Medicine Pipe Woman	F	Wife	31
1645	Sophia F. Tail	F	Dau	5
1646	Mollie F Tail	F	Dau	1
#1647	Philip Flat Tail	M	Father	21
1648	Nellie Flat Tail	F	Wife	20
1649	John Flat Tail	M	Son	1
#1650	Harry No Chier[sic]	M	Hus	28
1651	Big Stone	F	Wife	16
#1652	Joseph Spanish	M	Hus	27
1653	Margaret Spanish	F	Wife	35
1654	Agnes Clark	F	Dau	15
1655	Wm Clark	F	Wid	70
#1656	Chas Iron Breast	M	Father	22
1657	Different Woman	F	Wife	28
1658	Ellen Iron Breast	F	Dau	1
1659	Mrs Night Rider	F	Wid	50
#1660	George Prairie Chicken	M	Father	27
1661	Hannah P Chicken	F	Wife	22
1662	Thos P Chicken	M	Son	2
1663	Cecil P Chicken	F	Dau	4
#1664	Chicken Shoe	M	Father	27
1665	Medicine Star	F	Wife	32
1666	Frank C Shoe	M	Son	2
1668	Maggie C Shoe	F	Dau	4
#1669	Mike Day Rider	M	Father	29
1670	Hellen Day Rider	F	Wife	21
1671	Oliver Day Rider	M	Son	5
1672	George Day Rider	M	Son	3
1673	Jack Day Rider	M	Son	1
#1674	Peter Old Rock	M	Hus	25
1675	Rosa Old Rock	F	Wife	17
#1676	Tail Feathers	M	Father	48
1677	Petrified Stone	F	Wife	30

Census of the [Piegan] Indians of [Blackfeet] Agency, [Montana] taken by United States Indian Agent, , 18

No.	English Name	Sex	Relation	Age
1678	Wm Tail Feathers	M	Son	11
1679	Chas Tail Feathers	M	Son	10
1680	Peter Tail Feathers	M	Son	4
1681	Wm Tail Feathers	M	Son	3
#1682	Aims Back	M	Father	28
1683	Emma Aims Back	F	Wife	24
1684	Thos Aims Back	M	Son	6
1685	Mary Aims Back	F	Dau	1
#1686	Adam White Man	M	Hus	26
1687	Annie White Man	F	Wife	22
#1688	Mrs Pete Champite[sic]	F	Wid	30
1689	George Champine	M	Son	8
1690	Peter Champine	M	Son	1
1691	Maggie Champine	F	Dau	5
#1692	Josephine Sullivan	F	Wid	23
#1693	Good Strike	F	Wid	80
#1693[sic]	Duck Head	M	Father	36
1694	Elizabeth Duck Head	F	Wife	29
1695	Peter Duck Head	M	Son	9
1696	Josephine Duck Head	F	Dau	13
1697	Mary Duck Head	F	Dau	4
1698	Louise Duck Head	F	Dau	1
#1699	Tail Feathers Coming	M	Father	53
1700	Mollie Tail Feathers Coming	F	Wife	32
1701	Cecil Tail Feathers Coming	F	Dau	14
1702	Susie Tail Feathers Coming	F	Dau	5
1703	Mary Tail Feathers Coming	F	Dau	4
#1704	Wins Many Guns	F	Wid	51
1705	Mary Tail Feathers Coming	F	G-dau	7
#1706	Paul	F	orphan	7
#1707	Black Boy	F	Wid	43
1708	Ruben Black Boy	M	Son	13
#1709	Susan Schultz	F	Wife	36
1710	Hart Schultz	M	Son	17
#1711	Weasel Head	M	Father	37
1712	Mary Head	F	Wife	48
1713	Isaac Weipert	M	Son	23
1714	Peter Weasel Head	M	Son	11
1715	John Weasel Head	M	Son	10
1716	Thos Weasel Head	M	Son	4
1717	Mary Weasel Head	F	Dau	16
1718	Lizzie Weasel Head	F	Dau	9

Census of the [Piegan] Indians of [Blackfeet] Agency, [Montana] taken by United States Indian Agent, , 18

No.	English Name	Sex	Relation	Age
1719	John Weasel Head	M	Son	6
#1720	Maggie Albertson	F	Wife	44
1721	Arthur Albertson	M	Son	21
1722	Robert Albertson	M	Son	11
1723	Mary Albertson	F	Dau	5
1724	Julia Albertson	F	Dau	2
#1725	Calf Boss Ribs	M	Hus	58
1726	Medicine Lodge	F	Wife	53
1727	Joe Calf Boss Ribs	M	Son	4
1728	Minnie Calf Boss Ribs	F	Dau	7
#1729	Barney Calf Boss Ribs	M	Hus	26
1730	Mary Calf Boss Ribs	F	Wife	16
#1731	Able Skunk Cap	M	Sing	25
1732	Strikes Last	F	Moth	58
#1733	Young Mountain Chief	M	Hus	41
1734	Cecil Y.M. Chief	F	Wife	29
#1735	New Robe	M	Father	46
1736	Yells In the Water	F	Wife	36
1737	Short Nose	F	Wife	55
1738	Chas New Robe	M	Son	16
#1739	Tearing Lodge	M	Hus	61
1740	Lone Cut	F	Wife	53
#1741	Wakes Up last	M	Father	34
1742	Mollie Wakes Up Last	F	Wife	21
1743	Stephen Wakes Up Last	M	Bro	26
1744	Pretty Fly	F	Dau	2
1745	Julia Wakes Up Last	F	Dau	1
#1746	Sam Randall	M	Sing	27
#1747	Harry Face	M	Father	40
1748	Susie Face	F	Wife	30
1749	Glass Woman	F	Wife	28
1750	John H Face	M	Son	5
1751	Cecil H Face	F	Dau	14
1752	Jas H Face	M	Son	3
1753	Jennie H Face	F	Dau	1
#1754	After Buffalo	M	Wife	48
1755	Daisy After Buffalo	F	Wife	27
1756	Joe After Buffalo	M	Son	6
1757	Chas After Buffalo	M	Son	3
1758	Louise After Buffalo	F	Dau	1
#1759	No Runner	M	Hus	51
1760	White Woman	F	Wife	60

Census of the [Piegan] Indians of [Blackfeet] Agency, [Montana]
taken by United States Indian Agent, , 18

No.	English Name	Sex	Relation	Age
#1761	Kidney	M	Father	30
1762	Mary Kidney	F	Wife	23
1763	John Kidney	M	Son	2
#1764	Many Guns	M	Father	37
1765	Josephine Many Guns	F	Wife	18
1766	Jas Many Guns	M	Son	1
#1767	Little Dog	M	Father	45
1768	Wades In	F	Wife	19
1769	Harrison L Dog	M	Son	14
1770	Mary Little Dog	F	Dau	2
#1771	Long Time Woman	F	Wid	55
#1772	Rattler	M	Father	67
1773	Spear Woman	F	Wife	45
1774	Elmer Rattler	M	Son	26
#1775	Mad Plume	M	Father	56
1776	Kills In Night	F	Wife	43
1777	Richard Mad Plume	M	Son	15
1778	George Mad Plume	M	Son	6
1779	Mike Mad Plume	M	Son	5
1780	John Mad Plume	M	Son	3
1781	Julia Mad Plume	F	Dau	13
#1782	Wolf Eagle	M	Hus	48
1783	Blanket Woman	F	Wife	42
1784	Kills In Night	F	Wife	30
#1785	Fish	M	Father	24
1786	Lone Rock	F	Wife	22
1787	Joseph Fish	M	Son	1
#1788	Fisher	F	Wid	70
#1789	Joe Calf Robe	M	Father	28
1790	Annie Calf Robe	F	Wife	26
1791	Mink	M	Son	1
#1792	Albert Calf Robe	M	Son	19
1793	Bad Woman	F	Moth	48
#1794	Fast Buffalo Horse	F	Moth	45
1795	Joe Fast Buffalo Horse	M	Son	23
1796	Albert Fast Buffalo Horse	M	Son	22
1797	Jas Fast Buffalo Horse	M	Son	11
#1798	Alex Marceau	M	Father	36
1799	Theresa Marceau	F	Wife	25
1800	Louise Marceau	F	Dau	7
1801	Annie Marceau	F	Dau	3
1802	Agnes Marceau	F	Dau	1

Census of the   [Piegan]   Indians of [Blackfeet] Agency, [Montana]
taken by   United States Indian Agent,   , 18

No.	English Name	Sex	Relation	Age
#1803	Louis Marceau	M	Hus	33
1804	Rosa Marceau	F	Wife	24
#1805	Blackfoot Woman	F	Moth	50
1806	John Big Lake	M	Son	20
1807	Mike Blackfoot Woman	M	Son	21
1808	Mary Blackfoot Woman	F	Dau	8
#1809	Good Stabbing	M	Hus	33
1810	Medicine Woman	F	Wife	35
#1811	Wolf Medicine	M	Father	40
1812	First Strike	F	Wife	31
1813	Wesley Wolf Plume	S	Son	13
#1814	Good Strike	F	Wid	80
#1815	Richard Calf Robe	M	Hus	26
1816	Annie Calf Robe	F	Wife	24
1817	First Strike	F	Moth	45
#1818	Iron Pipe	M	Father	41
1819	Both Goes In	F	Wife	33
1820	Joe Iron Pipe	M	Son	13
1821	Chas Iron Pipe	M	Son	5
1822	Jas Iron Pipe	M	Son	3
1823	Joe P Iron Pipe	M	Son	1
1824	Maggie Iron Pipe	F	Dau	11
#1825	Red Horn	M	Wid	59
#1826	Short Face	M	Sing	29
1827	Double Strike	F	Moth	61
#1828	Crow Eyes	M	Father	42
1829	Running Rattler	F	Wife	24
1830	Takes Gun	M	Son	5
1831	Annie Crow Eyes	F	Dau	2
#1832	Big Crow	M	Father	42
1833	Maggie Big Crow	F	Wife	30
1834	Cecil Big Crow	F	Dau	12
#1835	Joe Wall	M	Wdr	47
#1836	Spotted Bear #2	M	Father	42
1837	Jas Spotted Bear	M	Son	9
1838	Minnie Spotted Bear	F	Dau	10
#1839	Pete Spotted Bear #2	F	moth	58
1840	Josephine Marceau	F	Dau	14
#1841	Frank Vielle	M	Father	30
1842	Susie Vielle	F	Wife	26
1843	Jack Vielle	M	Son	5
1844	Jos Vielle	M	Son	2

Census of the   [Piegan]   Indians of [Blackfeet] Agency, [Montana]
taken by   United States Indian Agent,   , 18

No.	English Name	Sex	Relation	Age
#1845	Mrs Eddie Jack	F	Wid	34
1846	John Two Guns	M	Son	18
1847	Eddy Jack	M	Son	1
1848	Minnie Jack	F	Dau	5
1849	Cecil Jack	F	Dau	11
1850	Maggie Two Guns	F	Dau	11
#1851	Lone Wolverine	F	Wid	65
#1852	White Quiver	M	Father	39
1853	Minnie Quiver	F	Wife	39
1854	Benj. Quiver	M	Son	16
1855	Josephine Quiver	F	Dau	3
1856	Maggie Quiver	F	Dau	9
#1857	Joe Evans	M	Father	27
1858	Mary C Evans	F	Wife	20
1859	Jas Evans	M	Son	4
1860	Irene Evans	F	Dau	1
#1861	Bad Old Man	M	Father	65
1862	Annie Bad Old Man	F	Wife	53
1863	Mike Bad Old Man	M	Son	18
#1864	Bear Shoe	M	Father	38
1865	Daisy Bear Shoe	F	Wife	17
1866	Katie Bear Shoe	F	Dau	2
#1867	Big Lodge Pole	M	Father	39
1868	Mary Big Lodge Pole	F	Wife	50
1869	Sam Choat	M	Son	22
1870	Peter Lodge Pole	M	Son	15
#1871	Ellen McMullen	F	Wife	18
#1874	Mary Phemister	F	Moth	43
1872	George Phemister	M	son	12
#1873	Frank Choat	M	Father	27
1874	Jennie Choat	F	Wife	35
1875	Mary Choat	F	Dau	1
1876	Jas Choat	M	Son	5
#1877	Chas Rose	M	Father	40
1878	Agnes Rose	F	Wife	30
1879	Jas Rose	M	Son	6
1880	Wm Rose	M	Son	7
1881	Alice Rose	F	Dau	8
1882	Julia Rose	F	Dau	10
1883	Maggie Rose	F	Dau	18
1884	Susie Rose	F	Dau	3
1885	Jennie Rose	F	Dau	1

Census of the [Piegan] Indians of [Blackfeet] Agency, [Montana] taken by United States Indian Agent, , 18

No.	English Name	Sex	Relation	Age
#1886	Louise Higgins	F	Wife	45
1887	Emma Croff	F	Dau	20
1888	Alice Higgins	F	Dau	10
1889	Henry Higgins	M	Son	15
#1890	Minnie Crawford	F	Wife	33
1891	Jas Crawford	M	Son	1
1892	Ellen Crawford	F	Dau	4
1893	Emma Crawford	F	Dau	8
1894	Joe Crawford	M	Son	3
#1895	Belle Ripley	F	Wife	44
#1896	Minnie Ripley	F	Wife	16
1897	Peter Ripley	M	Son	1
#1898	Henry Heavy Gun	M	Father	29
1899	Mary Heavy Gun	F	Wife	30
1900	Jack Heavy Gun	M	Son	1
1901	Arthur Heavy Gun	M	Son	1
#1902	Mary Hazlett	F	Moth	21
1903	Gulder Hazlett	M	Son	1
#1904	Philamon St Goddard	F	Wife	30
1905	Agnes St Goddard	F	Dau	10
#1906	Lena St Goddard	F	Dau	5
1907	Archie St Goddard	M	Son	1
#1908	Chas Juno	M	Sing	24
#1909	Kicking Woman	M	Hus	50
1910	Looks Last	F	Wife	50
1911	Dan Pias	M	Sing	12
#1912	Heavy Gun	M	Hus	44
1913	Good Woman	F	Wife	33
1914	Goes In Last	F	Wife	29
#1915	Garrett White	M	Hus	24
#1916	Chief All Over	M	Father	48
1917	Medicine Stone	F	Wife	42
1918	Geo Chief All Over	M	Son	10
#1919	Many Guns	M	Father	39
1920	Mouse Woman	F	Wife	42
1921	Thos Many Guns	M	Son	5
#1922	Shoots One Another	M	Father	36
1923	Mary Shoots Another	F	Wife	44
1924	Joe Shoots Another	M	Son	16
1925	Josephine Weatherwax	F	Dau	20
1926	Jennie Shoots Another	F	Dau	1
#1927	Long Time Sleeping	M	Father	31

Census of the [Piegan] Indians of [Blackfeet] Agency, [Montana]
taken by United States Indian Agent, , 18

No.	English Name	Sex	Relation	Age
1928	Calls Buck	F	Wife	32
1929	Joe Long Time Sleeping	M	Son	7
1930	Wm Long Time Sleeping	M	Son	3
1931	Good Catch	F	Dau	5
1932	Mary Long Time Sleeping	F	Dau	1
#1933	Hits On Top	F	Wid	50
#1934	Dan Lone Chief #2	F	Wid	56
#1935	Black Bull	M	Hus	32
1936	Dress Woman	F	Wife	48
1937	Good Steal	F	Dau	2
#1938	Lawrence Faber	M	Father	26
1939	Annie Faber	F	Wife	22
1940	Mary Faber	F	Dau	1
#1941	Small Face	M	Wid	50
1942	Hellen Faber	F	Adp-dau	3
#1943	Day Rider	M	Father	25
1944	Mollie Rider	F	Wife	31
1945	Joe Rider	M	Son	4
1946	Morning Owl	F	Dau	2
1947	George Day Rider	M	Son	8
1948	Cecil Day Rider	F	Dau	1
#1949	Ellen McMullen	F	Wife	18
#1950	Head Carrier	M	Father	74
1951	Caught	F	Wife	60
1952	Sitting Up	F	Wife	40
1953	John Head Carrier	M	Son	18
#1954	Joe Cayton	M	Hus	24
1955	Mary Cayton	F	Wife	19
#1956	Bead Woman	F	Moth	50
1957	Isabelle Running Rabbit	F	Ad-dau	12
#1958	Joe Kossuth	M	Father	25
1959	Different Woman	F	Wife	43
1960	Miles Running Wolf	M	S-son	20
1961	John Running Wolf	M	S-son	13
1962	George Running Wolf	M	S-son	12
1963	Jas Running Wolf	M	S-son	9
1964	Joe Running Wolf	M	S-son	7
#1965	Spotted Calf	M	Hus	72
1966	Mink Woman	F	Wife	66
#1967	Joe Trombly	M	Hus	42
1968	Julia Trombly	F	Wife	47
#1969	Dan Lone Chief #1	M	Father	26

Census of the [Piegan] Indians of [Blackfeet] Agency, [Montana] taken by United States Indian Agent, , 18

No.	English Name	Sex	Relation	Age
1970	Ellen Lone Chief	F	Wife	47
1971	Jas. Lone Chief	M	Son	1
1972	Susan Williamson	F	Ad dau of #2082	3
#1973	Dan Lone Chief #3	F	Wid	65
#1974	Double Runner	M	Father	54
1975	Long Time Woman	F	Wife	50
#1976	Turtle	M	Father	39
1977	Minnie Turtle	F	Wife	27
1978	Mary Turtle	F	Dau	1
1979	Edward Double Runner	M	Son	22
1980	Paul Double Runner	M	Son	14
1981	Many Guns	M	Son	27
#1982	Margaret De Champ	F	Wid	67
#1983	Julia Reevis	F	Moth	42
1984	Emmit Auger	M	Son	19
#1985	Octavia Gulick	F	Wife	35
#1986	Running Owl	M	Father	33
1987	Kills Twice	F	Wife	40
1988	Susie Big Road	F	Ad-dau	12
1989	Short Woman	F	Dau	12
1990	Anna Running Owl	F	Dau	2
#1991	Arrow Maker	M	Father	43
1992	Mary Arrow Maker	F	Wife	45
1993	Julia Arrow Maker	F	Dau	6
#1994	Kills Close	F	Wid	70
#1995	Big Plume	M	Father	66
1996	Catches On Top	F	Wife	42
1997	Jerry Big Plume	M	Son	22
1998	Louise Big Plume	F	Dau	6
#1999	Agnes Big Road	F	Sing	19
2000	Round Man	M	Bro	4
#2001	Old Chief	M	Father	47
2002	Morning Woman	F	Wife	37
2003	John Old Chief	M	Son	17
2004	Paul Old Chief	M	Son	2
2005	Arthur Old Chief	M	Son	8
2006	Mary Old Chief	F	Dau	11
2007	Cecil Old Chief	F	Dau	1
#2008	Young Bear Chief	M	Father	44
2009	Good Shield	F	Wife	36
2010	Elk Woman	F	Wife	30
2011	Eddy Bear Chief	M	Son	18

Census of the   [Piegan]   Indians of [Blackfeet] Agency, [Montana]
taken by   United States Indian Agent,   , 18

No.	English Name	Sex	Relation	Age
2012	Sebastian Bear Chief	M	Son	6
2013	John Bear Chief	M	Son	8
2014	Maggie Bear Chief	F	Dau	13
#------	(Jerry Big Plume)			
2015	Josephine Big Plume	F	Wife	18
#2016	Old Man Chief	M	Father	36
2017	Annie Old Man Chief	F	Wife	28
2018	Jas Old Man Chief	M	Son	5
2019	Thos Old Man Chief	M	Son	2
2020	Wm Old Man Chief	M	Som[sic]	1
#2021	Drags His Robe	M	Father	41
2022	Crow Woman	F	Wife	50
2023	Mary Drags Her Robe	F	Dau	4
#2024	Mary Stuart	F	Moth	34
2025	Jennie Stuart	F	Dau	17
2026	Clara Stuart	F	Dau	14
2027	Mollie Stuart	F	Dau	10
2028	Cecil Stuart	F	Dau	7
2029	Maggie Stuart	F	Dau	4
#2030	Louis Champine	M	Father	36
2031	Daisy Champine	F	Wife	39
2032	George Champine	M	Son	10
2033	Pete Champine	M	Son	6
2034	Mary Champine	F	Dau	3
2035	Mary Ann Champine	F	Dau	1
#2036	Every Body Talks About	M	Father	48
2037	Strikes Back	F	Wife	49
2038	Hate Woman	F	Wife	40
2039	Louis E.B.T. About	M	Son	10
2040	Paul E.B.T. About	M	Son	7
2041	George E.B.T. About	M	Son	9
2042	Mollie E.B.T. About	F	Dau	1
#2043	Josephine Hall	F	Wife	27
2044	Pat Hall	M	Son	7
2045	David Hall	M	Son	5
2046	Wm Hall	M	Son	2
2047	Mary Hall	F	Dau	10
#2048	John Eagle Ribs	M	Father	23
2049	Louise Eagle Ribs	F	Wife	26
2050	Jennie Eagle Ribs	F	Dau	1
#2051	Red Head	M	Hus	39
2052	Two Strikes	F	Wife	42

Census of the [Piegan] Indians of [Blackfeet] Agency, [Montana] taken by United States Indian Agent, , 18

No.	English Name	Sex	Relation	Age
#2053	Maggie Nichols	F	Wife	29
2054	Edith Innman	F	Dau	14
2055	Ollie Nichols	F	Dau	11
2056	Cecil Nichols	M	Son	5
#2057	Isa belle Thomas	F	Wife	54
2058	Ada Thomas	F	Dau	27
#2059	John Kicking Woman	M	Father	24
2060	Jennie Kicking Woman	F	Wife	32
2061	Mary Johnson	F	Dau	20
2062	Ida Johnson	F	Dau	11
2063	Belle Johnson	F	Dau	17
2064	Jas Johnson	M	Son	13
2065	Leo Kicking Woman	M	Son	11
#2066	Wm Johnson	M	Sing	19
2067	Takes Down	F	G-moth	50
#2068	Susan Williamson	F	Wife	38
2069	Henry Williamson	M	Son	19
2070	Wm Williamson	M	Son	17
2071	Mary Williamson	F	Dau	14
2072	Gertrude Williamson	F	Dau	12
2073	Susan Williamson	F	Ad-dau	3
#2074	Mary Morgan	F	Moth	40
2075	George Morgan	M	Son	21
2076	Jesse Morgan	M	Son	19
2077	Elizabeth Morgan	F	Dau	17
2078	Louis Morgan	M	Son	15
2079	Nellie Morgan	F	Dau	13
2080	Mack Morgan	M	Son	11
2081	Fannie Morgan	F	Dau	9
2082	Agnes Morgan	F	Dau	7
2083	Agnes Morgan	F	Dau	7
2084	Katie Morgan	F	Dau	2
2085	John Morgan	M	Son	1

Census of the Blackfeet,

Montana, 1901

| 46018 | **OFFICE OF**
Indian Affairs,
Rec. SEP. 3 | 1901 |

Blackfeet Agency
Census of Indians

CENSUS of the -PIEGAN- Indians of BLACKFEET Agency, MONTANA taken by JAMES H. MONTEATH United States Indian Agent, AUGUST 15th, 1901

No.	English Name	Sex	Relation	Age
1#	Charles Martain	M	Father	33
2	Ross Martain	M	Son	6
3	Rena Martain	F	Dau	2
4	Floyd Martain	M	Son	7-mo
5#	George Pablo	M	Father	32
6	Maggie Pablo	F	Wife	23
7	Emma Pablo	F	Dau	8
8	Christina Pablo	F	Dau	5
9	Agnes Pablo	F	Dau	4
10	Eva Pablo	F	Dau	2
11	Genevieve Pablo	F	Dau	3-mo
12	Lazy Boy	M	Father	47
13	Shaddow	F	Wife	33
14	Tom Lazy Boy	M	Son	21
15	Sam Lazy Boy	M	Son	6
16	Mack Lazy Boy	M	Son	4
17	Anna Lazy Boy	F	Dau	9
18	Drags Behind	M	Father	47
19	Going In Last	F	Wife	60
20	Weasel Tail	M	Father	41
21	Throwing Down	F	Wife	37
22	Emma Weasel Tail	F	Dau	17
23	Louise Weasel Tail	F	Dau	6
24	John Weasel Tail	M	Son	3
25	James Weasel Tail	M	Son	1
26#	Three Bears	M	Father	49
27	Crow Head	F	Wife	52
28	Joe Three Bears	M	Son	6
29	Different Petrified Rock	F	Dau	10
30#	No Chief	M	Father	60
31	Strikes In The Front	F	Wife	50
32	John Mountain Chief	M	Son	23
33	Jim Big Top	M	Son	26
34#	Mike Little Dog	M	Father	28
35	Good Tried Woman	F	Wife	19
36	Good Stealing	F	Dau	2
37#	Jim No Chief	M	Father	30
38	Fetching Back	F	Wife	18
39	Fine Driving Back	F	Dau	4
40	Medicine Singer	F	Dau	2
41#	Takes Gun Alone	F	Widow	50

CENSUS of the -PIEGAN- Indians of BLACKFEET Agency, MONTANA taken by JAMES H. MONTEATH United States Indian Agent, AUGUST 15th, 1901

No.	English Name	Sex	Relation	Age
42#	Medicine Singer	F	Widow	111
43#	Takes Gun On Top	M	Father	31
44	Yellow Bird	F	Wife	37
45	Spotted Woman	F	Dau	8
46	Just Can See Him	F	Dau	1
47#	David Duvall	M	Father	23
48	Gretchen	F	Wife	23
49#	Black Face Man	M	Father	45
50	Bead Woman	F	Wife	24
51	Red Petrified Rock	F	Dau	6
52	Yellow Ground Hog	F	Dau	4
53#	Blanket Woman	F	Moth	45
54	Dan Bull Plume	M	Son	23
55	Round Face	F	Dau	2
56#	Bird Rattler	M	Fath	46
57	Sitting Under	F	Moth	29
58	Way Off In Sight	F	Dau	3
59#	Charges On Both Sides	F	Widow	50
60#	Cow Hide Robe	M	Father	32
61	Rachel Cow Hide Robe	F	Wife	23
62	Black Young Man	M	Son	4
63#	Rides In the Middle	M	Father	34
64	Slim Woman	F	Wife	35
65	Squirrel Woman	F	Dau	5
66	Levi Rides In the Middle	M	Son	13
67#	Fred Black Man	M	Single	20
68	Short Face	M	Single	28
69#	Irvin Little Plume	M	Father	26
70	Small Woman	F	Wife	22
71	John Little Plume	M	Son	2
72	Single Woman	F	Dau	5
73#	Womans Word	F	Widow	80
74#	Cold Body	M	Father	28
75	Mary Cold Body	F	Wife	40
76	Cecile Cold Body	F	Dau	7
77	Peter Grant	M	S-Son	14
78	Maggie Cold Body	F	Dau	10
79#	Black Weasel	M	Father	35
80	Sparks	F	Wife	44
81	Going Ahead Alone	M	Son	5
82#	Clears Up	M	Father	28

CENSUS of the -PIEGAN- Indians of BLACKFEET Agency, MONTANA taken by JAMES H. MONTEATH United States Indian Agent, AUGUST 15th, 1901

No.	English Name	Sex	Relation	Age
83	Hollowing at Night	F	Wife	30
84	George Clears Up	M	Son	3
85	(Infant)	F	Dau	1-wk
86#	Julia Cobell	F	Single	22
87#	Mary Cobell	F	Widow	68
88	James Cobell	M	Son	30
89	Joseph Cobell	M	Son	21
90	George Cobell	M	Son	19
91	Johnny Cobell	M	Son	17
92	Bessie Cobell	F	Dau	13
93	Wm Cobell	M	Son	11
94	Thos. Cobell	M	Son	20
95#	John Kennedy	M	Father	31
96	Mary Kennedy	F	Wife	28
97	Johnny Potts	M	Son	11
98	Wm Kennedy	M	Son	2
99	(Infant)	F	Dau	7-wk
100#	Hairy Coat	M	Father	32
101	Mary hairy Coat	F	Wife	26
102	Perry Kennerly	M	Sing.	20
103#	Split Ears	M	Father	33
104	Good Killing	F	Wife	45
105	Maggie Split Ears	F	Dau	11
106	Susie Split Ears	F	Dau	8
107	Agnes Kennerly	F	Dau	15
108#	Wolf Chief	M	Father	32
109	Mrs Wolf Chief	F	Wife	18
110	(Infant)	M	Son	8-mo
111#	Emma Upham	F	Widow	38
112	Katie Upham	F	Dau	18
113	Jack Upham	M	Son	11
114	Myrtie Upham	F	Dau	8
115	(Infant)	F	Dau	1
116#	George Schmidt	M	Father	24
117	Rosa Schmidt	F	Wife	22
118#	Joseph Kipp	M	Father	49
119	Mary Kipp	F	Dau	12
120	James Kipp	M	Son	9
121	George Kipp	M	Son	3
122#	Dick Croff	M	Father	28
123	Maggie Croff	F	Wife	24

CENSUS of the -PIEGAN- Indians of BLACKFEET Agency, MONTANA taken by JAMES H. MONTEATH United States Indian Agent, AUGUST 15th, 1901

No.	English Name	Sex	Relation	Age
124	Arthur Croff	M	Son	4
125	Eva Croff	F	Dau	3
126#	Bad Marriage	M	Father	42
127	Little Fox	F	Wife	30
128	Joe Bad Marriage	M	Son	15
129	Jim Bad Marriage	M	Son	13
130	Last Bear Woman	F	Dau	6
131	Last Hollowing	F	Dau	3
132	Thos. Bad Marriage	M	Son	1
133#	Rosa Sharp	F	Wife	19
134	Julia Sharp	F	Dau	3
135	(Infant)	S	Son	1
136	Kills Across The Way	F	Widow	39
137#	Jack Miller	M	Father	55
138	Julia Miller	F	Wife	54
139#	Gambler	M	Father	38
140	Yellow Spot	F	Wife	39
141#	John Kills Across The Way	M	Father	27
142	Makes Signs	F	Wife	30
143	(Infant)	F	Dau	6-mo
144	---- ----	F	Dau	11
145#	Anthony Austin	M	Father	31
146	Susan Austin	F	Wife	40
147	Ira Burd	M	S-son	15
148	Phoebe Burd	F	S-dau	10
149#	Levi Burd	M	Father	24
150	Daisy Burd	F	Wife	20
151	Dorothy	F	Dau	3
152	(Infant)	F	Dau	1
153#	Bear Child	M	Father	48
154	Grain Woman	F	Wife	39
155	Wm Bear Child	M	Son	17
156	Josephine Bear Child	F	Dau	11
157	James Bear Child	M	Son	8
158	Louis Bear Child	M	Son	10
159	Benj Bear Child	M	Son	5
160#	George Horn	M	Father	31
161	Susan Horn	F	Wife	30
162	George Champine	M	S-Son	9
163	Maggie Champine	F	S-dau	5
164	Peter Champine	M	S-Son	3

CENSUS of the -PIEGAN- Indians of BLACKFEET Agency, MONTANA taken by JAMES H. MONTEATH United States Indian Agent, AUGUST 15th, 1901

No.	English Name	Sex	Relation	Age
165#	Theresa Pambrun	F	Wife	50
166	Percy Dennis	M	G-Son	19
167#	James Blood	M	Father	42
168	Paula Blood	F	Wife	22
169	John Blood	M	Son	2
170	Antoine Lewis	M	Neph	16
171#	Louis Pambrun	M	Father	43
172	Annie Pambrun	F	Wife	38
173	Edw Pambrun	M	Son	17
174	Dave Pambrun	M	Son	14
175	Isabella Pambrun	F	Dau	11
176	Geo. Pambrun	M	Son	7
177	Dora Pambrun	F	Dau	3
178#	Bessie Lahr	F	Single	17
179#	Double Rider	M	Father	45
180	Mary Double Rider	F	Wife	25
181	Ada Double Rider	F	Dau	11
182	Minnie Double Rider	F	Dau	5
183	Findian Double Rider	F	Dau	2
184#	Rachel Norris	F	Wife	28
185	Rosa Norris	F	Dau	12
186	Daniel Norris	M	Son	6
187	Dora Norris	F	Dau	3
188#	Good Gun	M	Sing	38
189	Kills On Top	F	Moth	60
190#	Rattling Barry Carrier	F	Widow	44
191	Little Fox	F	Dau	14
192	Different Child	F	Dau	11
193	(Infant)	M	Son	1
194#	Eagle Child	M	Father	43
195	Rushes On Both Sides	F	Wife	45
196	Jas Eagle Child	M	Son	14
197	Wild Gun	M	Son	5
198	Fringe Gun	M	Son	1
199	Strangle Wolf	M	Father	55
200	Dwarf	F	Wife	70
201#	Coat	M	Father	38
202	Broken Leg	F	Wife	36
203	Medicine	F	Dau	4
204	(Infant)	F	Dau	4-mo
205#	Frank Spearson	M	Father	45

CENSUS of the -PIEGAN- Indians of BLACKFEET Agency, MONTANA taken by JAMES H. MONTEATH United States Indian Agent, AUGUST 15th, 1901

No.	English Name	Sex	Relation	Age
206	Mary Spearson	F	Wife	31
207	Albert Spearson	M	Son	5
208#	Thomas Little Bear	M	Sing	38
209#	Flying	F	Widow	60
210#	Short Robe	M	Father	35
211	Rushes On Both Sides	F	Wife	39
212	Going After Water	F	Wife	29
213	Cecile Short Robe	F	Dau	10
214	Emma Short Robe	F	Dau	8
215	Anna Short Robe	F	Dau	9
216	Wm Short Robe	M	Son	2
217	Fred Big Top	M	Sing	21
218#	Three Guns	M	Father	32
219	Kills At Night	F	Wife	41
220	Diving All Round	F	Dau	2
221#	John Middle Calf	M	Father	55
222	Rolling Up A Calf	F	Wife	61
223	Mary Middle Calf	F	G-Dau	12
224#	Bear Medicine	M	Father	32
225	Ragged Woman	F	Wife	25
226	Wm Bear Medicine	M	Son	10
227	Maggie Bear Medicine	F	Dau	8
228	John Bear Medicine	M	Son	3
229	Had Teeth	F	Dau	2
230	(Infant)	M	Son	4-mo
231#	James Ground	M	Father	25
232	Double Face	F	Wife	24
233	George Ground	M	Son	3
234#	Ground	Single		48
235#	Boy	M	Father	60
236	Black Face	F	Wife	58
237	Raymond Boy	M	Son	11
238	Oscar Boy	M	Son	13
239#	Arrow Top Knott[sic]	M	Father	34
240	Squirrel	F	Wife	37
241	Antoine Arrow Top Knot	M	Son	4
242	Phillip Arrow Top Knot	M	Son	13
243	Silas Arrow Top Knot	M	Son	11
244#	Bull Calf	M	Father	53
245	Blanket Woman	F	Wife	63
246	John Bull Calf	M	Son	14

CENSUS of the -PIEGAN- Indians of BLACKFEET Agency, MONTANA taken by JAMES H. MONTEATH United States Indian Agent, AUGUST 15th, 1901

No.	English Name	Sex	Relation	Age
247#	Good Killing	F	Widow	80
248#	Heavy Runner	M	Father	35
249	No Petrified Rock	F	Wife	28
250	Blue Bead	F	Wife	29
251	George Heavy Runner	M	Son	12
252	Wood Heavy Runner	M	Son	11
253	Coming With a Gun	M	Son	3
254	Funny Gun	M	Son	1
255	Sweet Grass	F	Dau	4
256	Rosa Heavy Runner	F	Dau	8
257	Coyote Woman	F	Dau	6
258#	Antoine Chouquette	M	Single	57
259#	Strikes #3	F	Widow	60
260	Wild Gun	M	G-Son	5
261#	Rides Behind	M	Fater[sic]	46
262	Lone Crow	F	Wife	39
263#	Makes Cold Weather	M	Father	34
264	Spear Woman	F	Wife	33
265	Joe Makes Cold Weather	M	Son	6
266#	Maggie Wetzel		Widow	40
267	Wm Wetzel	M	Son	20
268#	Joe Livermore	M	Father	36
269	Clara Livermore	F	Dau	8
270	Lillie Livermore	F	Dau	6
271#	Pearl Haggerty	F	Wife	24
272	Wm. Wright Haggerty	M	Son	1
273#	Rides at the Door	M	Father	34
274	Mary Rides At the Door	F	Wife	30
275	Richard Rides at the Door	M	Son	11
276	Louise Rides at the Door	F	Dau	8
277	Frank Rides at the Door	M	Son	5
278	James Rides at the Door	M	Son	3
279	(Infant)	M	Son	1
280#	Frank Racine	M	Father	24
281	Nettie Racine	F	Wife	18
282	(Infant)	M	Son	6-mo
283#	Louise Aubrey	F	Wife	43
284	Alice Aubrey	F	Dau	23
285	Rosa Aubrey	F	Dau	20
286	Thos. Aubrey	M	Son	17
287	Lucy Aubrey	F	Dau	14

CENSUS of the -PIEGAN- Indians of BLACKFEET Agency, MONTANA taken by JAMES H. MONTEATH United States Indian Agent, AUGUST 15th, 1901

No.	English Name	Sex	Relation	Age
288	Dora Aubrey	F	Dau	13
289	May Aubrey	F	Dau	8
290	Philip Aubrey	M	Son	11
291	Janette Aubrey	F	Dau	6
292	Cal. Aubrey	M	Son	2
293#	Maggie Kennerly	F	Wife	44
294	Catherine Gobert	F	Dau	17
295	Agnes Gobert	F	Dau	15
296	Anna Kennerly	F	Dau	13
297	James Kennerly	M	Son	5
298	Lee Kennerly	M	Son	2
299	Jerome Kennerly	M	Son	12
300#	Mike Short Man	M	Father	44
301	Sophronia Short Man	F	Wife	34
302#	Many Hides	M	Father	27
303	Maggie Many Hides	F	Wife	18
304	Under Bear	M	Son	3
305	(Infant)	F	Dau	7-mo
306#	Iron Woman	F	Widow	77
307#	John Shorty	M	Father	48
308	White Petrified Rock	F	Wife	25
309	Medicine Old Woman	F	Ad-Dau	4
310#	Jim Bear Skin	M	Father	25
311	Jeanette Bear Skin	F	Wife	19
312	Coming Wind	F	Dau	2
313#	Henry Merchant	M	Father	28
314	Emma Merchant	F	Wife	17
315#	Esther Carney	F	Wife	30
316#	White Antelope	M	Father	49
317	Giving Things to the Sun	F	Wife	40
318	Jas Cream Antelope	M	Son	14
319	Jos Cream Antelope	M	Son	4
320#	Frank Guardipee	M	Father	30
321	Mary Guardipee	F	Wife	22
322	Frank Guardipee Jr	M	Son	5
323	Eli Guardipee	M	Son	2
324#	Bear Paw	M	Father	49
325	Different Kills	F	Wife	35
326	Minnie Bear Paw	F	Dau	12
327	John Bear Paw	M	Son	5
328	Joe Bear Paw	M	Son	3

CENSUS of the -PIEGAN- Indians of BLACKFEET Agency, MONTANA taken by JAMES H. MONTEATH United States Indian Agent, AUGUST 15th, 1901

No.	English Name	Sex	Relation	Age
329	Thos Bear Paw	M	Son	2
330#	Henry Under Bear	M	Father	25
331	Mary Under Bear	F	Wife	35
332	Charles Nequette	M	S-Son	18
333	John Nequette	M	S-Son	14
334#	Joe Nequette	M	Single	23
335#	Chief Coward	M	Father	48
336	Antelope Woman	F	Wife	50
337	Victor Chief Coward	M	Son	21
338	Good Looking Crow Woman	F	Dau	8
339#	Goes All Around	F	Widow	51
340	Alonzo Skunk Cap	M	Son	11
341#	Sophia Powell	F	Wife	28
342	Lorenzo Powell	M	Son	2
343	Lizzie Ellen Powell	F	Dau	10-M
344	Maggie Powell	F	Dau	15
345#	Ben De Roche	M	Father	38
346	Sallie Mary De Roche	F	Wife	38
347	Charles De Roche	M	Son	18
348#	William Goss	M	Father	24
349	Maggie Goss	F	Wife	21
350#	Maggie Goss	F	Wife	44
351	Nellie Goss	F	Dau	19
352	Caroline Goss	F	Dau	17
353	Susie Goss	F	Dau	14
354	Nate Goss	M	Son	14
355	Maggie Goss	F	Dau	12
356	George Goss	M	Son	10
357	Albert Goss	M	Son	7
358	Francis Goss	M	Son	5
359	Phena Goss	F	Dau	1
360#	Albert Goss	M	Father	27
361	Mary Goss	F	Wife	26
362	Albert Goss	M	Son	3
363	Mamie Goss	F	Dau	2
364#	Loamie Goss	M	Single	22
365#	Slim Tail	M	Father	38
366	Rosa Slim Tail	F	Wife	43
367#	Charles De Laney	F	Father	28
368	Viola De Laney	F	Wife	20
369	Fred De Laney	M	Son	7-mo

CENSUS of the -PIEGAN- Indians of BLACKFEET Agency, MONTANA taken by JAMES H. MONTEATH United States Indian Agent, AUGUST 15th, 1901

No.	English Name	Sex	Relation	Age
370	Margaret De Laney	F	Dau	2
371#	Strikes Back	F	Widow	60
372	Good Slaughter	F	Dau	10
373#	Wolf Calf	F	Widow	80
374#	Wm Smith	M	Single	26
375#	Sharps	M	Father	46
376	Spear Woman	F	Wife	45
377	Peter Smith	M	Ad-Son	19
378#	Little Young Man	M	Father	44
379	Cuts On Both Sides	F	Wife	60
380	?	M	Ad-Son	11
381#	Black Sarcee	M	Hus	37
382	Kills A Long Way	F	Wife	50
383#	Cut Finger	M	Father	55
384	Strikes Herself	F	Wife	30
385	Ernest Cut Finger	M	Son	20
386	Maggie Cut Finger	F	Dau	6
387	Thos Cut Finger	M	Son	5
388	Owl On Top	M	Son	2
389#	Mud Head	M	Father	31
390	White Horse Rider	F	Wife	37
391	Setting East	M	Son	15
392	Tallow Mud Head	M	Son	3
393#	Home Gun	M	Father	38
394	Many Pipes	F	Wife	25
395	Mary Home Gun	F	Dau	4
396	Paul Home Gun	M	Son	5
397	Dan Home Gun	M	Son	2
398#	John Morgan	M	Father	36
399	Lucy Morgan	F	Wife	26
400	Dave Morgan	M	Son	9
401	Joseph Morgan	M	Son	6
402	Mary Morgan	F	Dau	3
403#	Many Tail Feathers	M	Father	53
404	Long Time Bear Woman	F	Wife	30
405	Jennie Many Tail Feathers	F	Dau	12
406	Bertha Many Tail Feathers	F	Dau	9
407	Already Heard	F	Dau	5
408	Strikes In the Front	F	Dau	2
409#	Shoots First	M	Father	27
410	Calf Tail	F	Wife	38

CENSUS of the -PIEGAN- Indians of BLACKFEET Agency, MONTANA taken by JAMES H. MONTEATH United States Indian Agent, AUGUST 15th, 1901

No.	English Name	Sex	Relation	Age
411	Maggie Shoots First	F	Dau	2
412	Henry Marceau	M	S-Son	19
413#	John Black Bear	M	Father	28
414	Mary Black Bear	F	Wife	23
415	(Infant)	F	Dau	5-mo
416#	Old Person	M	Father	35
417	Iron Crow	F	Wife	25
418	Jennie Old Person	F	Dau	9
419	Edna Old Person	F	Dau	6
420	Anthony Old Person	M	Son	2
421	Juniper Old Person	M	Bro-Law	22
422#	Catches In the Brush	F	Wid	60
423#	Black Bear	M	Father	57
424	Many Snakes	F	Wife	45
425#	Medicine Owl	M	Father	35
426	Sheep Woman	F	Wife	40
427#	Blackfoot Child	M	Father	45
428	Buffalo Trail	F	Wife	50
429	Blanket Woman	F	Dau	5
430#	Mary Dunbar	F	Wife	28
431	Jane Dunbar	F	Dau	12
432	Frances Dunbar	F	Dau	8
433	Andrew Dunbar	M	Son	10
434	Carrie Dunbar	F	Dau	6
435	Esther Dunbar	F	Dau	4
436	James Dunbar	M	Son	2
437	Hazel Dunbar	F	Dau	1-mo
438#	Joe Brown	M	Father	26
439	Frances Brown	F	Wife	24
440	Wesley Brown	M	Son	3
441	Al. Brown	M	Son	1
442#	Horrace J. Clark	M	Father	54
443#	Malcolm Clark	M	Father	24
444	Ella J. Clark	F	Wife	26
445#	Thomas Dawson	M	Father	39
446	Isabel Dawson	F	Wife	37
447	Fred Patterson	M	Ad-Son	7
448	Malcolm Patterson	M	Ad-Son	5
449	Helen Patterson	F	Ad-Dau	3
450	Lorena Dawson	F	Ad-Dau	16
451#	Frank Munroe Jr	M	Father	32

CENSUS of the -PIEGAN- Indians of BLACKFEET Agency, MONTANA taken by JAMES H. MONTEATH United States Indian Agent, AUGUST 15th, 1901

No.	English Name	Sex	Relation	Age
452	Louise Munroe	F	Wife	25
453#	Baptiste Rondin	M	Father	40
454	Mary Rondin	F	Wife	48
455	Richard Rondin	M	Son	22
456	Samuel Rondin	M	Son	15
457	Phillip Rondin	M	Son	1
458	Louise Rondin	F	Dau	13
459	Mary Rondin	F	Dau	9
460	Nancy Rondin	F	Dau	5
461	Isabel Rondin	F	Dau	3
462#	Double Cloth	F	Widow	55
463	Lone Mouse	M	Son	28
464	Shoots Close	M	Son	16
465	John West Wolf	M	Son	5
466	George West Wolf	M	Son	15
467#	Medicine Weasel	M	Father	58
468	Good Cutting	F	Wife	40
469	Eagle Face	F	Wife	35
470	Crow Woman	F	Dau	6
471	Goes In Last	F	Dau	1
472	Theresa Medicine Weasel	F	Dau	10
473#	Bad Woman	F	Wife-468	50
474	Talks	F	Widow	70
475#	Catches Last	F	Widow	40
476	Geo. Bull Child	M	Son	9
477#	Tallow Ashley	M	Father	33
478	Rosa Ashley	F	Wife	26
479	Louis Ashley	M	Son	4
480	Mary Ashley	F	Ad-Dau	4
481#	Dog Ears	M	Father	26
482	Louise Dog Ears	F	Wife	24
483	Red Mouse	M	Son	2
484#	Percy Bull Child	M	Sing	19
485#	Baptiste West Wolf	M	Father	24
486	Annie West Wolf	F	Wife	17
487#	Looking for Smoke	M	Father	41
488	Louis Looking For Smoke	M	Son	9
489#	Wood Chief Woman	F	Widow	45
490	Kills One Another	F	Dau	7
491#	Sam Smith	M	Sing	21
492#	Lizzie Smith	F	Widow	50

CENSUS of the -PIEGAN- Indians of BLACKFEET Agency, MONTANA taken by JAMES H. MONTEATH United States Indian Agent, AUGUST 15th, 1901

No.	English Name	Sex	Relation	Age
493#	Charles Chouquette	M	Father	39
494	Louise Chouquette	F	Wife	40
495	Josephine Chouquette	F	Dau	17
496	Henry Bird	M	Single	19
497	Thomas Bird	M	Sing	17
498#	Henry Main	M	Father	22
499	Mary Main	F	Wife	22
500	(Infant)	F	Dau	5-mo
501#	Isabella Main	F	Wife	35
502	Lizzie Main	F	Dau	6
503	Alice Main	F	Dau	8
504#	John Ground	M	Fatjer[sic]	28
505	Mary Ground	F	Wife	19
506	Evelina Ground	F	Dau	7-mo
507#	Wm Sherman	M	Father	30
508	Genevieve Sherman	F	Wife	23
509	Mary Sherman	F	Dau	4
510	Charles Sherman	M	Son	2
511	Martin Sherman	M	Son	1
512	James Clark	M	Neph	19
513#	Iron	M	Father	75
514	Kills In the Middle	F	Wife	55
515#	Julia Pendergrass	F	Wife	30
516	Millie Pendergrass	F	Dau	4
517	George Pendergrass	M	Son	2
518	Phil Pendergrass	M	Son	1
519#	Ear Ring	M	Father	47
520	Susie Ear Ring	F	Wife	45
521	James Ear Ring	M	Son	17
522	Bird Ear Ring	M	Son	15
523#	Eagle Tail Feathers	M	Father	50
524	Pretty Snake	F	Wife	70
525	Yellow Weasel Woman	F	Dau	12
526	Blanket Woman	F	Dau	6
527#	Root Digger	F	Widow	80
528#	Chief Elk	M	Father	68
529	Last Star	F	Wife	50
530#	Lois Ell	M	Father	29
531	Annie Ell	F	Wife	20
532	Johnny Ell	M	Son	4
533	Louis Ell Jr	M	Son	1

CENSUS of the -PIEGAN- Indians of BLACKFEET Agency, MONTANA taken by JAMES H. MONTEATH United States Indian Agent, AUGUST 15th, 1901

No.	English Name	Sex	Relation	Age
534#	Rabbit Old Woman	F	Wife	35
535	Looking Glass	M	Son	4
536#	Many White Horses	M	Father	70
537	Thunder Nest	F	Wife	34
538	Small Teeth	M	Son	10
539	Crow	M	Son	5
540	Medicine Child	F	Dau	4
541	Flying Down	M	Son	6-mo
542#	Long Time Old Woman	F	Widow	20
543#	Kills By Mistake	F	Widow	70
544#	Hits In the Water	F	Widow	69
545#	Morning Plume	M	Father	56
546	Snake Woman	F	Wife	41
547	Battle Good Looking Woman	F	Dau	5
548	(Infant)	M	Son	1
549#	Wolverine	M	Father	30
550	Walking Backwards	F	Wife	24
551	Many Owls	M	Son	8
552	Joe Wolverine	M	Son	6
553	Red Holler	F	Dau	4
554	First Coyote	M	Son	1
555#	Susan Sherman	F	Wife	61
556	Alex Sherman	M	Son	22
557	Robert Sherman	M	Son	20
558	Sophie Sherman	F	Dau	18
559	Emma Sherman	F	Dau	16
560	Eva Sherman	F	Dau	1
561#	Pete After Buffalo	M	Father	38
562	Cut Nose	F	Wife	30
563	Joe After Buffalo	M	Son	6
564	Annie After Buffalo	F	Dau	5
565	Cecile Agter[sic] Buffalo	F	Dau	2
566	(Infant)	M	Son	6-mo
567#	Crane Woman	F	Widow	60
568#	Mrs Pete After Buffalo	F	Wife	29
569	Agnes After Buffalo	F	Dau	6
570	Maggie After Buffalo	F	Dau	4
571	James After Bufalo	M	Son	1
572	Charles After Buffalo	M	Son	9
573#	Strikes First	F	Widow	53
574#	Yellow Wolf	M	Father	50

CENSUS of the -PIEGAN- Indians of BLACKFEET Agency, MONTANA taken by JAMES H. MONTEATH United States Indian Agent, AUGUST 15th, 1901

No.	English Name	Sex	Relation	Age
575	Double Iron Woman	F	Wife	29
576	Mollie Yellow Wolf	F	Dau	2
577	(Infant)	F	Dau	1
578#	Bear Skin	M	Wdr	69
579#	Cecile Sanderville	F	Wife	32
580	Mollie Yellow Wolf	F	Dau	8
581	(Infant)	M	Son	6-mo
582#	Sam Middle Calf	M	Father	20
583	Agnes Middle Calf	F	Wife	18
584#	Night Shoot	M	Father	37
585	Scraping Hide	F	Wife	23
586	George Night Shoot	M	Son	4
587	Joseph Night Shoot	M	Son	11
588	Maggie Night Shoot	F	Dau	3
589	Double Kills	F	Dau	1
590#	Mary Kaiser	F	Widow	70
591#	Shorty White Grass	M	Father	61
592	Kill At Night	F	Wife	43
593	Catches Twice	F	Wife	24
594	Ross White Grass	M	Son	3
595	John White Grass	M	Son	6
596	Angeline White Grass	F	Dau	6-mo
597#	Joe Shorty	M	Father	32
598	Mary Shorty	F	Wife	26
599	Susanna Shorty	F	Dau	5
600	Rosa Shorty	F	Dau	2
601	Short Woman	F	Dau	1
602	(Infant)	F	Dau	6-mo
603	Joseph Shorty	M	Son	7
604#	Wallace Night Gun	M	Father	24
605	Mary Night Gun	F	Wife	20
606	(Infant)	F	Dau	1
607#	Weasel Fat	M	Father	48
608	Good Shield	F	Wife	37
609	Many Tail Feathers #2	F	Wife	80
610	Cree Woman	F	Dau	26
611#	Webster Galbreath	M	Sing	20
612	Jesse Sample	M	Sing	24
613#	Wolf Tail	M	Father	46
614	Ivory Woman	F	Wife	31
615	Wolf Talking	M	Son	6

CENSUS of the -PIEGAN- Indians of BLACKFEET Agency, MONTANA taken by JAMES H. MONTEATH United States Indian Agent, AUGUST 15th, 1901

No.	English Name	Sex	Relation	Age
616	Small Face	F	Dau	5
617	Julia Wolf Tail	F	Dau	13
618	Cecile Stevenson	F	S-Dau	7
619#	Takes Gun	M	Father	40
620	Minnie Takes Gun	F	Wife	23
621	Billy Takes Gun	M	Son	3
622	(Infant)	M	Son	6-mo
623	Eliza Galbreath	F	Wife	51
624	Lizzie Galbreath	F	Dau	16
625	Mary Galbreath	F	Dau	14
626	Jack Galbreath	M	Son	17
627	Phoebe Galbreath	F	Dau	12
628#	Susan Arnoux	F	Wife	43
629	Marian Arnoux	M	Son	18
630	George Arnoux	M	Son	16
631#	Monroe Arnoux	M	Sing	22
632#	Heading Off	F	Widow	83
633#	White Calf #2	F	Wife	50
634	Steals Inside	F	Dau	10
635	Diving Around	F	Dau	8
636#	Two Guns	M	Father	30
637	Taking Something	F	Wife	20
638	Small Otter	M	Son	2
639#	Pete Cadotte	M	Father	28
640	Lucy Cadotte	F	Wife	23
641	Rhoda Cadotte	F	Dau	4
642	Charles Cadotte	M	Son	3
643#	Joe Bull Child	M	Father	22
---	Catching	F	Wife	22
645	(Infant)	M	Son	1
646#	Catches On Both Sides	F	Widow	69
647#	Bull Child	M	Father	61
648	Fine Catcher	F	Wife	43
649	Geo Bull Child	M	Son	10
650	Drives Double Back	F	Dau	5
651#	Good Medicine Pipe	F	Wid	46
652	Mary Butterfly	F	Dau	10
653#	Herman Dusty Bull	M	Father	27
---	Louise Dusty Bull	F	Wife	19
655	Ralph Dusty Bull	M	Son	3
656	Rhoda Dusty Bull	F	Dau	1

CENSUS of the -PIEGAN- Indians of BLACKFEET Agency, MONTANA taken by JAMES H. MONTEATH United States Indian Agent, AUGUST 15th, 1901

No.	English Name	Sex	Relation	Age
657#	Mad Wolf	M	Father	63
658	Giving Things to the Sun	F	Wife	56
659	Charles Mad Wolf	M	Son	20
660	Mark Mad Wolf	M	Son	11
661#	James Many Tail Feathers	M	Father	24
662	Josephine M.T. Feathers	F	Wife	16
663#	Joseph Young Eagle	M	Father	47
664	Spotted Back	F	Wife	27
665	Joseph Young Eagle	M	Son	3
666	Sitting With Face Together	M	Son	2
667#	Dry Goods Woman	F	Widow	75
668	Annie Marceau	F	G-Dau	16
669#	Catches On Top	F	Widow	56
670#	Stingy	M	Father	55
671	Kills First	F	Wife	56
672	Mary Stingy	F	Dau	5
673	Wm Stingy	M	Son	8
674#	Nick Green	M	Faher[sic]	31
675	Long Time Bird	F	Wife	40
676	(Infant)	M	Son	6-mo
---	Fred Girard	M	Sing	28
678#	Charles Conway	M	Father	24
679	Laura Conway	F	Wife	18
680	John Conway	M	Son	1
681#	Kate Cross Guns	F	Widow	47
682	Willie Conway	M	Son	18
683	Preeley Cross Guns	M	Son	5
684	James Cross Guns	M	Son	3
685	John Stink Teat	M	Ad-Son	2
686#	Emily E/dridge[sic]	F	Wife	37
687#	Black Coyote	M	Father	70
688	Annie Black Coyote	F	Dau	20
689#	Ross White Grass	M	Father	24
690	Minnie White Grass	F	Wife	30
691#	Steve Henault	--	Father	27
692	Mary Henault	F	Wife	18
693#	Stabs Down	M	Father	30
694	Blanket Woman	F	Wife	24
695	John Stabs Down	M	Son	3
696	Wm Stabs Down	M	Son	1
697#	Cecile Hunsberger	F	Widow	60

CENSUS of the -PIEGAN- Indians of BLACKFEET Agency, MONTANA taken by JAMES H. MONTEATH United States Indian Agent, AUGUST 15th, 1901

No.	English Name	Sex	Relation	Age
698	Clara Hunsberger	F	Dau	21
699	Gus Hunsberger	M	Son	18
700	Thos Hunsberger	M	Son	25
701#	James White Calf	M	Father	35
702	Mary White Calf	F	Wife	19
703	Rosa White Calf	F	Dau	8-mo
704#	White Calf	M	Father	74
705	Catches Two	F	Wife	50
706#	Went In Herself	F	Widow	46
707	Louise Lodge Pole	F	Dau	22
708#	Eli Guardipee	M	Father	44
709	Sadie Guardipee	F	Wife	31
710	Thos Guardipee	M	Son	21
711	Frank Guardipee	M	Son	16
712	Charles Guardipee	M	Son	13
713	Josephine Guardipee	F	Dau	11
714	Louise Guardipee	F	Dau	8
715	Agnes Guardipee	F	Dau	5
716#	James Douglas	M	Father	29
717	James Archibald Douglas	M	Son	6
718	Arthur Williams Douglas	M	Son	2
719	Lyda Eveline Douglas	F	Dau	4
720	Cherry Agnes Douglas	F	Dau	1
721#	Wm Douglas	M	Father	26
722	May Douglas	F	Dau	2
723	(Infant)	--	Dau	6-mo
724#	Eli Rider	M	Father	28
725	Already Has Teeth	F	Mother	21
726	Henry Rider	M	Son	3
727	Mary Rider	F	Dau	7-mo
728#	Bear Head	M	Father	42
729#	Heavy Breast	M	Father	55
730	Laying for Them	F	Wife	48
731	Fine Spear	F	Wife	37
732#	Owen Heavy Breast	M	Father	21
733	Lone Woman	F	Wife	24
734#	John Munroe	M	Father	75
735	Angus Munroe	M	Son	14
736#	John Hunsberger	M	Father	30
737	Mary Hunsberger	F	Wife	26
738	John Hunsberger	M	Son	2

CENSUS of the -PIEGAN- Indians of BLACKFEET Agency, MONTANA taken by JAMES H. MONTEATH United States Indian Agent, AUGUST 15th, 1901

No.	English Name	Sex	Relation	Age
739	Thomas Hunsberger	M	Son	7-mo
740#	John Don't Go Out	M	Father	60
741	Blanket Woman	--	Wife	62
742#	Wipe His Eyes	M	Father	36
743	Takes Gun	F	Wife	40
744	Evening Star	F	Dau	4
745	(Infant)	M	Son	1
746#	James Perrine	M	Father	31
747	Wm Perrine	M	Son	7
748	Florence Perrine	F	Dau	5
749	Annie Perrine	F	Dau	4
750	Stella Perrine	F	Dau	2
751#	Louis Matt	M	Father	44
752	Julia Alice Matt	F	Dau	6
753	Francis Matt	M	Son	4
754	Lena Matt	F	Dau	2
755	Albert Matt	M	Son	1
756	Louis Matt	M	Son	21
757#	Machiel Matt	M	Sing	19
758#	Mary Davis	F	Wife	23
759	Hattie Davis	F	Dau	5
760#	Mattie Bird	F	Wife	35
761	Martha Bird	F	Dau	18
762	Sampson Bird	M	Son	16
763	Chrles[sic] Bird	M	Son	12
764	Johnson Bird	M	Son	10
765	Millie Bird	F	Dau	8
766	Henry Bird	M	Son	5
767	George Bird	M	Son	3
768	Oscar Bird	M	Son	1
769#	John Kicking Woman	M	Father	26
770	Fine Kills	F	Wife	30
771	James Johnson	M	S-Son	12
772	Ida Johnson	F	S-Dau	11
773	Mary Johnson	F	S-Dau	23
774	Belle Johnson	F	S-Dau	15
775#	Edward Billeadeaux	M	Father	38
776	Virginia Billeadeaux	F	Wife	33
777	Carl Billeceaux[sic]	M	Son	8
778	Genevieve Billedeaux	F	Dau	6
779	Martha Billedeaux	F	Dau	5

CENSUS of the -PIEGAN- Indians of BLACKFEET Agency, MONTANA taken by JAMES H. MONTEATH United States Indian Agent, AUGUST 15th, 1901

No.	English Name	Sex	Relation	Age
780	Edward Billedeaux	M	Son	2
781	Mitchell Billedeaux	M	Son	1
782#	Mary Howard	F	Widow	54
783	Walter Howard	M	Son	18
784	Big Woman	F	Widow	20
785	Black Face	F	Dau	13
786#	Mary Stone	F	Wife	38
787	Henry Stone	M	Son	6
788	Joseph Stone	M	Son	3
789	Frank Stone	M	Son	2
790	(Infant)	M	Son	3-mo
791#	Peter Oscar	M	Single	35
792#	Xavier Billedeaux	M	Father	44
793	Salina Billedeaux	F	Wife	38
794	William Billedeaux	M	Son	12
795	Charles Billedeaux	M	Son	12
796	Warren Billedeaux	M	Son	10
797	Greely Billedeaux	M	Son	6
798	Mabel Billedeaux	F	Dau	4
799	Celina Billedeaux	F	Dau	2
800#	Runnisng[sic] Fisher	M	Father	37
801	Rushing Alone	F	Wife	36
802	First Rusher	M	Son	5
803	Don't Care for Anything	F	Dau	6
804#	Leggins	F	Widow	60
805#	Yellow Owl	M	Father	26
806	Bawling In the Water	F	Wife	20
807	Waiting along time to Fly	M	Son	2
808#	Wm Hungry	M	Son	24
809	First Gun	F	Moth	51
810	Ezra Piegan	M	Son	10
811#	Mike Berry Child	M	Father	28
812	Hits The Back	F	Dau	29
813	Annie Berry Child	F	Dau	5
814	Joseph Berry Child	M	Son	1
815#	John Night Gun	M	Father	30
816	Minnie Night Gun	F	Wife	22
817#	Lucy Night Gun	F	Dau	6
818	Josephine Night Gun	F	Dau	3
819#	Maggie Peterson	F	Wife	41
820	Oscar Peterson	M	Son	21

CENSUS of the -PIEGAN- Indians of BLACKFEET Agency, MONTANA taken by JAMES H. MONTEATH United States Indian Agent, AUGUST 15th, 1901

No.	English Name	Sex	Relation	Age
821	Walter Peterson	M	Son	19
822	Frank Peterson	M	Son	17
823	Melvin Peterson	M	Son	15
824	Mitchell Peterson	M	Son	14
825#	Mary Lemon	F	Wife	32
826	Lee Lemon	M	Son	4
827	Amie Lemon	F	Dau	6
828	John Lemon	M	Son	10
829	Louise Lemon	F	Dau	8
830	(Infant)	M	Son	6-mo
831#	Nellie Hagen	F	Dau	9
832	Sallie Hagen	F	Dau	3
833	Maggie Hagen	F	Dau	15
834	Sadie Hagen	F	Dau	4
835#	John Merchant	M	Sing	25
836#	Dick Lucero	M	Single	22
837#	Morning Eagle	--	Father	80
838	Strikes On Top	F	Wife	45
839	Many Yells	M	Son	12
840	Rattling Running On Top	M	Son	7
841	Two Rabbits	M	Son	4
842#	Little Owl	M	Father	27
843	Mary Little Owl	F	Wife	22
844	Fox Woman	F	Dau	3
845	(Infant)	M	Son	6-mo
846	Good Kill	F	Widow	90
847#	Julia Thomas	F	Wid	28
848	Geo Thomas	M	Son	6
849	Nora Thomas	F	Dau	3
850	Many Necklace	F	Widow	64
851#	Big Spring	M	Father	35
852	No Owl Woman	F	Wife	40
853	Small Face	F	Wife	22
854	Heavy Hair	F	Dau	1
855#	Mrs Bull Shoe	F	Widow	47
856	Different Nation	F	Dau	6
857	Lou Paisley	F	Wife	38
858	George Paisley	M	Son	16
859	Allen Paisley	M	Son	11
860	Mattie Paisley	F	Dau	9
861	Chauncy Paisley	M	Son	4

CENSUS of the -PIEGAN- Indians of BLACKFEET Agency, MONTANA taken by JAMES H. MONTEATH United States Indian Agent, AUGUST 15th, 1901

No.	English Name	Sex	Relation	Age
862#	Two Strikes	F	Widow	50
863#	Margaret Schmidt	F	Wife	50
864	Karl Schmidt	M	Son	25
865	Alex Schmidt	M	Ad-Son	40
866#	Last Star	M	Father	32
867	White Horse Rider	F	Wife	22
868	Takes Gun Inside	M	Son	5
869	Theodore Last Star	M	Son	12
870#	Josephine Gilham	F	Wife	30
871	Anthony Gilham	M	Son	11
872	Wm Gilham	M	Son	8
873#	Sallie Allison	F	Wife	27
874	Annie Allison	F	Dau	1
875	Willie Allison	M	Son	4
876	Lafayette Allison	M	Son	6
877	James Allison	M	Son	2
878#	New Breast	M	Father	34
879	Long Face	F	wife	40
880	Janet Coe	F	Dau	16
881	James Coe	M	Son	14
882#	Marry Romsay	F	Wife	25
883	Jesse Romsay	M	Son	5
884	Malvin Romsay	M	Son	2
885#	Mary Luken	F	Wife	50
886	John Luken	M	Son	20
887	Peter Luken	M	Son	18
888#	Dora Luken	F	Sing	24
889#	Mandan Woman	F	Widow	75
890#	John Vielle	M	Father	35
891	Kills a Long Way	F	Wife	25
892	Francis Vielle	M	Son	10
893	Mary Vielle	F	Dau	8
894	Wm Vielle	M	Son	5
895	Annie Vielle	F	Dau	2
896#	Julis Momberg	F	Wife	29
897	Lewis Jacob Momberg	M	Son	4
898	Mabel Momberg	F	Dau	1
899	Maud Momberg	F	Dau	1
900#	George Wren	M	Father	34
901	Susie Wren	F	Wife	30
902#	James Grant	M	Father	28

CENSUS of the -PIEGAN- Indians of BLACKFEET Agency, MONTANA taken by JAMES H. MONTEATH United States Indian Agent, AUGUST 15th, 1901

No.	English Name	Sex	Relation	Age
903	Josephine Grant	F	Wife	26
904#	Frank Marceau	M	Father	24
905	Mabel Marceau	F	Wife	18
906#	Charles Marceau	M	Father	26
907#	Medicine Boss Ribs	--	Father	55
908	Black Face Woman	F	Wife	48
909	Maggie Medicine Boss Ribs	F	Dau	4
910#	John Kipp	M	Father	40
911	Calf Woman	F	Wife	40
912	Jack Kipp	M	Son	14
913	Joe Kipp	M	Son	13
914	Wm Kipp	M	Son	9
915	Julia Kipp	F	Dau	6
916	Sadie Kipp	F	Dau	1
917#	Many Cuts	F	Widow	60
918#	Matt Lytle	M	Father	27
919#	Katie Lytle	F	Wife	22
920	Matt Lytle	M	Son	2
921	James Lytle	M	Son	1
922#	Dog Taking Gun	M	Father	34
923	Cutting Herself	F	Wife	26
924	Medicine Road	F	Dau	1
925#	Spotted Head	M	Single	70
926#	Takes Gun Up	M	Father	35
927	Strikes In the Front	F	Wife	40
928	Austin Hits In The Front	M	Son	13
929#	Frank Munrow	M	Father	55
930	Kills on the Shore	F	Wife	49
931	Louis Munroe	M	Son	20
932	Antoine Munroe	M	Son	13
933#	Two Bear Woman	F	Wid	53
934	Orrie Sheriff	M	Son	21
935#	Eddie Gobert	M	Single	21
936#	Charles Buck	M	Father	26
937	Spyna Buck	F	Wife	25
938#	Nellie Schildt	--	Wife	38
939	Joseph Schildt	M	Son	20
940	Harry Schildt	M	Son	16
941	Andrew Schildt	M	Son	11
942	Augusta Schildt	F	Dau	9
943	Mary Schildt	F	Dau	7

CENSUS of the -PIEGAN- Indians of BLACKFEET Agency, MONTANA taken by JAMES H. MONTEATH United States Indian Agent, AUGUST 15th, 1901

No.	English Name	Sex	Relation	Age
944	Irene Schildt	F	Dau	4
945	Stillman Schildt	M	Son	2
946#	Mary Jackson	F	Widow	27
947	Minnie Jackson	F	Dau	11
948	Maggie Jackson	F	Dau	6
949	Annie Jackson	F	Dau	4
950	Thos Jackson	M	Son	13
951	Julia Jackson	F	Dau	3
952#	Augustus Augers	M	Sing	22
953#	Emily Fox	Wid	Widow	60
954	Eliza Jackson	F	G-Dau	17
955#	Plume Woman	F	Widow	55
956	Ragged	M	Son	2
957#	Dick Kipp	M	Father	39
---	Mary Kipp	F	Wife	29
959	Louis Kipp	M	Son	10
960	Cora Kipp	F	Dau	13
961	George Kipp	M	Son	5
962	Cecile Kipp	F	Dau	2
963#	Mary Higgins	F	Wife	24
964	May Higgins	F	Dau	5
965	Charles Higgins	M	Son	3
966	John Higgins	M	Son	2
967#	Julia Reevis	F	Wife	35
968	Francis Reevis	M	Son	13
969	Amie Reevis	F	Dau	15
970	Emmett Augers	M	Son	20
971#	Chief In the Middle	M	Father	27
972	Mary Chief In the Middle	F	Wife	27
973	Long Time Medicine Pipe Woman	F	Widow	57
974#	Chas. Reevis	M	Father	26
975	Strikes First	F	Wife	31
976	Fine Gun Woman	F	Dau	3
977	Louis Reevis	M	Son	1
978	Joe Reevis	M	Son	6
979#	Beaver Woman	F	Widow	70
980	Many Guns	M	G-Son	11
981	Sam Scabby Robe	M	Son	16
982#	Mary Devereaux	F	Wife	50
983	Charles Devereaux	M	Son	21
984	Jason Devereaux	M	Son	5

CENSUS of the -PIEGAN- Indians of BLACKFEET Agency, MONTANA taken by JAMES H. MONTEATH United States Indian Agent, AUGUST 15th, 1901

No.	English Name	Sex	Relation	Age
985	Wild Cat	F	Dau	9
986#	Henry Devereaux	M	Sing	23
987	Joe Howard	--	Father	23
988	Annie Howard	F	Wife	18
989	Carrie Monroe	--	Wife	30
990	Mabel Monroe	F	Dau	8
991	Jesse Monroe	M	Son	5
992	Joe Monroe	M	Son	3
993	Grinnell Monroe	M	Son	1
994#	Lucy Cook	F	Wife	29
995	Loretta Cook	F	Dau	5
996	Isabella Cook	F	Dau	8
997#	Joe Still Smoking	--	Father	25
998	Minnie Still Smoking	F	Wife	18
999	Susan Still Smoking	F	Dau	6-mo
1000#	Geneva Stewart	F	Wife	31
1001	Earl Stewart	M	Son	9
1002	James Stewart	M	Son	5
1003	Vera Stewart	F	Dau	3
1004	Virginia Stewart	F	Dau	2
1005	Jesse Stewart	M	Son	6-mo
1006#	Sarah Brown	F	Wife	45
1007	Jesse Brown	M	Son	19
1008	Leo Brown	M	Son	5
1009#	James W. Brown	M	Father	29
1010#	Victoria Brown	F	Wife	23
1011	Sarah Adele Brown	F	Dau	2
1012	Wm Upham	M	Father	30
1013	Bells Coming	F	Wife	27
1014	Joe Brown Upham	M	Son	3
1015#	William Kipp	M	Faher[sic]	25
1016	Elizabeth Kipp	F	Wife	23
1017	Ursula Kipp	F	Dau	2
1018	Bernice Kipp	F	Dau	1
1019#	Thos Vielle	M	Sing	23
1020#	Josephine Sullivan	F	Widow	25
1021#	Rosa Ward	F	Wife	34
1022	James Ward	M	Son	10
1023	George Ward	M	Son	8
1024	Mary Rose Ward	F	Dau	6
1025	Emma Ward	F	Dau	3

CENSUS of the -PIEGAN- Indians of BLACKFEET Agency, MONTANA taken by JAMES H. MONTEATH United States Indian Agent, AUGUST 15th, 1901

No.	English Name	Sex	Relation	Age
1026	William Ward	M	Son	1
1027#	Eliza McGowan	F	Wife	25
1028	Jeanette Marie McGowan	F	Dau	4
1029	Georgiani McGowan	F	Dau	2
1030#	Wm Lewis	M	Father	60
1031	Antoine Lewis	M	Son	16
1032	Peter Lewis	M	Son	3
1033	Sarah Lewis	F	Dau	2
1034	Betsey Lewis	F	Dau	1
1035	Joseph Narcius Lewis	M	Son	3-mo
1036#	Mary Norman	F	Wife	25
1037	Lena Norman	F	Dau	6
1038	Adolph Norman	M	Son	4
1039	Alfred Norman	M	Son	3
1040#	Pressley Houk	M	Father	24
1041	Margaret E Houk	F	Wife	17
1042	Ellenor Houk	F	Dau	1
1043#	Alex DuBrey	M	Father	38
1044	Joe DuBrey	M	Son	3
1045	George DuBrey	M	Son	2
1046#	Mary Powell	F	Wife	50
1047	Charles Powell	M	Son	23
1048	Jesse Powell	M	Son	18
1049	Susan Powell	F	Dau	14
1050	Jennie DeWolf	F	Dau	19
1051	Maggie Powell	F	Dau	1
1052#	Malinda Wren	F	Widow	52
1053	John Wren	M	Son	20
1054	Robert Wren	M	Son	17
1055	Dora Wren	F	Dau	15
1056	William Wren Wren[sic]	M	Son	12
1057	Lillie Wren	F	Dau	10
1058	Ida Wren	F	Dau	8
1059	Malinda Wren	F	Dau	6
1060#	Louis Cobell	M	Father	46
1061	Peter Cobell	M	Son	17
1062	Clara Cobell	F	Dau	14
1063	Julius Cobell	M	Son	6
1064	Louise Cobell	F	Dau	5
1065	Dewey Cobell	M	Son	2
1066	Thos. Rob't Cobell	M	Son	1

CENSUS of the -PIEGAN- Indians of BLACKFEET Agency, MONTANA taken by JAMES H. MONTEATH United States Indian Agent, AUGUST 15th, 1901

No.	English Name	Sex	Relation	Age
1067#	Angeline Connelly	F	Widow	27
1068	John Connelly	M	Son	11
1069	Bryan Connelly	M	Son	15
1070	Victor Connelly	M	Son	13
1071	Mary Connelly	F	Dau	17
1072	Rose Connelly	F	Dau	16
1073#	Rose Hinkel	F	Wife	39
1074	George Hinkle	M	Son	19
1075	William Hinkle	M	Son	17
1076	Lizzie Hinkle	F	Dau	15
1077	Mamie Hinkle	F	Dau	13
1078#	Alex Fox	M	Father	23
1079	Mabel Fox	F	Dau	1
1080#	George Croff	M	Single	23
1081#	Frank Bostwick	M	Father	38
1082	Louise Bostwick	F	Wife	27
1083	John Bostwick	M	Bro	24
1084	Henry Bostwick	M	Son	8
1085	George Bostwick	M	Son	6
1086	William Bostwick	M	Son	5
1087	Annie Bostwick	F	Dau	2
1088#	Helen Iron	F	Wife	30
1089	Louise Paul	F	Wife	44
1090	Solomon Paul	M	Son	22
1091	Albert Paul	M	Son	20
1092	Philip Paul	M	Son	17
1093	Eddie Paul	M	Son	15
1094	Rosina Paul	F	Dau	12
1095	Oliver Paul	M	Son	10
1096	William Paul	M	Son	7
1097	Celina Paul	F	Dau	5
1098#	James Houseman	M	Father	34
1099	Thomas Jackson	M	S-Son	13
1100	Joseph Houseman	M	Son	11
1101	Mary Houseman	F	Dau	10
1102	Geneva Houseman	F	Dau	7
1103	Maggie Houseman	F	Dau	2
1104	Frank Houseman	M	Son	1
1105#	Vina Hall	F	Wife	22
1106	Elsie Hall	F	S-Dau	3
1107	Abner Hall	M	Son	2

CENSUS of the -PIEGAN- Indians of BLACKFEET Agency, MONTANA taken by JAMES H. MONTEATH United States Indian Agent, AUGUST 15th, 1901

No.	English Name	Sex	Relation	Age
1108	Ruth Hall	F	Dau	1
1109#	Harry No Chief	M	Father	27
1110	Red Buffalo Stone	F	Wife	17
1111	Harry No Chief	M	Son	6-mo
1112#	Chief Crow	M	Father	45
1113	Strikes With A Gun	F	Wife	50
1114	James Chief Crow	M	Son	20
1115	Alfred Chief Crow	M	Son	17
1116	Yells Last Woman	F	Dau	10
1117#	Alice Burd	F	G-Widow	21
1118#	Many Guns	M	Father	42
1119	Mouse Woman	F	Wife	43
1120	Thos. Many Guns	M	Son	6
1121#	Laura Van Senden	F	Wife	18
1122#	Stuart Hazlett	M	Single	18
1123#	George W. Cook	M	Father	39
1124	Julia Cook	F	Wife	28
1125#	Rene Comelle	F	Sing	25
1126#	Wm D. Murphy	M	Sing	19
1127	Hamlin H. Murphy	M	Bro	14
1128	Harlin Murphy	M	Bro	12
1129	Albert H. Murphy	M	Bro	9
1130#	Paul Austin	M	Father	34
1131	Louise Austin	F	Wife	38
1132	Maud Davis	F	Dau	10
1133	Agnes Schubert	F	Dau	7
1134	Wm Austin	M	Son	2
1135#	George Prairie Chicken	M	Father	28
1136	Johanna Prairie Chicken	F	Wife	24
1137	Thomas Prairie Chicken	M	Son	3
1138	Cecile Prairie Chicken	F	Dau	5
1139	(Infant)	M	Son	4-mo
1140#	Steve Mad Man	M	Single	23
1141#	Joseph Wall	M	Widower	58
1142#	Rushes Home	F	Widow	30
1143	Irvin Bear Leggins	M	Son	4
1144	(Infant)	F	Dau	4-mo
1145#	Every Body Looks At	M	Father	45
1146	Minnie Last Coyote	F	Dau	6
1147#	Four Horns	M	Father	50
1148	Short Woman	F	Wife	38

CENSUS of the -PIEGAN- Indians of BLACKFEET Agency, MONTANA taken by JAMES H. MONTEATH United States Indian Agent, AUGUST 15th, 1901

No.	English Name	Sex	Relation	Age
1149	Jas Four Horns	M	Son	7
1150	Benj. Four Horns	M	Son	22
1151	Louis Four Horns	M	Son	3
1152#	Spotted Calf	M	Father	74
1153	Mink Woman	F	Wife	64
1154#	Rattler	M	Father	54
1155	Spear Woman	F	Wife	40
1156	Elmer Rattler	M	Son	23
1157#	Albert Calf Robe	M	Son	25
1158	Strikes First	F	Mother	60
1159#	Kills at the Edge	F	Moth	60
1160	George Four Horns	M	Son	20
1161#	Chief All Over	M	Father	48
1162	Little Petrified Rock	F	Wife	50
1163	George Chief All Over	M	Son	11
1164#	Good Stabbing	M	Father	35
1165	Medicine Hollering Woman	F	Wife	39
1166#	Kicking Woman	F	Wid	61
1167#	Wolf Eagle	M	Father	49
1168	Kills In the Night	F	Wife	36
1169	Blanket Woman	F	Wife	43
1170#	Iron Eater	M	Father	49
1171	Long Time Rock	F	Wife	38
1172	Black Cloth Woman	F	Wife	35
1173	Isabel Iron Eater	F	Dau	14
1174	Rosa Iron Eater	F	Dau	10
1175	Button Woman	F	Dau	3
1176	Medicine Smoke Woman	F	Dau	1
1177#	Flint Smoker	M	Father	41
1178	Under Beaver	F	Wife	40
1179	Peter Flint Smoker	M	Son	18
1180	James Flint Smoker	M	Son	10
1181#	Isabel Iron Crow	F	Sing	15
1182#	Josephine Hall	F	Wife	26
1183	Patrick Hall	M	Son	10
1184	David Hall	M	Son	7
1185	William Hall	M	Son	5
1186	James Hall	M	Son	1
1187	Mary Pablo	F	Dau	1
1188#	John Eagle Ribs	M	Father	35
1189	Louise Eagle Ribs	F	Wife	25

CENSUS of the -PIEGAN- Indians of BLACKFEET Agency, MONTANA taken by JAMES H. MONTEATH United States Indian Agent, AUGUST 15th, 1901

No.	English Name	Sex	Relation	Age
1190	Last Light To Come Over The Hill	F	Dau	2
1191#	Tearing Lodge	M	Father	65
1192	Cuts With Many	F	Wife	54
1193#	Boy Chief	M	Father	43
1194	Last Gun Woman	F	Wife	29
1195	Clara Boy Chief	F	Dau	5
1196	Emma Boy Chief	F	Dau	3
1197	William Boy Chief	M	Son	8
1198	Dennis Boy Chief	M	Son	10
1199#	Eagle Head	M	Father	67
1200	White Tail Feathers	F	Wife	54
1201	James Eagle Head	M	Son	15
1202	Maggie Eagle Head	F	Dau	11
1203#	Big Beaver	M	Father	40
1204	Annie Big Beaver	F	Wife	32
1205	Eddie Big Beaver	M	Son	16
1206	Aaron Big Beaver	M	Son	14
1207	Rosa Big Beaver	F	Dau	6
1208	George Big Beaver	M	Son	2
1209#	Bear Shoe	M	Father	38
1210	Daisy Big Beaver	F	Wife	16
1211	Catherine Big Beaver	F	Dau	2
1212#	Antoine Mountain Chief	M	Single	22
1213#	Mountain Chief	M	Father	53
1214	Nothing Gun	F	Wife	42
1215	Walter Mountain Chief	M	Son	19
1216	Old Mouse	F	Dau	6
1217	Hears All Languages	F	Dau	5
1218#	Thekla Mountain Chief	F	Mother	21
1219	Louis Navaro	M	Son	3
1220#	Maggie Albertson	M[sic]	Wife	42
1221	Arthur Walters	M	Son	21
1222	George Walters	M	Son	26
1223	Robert Albertson	M	Son	9
1224	Old Person Woman	F	Dau	6
1225	Rattles With Many	F	Dau	4
1226#	Louis Marceau	M	Father	35
1227	Rosa Marceau	F	Wife	24
1228#	Minnie Ripley	F	Moth	19
1229	Peter Ripley	M	Son	1
1230#	Richard Calf Robe	M	Father	23

CENSUS of the -PIEGAN- Indians of BLACKFEET Agency, MONTANA taken by JAMES H. MONTEATH United States Indian Agent, AUGUST 15th, 1901

No.	English Name	Sex	Relation	Age
1231	Anna Calf Robe	F	Wife	22
1232	(Infant)	F	Dau	6-mo
1233#	Strikes Back	F	Moth	50
1234	Rape Woman	F	Dau	4
1235#	Frank Calf Robe	M	Father	29
1236	Kills Across	F	Wife	26
1237	Thos Calf Robe	M	Son	4
1238#	Mrs Calf Robe	F	Widow	45
1239#	Fish	M	Father	23
1240	Lone Rock	F	Wife	24
1241#	Day Rider	M	Father	28
1242	Crawls Away	F	Wife	30
1243	Joe Day Rider	M	Son	5
1244	Morning Owl Woman	F	Dau	3
1245	Peter Day Rider	M	Son	1
1246	Geo Day Rider	M	Son	16
1247#	Head Carrier	M	Father	89
1248	Catches	F	Wife	60
1249	John Head Carrier	M	Son	22
1250#	Barney Calf Ribs	M	Father	27
1251	Good Attack Woman	F	Wife	18
1252	(Infant)	F	Dau	3-mo
1253	Calf Boss Ribs	M	Father	59
1254	Made A Medicine Lodge Suddenly	F	Wife	56
1255	Minnie Calf Boss Ribs	F	Dau	8
1256	Joseph Calf Boss Ribs	M	Son	6
1257#	Owl Top Feathers	M	Father	39
1258	Black Point Woman	F	Wife	43
1259	Drives Back Good	F	Dau	15
1260#	Lone Cut	F	Widow	73
1261#	Poor Woman	F	Widow	54
1262#	Old Coyote	M	Father	35
1263	Orphan Woman	F	Wife	44
1264	Phillip Wells	M	Son	19
1265#	Black Face	F	Widow	60
1266	Goes To War Alone	M	Son	6
1267#	Big Plume	M	Father	57
1268	Catches On The Top	F	Wife	44
1269	Louise Big Plume	F	Dau	8
1270#	Jerry Big Plume	M	Father	22
1271	Josephine Big Plume	F	Wife	19

CENSUS of the -PIEGAN- Indians of BLACKFEET Agency, MONTANA taken by JAMES H. MONTEATH United States Indian Agent, AUGUST 15th, 1901

No.	English Name	Sex	Relation	Age
1272#	Black Boy	M	Father	44
1273	Anthelia Black Boy	F	Wife	16
1274	Fisher Black Boy	M	Son	13
1275#	Calf Tail	M	Father	41
1276	Different Gun Woman	F	Wife	44
1277	Earnest Calf Tail	M	Son	14
1278	(Infant)	F	Dau	6-mo
1279#	Coming Owl	F	Widow	62
1280#	Gambler	M	Father	45
1281	Anna Gambler	F	Wife	50
1282	Yellow Light	F	Dau	5
1283#	Owl Child	M	Father	46
1284	Mollie Owl Child	F	Wife	34
1285	Susan Owl Child	F	Dau	20
1286	John Owl Child	M	Son	18
1287	Isabel Owl Child	F	Dau	13
1288	Joseph Owl Child	M	Son	11
1289	Louis Owl Child	M	Son	6
1290	Anna Owl Child	F	Dau	5
1291	William Owl Child	M	Son	3
1292#	Richard Sanderville	M	Father	34
1293	Nancy Sanderville	F	Wife	24
1294	Agnes Sanderville	F	Dau	12
1295	Bridget Sanderville	F	Dau	2
1296	(Infant)	M	Son	6-mo
1297#	Michael Day Rider	M	Father	29
1298	Helen Day Rider	F	Mother	24
1299	Oliver Day Rider	M	Son	6
1300	George Day Rider	M	Son	2
1301	Jack Day Rider	M	Son	2
1302	(Infant)	F	Dau	5-mo
1303#	Yells In Water	M	Father	27
1304	Assorted Gun Woman	F	Wife	24
1305	John Yells In The Water	M	Son	10
1306	George Yells In The Water	M	Son	2
1307#	Wolf Head	M	Father	52
1308	Sings In the Air	F	Wife	44
1309	Alex Wolf Head	M	Son	11
1310#	Alex Guardipee	M	Father	36
1311	Grass Snake	F	Wife	23
1312	John Guardipee	M	Son	6

CENSUS of the -PIEGAN- Indians of BLACKFEET Agency, MONTANA taken by JAMES H. MONTEATH United States Indian Agent, AUGUST 15th, 1901

No.	English Name	Sex	Relation	Age
1313	Katie Guardipee	F	Dau	10
1314	(Infant)	F	Dau	6-mo
1315#	Good Strike	F	Widow	60
1316	Esther Running Rabbit	F	Dau	16
1317#	Stabs By Mistake	M	Father	32
1318	Steals In The Day Woman	F	Wife	28
1319	Red Boy	M	Son	5
1320	Louise Stabs By Mistake	M	Son	3
1321	Maggie Stabs By Mistake	F	Dau	1
1322#	Weasel Head	M	Father	36
1323	Old Form	F	Wife	48
1324	Kills Close Woman	F	Dau.	15
1325	Charles Weasel Head	M	Son	13
1326	Peter Weasel Head	M	Son	10
1327	Good Looking Woman	F	Dau	6
1328	John Weasel Head	M	Son	5
1329	Thos Weasel Head	M	Son	3
1330	Goes To War Good	M	Son	13
1331#	George Eats Alone	M	Single	21
1332#	Jack Big Moon	M	Father	53
1333	Long Time Calf	F	Wife	38
1334#	Medicine Bull	M	Father	41
1335	Sore Back	F	Wife	34
1336	Thos. Medicine Bull	M	Son	4
1337	Coyote Woman	F	Dau	3
1338#	Henry Head Carrier	M	Father	37
1339	Good Victory	F	Wife	47
1340	Goes In Two Places	F	Dau	3
1341#	Mrs Eddie Jack	F	Widow	38
1342	John Two Guns	M	Son	20
1343	Eddy Jack	M	Son	1
1344	Juanique Jack	F	Dau	6
1345	Cecile Jack	F	Dau	4
1346#	Long Time Wolverine	F	Widow	58
1347	Little Bull #2	F	Wife	46
1348	Tail Feathers Coming #1	M	Father	56
1349	Snake Woman	F	Wife	32
1350	Cecile Tail Feathers Coming	F	Dau	14
1351	Rabbit	F	Dau	5
1352	Double Steal	F	Dau	3
1353	Paul	F	G-Dau	11

CENSUS of the -PIEGAN- Indians of BLACKFEET Agency, MONTANA taken by JAMES H. MONTEATH United States Indian Agent, AUGUST 15th, 1901

No.	English Name	Sex	Relation	Age
1354#	Tail Feathers Coming #2	F	Mother	76
1355	Broad Woman	F	Dau	10
1356#	Wm Russell	M	Father	47
1357	Mary Russell	F	Wife	41
1358	George Russell	M	Son	16
1359	Joseph Russell	M	Son	12
1360	Wm Russell	M	Son	10
1361	Henry Russell	M	Son	3
1362#	Alfred Trombly	M	Father	23
1363	Cecile Trombly	F	Wife	18
1364	(Infant)	F	Dau	6-mo
1365#	Mrs Arrow Maker	F	Widow	40
1366	Strikes On the Floor	F	Dau	8
1367#	Lawrence Faber	M	Father	27
1368	Annie Faber	F	Wife	23
1369	Kazy Faber	F	Dau	1
1370#	Small Face	F	Widow	53
1371	Hellen Faber	F	G-Dau	5
1372#	Young Running Rabbit	M	Father	64
1373	Old Woman	F	Wife	42
1374	Susie Running Rabbit	F	Dau	2
1375	Julia Running Rabbit	F	Dau	13
1376	Isabel Running Rabbit	F	Dau	7
1377#	Double Blaze Jackson	M	Father	43
1378	Medicine Beaver	F	Wife	50
1379	Richard Jackson	M	Son	4
1380	Louis Jackson	M	Son	5
1381	Frank Jackson	M	Son	16
1382	Joseph Jackson	M	Son	29
1383#	Singing	F	Widow	70
1384#	Under Otter	F	Widow	70
1385#	Bad OOld[sic] Man	M	Father	70
1386	Strikes By Mistake	F	Wife	60
1387	Mack Bad Old Man	M	Son	19
1388#	Mike Big Lake	M	Father	23
1389	Round Head	F	Wife	17
1390#	Blackfoot Woman	F	Wid	60
1391	John Big Lake	M	Son	19
1392	Maniase Big Lake	F	Dau	13
1393#	Susan Schultz	F	Wife	40
1394	Hart Schultz	M	Son	19

CENSUS of the -PIEGAN- Indians of BLACKFEET Agency, MONTANA taken by JAMES H. MONTEATH United States Indian Agent, AUGUST 15th, 1901

No.	English Name	Sex	Relation	Age
1395#	Jessie Pepion	F	Wife	30
1396	Tom Pepion	M	Son	6
1397	Lucius Pepion	M	Son	3
1398	Victor Pepion	M	Son	2
1399#	Red Head	M	Father	43
1400	Strikes Twice	F	Wife	52
1401	Running Owl	M	Father	38
1402	Kills Two	F	Wife	48
1403	Short Woman	F	Dau	10
1404	Round Robe	M	Son	4
1405	Last Iron Woman	F	Dau	3
1406#	Kills Close	F	Widow	80
1407#	Agnes Big Road	F	Sing	21
1408#	Joe Calf Robe	M	Father	27
1409	Medicine Big Head	F	Wife	26
1410	Mink Calf Robe	M	Son	2
1411#	Skunk Woman	F	Widow	25
1412	Takes Alone	M	Son	3
1413	Good Rider	M	Son	2
1414	Steal Woman	F	Dau	1
1415#	Sam Randall	M	Single	28
1416#	Joe Evans	M	Father	28
1417	Mary Cecile Evans	F	Wife	20
1418	James Evans	M	Son	5
1419	Irene Evans	F	Dau	2
1420#	The Bite	M	Father	49
1421	Kills for Nothing	F	Wife	42
1422	Harry Bite	M	Son	16
1423	Minnie Bite	F	Dau	8
1424	Rosa Bite	F	Dau	2
1425	Thos Bite	M	Son	3
1426#	Wakes Up Last	M	Father	33
1427	Mollie Wakes Up Last	F	Wife	21
1428	Pretty Bird	F	Dau	4
1429	Julia Wakes Up Last	F	Dau	2
1430#	Catching Him Down	F	Wife	42
1431	Jingles In the Air	M	Son	5
1432#	Wolf Plume	M	Father	41
1433	Strikes First	F	Wife	33
1434	Wesley Wolf Plume	M	Son	14
1435	Lizzie Wolf Plume	F	Dau	1

CENSUS of the -PIEGAN- Indians of BLACKFEET Agency, MONTANA taken by JAMES H. MONTEATH United States Indian Agent, AUGUST 15th, 1901

No.	English Name	Sex	Relation	Age
1436#	Going to Move	M	Father	49
1437	Hide Scraper	F	Wife	50
1438	James Going to Move	M	Son	18
1439#	Dry Limb	M	Father	24
1440	Rag Woman	F	Wife	21
1441	Little Bull #1	M	Father	56
1442	Steals Good Woman	F	Wife	41
1443	Takes Two Guns	M	Son	5
1444#	Found A Gun	M	Single	21
1445#	Little Otter	F	Widow	60
1446#	Spotted Eagle	M	Father	60
1447	Gives To One Another	F	Wife	50
1448	John Spotted Eagle	M	Son	20
1449	Asks For Many	M	Son	9
1450#	Morning Gun	M	Father	35
1451	Otter Woman	F	Wife	23
1452	Emma Morning Gun	F	Dau	3
1453	Rosa Morning Gun	F	Dau	2
1454	John Morning Gun	M	Son	1
1455	Flies In Water	M	Son	5
1456	Joseph Morning Gun	M	Son	10
1457#	Medicine Stab	M	Father	49
1458	Cut Body	F	Wife	38
1459#	Old Chief	M	Father	50
1460	Morning Woman	F	Wife	43
1461	John Old Chief	M	Son	19
1462	Medicine Girl	F	Dau	12
1463	Robert Old Chief	M	Son	9
1464	Paul Old Chief	M	Son	3
1465#	Running Crane #2	F	Widow	50
1466	Little Rock	F	Widow	60
1467	James Running Crane	M	Son	9
1468#	Hairy Face	M	Father	41
1469	Rag Woman	F	Wife	30
1470	Bead Woman	F	Wife	24
1471	Blind Woman	F	Dau	14
1472	Took After Them Home	M	Son	8
1473	First One	M	Son	3
1474	Mollie Hairy Face	F	Dau	2
1475#	Yellow Kidney	M	Father	31
1476	Maggie Yellow Kidney	F	Wife	29

CENSUS of the -PIEGAN- Indians of BLACKFEET Agency, MONTANA taken by JAMES H. MONTEATH United States Indian Agent, AUGUST 15th, 1901

No.	English Name	Sex	Relation	Age
1477	Medicine Otter	M	Son	5
1478	Yelled There Before	F	Dau	2
1479	Short Quill Woman	F	Dau	14
1480#	Abel Skunk Cap	M	Single	25
1481	Little Girl	F	Mother	60
1482#	Wades In Water	M	Father	32
1483	Lucy Wades In Water	F	Wife	25
1484#	Adam Whiteman	M	Father	26
1485	Anna Whiteman	F	Wife	22
1486#	Old Man Chief	M	Father	31
1487	Rosa Old Man Chief	F	Wife	26
1488	James Old Man Chief	M	Son	6
1489	Thos Old Man Chief	M	Son	2
1490	(Infant)	M	Son	5-mo
1491#	Joe Bull Shoe	M	Father	23
1492	Dirty Face	F	Mother	37
1493	Patrick Bull Shoe	M	Brother	14
1494#	Bull Shoe #2	F	Widow	40
1495	Big Woman	F	Widow	43
1496#	Catches First	F	Widow	78
1497#	John Pepion	M	Father	30
1498	Cecile Pepion	F	Wife	29
1499#	Cecile Pepion	F	Single	26
1500#	Louise Pepion	F	Single	23
1501	Charles No Coat	M	Single	23
1502#	No Coat	M	Father	43
1503	Kills for Nothing	F	Wife	33
1504	Annie No Coat	F	Dau	8
1505#	Shoots Another	M	Father	37
1506	Bird Tail Woman	F	Wife	40
1507	Joseph Weatherwax	M	Son	17
1508	Yells On The Way Home	F	Dau	2
1509	Josephine Weatherwax	F	Dau	21
1510#	Iron Pipe	--	Father	42
1511	Goes In Two Places	F	Wife	35
1512	Joseph Iron Pipe	M	Son	13
1513	Maggie Iron Pipe	F	Dau	12
1514	John Iron Pipe	M	Son	6
1515	Shines Again	M	Son	5
1516	Shoots Close	M	Son	2
1517#	Red Horn	F	Widow	65

CENSUS of the -PIEGAN- Indians of BLACKFEET Agency, MONTANA taken by JAMES H. MONTEATH United States Indian Agent, AUGUST 15th, 1901

No.	English Name	Sex	Relation	Age
1518	Mamie Crawford	F	Wife	40
1519	Joseph Crawford	M	Son	3
1520	James Crawford	M	Son	2
1521	Hellen Crawford	F	Dau	5
1522	Emma Crawford	F	Dau	9
1523#	Belle Ripley	F	Widow	50
1524	David Ripley	M	Son	30
1525#	Dives Long Way	F	Widow	80
1526#	White Dog	M	Father	49
1527	Medicine Pipe Woman	F	Wife	21
1528#	Iron Necklace	M	Father	30
1529	Kills Inside	F	Wife	24
1530	Anna Iron Necklace	F	Dau	8
1531#	War Bonnet	M	Father	26
1532	Victory Before Time	F	Wife	30
1533	James War Bonnet	M	Son	4
1534	Thos War Bonnet	M	Son	2
1535#	Big Lodge Pole	M	Father	40
1536	Mary Big Lodge Pole	F	Wife	58
1537	Peter Big Lodge Pole	M	Son	16
1538	Sam Choate	M	Son	22
1539#	Felix Marrow Bones	M	Father	29
1540	Fanny Marrow Bones	F	Wife	17
1541	(Infant)	M	Son	6-mo
1542#	Little White Woman	F	Widow	65
1543#	Henry No Bear	M	Father	34
1544	Sure Woman	F	Wife	28
1545	Thomas No Bear	M	Son	5
1546	Rosa No Bear	F	Dau	2
1547	Last Coyote	F	Widow	56
1548#	Joseph Wall	M	Widower	58
1549#	Thomas Spotted Eagle	M	Hus	27
1550	Matilda Spotted Eagle	F	Wife	17
1551#	Long Time Woman	F	Single	54
1552#	Louis Trombly	M	Fath	30
1553	Maggie Trombly	F	Wife	28
1554	Isaac Trombly	M	Son	5
1555	Joseph Trombly	M	Son	3
1556	George Trombly	M	Son	2
1557	(Infant)	F	Dau	3-mo
1558#	Little Plume	M	Father	47

CENSUS of the -PIEGAN- Indians of BLACKFEET Agency, MONTANA taken by JAMES H. MONTEATH United States Indian Agent, AUGUST 15th, 1901

No.	English Name	Sex	Relation	Age
1559	Cuts Different	F	Wife	41
1560	James Little Plume	M	Bro	22
1561	Millie Little Plume	F	Dau	12
1562	Louis Little Plume	M	Son	11
1563	Josephine Little Plume	F	Dau	8
1564	Peter Little Plume	M	Son	7
1565	Joseph Little Plume	M	Son	6
1566	Mary Little Plume	F	Dau	6
1567	Annie Little Plume	F	Dau	9-mo
1568#	Stretched Out	M	Sing	38
1569#	Duck Head	M	Father	35
1570	Lizzie Duck Head	F	Wife	29
1571	Louise Duck Head	F	Dau	3
1572	Josephine Duck Head	F	Dau	11
1573	Peter Duck Head	M	Son	9
1574	Mary Duck Head	F	Dau	5
1575#	Henry Heavy Gun	M	Father	21
1576	Mary Heavy Gun	F	Wife	31
1577	Jack Heavy Gun	M	Son	1
1578	Arthur Heavy Gun	M	Son	1
1579#	Eddie Running Crane	M	Father	27
1580	Nellie Running Crane	F	Wife	23
1581	Peter Running Crane	M	Son	4
1582	Paul Running Crane	M	Son	1
1583#	After Buffalo	M	Father	49
1584	Tatsey After Buffalo	F	Wife	26
1585	Louise After Buffalo	F	Dau	1
1586#	Alex Marceau	M	Father	36
1587	Theresa Marceau	F	Wife	27
1588	Louise Marceau	F	Dau	8
1589	Anna Marceau	F	Dau	3
1590#	Red Fox	M	Father	28
1591	Good Victory	F	Wife	25
1592	John Red Fox	M	Son	4
1593	James Red Fox	M	Son	3
1594#	Little Dog	M	Father	47
1595	Walks In Water	F	Wife	21
1596	Medicine Rattling Running	F	Dau	4
1597	Harrison Little Dog	M	Son	18
1598#	Buffalo Growing	M	Father	43
1599	Shield Woman	M	Wife	41

CENSUS of the -PIEGAN- Indians of BLACKFEET Agency, MONTANA taken by JAMES H. MONTEATH United States Indian Agent, AUGUST 15th, 1901

No.	English Name	Sex	Relation	Age
1600#	Peter Spotted Bear	M	Father	20
1601	Anna Spotted Bear	F	Wife	18
1602	Rosa Spotted Bear	F	Dau	2
1603	John Spotted Bear	M	Son	1
1604#	Spotted Bear #1	M	Father	75
1605	Wet Teeth	F	Wife	40
1606	Perry Spotted Bear	M	Son	9
1607#	Takes Iron Gun	F	Widow	80
1608#	Wild Gun	M	Father	47
1609	Tiger Woman	F	Wife	48
1610	Julia Wild Gun	F	Dau	2
1611#	Mittens	M	Father	32
1612	Strikes Near	F	Wife	22
1613	Kills In The Night	F	Dau	10
1614	James Mittens	M	Son	7
1615	John Mittens	M	Son	5
1616	A Lone Light	F	Dau	3
1617#	Thomas Two Stabs	M	Father	42
1618	Maggie Two Stabs	F	Wife	33
1619	Joseph Two Stabs	M	Son	9
1620	Louis Two Stabs	M	Son	5
1621	Louise Two Stabs	F	Dau	3
1622#	Double Runner	M	Father	56
1623	Long Time Squirrel	F	Wife	53
1624	Edward Double Runner	M	Son	23
1625	Paul Double Runner	M	Son	11
1626#	Edgar Double Runner	M	Single	25
1627#	Painted Wings	M	Father	67
1628	Strikes On the Top	F	Wife	56
1629	Little Blaze	M	Son	26
1630#	Running Crane #1	M	Father	74
1631	White Woman	F	Wife	50
1632#	Chewing Black Bones	M	Father	35
1633	Mollie Chewing Black Bones	F	Wife	31
1634	John Chouquette	M	Son	15
1635	George Chewing Black Bones	M	Son	8
1636	Isabel Chewing Black Bones	F	Dau	13
1637	Agnes Chewing Black Bones	F	Dau	10
1638	Maggie Chewing Black Bones	F	Dau	5
1639#	Frank Rider	M	Father	34
1640	Maggie Rider	F	Wife	17

CENSUS of the -PIEGAN- Indians of BLACKFEET Agency, MONTANA taken by JAMES H. MONTEATH United States Indian Agent, AUGUST 15th, 1901

No.	English Name	Sex	Relation	Age
1641	Chewing Black Bones #2	F	Widow	80
1642#	Fine Bull	M	Father	53
1643	Scattered Woman	F	Wife	40
1644	Yellow Spider	F	Dau	10
1645	Lucy Fine Bull	F	Dau	7
1646	James Fine Bull	M	Son	5
1647	Stabs Him Down	M	Son	13
1648	Maggie Fine Bull	F	Dau	2
1649#	Buffalo Hide	M	Father	35
1650	Spotted Woman	F	Wife	27
1651	Thomas Buffalo Hide	M	Son	10
1652	Yellow Buffalo Hide	M	Dau	2
1653#	Good Looking Woman	F	Widow	80
1654#	White Quiver	M	Father	42
1655	Wing	F	Wife	42
1656	Benj. White Quiver	M	Son	16
1657	Maggie White Quiver	F	Dau	9
1658	Josephine White Quiver	F	Dau	4
1659#	Green Grass Bull	M	Father	39
1660	Young Man	M	Son	12
1661#	James Spotted Eagle	M	Father	23
1662	Mary Spotted Eagle	F	Wife	19
1663#	Big Smoke	M	Father	74
1664	Water Black Bird	F	Wife	43
1665	Long Time Buffalo Stone	M	Son	2
1666#	Dan Lone Chief #1	--	Father	27
1667	Ellen Lone Chief	F	Wife	25
1668	Dan Lone Chief	M	Son	1
1669#	John Calf Tail	M	Father	22
1670	Susan Calf Tail	F	Wife	16
1671#	LongTime Rock	M	Father	35
1672	Annie Long Time Rock	F	Wife	23
1673	George Long Time Rock	M	Son	4
1674	Small Young Man	M	Son	2
1675	Tail Feathers	M	Father	53
1676	Sure Buffalo Stone	F	Wife	40
1677	William Tail Feathers	M	Son	12
1678	Charles Tail Feathers	M	Son	10
1679	Small Mink	F	Dau	6
1680	Steals Alone	F	Dau	4
1681#	Elmer Butterfly	M	Father	27

CENSUS of the -PIEGAN- Indians of BLACKFEET Agency, MONTANA taken by JAMES H. MONTEATH United States Indian Agent, AUGUST 15th, 1901

No.	English Name	Sex	Relation	Age
1682	Long Time Hawk	F	Wife	20
1683	Joseph Butterfly	M	Son	6
1684	Snake Old Woman	F	Dau	5
1685	Takes Gun Himself	M	Son	2
1686	(Infant)	M	Son	5-mo
1687#	Petrified	F	Widow	59
1688#	Swims Under	M	Father	31
1689	Mink Woman	F	Wife	18
1690#	Big Crow	M	Father	42
1691	Takes Double Gun	F	Wife	32
1692	Little Hawk Woman	F	Dau	13
1693#	Cree Medicine	M	Father	42
1694	Cecile Cree Medicine	F	Wife	36
1695	Maggie Cree Medicine	F	Dau	10
1696#	Every Body Talks About	M	Father	49
1697	Strikes Back	F	Wife	51
1698	Clumsy Woman	F	Wife	38
1699	Louis E.B.T. About	M	Son	12
1700	George E.B.T. About	M	Son	2
1701	Antoine E.B.T. About	M	Son	2
1702	Singing Inside	F	Dau	6
1703#	Big Wolf Medicine	M	Father	34
1704	Good Clean Up	F	Wife	40
1705	Mary Ann Big Wolf Medicine	F	Dau	10
1706	Light Face	F	Dau	9
1707#	First One Russell	M	Father	29
1708	Isabelle Russell	F	Wife	20
1709	Joseph Russell	M	Son	1
1710#	Thos Kiyo	M	Father	41
1711	Mary Kiyo	F	Wife	26
1712	William Kiyo	M	Son	5
1713	Nellie Kiyo	F	Dau	2
1714#	Mabel Davis	F	Single	16
1715#	Albert Mad Plume	M	Father	27
1716	Susan Mad Plume	F	Wife	24
1717	Maggie Mad Plume	F	Dau	4
1718	Joseph Mad Plume	M	Son	3
1719	Mary Mad Plume	F	Dau	1
1720#	Mary Teasdale	F	Wife	70
1721	Nellie Teasdale	F	Dau	17
1722#	Mad Plume	M	Father	51

CENSUS of the -PIEGAN- Indians of BLACKFEET Agency, MONTANA taken by JAMES H. MONTEATH United States Indian Agent, AUGUST 15th, 1901

No.	English Name	Sex	Relation	Age
1723	Kills In The Night	F	Wife	40
1724	Richard Mad Plume	M	Son	19
1725	Julia Mad Plume	F	Dau	18
1726	Maggie Mad Plume	F	Dau	4
1727	Charles Mad Plume	M	Son	3
1728#	Richard Grant	M	Father	24
1729	Rosa Grant	F	Wife	22
1730	James Grant	M	Son	1
1731	(Infant)	F	Dau	6-mo
1732#	New Robe	M	Father	48
1733	Sharpe Faced Woman	F	Wife	57
1734	Squeal In the Night	F	Wife	36
1735	Joseph New Robe	M	Son	15
1736	(Infant)	M	Son	6-mo
1737#	Louis Champine	M	Father	38
1738	Busy Champine	F	Wife	40
1739	George Champine	M	Son	10
1740	Peter Champine	M	Son	6
1741	Mary Champine	F	Dau	5
1742	Mary Ann Champine	F	Dau	2
1743#	Curlew	F	Widow	70
1744#	Big Tiger Woman	F	Widow	38
1745	James Tiger Woman	M	G-Son	10
1746	Minnie Tiger Woman	F	G-Dau	11
1747#	Yellow Kidney	M	Father	29
1748	Mary Kidney	F	Wife	26
1749	Joseph Kidney	M	Son	2
1750	(Infant)	F	Dau	6-mo
1751#	Crow Eyes	M	Father	44
1752	Running Rattle	F	Wife	30
1753	Takes Gun In The Brush	M	Son	5
1754	Katie Crow Eyes	F	Dau	3
1755	(Infant)	F	Dau	9-mo
1756#	Strike Back	F	Mother	45
1757	Charles Under Bull	F	Son	13
1758	Peter Under Bull	F[sic]	Son	7
1759#	Almost Killed	F	Widow	80
1760#	Joe Trombly	M	Father	42
1761	Julia Trombly	F	Wife	47
1762#	Isabella Trombly	F	Widow	67
1763#	Small Woman	F	Widow	69

CENSUS of the -PIEGAN- Indians of BLACKFEET Agency, MONTANA taken by JAMES H. MONTEATH United States Indian Agent, AUGUST 15th, 1901

No.	English Name	Sex	Relation	Age
1764#	Frank Vielle	M	Father	33
1765	Anna Vielle	F	Wife	38
1766	Jack Vielle	M	Son	5
1767	James Vielle	M	Son	2
1768	(Infant)	M	Son	4-mo
1769#	John Gobert	M	Father	31
1770	Susan Gobert	F	Wife	23
1771	Nellie Gobert	F	Dau	3
1772	Mary Gobert	F	Dau	2
1773#	Philomena St Goddard	F	Wife	32
1774	Agnes St Goddard	F	Dau	11
1775	Alamena St Goddard	F	Dau	6
1776	Archibald St Goddard	M	Son	1
1777#	Louis Croff	M	Father	28
1778	Louise Croff	F	Wife	29
1779	Edward Croff	M	Son	1
1780#	Oliver Sanderville	M	Father	41
1781	Mary Sanderville	F	Wife	36
1782	John Sanderville	M	Son	14
1783#	Joe Fast Buffalo Horse	M	Single	25
1784	Albert Fast Buffalo Horse	M	Brother	24
1785	James Fast Buffalo Horse	M	Brother	15
1786#	Drags His Robe	M	Father	41
1787	Saucy Woman	F	Wife	52
1788	Chipp Drags His Robe	F	Dau	4
1789#	Thunder Woman	F	Widow	68
1790#	Charles White Swan	M	Father	23
1791	Went In First	F	Wife	16
1792#	Joe Kossuth	M	Father	26
1793	Mary Kossuth	M	Wife	40
1794	Miles Running Wolf	M	S-Son	20
1795	Herbert Running Wolf	M	S-Son	16
1796	Homer Running Wolf	M	S-Son	14
1797	George Running Wolf	M	S-Son	11
1798	James Running Wolf	M	S-Son	6
1799#	Many Guns	M	Father	43
1800	Josephine Many Guns	F	Wife	19
1801	Just Heard Him	M	Son	1
1802#	No Runner	M	Father	59
1803	White Woman	F	Wife	57
1804#	Charles Iron Breast	M	Father	26

CENSUS of the -PIEGAN- Indians of BLACKFEET Agency, MONTANA taken by JAMES H. MONTEATH United States Indian Agent, AUGUST 15th, 1901

No.	English Name	Sex	Relation	Age
1805	Nellie Iron Breast	F	Wife	29
1806	Long Time Buffalo Stone	F	Dau	1
1807	Curly Bear	M	Father	54
1808	Free Will	F	Wife	38
1809	Go In Often	F	Wife	37
1810	Charles Curly Bear	M	Son	20
1811	Captures In the Night	F	Dau	8
1812	Old Man	M	Son	5
1813	Old Woman	F	Dau	4
1814	Long Time Black Bird	M	Son	3
1815	(Infant)	F	Dau	5-mo
1816#	Nelson Henault	M	Single	21
1817#	Maggie Henault	F	Wife	50
1818	Moses Henault	M	Son	13
1819	Clara Henault	F	Dau	11
1820#	Charles Juneau	M	Single	23
1821#	Peter Lauzon	M	Single	21
1822#	Peter Marceau	M	Single	28
1823#	Catches at the Edge of the Water	F	Widow	80
1824#	Margaret Marceau	F	Widow	56
1825	Josephine Marceau	F	Dau	14
1826#	Flat Tail	M	Father	51
1827	Medicine Pipe Woman	F	Wife	40
1828	Sophia Flat Tail	F	Dau	7
1829	Anna Flat Tail	F	Dau	2
1830#	Peter Old Rock	M	Father	25
1831	Rosa Old Rock	F	Wife	16
1832	(Infant)	F	Dau	4-mo
1833#	Louis Chicken Shoe	M	Orphan	4
1834	Yellow Top Knot	F	Orphan	5
1835	Susie Chicken Shoe	F	Orphan	15
1836#	Frank Donovan	M	Father	23
1837	Jenie Donovan	F	Wife	20
1838	Yellow Fly	M	Son	1
1839	Two Strikes	F	Widow	68
1840#	James Gambler	M	Father	26
1841	Anna Gambler	F	Wife	22
1842	Pretty Buffalo Stone	F	Dau	2
1843	(Infant)	F	Dau	4-mo
1844#	Young Running Crane	--	Fateher[sic]	46
1845	Buffalo Stone Woman	F	Wife	48

CENSUS of the -PIEGAN- Indians of BLACKFEET Agency, MONTANA taken by JAMES H. MONTEATH United States Indian Agent, AUGUST 15th, 1901

No.	English Name	Sex	Relation	Age
1846	John Y.R. Crane	M	Son	16
1847	Went In By Mistake	F	Dau	5
1848#	Young Man Chief	M	Father	44
1849	Cecile Young Man Chief	M	Wife	31
1850	(Infant)	F	Dau	5-mo
1851#	Aims Back	M	Father	30
1852	Minnie Aims Back	F	Wife	20
1853	Thomas Aims Back	M	Son	7
1854	Maggie Aims Back	F	Dau	2
1855#	The Horn	M	Father	69
1856	Good Looking	F	Wife	60
1857	Harry Horn	M	Son	22
1858#	Calf Looking	M	Father	57
1859	Weasel Went	F	Wife	80
1860	Paul Calf Looking	M	Son	24
1861	Takes Gun At Night	M	Son	10
1862	Sitting In The Road	F	Moth	89
1863#	Kills Inside	F	Widow	90
1864	William Johnson	M	G-Son	18
1865#	Frank Pepion	M	Single	20
1866	Chester Pepion	M	Bro	17
1867#	Like Marrow Bones	M	Father	60
1868	Takes Good Gun	F	Wife	78
1869#	Peter Guardipee	M	Single	39
1870#	Louise Guardipee	F	Widow	60
1871	John Guardipee	M	Son	19
1872#	Joe Spanish	M	Father	30
1873	Kills First	F	Wife	40
1874	William Spanish	M	Son	7
1875	Agnes Clark	F	S-dau	16
1876#	Takes Gun Both Sides	M	Father	31
1877	One Strike	F	Wife	32
1878	Medicine Black Bird	M	Son	5
1879	Pussy Takes Gun Both Sides	F	Dau	2
1880	Sophia Takes Gun Both Sides	F	Dau	1
1881#	Catches In Side	F	Widow	65
1882	Lone Cut	F	Widow	90
1883#	Red Plume	M	Father	56
1884	Catches First	F	Mother	43
1885	Peter Red Plume	M	Son	3
1886#	Hits On Top	F	Widow	50

CENSUS of the -PIEGAN- Indians of BLACKFEET Agency, MONTANA taken by JAMES H. MONTEATH United States Indian Agent, AUGUST 15th, 1901

No.	English Name	Sex	Relation	Age
1887#	Good Strike	F	Widow	90
1888#	Mary Hazlett	F	Mother	22
1889	Gerald Hazlett	M	Son	2
1890#	Long Time Old Woman	F	Widow	60
1891#	Margaret DeChamp	F	Widow	68
1892#	White Man	M	Father	52
1893	Many Victories	F	Wife	37
1894	Sweet Grass Woman	F	Wife	33
1895	John White Man	M	Son	22
1896	Peter White Man	M	Son	20
1897	James White Man	M	Son	3
1898	Mary White Man	F	Dau	5
1899#	Long Time Sleeping	M	Father	32
1900	Calling Back	F	Wife	33
1901	Lohn[sic] Long Time Sleeping	M	Son	7
1902	Joseph Long Time Sleeping	M	Son	3
1903	Catches Good	F	Dau	5
1904	Sing By Mistake	F	Dau	1
1905#	Cold Feet	M	Father	57
1906	Good Cut	F	Wife	44
1907#	Young Bear Chief	M	Father	44
1908	Good Shield Woman	F	Wife	41
1909	Elk Yells In the Water	F	Wife	39
1910	Maggie Bear Chief	F	Dau	39
1911	John Bear Chief	M	Son	14
1912	John Bear Chief	M	Son	12
1913	Edward Bear Chief	M	Son	22
1914	Lucy Bear Chief	F	Dau	1
1915	Phoebe Bear Chief	F	Dau	6
1916	George Bear Chief	M	Son	7
1917	(Infant)	M	Son	2-mo
1918#	Turtle	M	Father	31
1919	Mary Ann Turtle	F	Wife	21
1920#	Moniac Simons	F	Widow	70
1921#	Millie La Breeche	F	Wife	50
1922	Leonore La Breeche	F	Dau	21
1923	Emily La Breeche	F	Dau	19
1924	Jessie La Breeche	F	Dau	16
1925	Phillip LaBreeche	M	Son	14
1926#	Black Bull	M	Father	33
1927	Dressed Like A Woman	F	Wife	40

CENSUS of the -PIEGAN- Indians of BLACKFEET Agency, MONTANA taken by JAMES H. MONTEATH United States Indian Agent, AUGUST 15th, 1901

No.	English Name	Sex	Relation	Age
1928	Good Steal	F	Dau	3
1929#	David La Breeche	M	Father	28
1930	Minnie La Breeche	F	Wife	29
1931	Charles La Breeche	M	Son	5
1932	Clarence La Breeche	M	Son	3
1933	Violet La Breeche	F	Dau	2
1934#	Medor La Breeche	M	Single	24
1935#	Frank Choate	M	Father	28
1936	Rosaline Choat[sic]	F	Wife	36
1937	James Choate	M	Son	6
1938	Mary Choate	F	Dau	2
1939#	Comes In The Night	M	Father	47
1940	Double Charge	F	Wife	26
1941	Cecil Comes In the Night	F	Dau	6
1942	Minnie Comes In the Night	F	Dau	5
1943	Jamea[sic] Comes In the Night	M	Son	2
1944	Julia Comes In the Night	F	Dau	2
1945	(Infant)	M	Son	5
1946#	Joseph Kills In the Brush	F	Widow	70
1947#	Sure Chief	M	Father	33
1948	Birds Wing	F	Wife	30
1949	Phillip Sure Chief	M	Son	6
1950	William Sure Chief	M	Son	4
1951	George Sure Chief	M	Son	2
1952#	Strikes With A Gun	F	Wife	60
1953#	George Choat	M	Father	25
1954	Funny Choat	F	Wife	22
1955#	Phillip Flat Tail	M	Father	25
1956	Anna Flat Tail	F	Wife	19
1957	Charles Flat Tail	M	Son	1
1958#	Night Gun	M	Father	29
1959	Stella Night Gun	F	Wife	16
1960#	Joseph Night Gun	M	Son	1
1961	Strikes In The Edge of the Water	F	Widow	80
1962#	Charles Rose	M	Father	43
1963	Agnes Rose	F	Wife	38
1964	Maggie Rose	F	Dau	20
1965	William Rose	M	Son	11
1966	Julia Rose	F	Dau	15
1967	Alice Rose	F	Dau	4
1968	Lorene Rose	F	Dau	4

CENSUS of the -PIEGAN- Indians of BLACKFEET Agency, MONTANA taken by JAMES H. MONTEATH United States Indian Agent, AUGUST 15th, 1901

No.	English Name	Sex	Relation	Age
1969	(Infant)	F	Dau	1
1970#	Eagle Flagg	M	Father	74
1971	Bounds Up	F	Wife	69
1972	Annie Eagle Flagg	F	Dau	18
1973#	Eagle	M	Father	33
1974	Medicine Beaver	F	Wife	26
1975	William Eagle	M	Son	4
1976#	Calf Woman	F	Widow	80
1977#	Garrett White	M	Father	26
1978#	Ellen Edwards	F	Wife	30
1979	William Edwards	M	Son	12
1980	Thomas Edwards	M	Son	10
1981	Fanny Edwards	F	Dau	9
1982	Lizzie Edwards	F	Dau	8
1983	John Edwards	M	Son	4
1984	Rosa Edwards	F	Dau	3
1985#	Louise Higgins	F	Wife	52
1986	Emma Croff	F	Dau	21
1987	Alice Higgins	F	Dau	13
1988	Henry Higgins	M	Son	16
1989#	William Croff	M	Single	26
1990#	Mary Stuart	F	Wife	36
1991	Jennie Stuart	F	Dau	18
1992	Clara Stuart	F	Dau	15
1993	Mollie Stuart	F	Dau	10
1994	Cecelia Stuart	F	Dau	7
1995	Mazie Stuart	F	Dau	4
1996#	Bead Woman	F	Mother	45
1997	Isabel Cayton	F	Dau	12
1998#	Joseph Cayton	M	Father	23
1999	Mary Cayton	F	Wife	19
2000#	Mary Jane White	F	Wife	26
2001	Cora White	F	Dau	7
2002	Lorenzo White	M	Son	6
2003	Melvina White	F	Dau	4
2004#	Alice Rutherford	F	Single	21
2005	Henry Rutherford	M	Bro	11
2006	William Rutherford	M	Bro	17
2007#	Richard Rutherford	M	Father	24
2008	Eliza Rutherford	F	Wife	24
2009	Edna Rutherford	F	Dau	2

CENSUS of the -PIEGAN- Indians of BLACKFEET Agency, MONTANA taken by JAMES H. MONTEATH United States Indian Agent, AUGUST 15th, 1901

No.	English Name	Sex	Relation	Age
2010	Dewey Rutherford	M	Son	1
2011#	Joseph McKnight	M	Father	26
2012	Lucy McKnight	F	Wife	24
2013	Irene McKnight	F	Dau	4
2014	Aaron McKnight	M	Son	2
2015	Nancy McKnight	F	Dau	1
2016#	Anna Fisher	F	Wife	30
2017	James Fisher	M	Son	14
2018	Eugene Fisher	M	Son	2
2019#	Aggie Pias	F	Single	14
2020	Daniel Pias	M	Bro	12
2021#	Joseph Tatsey	M	Father	37
2022	Annie Tatsey	F	Wife	28
2023	Josephine Tatsey	F	Dau	12
2024	Hattie Tatsey	F	Dau	9
2025	John Tatsey	M	Son	6
2026	Joseph Tatsey	M	Son	4
2027	Elixabeth[sic] Tatsey	F	Dau	2
2028#	Susan Tatsey	F	Widow	80
2029#	John White Calf	M	Father	40
2030	Weasel Tail Woman	F	Wife	30
2031	Steals from one Another	F	Dau	2
2032	Mans Face	F	Dau	15
2033#	Minnie La Mott	F	Single	18
2034	Jennie La Mott	F	Sister	16
2035	Joseph La Mott	M	Bro	14
2036#	Robert Hamilton	M	Father	31
2037	Rosa Hamilton	F	Wife	27
2038	Theo Hamilton	F	Dau	1
2039#	Oliver Racine	M	Father	22
2040	Belle Racine	F	Wife	19
2041	Joseph Racine	M	Son	1
2042#	Thos. Bogie	M	Single	24
2043#	Diving At The Shore	F	Wife	42

Decrease caused by a number of families being stricken from the rolls by recent Council proceedings subject to approval of the Hon. Sec'y of the Interior.

Index

----, Robert 39
(INFANT) 9,11,12,14,15,16,17,19,
20,21,22,23,24,25,26,27,29,30,32,33,
251,252,253,254,255,256,259,261,262,
263,264,265,266,267,268,269,276,279,
280,281,282,285,286,290,291,292,293,
294,295,296,297
? 258
2 STABS, Maggie 4
A BACK
    Emley 17
    John 17
A BUFFALO
    Ammie 56
    Annie 112
    Fanny 112
    Isabel 56,112
    Joe 112
    John 56
    Susan 56
    Xzever 56
A LONE LIGHT 288
A T KNOT
    Antoine 110
    Louise 110
    Philip 110
    Stink 110
A T KNOTT
    Geo 46
    Louize 46
    Philip 46
    Silas 46
ABBOT, Maggie 163
ACOWAS 111
ACTIVE BIRD 107,166
AFTER BUFFALO 7,26,70,78,135,
    238,287
    Agnes 210,262
    Anna 205
    Annie 262
    Cecil 205
    Charles 262
    Chas 238
    Daisy 78,238
    James 135,262
    Joe 238,262
    John 78,210
    Jos 205
    Joseph 70
    Louise 238,287
    Maggie 262
    Mrs Pete 210,262
    Pete 55,205,262
    Peter 112
    Tatsey 287
AFTER BUFFALO #2 135
AGTER BUFFALO, Cecile 262
AIMS BACK 17,70,135,237,294
    Emma 70,135,237
    Joseph 135
    Maggie 294
    Mary 237
    Minnie 294
    Thomas 135,294
    Thos 70,237
ALBERTSON
    Arthur 24,238
    Geo 24
    Julia 135,238
    Maggie 24,73,135,238,278
    Mary 24,135,238
    Mau 135
    Robert 24,135,238,278
ALEKIS 113
ALL THE TIME HEARD 53
ALLISON
    Allen 120,162
    Anna 219
    Annie 270
    Infant 120,162
    James 270
    Jas 219
    Lafayette 219,270
    Laffiatte 39
    Maggie 39,219
    Sallie 120,162,219,270
    Sally 39
    Wendell 120,162
    Wendle 39
    William 39
    Willie 120,162,270
    Winslow 219
    Wm 219
    Zella 219
ALMOST KILLED 31,81,135,
    231,291

Index

ALREADY HAD TEETH 49,210
ALREADY HAS TEETH 266
ALREADY HEARD................46,258
ALREADY KILLED 108,188
ANDERSON
   Collins...208
   Phena M...208
ANTELOPE WOMAN ..126,194,197,
  204,257
ANTILOPE
   Chas 36
   Jas 36
   Mary...36
ANTILOPE WOMAN 44
ANTILPOE, Wallace.......................36
ANTILPOE WOMAN 45
ANTOINE.......................47,163,201
   Sophia..201
APPROACH FROM ALL SIDES .....
  188
APPROCHED FROM ALL SIDES...
  108
ARNOUX
   Frankie 36
   Geo...36
   George.............. 100,162,219,264
   Marian.....................................219,264
   Marion...........................36,100,162
   Monroe...........36,100,162,219,264
   Susan..............36,100,162,219,264
ARROW MAKER 12,88,244
   Julia..244
   Maggie 88
   Mary..244
   Mrs...282
ARROW TOP KNOT 110,207
   Antoine 254
   Phillip..254
   Silas...254
ARROW TOP KNOTT............46,254
ARROW TOPKNOT, Arrow........162
ASHLEY
   John..202
   Lewis...52
   Louis 116,162,202,260
   Mary.................... 116,162,202,260
   Nellie...52
   Rosa..202,260

Talaho..52
Tallow................. 116,162,202,260
ASKS FOR MANY 284
ASSORTED GUN WOMAN 280
AUBARY
   Alice 55
   Dora...55
   Janette...55
   Laura..55
   Lou...55
   May...55
   Philip...55
   Rose...55
   Thos..55
AUBERY, Louize...............................55
AUBREY
   Alice 118,162,218,255
   Cal 256
   Carrol.. 162
   Dora.................... 118,162,256
   Dorae 218
   Janette....................... 162,218,256
   Jeanette.. 118
   Karl.. 218
   Laura....................... 118,162,218
   Louise 118,162,255
   Louize... 218
   Lucy................ 118,162,218,255
   May................. 118,162,218,256
   Philip 118,162,219,256
   Rosa................. 118,162,218,255
   Thomas 162
   Thos........................ 118,219,255
AUGER
   Augustine................................. 225
   Emmit 244
AUGERS
   August 155
   Augustus.................................. 272
   Emma 155
   Emmet 155
   Emmett 272
   Frances 155
AUGUST....................................... 211
AUSTIN
   Agnes................................. 163,232
   Annie 232
   Anthony 37,116,163,210,252

Index

Fanny 127
Jas 232
Jennie 232
Louise 127,163,276
Mabel 127,163
Maude 163
Paul 127,163,232,276
Susan 37,163,210,252
Susin 116
Willie 163
AUTIN, Wm 276
B BEAR, John 116
B BEAVER
   Aaron 22
   Eddy 22
B BONES
   Issabella 9
   Jennie 9
   Maggie 9
   Mary 9
B BOY, Rheuben 96
B BULL, Jennie 5
B CALF
   Chas 41
   John 103
B CHIEF
   Authelia 91
   Dennis 91
   Edward 90
   Edward B 8
   Geo 8
   Isabella 90
   Issabella B 8
   Joe 90
   John 8,90
   Josephine 8
   Maggie 8,90
   Mary 8
   Sabastian 8
   Sebastin 90
   Wm 26,91
B CHILD
   Annie 28
   Ben 119
   Geo 51
   Grace 52,115,165
   Irene 52,115,165
   Jas 119

Joe 51
Joseph 107
Josephene 119
Louis 119
Maggie 107
Mark 51
Percy 107
William 119
B EYES, Mary 19
B F MAN, John 167
B F WOMAN
   John 90
   Mary 90
   Mike 90
B FACE, Roselia 21
B HEAD, Mary 116
B HIDE
   Billy 137
   Cecil 32
   Jennie 137
   Peter 32
B JOHN
   Jack 40
   Jerry 40
   Josepg 40
   William 40
B LEGGINS
   Mary 11,89
   Peter 89
   Rachel 11,89
B LOOKS, Puss 165
B MARRIED, Joseph 52
B MEDICINE
   Joseph 111
   Maggie 111
   Willie 111
B MOON, Annie 95
B O MAN
   John 95
   Sallie 95
B PAW
   Jim 108
   John 108
   Minnie 107
B PLUME
   Jerry 8,90
   Louese 8
   Louise 90

Index

Thos 90
B R HUNTER
   Ammie 43
   Maggie 43
B RATTLER, Elmer 61
B SHOE
   Claud 13
   Daisy 93
B SKIN, Geneva 104
B W MEDICINE, Lucy 30
B WEASEL, James 166
BAD BOY 42,53,106,164
BAD EYES 93,139
BAD FOOT 108
BAD GROWTH 211
BAD MAN, Steven 37
BAD MARRIAGE 165,202,252
   Jim 252
   Joe 252
   Thos 252
BAD MARRIED 52,119
BAD OLD MAN 94,137,241
   Annie 241
   John 137
   Mack 282
   Mike 241
   Sallie 137
BAD OOLD MAN 282
BAD WOMAN 7,67,136,212,
   239,260
BAR WOMAN 136
BARK 113
BATTLE GOOD LOOKING WOMAN
   262
BAWLING IN THE WATER 268
BAYONET 110,179,213
BEAD WOMAN 3,74,83,135,166,
   203,243,250,284,297
BEAR
   ---- 25
   Annie 227
   Chas 227
   Frank 227
   Jennie 227
   Mary 42,227
   Minnie 227
   Wm 227
BEAR CHIEF

Eddy 244
Edward 161,295
George 295
Isabel 161
Joe 65,161
John 161,245,295
Lucy 295
Maggie 3,65,138,161,232,
   245,295
Phoebe 295
Sebastian 161,245
Susie 3,65,138
Widow No 1 3
BEAR CHIEFS WINDOW NO 2 3
BEAR CHILD 35,119,164,204,252
   Ben 35,164
   Benj 204,252
   James 164,204,252
   Jas 35
   Josepene 35
   Josephine 164,204,252
   Lewis 35
   Louis 164,204,252
   Mattie 35
   Oats 164
   William 35,164
   Wm 204,252
BEAR HEAD 53,116,164,213,266
   Albert 164
   Cree 213
   Julia 164
   Mary 53
BEAR LEADER 104,191
BEAR LEGGINGS 52
BEAR LEGGINS 11,88,136,215
   Irvin 276
   Mary 136
   Peter 136
   Rachel 136
BEAR MEDICINE 46,111,165,
   213,254
   John 213,254
   Joseph 165
   Maggie 46,165,213,254
   Peter 46
   Robert 46
   Willie 165
   Wm 213,254

Index

BEAR PAW 45,107,164,207,256
    Baptiste 207
    James 164
    Jim 45
    Joe 256
    John 45,164,207,256
    Minnie 164,256
    Otto 207
    Thos 257
BEAR SHOE 23,93,137,241,278
    Daisy 137,241
    Katie 241
    Minnie 137
    Mrs 23
BEAR SKIN 53,104,119,164,
    165,209,263
    Geneva 164,209
    Jeanette 256
    Jim 256
    Mary 164
BEAR SKIN #2 197
BEARS, Mary 114
BEAVER
    Aaron 234
    Alfred 190
    Annie 234
    Eddie 234
    George 234
    Rosa 234
BEAVER EYES 19
    Dave 19
    Patrick 19
BEAVER WOMAN ... 85,167,205,272
BEGS PLENTY 95,156
BELEDEAUX
    Chas 37
    Earl 37
    Eddie 37
    Genevive 37
    Mable 37
    Puss 37
    Selena 37
    Warren 37
    William 37
    Xiver 37
BELL COMING 97,192
BELLS COMING 273
BERRIE CARRIER 28

BERRY CARRIER 84,166,209
BERRY CHILD
    Anna 183
    Annie 268
    Henry 204
    Joseph 268
    Mike 106,183,204,268
BERRY WOMAN 91
BIG BEAVER 21,69,136,234,278
    Aaron 278
    Annie 278
    Catherine 278
    Daisy 278
    Eddie 69,136,278
    Emma 69
    George 278
    Hiram 69
    Horace 136
    James 136
    Jas 69
    Minnie 69,136
    Rosa 278
BIG CHICKEN HAWK 30
BIG CROW 31,80,137,240,290
    Cecil 31,81,137,240
    Maggie 240
BIG EAGLE 114,193
BIG GUN WOMAN 71,150
BIG HEAD 71,140
    Chas 140
    Mary 17
    Thos 71
BIG LAKE
    John 161,240,282
    Maniase 282
    Mike 282
BIG LODGE POLE 20,72,136,
    241,286
    Mary 241,286
    Peter 286
BIG MOON 23
    Anna 146
    Jack 95,146,232,281
BIG MOUTH SPRING 83
BIG NOSE, Mrs 188
BIG OLD WOMAN 120,166
BIG PINE TREE 205
BIG PLUME 8,90,161,244,279

Index

Agnes 244
Daniel 83
Jerry 161,244,245,279
Josephine 245,279
Louise 161,244,279
Thomas 161
BIG ROAD
    Agnes 136,283
    Mary 125
    Minnie 136
    Susie 244
BIG RUMP 209
BIG SMOKE 136,289
    Joe 136
BIG SNAKE 3,74,235
BIG SPRING 61,166,216,269
    Anna 83
    Chas 83
    John 83
BIG SPRINGS, John 177
BIG STONE 236
BIG TIGER 17,232
BIG TIGER WOMAN 136,291
BIG TIP, Fred 217
BIG TOP 113,207
    Fred 254
    Jim 203,249
BIG WOLF MEDICINE ... 30,235,290
    Ellen 236
    Mary Ann 290
BIG WOMAN 11,13,41,76,102,
    215,268,285
BIGTOP
    Fred 173
    Jim 178
BILLEDEAUX
    Carl 114,205,267
    Carrol 166
    Celina 268
    Charles 268
    Chas 115,165,217
    Ed 114,166
    Eddie 114,166
    Edward 205,267,268
    Geneviein 114
    Genevieve 205,267
    Greeley 115
    Greely 165,217,268

Jeniveve 166
Mabel 115,165,268
Mable Catharine 217
Martha 114,166,205,267
Mitchell 268
Mitchell Joseph 205
Puss 166
Salina 165,217,268
Selena 115
Virginia 114,267
Warren 268
Wearen 115
Weren 217
Wern 165
William 268
Willie 115,165
Wm 217
Xavier 115,165,217,268
BILLIDEAUX
    Edward 205
    Virginia 205
BIRD
    Charles 198
    Chrles 267
    George 198,267
    Henry 198,216,261,267
    John 198
    Johnson 267
    Martha 198,267
    Mattie 198,267
    Millie 198,267
    Oscar 267
    Sam 198
    Sampson 267
    Thomas 261
BIRD RATTLE 60
BIRD RATTLER 83,166,203,250
BIRD TAIL WOMAN 285
BIRD WING 230
BIRD WINGS CHIEF 26
BIRD WOMAN 94,155
BIRDS WING 296
BITE
    Harry 283
    Howard 13
    John 92,137,227
    Lucy 227
    Minnie 13,92,137,227,283

Index

Rosa 283
   Sheridan 13
   Thos 13,283
BLACK BEAR ... 52,116,165,197,259
   John 167,197,259
   Mary 259
BLACK BIRD 5,136,235
BLACK BLANKET 109
BLACK BLANKET WOMAN 122
BLACK BONES, Cecil 235
BLACK BOY 6,68,135,237,280
   Anthelia 280
   Fisher 280
   Reuben 135
   Ruben 6,237
BLACK BULL 5,66,136,243,295
   Jennie 66
   Mary 66
BLACK CAYOTE 96
BLACK CLOTH WOMAN 49,
.... 198,277
BLACK COYOTE 167,206,265
   Annie 265
   Minnie 265
   Ross 265
BLACK DRESS WOMAN 6
BLACK FACE 21,215,227,228,
.... 254,268,279
   Henry 228
BLACK FACE MAN 83,166,
.... 203,250
   John 83
BLACK FACE WOMAN 43,104,
.... 201,271
BLACK LOOKS 106,165
   Jim 44
   Puss 45
BLACK MAN, Fred 250
BLACK POINT WOMAN 279
BLACK RIDER 198
BLACK SARCEE 59,115,165,
.... 199,258
BLACK SMOKE 44,193
BLACK SNAKE 47,112
BLACK WEASEL 84,106,166,
.... 211,250
BLACK WEASLE 58
BLACK YOUNG MAN 202,250

BLACKFACE WOMAN 182
BLACKFOOT CHILD 52,115,165,
.... 199,259
BLACKFOOT WOMAN 8,90,
.... 161,240,282
   John 8
   Mary 8,161,240
   Mike 161,240
BLACKSNAKE WOMAN 165
BLANKET 61,166
BLANKET WOMAN 21,31,41,
67,80,82,83,87,103,119,146,149,160,
164,167,171,177,198,199,200,203,204
,208,228,239,250,254,259,261,265,
.... 267,277
BLIND GIRL 30
BLIND WOMAN 80,284
BLOOD
   Antoine 199
   Austin 177
   Autern 84
   Fannie 84
   Fanny 177
   Herman 177
   James 199,253
   Jim 28,84,177
   John 199,253
   Paula 253
   Polly 28
BLOOD WOMAN 122,146,205
BLUE BEAD 207,255
BLUE BEADS 104
BLUE BEEDS 42
BLUE OWL 112,170
BLUE WOMAN 96,167,206
BOB TAIL HORSE 5
   Bob 74
   Joe 74,233
   John 5
   Joseph 5
   Mre 233
BOB TAIL MOUSE 106
BOBTAIL HORSE 135
   Joe 135
BOBTAIL MOUSE 166
BOGIE, Thos 298
BOGY
   Thomas 163

Index

Tom 100
BOSS RIB HUNTER 43
BOSS RIBS
    Emma 182
    Joseph 139
    Maggie 182,201
    Minnie 10,139
BOSS WOMAN, Joe 10
BOSTWICK
    Alice 218
    Anna 218
    Annie 163,275
    Billy 163
    Francis 218
    Frank 60,105,163,218,275
    Geo 60,105
    George 163,218,275
    Henry 60,105,163,218,275
    John 105,163,218,275
    Lena 218
    Louise 275
    Louize 60,218
    Mary 105,163
    William 60,275
    Wm 105,218
BOTH GO IN 146
BOTH GOES IN 68,78,240
BOUNCES UP 6,66,141,229
BOUNDS UP 297
BOW LEGS 203
BOY 42,106,164,210,254
    Oscar 42,164,254
    Raymond 254
BOY CHIEF 26,91,135,228,278
    Annie 228
    Anthelia 26
    Clara 278
    Dennie 228
    Dennis 278
    Emma 228,278
    Susie 228
    William 278
    Wm 228
BOY CHILD, Michael 28
BREAKS GOOD 59,111,191
BRIAR 14
BRIAR WOMAN 235
BRIER 150,228

BROAD FEET 45
BROAD FOOT 181
BROAD WOMAN 282
BROKEN LEG 108,169,199,253
BROKER LEG 45
BROWN
    Al 259
    Frances 167,259
    Franky 220
    James W 273
    Jesse 36,100,163,221,273
    Joe 167,259
    Joseph 36,220
    Leo 36,100,163,221,273
    Sarah 36,100,163,221,273
    Sarah A 221
    Sarah Adele 163,273
    Victoria 163,221,273
    Wesley 167,220,259
    William 36,163
    Wm 100,221
BRYER 77
BUCK
    Charles 106,271
    Chas 41,164,216
    Spina 106
    Spyna 41,164,216,271
BUCK SKIN RIDER 103
BUCKLEY
    Infant 127
    Matilda 126
    Mattie 203
BUCKSKIN HORSE 234
BUCKSKIN RIDER 77,140
BUCKSKIN WOMAN 177
BUFFALO
    Chas 26
    Daisy 26,135
    John 135
BUFFALO CHILD 52
BUFFALO GROWING 20,93,
    137,227,287
BUFFALO HIDE 32,85,137,
    214,289
    James 137
    Mary 137
    Thomas 289
    Wm 85

Index

Yellow..................................289
BUFFALO HIDE NO 2 85
BUFFALO HORSE
   Albert..................................143
   James..................................143
   Joe......................................143
BUFFALO ROAD 115,165
BUFFALO STONE WOMAN......293
BUFFALO TRAIL.................199,259
BULL
   Josephine............................228
   Thos 226
BULL CALF 40,103,164,208,254
   Chas 164
   John..............................208,254
BULL CHILD............51,61,107,166,
  200,264
   Geo...............................260,264
   Joe......................................264
   Joseph 166,200,216
   Maggie................................166
   Percy 166,260
   Puss......................................51
   Thos 200
BULL CHILD 2..............................51
BULL PLUME.............................166
   Dan...............................203,250
   Eddie..................................100
BULL SHOE....................13,136,234
   Joe.....................76,136,234,285
   Joseph 13
   Mrs......................................269
   Pat.................................76,136
   Patrick............................13,285
BULL SHOE #2....................136,285
BULL SHOE NO 1 76
BURD
   Phoebe................................210
   Alice...............38,117,166,210,276
   Charley...............................164
   Chas 127
   Daisy....................99,163,252
   Daisy D 163
   Dorthy................................224
   George................................164
   Henry 127
   Hwney................................164
   Infant..................................127

Ira 99,163,210,252
Ire 38
Johnson............................127,164
Levi.................37,99,163,224,252
Martha 127,164
Mattie 127,164
Nellie 164
Phebe 38
Phoebe 99,163,252
Sam.......................................127
Samson 164
BUSY WOMAN 9,140
BUTTER FLY 81
   Elmer 232
   Joe 232
   John 232
   Maryan 81
BUTTERFLY 30
   Elmer 30,80,137,289
   Joseph..................................290
   Mary 30,80,137,264
   Mrs 137
   Saatal 30
BUTTON WOMAN.....................277
C ANTELOPE
   James 169
   Jas.......................................102
C B BONES
   Isabella 161
   Isabelle..................................89
   John 161
   Julia 161
   Maggie................................161
   Mary 89,161
C BEAR
   Annie 4
   Chas..4
   Jennie......................................4
   Maggie....................................4
   Minnie 4
   Philip 4
   Willie 4
C BODY
   Cecil 87
   Maggie..................................87
   Mary 87
   Pete 87
C COWARD, Victor....................107

Index

C CROW
- Alfred 88
- Jas 88
- John 88
- Maggie 88

C FINGER
- Ernest 124
- Josephene 124
- Maggie 124
- Paul 124
- Thos 124

C GUN
- Kate 105
- Presly 105

C GUNS, Presley 167

C I NIGHT
- Cecil 140
- James 140
- Minnie 140

C MEDICINE
- Chas 46
- Joseph 46
- Josephine 46
- Mary 46

C RIBS
- Joe 93
- Minnie 93

C SHIELD, Geo 126

C SHOE
- Frank 11,236
- Joseph 11
- Maggie 236
- Mary 11,92

C TAIL
- Charley 19
- Ernest 19
- Mary 20

CADOTT
- Lucy 89
- Peter 89
- Rosa 89

CADOTTE
- Charles 264
- Jennie 169
- Lucy 11,169,264
- Pete 11,169,215,264
- Rhoda 11,264
- Rosa 169

CALF BOSS RIBS 93,139,238,279
- Barney 238
- Joe 238
- Joseph 279
- Mary 238
- Minnie 238,279

CALF BOSS RIBS 10

CALF LOOKING 17,71,138, 228,294
- Paul 17,71,138,228,294

CALF RIBS
- Austin 86
- Barnet 93
- Barney 10,136,279
- Joe 86
- John 28,177

CALF ROBE 7,19,67,138
- Albert 7,239,277
- Anna 279
- Annie 239,240
- Emma 7,67,138
- Frank 18,125,140,227,279
- Jennie 18
- Joe 7,138,239,283
- Joseph 67
- Minnie 140,227
- Mrs 279
- Richard 7,19,67,136,240,278
- Thos 279

CALF SHIELD 44,126,170,213
- Geo 44

CALF TAIL 75,138,232,258,280
- Earnest 138
- Ernest 75,232,280
- John 75,138,232,289
- Susan 289

CALF WOMAN 23,40,70,102,138, 178,197,227,271,297

CALF WOMAN NO 2 86

CALLED FROM THE OTHER SIDE 207

CALLING BACK 295

CALLING ONE OTHER 19

CALLS AT NIGHT 113,169

CALLS BUCK 243

CAMP
- John 208
- Mary 208

Index

Susie 208
CAPTURES IN THE NIGHT 293
CARNEY
   Eliza 124
   Esther 167,256
CARSON, Chas 178
CASOOTH, Jos 23
CAT 215
CATCHES 18,26,279
CATCHES ANOTHER 148
CATCHES AT THE EDGE OF THE
   WATER 293
CATCHES BOTH SIDES 51,112,
   193,199
CATCHES EDGE WATER 12,77,
   139,235
CATCHES FIRST 27,48,76,139,
   214,234,285,294
CATCHES GOOD 295
CATCHES IN SIDE 27,215,294
CATCHES IN THE BRUSH 259
CATCHES IN WATER 90
CATCHES INSIDE 87,161
CATCHES LAST 107,170,202,260
CATCHES ON BOTH SIDES ....
   222,264
CATCHES ON GROUND 30
CATCHES ON THE TOP 279
CATCHES ON TOP 8,42,81,106,
   142,151,169,215,244,265
CATCHES TOGETHER 47,214
CATCHES TWICE 206,263
CATCHES TWO 110,112,193,266
CATCHES WHITE CALF 47
CATCHING 204,264
CATCHING HIM DOWN 283
CATCHING 200
CAUGHT 243
CAYTON
   Isabel 297
   Isabella 3
   Joe 74,135,243
   Joseph 3,297
   Mary 243,297
CHAMPIN
   Annie 12
   George 9,12
   Louie 9

Maggie 12
Mary 9
Pete 12
Peter 9
Susie 12
CHAMPINE
   Busy 291
   Daisy 245
   George 76,91,138,140,237,
   245,252,291
   Louie 91,140
   Louis 245,291
   Maggie 76,139,237,252
   Mary 91,140,245,291
   Mary Ann 245,291
   Mrs Pete 138
   Pete 76,91,139,140,245
   Peter 237,252,291
   Susie 76
CHAMPITE, Mrs Pete 237
CHARGED ALL AROUND 44
CHARGED ALONE 44
CHARGES 78,140,235
CHARGES BOTH SIDES .. 29,84,228
CHARGES ON BOTH SIDES 250
CHARGING WOMAN 85
CHEWING B BONES 161
CHEWING BACK BONES 9
CHEWING BLACK BONES
   89,234,288
   Agnes 235,288
   George 288
   Isabel 288
   Isabelle 235
   John 235
   Maggie 235,288
   Mary 234,235
   Mollie 288
CHEWING BLACK BONES #2 .. 289
CHICKEN 215
CHICKEN FRONT 52
CHICKEN SHOE 11,92,139
   John 139
   Louis 293
   Mary 139
   Peter 139
   Susie 293
CHICKEN WOMAN 54,80,160

Index

CHIEF 15
CHIEF ALL OVER 17,71,139,
.... 242,277
   Geo 17,71,242
   George 139,277
CHIEF COWARD 44,107,167,
.... 197,257
   Victor 167,257
CHIEF CROW 60,88,169,215,276
   Albert 169
   Alfred 276
   James 169,215,276
   John 160
CHIEF ELK 38,99,167,206,261
CHIEF IN FRONT 52,126
CHIEF IN THE MIDDLE 203,272
   Mary 272
CHILD, Cecil 113
CHIP MUNK 92
CHOAT
   Fannie 71,233
   Fanny 20
   Frank 20,71,241
   Funny 296
   Geo 20,71,233
   George 296
   Jas 241
   Jennie 241
   Josephine 20
   Mary 241
   Minnie 71
   Pete 20
   Rosaline 296
   Sam 241
   Sam'l 20
   Samuel 71
CHOATE
   Fanny 139
   Frank 140,296
   George 139
   James 140,296
   Mary 296
   Minnie 139
   Sam 286
   Samuel 139
CHOQUETT, Louise 24
CHOUQUETT, Henry 24
CHOUQUETTE

Antoine 113,209,255
Antone 167
Charles 261
Chas 113,168
Henry 79
John 79,161,223,288
Josephine 168,199,261
Louis 168
Louise 79,113,199,261
CLARK
   Agnes 117,236,294
   Anna 201
   Annie 102
   Ella J 220,259
   Geo 9,201
   Horace J 125
   Horrace 220
   Horrace J 259
   James 198,261
   Jas 9
   John 220
   Louese 9
   Louise 201
   Malcolm 220,259
   Robert 9,201
   Wm 117,236
CLARKE
   Agnes 189
   Anna 189
   Geo 102,137
   Horace 60,169
   James 137
   Jas 102
   John 60,125,169
   Loouisa 102
   Louise 137
   Malcolm 60,169
   Malcomn 125
   Robert 102,137
   William 189
CLEAN UP 77
CLEAN YO 159
CLEANS UP 83
CLEANS UP AT NIGHT 203
CLEAR UP 58
CLEARS UP 84,113,168,200,250
   George 201,251
   Mabel 85,113,169

310

Index

Rosa 85
Rose 113
CLOSE GUN 103
CLOTH WOMAN 28,50,57,58,
....................................61,84,111,190
CLUMSY WOMAN 290
COAT 108,169,199,253
   Harry 58
   Jenny 45
   Mary 45,58,169
COBELL
   Bessie 40,103,168,220,251
   Clara 103,168,220,274
   Dewey 103,168,220,274
   Geo 40,103
   George 168,219,251
   James 251
   Jas 220
   John 40,103,168,220
   Johnny 251
   Jos 103
   Joseph 40,168,220,251
   Josie 114
   Jule 103,168,220
   Julia 40,125,220,251
   Julius 274
   Louis 103,168,220,274
   Louise 103,168,274
   Louize 220
   Maggie 103,168
   Mary 40,102,114,168,219,251
   Mary R 103
   Mary Rose 168
   Norah 114
   Peter 103,168,220,274
   Thomas 220
   Thos 40,251
   Thos Rob't 274
   Tom 168
   Tommy 103
   William 40
   Willie 103,168
   Wm 220,251
COE
   Agnes 40,118,168
   James 118,168,270
   Janet 118,168,270
   Jas 40

Jenette 40
COLD BODY 29,87,169,210,250
   Cecelia 210
   Cecil 169
   Cecile 250
   Maggie 169,210,250
   Mary 29,169,250
   Mrs 210
   Pete 169
COLD FEET 11,89,139,235,295
COME WITH THE WIND 209
COMELLE, Rene 276
COMES IN NIGHT 10,78,139,235
   Cecil 78,235
   James 235
   Julia 235
   Minnie 78,235
   William 79
COMES IN THE NIGHT 296
   Cecil 296
   Jamea 296
   Julia 296
   Minnie 296
COMES OUT OF BRUSH 8
COMES SINGING 157
COMES TO MAKE DUST ...101,170
COMING OWL 280
COMING RATTLING 206
COMING WIND 256
COMING WITH A GUN 255
CONNELLY
   Angeline 168,275
   Angelline 220
   Brina 220
   Bryan 275
   George 275
   John 168,275
   Johnny 220
   Lizzie 275
   Mamie 275
   Mary 168,220,275
   Rosa 220
   Rose 168,275
   Victor 168,220,275
   William 275
CONNOLLY
   Angeline 103
   Boyan 103

Index

John 103
Mary 103
Rose 103
Victor 103
CONWAY
    Charles 265
    Chas 43,105,167,221
    Frank 43,167
    John 265
    Laura 221,265
    William 43
    Willie 105,167,221,265
COOK
    Geo 60
    Geo W 118,206
    George W 168,276
    Isabel 57,123,180
    Isabella 212,273
    Joseph 180
    Julia 60,168,276
    Julie 118
    Julis 206
    Laura 180
    Loratta 58,123
    Loretta 273
    Lucy 57,123,180,212,273
    Mountain W 212
COUUQUETTE, Charles 199
COW HIDE ROBE 83,202,250
    Grace 83
    Rachel 250
COWAY, Frank 105
COWHIDE ROBE 170
    Grace 170,202
COYOTE
    Alice 6
    Fanny 6
    Mary 227
    Philip 227
COYOTE WOMAN 207,255,281
CRADLE WOMAN 46,177
CRANE WOMAN 45,48,56,
   112,212,262
CRANING WOMAN 227
CRAWFORD
    Ellen 9,69,138,242
    Emma 242,286
    Hellen 286

James 286
Jas 242
Joe 69,138,242
John 69,138
Joseph 9,286
Mamie 69,138,286
Minnie 9,242
CRAWLING AWAY 12
CRAWLS AWAY 279
CREAM ANTELOPE 101,169,214
    James 214
    Jas 256
    Joe 214
    Jos 256
    Mrs 214
CREAM ANTILOPE 36
CREE MEDICINE 65,138,232,290
    Cecile 290
    Joe 138
    Maggie 290
CREE WOMAN 119,193,213,263
CRIES MEDICINE 46
CROFF
    Arthur 126,168,221,252
    Auther 38
    Dick 38,126,221,251
    Edward 229,292
    Emma 38,98,242,297
    Eva 168,221,252
    Geo 38
    George 98,275
    Infant 126
    John 123,167,229
    Lad 123
    Louis 292
    Louise 123,167,292
    Louize 229
    Maggie 38,126,168,221,251
    Richard 168
    William 39,297
    Willie 98
    Wm 229
CROFT
    John 20
    Lad 20
    Louese 20
CRONING OLD WOMAN 138
CROSS GUN 105

Index

CROSS GUNS 43,167
   James 221,265
   John 203
   Kate 265
   Katie 167
   Mrs 221
   Percy 43
   Preeley 265
   Pressey 221
   Rider 43
CROSSING WOMAN 31
CROW 262
   Albert 60
   Elizabeth I 96
   Jas 60
   Matilda I 96
CROW EYES 9,79,139,240,291
   Annie 240
   Katie 291
   Mary 139
   William 139
CROW GIRL 44,53
CROW GOOD LOOKING 197
CROW HEAD 47,57,212,249
CROW PITTIER 214
CROW W HORSES 101
CROW WHITE HORSES 194
CROW WOMAN 111,170,
   177,245,260
CROWING OLD WOMAN 67
CROWNING OWL WOMAN 7
CURLEW 53,116,168,291
CURLEY BEAR 4,66,138,227
   Anna 138
   Annie 66
   Charles 138
   Chas 66
   Jennie 66,138
   Mary 66,138
   Minnie 66,138
   William 138
   Wm 66
CURLY BEAR 293
   Charles 293
CUT BANK JOHN 40
CUT BODY 284
CUT DIFFERENT 287
CUT FINGER 53,124,169,201,258

Annie 202
Earnest 53,169
Ernest 201,258
Florence 53
Josephine 53,169,202
Lewis 53
Maggie 53,169,202,258
Thomas 169
Thos 53,202,258
CUT NOSE 112,186,205,262
CUTS, Mary 40
CUTS BOTH SIDES 70,146
CUTS DIFFERENT 86,148
CUTS FOR HERSELF 212
CUTS HERSELF 83,141
CUTS IN DIFFERENT PLACES ....
   213
CUTS INSIDE 88
CUTS ON BOTH SIDES 258
CUTS WITH MANY 278
CUTTING 109,184
CUTTING HERSELF 271
CUTTING WOMAN 88
D BEHIND, Geo 171
D BULL
   Louise 109,175
   Louize 49
   Ralph 175
   Thos 49
   Tom 109
D EARS, Mary 116
D H ROBE, Minnie 141
D HEAD
   Josephine 13
   Mary 13
D HIS ROBE, Chas 88
D RIDER
   Addie 45
   Annie 108
   Josephine 12
   Mary 45
   Minnie 45,108
D ROBE, Susie 11
D RUNNER
   Edgar 92
   Edward 9,92
   Paul 9,92
DAVIS

Index

Bryan.................55,117,170,219
Catherine........................55
Eddie............................55
Hattie............24,65,140,198,267
Mabel...........................290
Mary.............24,65,140,198,267
Maud............................276
Molley...........................54
Mollie..................117,170,219
Pearl................55,117,170,219
Thomas..........................170
Thos...................54,117,219
DAVLIN, Mollie.........127,209,216
DAWSON
   Erskins........................60
   Fanny.....................120,171
   Harold........................171
   Harrold.......................120
   Herald.........................60
   Irene.........................220
   Isabel.................60,120,259
   Isabella......................171
   Isabelle......................220
   James.....................171,221
   James, Jr.....................171
   Jas........................60,120
   Lorena.....................60,259
   Thomas....................220,259
   Thos...........................60
   Tom.......................120,171
   William....................60,171
   Wm............................120
DAY OLD WOMAN...................108
DAY RIDER........12,73,140,243,279
   Cecil.........................243
   Chas......................68,140
   Geo...........................279
   George............140,236,243,280
   Helen.................68,140,280
   Hellen........................236
   Jack......................236,280
   Joe..................12,140,279
   John..........................140
   Jos............................73
   Mary..........................141
   Michael...............68,140,280
   Mike..........................236
   Oliver............68,140,236,280

   Peter.........................279
DAYRIDER
   (Infant)........................6
   Hellen..........................6
   Michael.........................6
   Oliver..........................6
DE CAMPS, Margerete..............91
DE CHAMP, Margaret..............244
DE LANEY
   Charles.......................257
   Fred..........................257
   Margaret......................258
   Viola.........................257
DE ROCHE
   Ben.......................101,257
   Charles.......................257
   Chas..........................101
   Sallie........................101
   Sallie Mary...................257
DECHAMP, Margaret........8,141,295
DEER.............................18
DELANEY
   Charles.......................205
   Chas..................35,119,170
   Margaret......................170
   Viola.............35,119,170,205
DEMOTT
   Jenny..........................39
   Joseph.........................39
   Minnie.........................39
DENNIS
   Percy.....................186,253
   Perry..........................38
   Persy..........................98
DENOVAN, Frank...................31
DEROCHE
   Ben........................35,172
   Benj..........................205
   Charley.......................172
   Chas.......................35,205
   Sallie........................172
   Sally..........................35
DEVAL, David.....................52
DEVERAUX
   Abbie.........................216
   Anna..........................216
   Charles.......................216
   Jason.........................216

Index

Mary 216
DEVEREAUX
  Abbie 41
  Abby 170
  Ammie 41
  Annie 170
  Charles 272
  Chas 41,170
  Geo 170
  Henry 41,170,216,273
  Jason 41,272
  Mary 41,170,272
DEVEREUX
  Abby 106
  Annie 106
  Chas 106
  Henry 106
  Jason 106
  Mary 106
DEWOLF, Jennie 274
DIED FIRST 108,190
DIFFERENT CHILD 253
DIFFERENT CUT 52
DIFFERENT GUN 25,75,232
DIFFERENT GUN WOMAN 280
DIFFERENT KILLS 256
DIFFERENT NATION 269
DIFFERENT PERSON KILLED..107
DIFFERENT PERSONS KILLED ....
.... 164
DIFFERENT PETRIFIED ROCK .....
.... 249
DIFFERENT ROCK 103,175
DIFFERENT SHIELD 28,209
DIFFERENT SUGAR 22
DIFFERENT WOMAN 45,84,138,
.... 166,236,243
DIRTY FACE 13,76,136,234,285
DIVER 59,113
DIVES LONG WAY 74,140,
.... 157,286
DIVES LONG WAYS 52
DIVES LONG WOMAN 213
DIVING ALL ROUND 254
DIVING AROUND 112,193,264
DIVING AROUND BEHIND 214
DIVING AT SHORE 204
DIVING AT THE SHORE 298

DOG EAR 172
  Billy 172
  Mary 172
DOG EARS 116,260
  Louise 260
DOG EARSL 199
DOG MEDICINE 214
DOG TAKES GUN 212
DOG TAKING GUN... 32,83,141,271
DONAVON
  Frank 76
  Jane 76
DONIVAN
  Frank 141
  Jennie 141
DONOVAN
  Frank 293
  Jenie 293
DONT CARE 199
DON'T CARE FOR ANYTHING 268
DONT CARE FOR NOTHING 205
DON'T GO OUT, Mary 84
DON'T GO OUT 84,171
  John 267
DONT GO OUT, John 58,198
DONT LIKE TO BE A WOMAN ......
.... 215
DOROTHY 252
DOUBLE BLAZE 16
  Dick 69,146
  Frank 69
  Jackson 69,146
  Joe 69,146
  Louie 146
  Louis 69
  Oliver 69,146
DOUBLE CHARGE 296
DOUBLE CLEAN UP 113
DOUBLE CLEAR UP 170
DOUBLE CLOTH 50,112,171,
.... 199,260
DOUBLE FACE 198,254
DOUBLE FOX
  Fanny 142
  Mary 142
DOUBLE GO IN 144
DOUBLE GUN 31,106,165
DOUBLE HID 232

Index

DOUBLE IRON WOMAN 116,
.... 194,263
DOUBLE KILLS 263
DOUBLE OWL 112,170
DOUBLE RIDER 45,108,170,
.... 205,253
   Ada 253
   Anna 170
   Findian 253
   Mary 253
   Minnie 170,205,253
DOUBLE RUNNER 9,92,141,
.... 244,288
   Edgar 9,141,288
   Edward 244,288
   Paul 141,244,288
DOUBLE RUSH 10
DOUBLE STEAL 106,281
DOUBLE STEALING WOMAN ......
.... 197
DOUBLE STRIKE 20,31,240
DOUBLE WOLF 105
DOUBLR WOLF 60
DOUGLAS
   Annie C 171
   Archibald 217
   Arthur 172
   Arthur W 217
   Arthur Williams 266
   Cherry Agnes 266
   Edward 218
   Florence 171
   Henry 218
   James 171,217,266
   James Archibald 266
   James, Jr 171
   Jas 125
   Jas A 42,125
   Jim 42
   John 118
   Lida 42,125
   Lyda Eveline 266
   Lydia 172,217
   Mary 124
   May 266
   Mollie 218
   Peter 217
   William 43,171

Wm 124,266
DOY EARS 52
DRAGS BEHIND 83,171,209,249
DRAGS HER ROBE, Mary 245
DRAGS HIR ROBE 11
DRAGS HIS BLANKET 141
DRAGS HIS ROBE 11,88,141,
.... 245,292
   Chipp 292
DRAWS RATIONS 108,170
DRESS WOMAN 243
DRESSED LIKE A WOMAN 295
DRIVES BACK FINE 200
DRIVES BACK GOOD 279
DRIVES DOUBLE BACK 264
DRIVES LONG WAY 69
DRIVING BACK 107,166
DRIVING BACKWARD 200
DRY GOODS WOMAN 11,45,89,
.... 108,139,172,199,265
DRY LIMB 204,284
DRY ROX 30
DRY WOOD 172
DU BRELL, Alex 98
DUBRAY, Elix 38
DUBRELL, Lillie 98
DUBREY
   Alex 171,225,274
   George 225,274
   Joe 274
   Joseph 171,225
   Lily 171
DUCK HEAD 13,77,140,237,287
   Elizabeth 237
   Josephine 77,140,237,287
   Lizzie 287
   Louie 140
   Louise 237,287
   Mary 77,140,237,287
   Peter 13,77,140,237,287
DUNBAR
   Andrew 120,171,221,259
   Carrie 120,171,221,259
   Esther 120,171,221,259
   Frances 259
   Frank 120
   Frankie 171,221
   Hazel 259

Index

James 171,221,259
Jane 120,171,221,259
Jas 120
Mary 120,171,221,259
DUNOVON
   Frank 232
   Jennie 232
DUSTY BULL
   Herman 49,109,175,223,264
   James 223
   Louise 223,264
   Ralph 264
   Rhoda 264
DUVAL, David 84
DUVALL
   David 171,213,250
   Gretchen 213
DWARF 253
E B T ABOUT
   Antoine 290
   George 82,245,290
   Lomie 82
   Louis 245,290
   Mollie 82,245
   Paul 82,245
   Susie 82
E B TALKS
   Geo 32
   Louie 32
E B TALKS ABOUT
   Paul 32
   Susie 32
E CHILD
   Bark 172
   Cecil 172
   Fawn 172
   Geo 57
   Jonh 57
E FLAG
   Annie 6
   Emma 141
   Stella 6
E HEAD, Margaret 7
E/DRIDGE, Emily 265
EAGLE 23,91,142,227,297
   Mary 142
   William 297
   Wm 227

EAGLE CHILD 57,79,113,
.... 172,197,253
   James 79,197
   Jas 28,122,253
EAGLE FACE 21,109,184,212,260
EAGLE FLAG 6,66,141,229
   Anna 66,229
   Percy 229
   Stella 66
EAGLE FLAGG 297
   Annie 297
EAGLE HEAD 7,69,142,234,278
   James 142,278
   Jas 69,234
   Maggie 278
   Margaret 69,142,234
EAGLE RIBS 3
   Agnes 142
   Cecil 3,142
   Ceeila 66
   Jennie 245
   John 5,142,245,277
   Louisa 142,277
   Louise 245
   Mrs 66,141
   Susie 3,66
EAGLE TAIL 57
EAGLE TAIL FEATHERS 26,27,
.... 172,203,261
EAGLES RIBS, John 68
EAR RING 261
   Bird 261
   James 261
   Susie 261
EAR RINGS 48,212
   Bert 212
   Burd 48
   James 212
   Jim 48
   Suan 48
   Susan 212
EAR-RINGS 172
   Susan 172
EARRINGS 119
EAST WOMAN 121,172,205
EATS ALONE
   Geo 232
   George 95,146,281

Index

ECHO WOMAN 48
EDWARDS
   Elisabeth 65
   Elizabeth 3,141,229
   Ellen 3,65,141,228,297
   Fanny 3,141,229,297
   Funny 65
   John 3,65,141,229,297
   Lizzie 297
   Rosa 141,229,297
   Thomas 141,297
   Thos 3,65,229
   William 141,297
   Wm 3,65,228
EKIMO WOMAN 88
ELDRIDGE
   Emily 125,198
   Emma 172
ELIZABETH 220
ELK 76,152
   Elda 38
ELK NECKLACE 108,181
ELK ROBE 10,78,140,235
ELK WOMAN 36,116,184,244
ELK YELLS IN THE WATER 295
ELL
   Adah 172
   Alda 210
   Aldah 99
   Annie 261
   Chas 99,172,210
   Elda 38
   Johnny 261
   Levi 38
   Lois 261
   Louis 99,172,210
   Louis, Jr 261
ESQUIMO WOMAN 141
EVANS
   Irene 142,241,283
   James 14,142,283
   Jas 75,241
   Jim 60
   Joe 14,75,142,241,283
   Joseph 59
   Mary 14,75,142
   Mary C 59,241
   Mary Cecile 283

EVENING STAR 203,267
EVERY BODY LOOKS AT
   6,26,231,276
EVERY BODY TALKS ABOUT
   32,245,290
EVERYBODY LOOKS AT 142
EVERYBODY TALKS 142
   Louie 142
   Mollie 142
   Paul 142
   Susie 142
EVERYBODY TALKS ABOUT ... 82
F B HORSE
   Albert 18
   Joseph 18
F BULL
   Jas 96
   Lucy 96
F RIDER
   Irene 126
   Reney 110
F SMOKE, Louis 113
F TAIL
   Anna 89
   Jas 10
   Jimmy 89
   John 10
   Mollie 236
   Sofa 10
   Sofia 89
   Sophia 236
FABER
   Anna 143
   Annie 16,79,243,282
   Ellen 79
   Hellen 16,243,282
   Kazy 282
   Lawrence 15,79,143,243,282
   Mary 143,243
   Nancy 79
FACE
   Harry 30
   Susie 238
FACE TOGETHER 50
FAR AWAY WOMAN 46
FAST BUFFALO HORSE 18,239
   Albert 73,239,292
   James 292

Index

Jas 73,239	FIRST ONE 284
Joe 239,292	Louese 16
Jos 73	Louise 80
Mrs 73,143	FIRST ONE RUSSELL 92,143,
FAWN 113	 203,290
FEATHERS COMING	FIRST OWL 11
Cecil 10	FIRST PREPARED 28
Mary 10	FIRST RIDER 31,110
Susie 10	Rena 173
FELL NO IRON 21	FIRST RUNNER 187
FELL NO KIDNEY 27	FIRST RUSHER 268
FELL NO LIGHT 25	FIRST STIKE 159
FELL NO OWL 27	FIRST STRIKE 16,81,187,240
FELL NO SNAKE 11	FIRST STRIKES 85
FELL NOT PETRIFIED 11	FIRST WOMAN 176
FELLOW HORSE RIDER ... 13	FISH 143,239,279
FETCHING BACK 249	Joseph 239
FETCHING HER BACK 200	Josephene 82
FIGHTS IN FRONT 48	FISHER 31,143,239
FINDING 217	Anna 73,142,226,298
FINE BULL 15,96,143,233,289	Eugene 298
James 143,289	James 142,226,298
Jas 15,233	Jas 18,73
Lucy 143,233,289	Jesse 142
Maggie 233,289	FISHERE, Eugine 226
Rosa 15	FITZPATRICK
FINE CATCHER 264	Chas 173
FINE CATCHING 200	Kate 173
FINE CUTTER 212	Matt 115,173
FINE DRIVING BACK 249	FLAT FACE 52
FINE GUN WOMAN 204,272	FLAT TAIL 10,89,143,236,293
FINE KILL 173	Anna 143,293,296
FINE KILLS 113,217,267	Annie 33
FINE SLAUGHTER 205	Charles 296
FINE SPEAR 266	John 236
FINE WAR WOMAN 200	Nellie 236
FINE YOUNG MAN 31	Philip 33,89,143,236
FIRST CATCHER 216	Phillip 296
FIRST CHIEF 108	Sophia 143,293
FIRST CLEAN UP 66	FLIES IN WATER 77,284
FIRST CLEAR UP 158	FLINT SMOKE 228
FIRST COYOTE 262	Minnie 228
FIRST GO IN 146	FLINT SMOKER 113,142,277
FIRST GOES IN 93	James 143,277
FIRST GUN 268	Jas 70,228
FIRST KILLS 53	Peter 70,143,277
Agnes 53	FLINT SMOKES, Peter 228
Ben 53	FLYING 44,107,173,211,254

Index

FLYING BEAR 8
FLYING DOWN 262
FLYING HEN 51
FLYING IN WATER 14
FLYING SQUIRREL 110,162
FLYS IN WATER 150
FORD
    Adell 224
    Anna 224
    Corbett 224
    Daniel 224
    Dewey 225
    Ellen 224
    Emiline 224
    Florestine 224
    Henry 224
    Jeames 224
    Joseph 224
    Nelson 224
    Rosa 225
    Samuel 224
FOUND A GUN ... 28,87,143,214,284
FOUND HERSELF 111,193
FOUR BULLS 44,197
FOUR HORNS 22,75,142,234,276
    Benj 142,277
    Benjamin 22,75,234
    Geo 6,68
    George 144,234,277
    James 75,142
    Jas 22,234,277
    Louis 277
FOX 84,166
    Aleic 101
    Alex 173,225,275
    Amelia 35,101,172
    Anna 173
    Chas 231
    Elix 35
    Eliza 172,224
    Emily 224
    Infant 225
    Jas 231
    Lisa 36
    Mabel 275
    Peter 231
FOX WOMAN 269
FPX, Emily 272

FRD, Arthur 225
FREE WILL 293
FRENCH GUN COVER 200
FRINGE GUN 253
FRONT RIDER 48
FRONT RIDER, Rene 48
FUNNY GUN 255
G BOTH SIDES
    John 87
    Pete 87
G BULL
    Cecil 145
    George 145
    Joseph 8
    Mary 145
    Thos 8
G G BULL
    George 96
    Mary 96
G STABBING
    Anna 93
    Maggie 93
G T MOVE, Jas 231
GALBRAITH
    Amelia 37
    Annie 97
    Eliza 34,97
    John 34,97
    Lizzie 97
    Lizzy 34
    Mollie 97
    Phibe 34
    Phoebie 97
    Webster 34,97
GALBREATH
    Anna 173
    Eliza 173,219,264
    Jack 219,264
    John 173
    Lizzie 173,219,264
    Mary 264
    Mollie 173,219
    Phoebe 173,264
    Webster 173,219,263
GAMBLER 25,59,79,116,144,197,
    233,252,280
    ---- 25
    Anna 74,144,280,293

Index

Annie 5,25,79,233
  James 144,293
  Jas 5,74,233
  Jennie 25,233
  Jessie 79
  Louise 116,174
  Louize 59
  Mary 144,233
  Richard 79,144
GARDAFREE
  (Infant) 4
  Alex 4
  John 4
  Josephine 4
GARDIPEE, Mary 102
GARDUPIN 65
  Alex 65
  Frank 66
  John 66
  Louise 66
  Mary 66
  Pete 66
GATHER WOOD 59
GERARD, Fred 167
GILHAM
  Anthony 103,173,219,270
  Josephene 103
  Josephine 173,219,270
  William 173
  Wm 103,219,270
GILLIAM
  Anthony 40
  Josephene 40
  Julia 40
  William 40
GIRARD, Fred 105,221,265
GIVES BACK 230
GIVES GUN AWAY 101,194
GIVES PLENTY 82,158
GIVES TO ONE ANOTHER 284
GIVES TO SUN 181
GIVES TO THE SUN 102,109,169
GIVING THINGS TO THE SUN
  256,265
GIVING WAR CLUB 200
GLASS IN FRONT 200
GLASS WOMAN 30,146,238
GO IN OFTEN 293

GOBART
  Agnes 54
  Ammie 54
GOBERT
  Agnes 117,178,223,256
  Alice 33
  Anne 178
  Annie 117
  Catharine 219
  Catherine 117,170,256
  Ed 117,170
  Eddie 219,271
  John 33,74,144,226,292
  Mary 226,292
  Nellie 74,144,226,292
  Susan 292
  Susie 33,74,144,226
GOES ALL AROUND 257
GOES IN ALL AROUND 198
GOES IN ALL ARROUND 49
GOES IN ALL LODGES . 11,109,144
GOES IN BOTH 233
GOES IN BOTH PLACES 9
GOES IN BOTH SIDES 25
GOES IN FIRST 26
GOES IN HER SELF 41
GOES IN LAST 71,138,209,
  212,242,260
GOES IN PLACES 5
GOES IN TWO PLACES 281,285
GOES TO WAR ALONE 279
GOES TO WAR GOOD 281
GOES UP ALONE 84
GOING AFTER WATER 254
GOING AHEAD ALONE 250
GOING ALONE 211
GOING BACK 5
GOING IN LAST 249
GOING OVER 17
GOING TO GO IN 90
GOING TO MOVE 20,81,145,
  231,284
  James 284
GOING TO THE SUN 210
GOING UP HILL 58
GOO STABBING 240
GOOD ATTACK WOMAN 279
GOOD BEAR 19

Index

GOOD BEAR WOMAN..........91,145
GOOD BIRD WOMAN................198
GOOD CATCH 107,148,243
GOOD CATCHER 51
GOOD CHARGE............................136
GOOD CHARGING................87,149
GOOD CHASER 49
GOOD CHASES............................122
GOOD CLEAN UP.........21,68,77,80,
....160,235,290
GOOD CLEAR UP...............144,154
GOOD CRANE 49
GOOD CUT.............................21,295
GOOD CUTTING 260
GOOD FOR NOTHING 210
GOOD G WOMAN 94
GOOD GRASS WOMAN 177
GOOD GUN 84,188,209,253
GOOD KILL..................120,174,189,
....231,233,269
GOOD KILLER............31,49,58,103,
....123,209,214
GOOD KILLING............209,251,255
GOOD KILLS.................................85
GOOD L GIRL 86
GOOD L WOMAN........................94
GOOD LOOKING.............61,230,294
GOOD LOOKING CROW WOMAN
....107,167,257
GOOD LOOKING GIRL................15
GOOD LOOKING OWL..............199
GOOD LOOKING WOMAN ...25,73,
...................145,146,215,281,289
   John..73
GOOD MASSACRE................5,14,30
GOOD MEDICINE........................81
GOOD MEDICINE PIPE 174,264
GOOD MEDICINE RIPE 198
GOOD PAINTER 47
GOOD RIDER 106,179,210,283
GOOD RUSH................................28
GOOD SHEILD............................119
GOOD SHIELD..............8,49,90,161,
....193,244,263
GOOD SHIELD WOMAN 295
GOOD SINGER................52,115,180
GOOD SLAUGHTER 215,258
GOOD STAB................................144

   Maggie.....................................144
GOOD STABBING................93,277
GOOD STABING 26
   Annie..26
   Mary..26
GOOD STEAL......................243,296
GOOD STEALING................210,249
GOOD STEALING WOMAN 199
GOOD STEEL................................27
GOOD STRIKE.............12,65,87,93,
..........144,149,160,237,240,281,295
GOOD STRIKES 231
GOOD TIED WOMAN...............199
GOOD TRIED WOMAN............249
GOOD VICTORY................281,287
GOOD WOMAN............16,41,55,93,
....141,146,193,242
GOODS WOMAN 235
GOSS
   Abbot....................................... 173
   Albert.......43,104,105,173,218,257
   Albert R................................... 105
   Albert, Jr.................................. 173
   Caroline 43,173,257
   Carrie....................................... 105
   Carris....................................... 218
   Francis 43,104,173,218,257
   Geo 43
   George 104,173,218,257
   Gina 218
   Loamie................................43,257
   Loammie.................................. 218
   Lome.. 173
   Lomie 104
   Maggie....43,104,105,173,218,257
   Mamie...............................173,257
   Mammie................................... 218
   Mary....................................43,173
   Mary J................................105,218
   Nate 257
   Nathan 104,173,218
   Nellie 43,104,173,218,257
   Phena....................................... 257
   Susa... 218
   Susan... 43
   Susie 105,173,257
   William........................43,173,257
   Willie....................................... 104

Index

Wm 218
GOT GUN IN SIDE 58
GOT MANY DIFFERENT THINGS
.... 214
GRAIN WOMAN 204,252
GRANT
    Cecil 29
    Dick 210
    James 174,199,291
    Jim 53
    Josephene 54
    Josephine 174,199,271
    Maggie 29
    Pete 29
    Peter 250
    Richard 54,117,145,209,291
    Rosa 145,209,291
GRASS HOPPER 111
GRASS SNAKE 65,233,280
GRASS WOMAN 80
GRAY WHISKERS 94,155,230
GREEN
    Mary 202
    Nick 19,127,185,202,265
GREEN GRASS BULL 8,96,145,
.... 226,289
GRETCHEN 250
GROS VENTRES WOMAN 142
GROS-VENTRE WOMAN 24,75
GROUND 48,121,174,254
    Evelina 261
    George 254
    James 174,254
    Jas 48,121
    John 48,121,174,202,261
    Mary 174,202,261
    Minnie 48
GROUND SNAKE 15
GROUND SQUIREL 46
GROUNDS 198
    James 198
GROVE ANT WOMAN 22
GROVENT WOMAN 79
GUARDIPEE
    Agnes 107,174,266
    Alex 144,233,280
    Charles 266
    Chas 107,174,223,224

Eli 106,198,223,256,266
Ely 174
Frank 107,174,198,223,256,266
Frank, Jr 174,256
George 224
Joe 174
John 144,232,233,280,294
Josephene 107
Josephine 174,224,266
Kate 102
Katie 281
Kittie 144
Louisa 144
Louise 266,294
Louize 232
Maggie 144,224
Mary 107,174,198,256
Pete 144,232
Peter 294
Sadie 106,174,223,266
Thos 223,266
Tom 106,174
GUARDUPIN
    John 5
    Louese 5
    Pete 5
GUARTIPEE
    Chas 40,41
    Elli 41
    Francie 41
    Geo 41
    Josephene 41
    Kattie 40
    Maggie 41
    Mary 40
    Saddie 41
    Thos 41
GULICK, Octavia 244
GUN ALONE, Josephine 29
GUN FOR NOTHING 9
GUN FRINGE 101,194
GUN GUN WOMAN 150
H BREAST, Young 50
H COAT, Mary 123,176
H FACE
    Jas 238
    Jennie 238
    John 238

Index

H GUN
   Josephine 4
   Mary 49,122
   Paul 49,122
H RUNNER
   Geo 42,103
   Rosa 104
   Rose 42
HAD TEETH 254
HAGAN
   Esther 175
   Esturill 99
   Iswell 38
   Maggie 38,99,175
   Nellie 38,99,175
   Sadie 100,175
   Sallie 99,175
   Sally 38
HAGEN
   Maggie 222,269
   Mary 211
   Nellie 210,269
   Sadie 222,269
   Sallie 224,269
HAGGERTY
   Pearl 255
   Wm Wright 255
HAIRY COAT 123,176,214,251
   Mary 214,251
HAIRY FACE 80,284
   James 80
   Mollie 284
   Pete 80
HALL
   Abner 175,275
   David 68,145,245,277
   Elsie 97,175,275
   James 277
   John 68
   John P 145
   Josephine 68,145,245,277
   Mary 145,245
   Pat 245
   Patrick 277
   Ruth 276
   Vina 97,175,275
   W H 145
   William 277

Wm 68,245
HAMILTON
   Ella 42,104
   Ella J 175
   Grace 43
   Gracie 104
   Lucy 42,104
   Robert 42,126,175,205,298
   Rosa 175,205,298
   Theo 298
HANDS IT BACK 95,155
HARRISON
   Frank 127
   Jennie 127
HARRY FACE 146,238
   James 146
   Peter 146
HATE WOMAN 82,245
HATEING WOMAN 114
HATES WOMAN 142
HAWK, Presley 121
HAZLETT
   Baby 176
   Geo 117
   George 32
   Gerald 295
   Gulder 242
   Maggie 32
   Mary 58,117,176,242,295
   Stewart 222
   Stuart 276
   William 41
   Wm 124,208
HAZLETT WOMAN 80
HEAD, Mary 237
HEAD CARRIER 18,73,145,
.... 243,279
   Henry 89,233,281
   John 18,73,145,243,279
   Mary 73,145
HEAD WOMAN 30,80
HEADING OFF 56,123,176,
.... 198,264
HEARD FIRST 197
HEARD IT BEFORE 108,181
HEARS ALL LANGUAGES 278
HEAVY BREAST 50,123,176,
.... 214,266

Index

Owen 176,215,266
HEAVY GUN 26,93,145,242
   Arthur 242,287
   Henry 4,67,146,242,287
   Jack 242,287
   Josephine 67
   Mary 26,242,287
HEAVY HAIR 269
HEAVY RUNNER 42,103,175,
  207,255
   Geo 175,207
   George 255
   Jack 207
   Rosa 255
   Wood 255
HEAVY SET OF HAIR 212
HENAULT
   Caroline 198
   Clara 6,67,145,229,293
   Hesler 145
   Maggie 6,67,145,229,293
   Mary 265
   Moses 6,67,145,229,293
   Nelson 6,67,145,229,293
   Stephen 6,67,198
   Steve 145,265
HERAN
   Maggie 65
   Mary 65
HEWAS IN NIGHT 79
HIDE IN NIGHT 151
HIDE SCRAPER 284
HIDES BEHIND BLANKET .. 47,165
HIGANS
   Mary P 39
   May 39
HIGGANS
   Alice 38
   Henry 38
   Louise 38
HIGGINS
   Alice 98,242,297
   Charles 103,206,272
   Chas 175
   Henry 98,242,297
   John 206,272
   John E 175
   Louise 98,242,297

Mary 103,175,206,272
May 103,175,272
HIGH FORHEAD 199
HILL
   Daniel 226
   Fred 226
HINKEL
   Caroline 34
   Elizzie 207
   Geo 34,207
   Lizzie 34
   Mamie 34,207
   Rosa 207
   William 34
   Wm 207
HINKLE
   Geo 175
   George 97
   Lizzie 97,175
   Mamie 175
   Martha 97
   Rosa 97,175
   William 97
   Willie 175
HIRS IN SAME PLACE 109
HITS BACK 183
HITS DOWN 21
HITS FIRST 184
HITS IN FRONT 86,108,181
   Austin 28,177
   Joe 28,177
HITS IN SAME PLACE 184
HITS IN THE FRONT, Austin 271
HITS IN THE MIDDLE 209
HITS IN THE WATER 262
HITS IN WATER 59,113,146
HITS LAST 135,157
HITS ON TOP 54,76,81,91,146,
   151,152,232,243,294
HITS THE BACK 268
HITS WITH A GUN 215
HOLLOWING AT NIGHT 251
HOLLOWING LAST 215
HOME GUN 49,122,176,213,258
   Dan 258
   Mary 176,258
   Minnie 213
   Paul 176,213,258

Index

HOME RUSHING 215
HORN
   Geo 35,123
   George 176,204,252
   Harry 25,94,145,230,294
   Maggie 25
   Susan 252
HOUK
   Ellenor 274
   Margaret E 274
   Margaret 224
   Pressley 224,274
   Pressly 37
HOUKE, Presley 185
HOUSEMAN
   Frank 275
   Geneva 275
   James 275
   Joseph 275
   Maggie 275
   Mary 275
HOUSMAN
   Geneva 123
   James 174
   Jas 34,123
   Jenivene 34
   Joseph 34
   Josephene 123
   Josephine 34,174
   Mary 34,123,174
   Susan 34,123
   Thomas 174
   Thos 34,123
HOWARD
   Ammie 35
   Anna 175,206
   Annie 98,273
   Joe 175
   Joseph 35,98,205
   Jow 273
   Mary 35,98,175,205,268
   Walter 35,98,175,205,268
HOWLS AT NIGHT 200
HOWLS IN WATER 8
HUNCBUGER
   Cicelia 59
   Clara 59
   Guss 59

John 59
Thos 59
HUNGRY 27,87,113,176
   Austin 114,176
   Ezra 87
   Henry 27,87,216
   Isaac 27
   Jos 113
   Joseph 176
   Wm 268
HUNGRY WOMAN 51,101,
.... 194,215
HUNSBERGER
   Augustus 117,176
   Cecil 117,176,208
   Cecile 265
   Clara 117,176,208,266
   Gus 266
   Gussie 208
   Isaac 117,176
   John 117,175,208,266
   Mary 175,208,266
   Thomas 208,267
   Thos 117,266
   Tom 176
   Willie 175
   Wm 208
I NECKLACE, Minnie 16
IGNACE 112
IN THE WATER, John 25
INFANT 198,199,200,201,202,
203,205,206,207,210,211,212,213,215
,216,217,218,224
INFENT 50
INMAN
   Edith 75
   Ollie 75
INNMAN, Edith 246
IRON 48,111,176,198,261
   Helen 275
IRON BREAST
   Charles 292
   Chas 13,76,139,236
   Ellen 236
   Minnie 76,139
   Nancy 13
   Nellie 293
IRON CROW 259

Elizabeth 149	Monic 147
Isabel 277	Mrs Eddie 241,281
Isabella 228	Sarah 121
Mary 213	Skip 127
Matilda 228	JACKRABBIT WOMAN 51
Matildo 149	JACKSON
IRON EATER 6,67,97,228,277	Andrew 101
(Infant) 6	Anna 177
Isabel 277	Annie 105,224,272
Isabella 6	Billie 177
Issabella 67	Bouble B 234
Jennie 228	Dick 234
John 6	Double Blaze 282
Maggie 67,228	Eliza 101,272
Rosa 68,228,277	Frank 16,234,282
Susie 6,67,228	Hugh 44,105,177
IRON GUN	Joe 16
John 31	John 101,172
Lucy 31,82	Joseph 234,282
IRON NECKLACE 16,70,146,	Julia 177,224,272
.... 235,286	Lizzie 101
Anna 70,146,235	Louie 16
Annie 16	Louis 234,282
Minnie 70,146	Lucy 234
IRON PIPE 25,78,146,240,285	Maggie 44,105,177,224,272
Cecil 25	Mary 44,105,177,224,272
Charles 78,146	Michael 224
Chas 240	Millie 44,105
Joe 78,146,240	Milly 101
Joe P 240	Minnie 224,272
John 25,78,146,285	Oliver 16
Joseph 25,285	Richard 282
Maggie 78,146,240,285	Thomas 177,275
IRON WOMAN 7,10,30,36,41,45,	Thos 44,105,224,272
..... 93,103,164,176,185,206,208,256	William 44,177
IVOCKATOPSIS 180	Wm 105
IVORY WOMAN 217,263	JINGLES 28
IYOCKATOPSIS 115	JINGLES IN THE AIR 283
JACK	JOHNSON
Cecil 147,241	Belle 17,72,246,267
Cecile 281	Chas 17
Eddie 121,147	Homer 17
Eddy 15,241,281	Ida 17,72,147,246,267
Juanique 281	James 267
Maggie 121	Jas 17,72,246
Mary 121	Jennie 17,72,146
Minnie 241	Joe 147
Money 15	Mary ... 17,72,118,147,177,246,267

Index

William 147,294
Willie 17
Wm 72,246
JUMPER 206
JUNEAU
    Charles 293
    Chas 124
JUNO, Chas 242
JUST CAN SEE HIM 250
JUST HEARD HIM 292
K WAY, John 46
K WOMAN, John 93
KAISER, Mary 263
KEISER, Mary 105,178,200
KENNEDY
    John 43,124,125,225,251
    Mary 124,225,251
    Willie 225
    Wm 251
KENNERLEY
    Agnes 117
    Jas 117
    Jerome 117
    Maggie 117
KENNERLY
    Agnes 54,178,251
    Anna 256
    Annie 222
    Bert 56,179,209
    James 179,222,256
    Jas 54
    Jerome 54,179,222,256
    Lee 256
    Leo 179
    Lep 222
    Maggie 54,178,222,256
    Perry 56,179,209,251
KICKING WOMAN 26,93,147,
.... 242,277
    Jennie 246
    John 26,147,246,267
    Leo 246
KIDD
    Mary 18
    Thos 17
    Willie 18
KIDNEY 81,147,239
    Alice 82

John 147,239
Joseph 291
Mack 27,214
Maggie 160
Mary 81,147,160,239,291
Mike 160
Minnie 27
KILL ACROSS THE WAY, John 204
KILL AT NIGHT 263
KILL FORWARD 193
KILLA BY MISTAKE 200
KILLED & GOT AWAY 108,181
KILLS A LONG WAY 258,270
KILLS ACROSS 279
KILLS ACROSS THE WAY 204,252
    John 252
KILLS ACROSS WAY 46,178
    John 178
KILLS ALONE 36
KILLS ANOTHER 27,128,194
KILLS AT NIGHT .. 110,123,206,254
    Eneas 192
KILLS AT THE EDGE 277
KILLS AWAY OFF 59
KILLS BY MISTAKE 23,262
KILLS CLOSE ... 12,161,234,244,283
    Susie 161
KILLS CLOSE WOMAN 281
KILLS DIFFERENT 207
KILLS FAR 115,165
KILLS FIRST 47,95,117,151,
.... 189,220,265,294
KILLS FOR NOTHING 13,92,
.... 137,227,231,283,285
KILLS FORWARD 113
KILLS FUR 88
KILLS IN AIR 29,84,178
KILLS IN BRUSH . 32,83,87,147,149
KILLS IN FRONT 206
KILLS IN NIGHT 3,31,82,94,
.... 150,160,191,239
KILLS IN THE AIR 209
KILLS IN THE BRUSH. 211,214,235
    Joseph 296
KILLS IN THE MIDDLE 261
KILLS IN THE NIGHT 49,277,288,291
KILLS IN WATER
.... 6,36,61,68,144,188,212

Index

KILLS INSIDE 16,235,286,294
KILLS LONG WAY 211
KILLS ON THE MIDDLE 206
KILLS ON THE SHORE 271
KILLS ON TOP 6,68,253
KILLS ONE ANOTHER 204,260
KILLS PLENTY 235
KILLS TWICE 244
KILLS TWO 12,161,283
KILLS WATER 113
KILS LONG WAY 199
KIND WOMAN 50,123
KING
    Charley 178
    Chas 40,126
    Dewey 178
    Henry 40,126,178
    Jane 178
    Jas 40,126
    Lucy 40,125,178
    Sadie 126,178
    Sady 40
    William 40,126
    Willie 178
KIPP
    Bernice 273
    Calf W 223
    Cecelia 217
    Cecil 179
    Cecile 272
    Cora 54,125,179,217,272
    Dick 54,125,179,217,272
    Elizabeth 273
    Geo 54,115,125,178,179,208
    George 217,251,272
    Gro 54
    Hannah 125
    Jack 102,178,271
    James 178,208,251
    Jas 54,115
    Jeo 54
    Joe 102,115,178,271
    John 102,178,223,271
    Joseph 208,223,251
    Julia 102,178,223,271
    Lewis 54
    Libby 122
    Louis 125,179,217,272

    Martha 54,115,124
    Mary 54,115,125,178,
    208,251,272
    Rosas 217
    Sadie 223,271
    Susan 217
    Ursula 273
    William 54,273
    Willie 102,178
    Wm 115,217,223,271
KIPPP
    Joe 178
    Mary 54
KISER, Mary 42
KIYO
    Mary 290
    Nellie 290
    Thos 290
    William 290
KOSSUTH
    Joe 70,146,197,243,292
    Mary 292
KUKA, Martha 226
KYO
    Mary 72,147,230
    Nellie 230
    Thomas 147
    Thos 72,230
    William 147
    Wm 72,230
L BEAR
    James 106
    Mary 106
L BOY
    Annie 110
    Rebecca 110
    Sam 110
    Swan 110
    Tom 110
L CAYOTE, Fanny 95
L CHIEF, Ellen 91
L DOG
    Harrison 239
    Irene 86
L F SMOKE, Louis 113,180
L PLUME
    Jas 27,86
    Jennie 87

Joe	86
Louie	27,86
Mary	87
Mollie	86
Susie	86
L POLE, Mary	20

L T ROCK
Joe	148
Nellie	148

L T SLEEPING
James	148
John	19,148
Lizzie	19

LA BREECH
Chas	74,227
Clarence	74,227
David	74
Jessie	74,227
Laura	227
Leanora	74
Madore	227
Medora	74
Millie	74,227
Minnie	74,227
Nellie	74
Philip	227
Toxhiel	74
Viola	227

LA BREECHE
Charles	296
Clarence	296
David	227,296
Emily	295
Jessie	295
Leonore	295
Medor	296
Millie	295
Minnie	296
Phillip	295
Violet	296

LA MOTT
Jennie	98,298
Joseph	298
Minnie	298
LA PAGE, Phoebe	219

LABREECH
Chas	23
David	23
Jessie	23
Lena	22
Melvin	23
Millie	22
Minnie	23
Phill	23

LABREECHE
Chas	147
Clarrisia	147
David	147
Jessie	147
Joseph	147
Leanor	147
Medor	147
Millie	147
Minnie	147
LACY BOY, Mack	202

LAHR
Besie	253
Bessie	217
Henry	217
LAMA BEAR	210
LAME BEAR	42,106,179
James	179
Mary	179

LAMOTT
Joe	98
Minnie	98

LARB
Bessie	18
Henry	18,121,180
LAST BEAR	119,165
LAST BEAR WOMAN	53,202,252
LAST BOY	206
LAST CAYOTE NO 2	95
LAST COYOTE	6,68,148,226,286
Minnie	276
LAST GO IN	171
LAST GOES IN	141
LAST GUN	84,228
LAST GUN WOMAN	91,135,278
LAST HOLLOW	119,165
LAST HOLLOWING	252
LAST IRON WOMAN	283
LAST LIFE	200
LAST LIGHT TO COME OVER THE HILL	278
LAST SHOOT	119,165

Index

LAST STAR 32,83,99,167,180,
  206,209,261,270
  Helen 180
  Hellen 83
  Philip 32
  Theodore 270
  Tony 32
LAST STRIKE 10,65,147
LAST STRIKES 39,234
LAST WOLF 101,194
LAST YELLING WOMAN 202
LASY CUT 97
LAUZON, Peter 293
LAYING FOR THEM 266
LAYING LOW 50,123
LAYS FINE 198
LAZY BOY ... 48,95,110,180,202,249
  Anna 249
  Annie 180
  Goose 48
  Mack 249
  Mary 180
  Mike 180
  Sam 48,180,249
  Samuel 202
  Thos 48,202
  Tom 180,249
LAZY CUT 34,192
LAZY YOUNG MAN 110,179
  Lazy Yo 48
LEAD WOMAN 67,160
LEGGINS 86,199,268
LEHMAN
  Ammie 38
  Jessie 38
  John 38
  Lee 38
  Lewis 38
  Mary 38
LEMMON
  Emma 222
  John 222
  Lee 222
  Louise 222
  Mary 222
LEMON
  Annie 269
  Emma 99

Jessie 99
John 99,269
Lee 99,179,269
Louise 99,269
Mary 99,179,269
LEWIS
  Antoine 123,179,253,274
  Antone 34
  Baby 197
  Bessie 179
  Betsey 274
  Geo 34,123
  Joseph Narcius 274
  Margaret 34
  Margarete 123
  Pete 179
  Peter 34,274
  Piler 123
  Sarah 34,123,179,197,274
  William 34,179
  Wm 123,197,274
LIGHT FACE 290
LIGHTS AT NIGHT 215
LIKE MARROW BONES 294
LIKES MARROW BONES 226
LINX WOMAN 81
LIPPINCOTT
  Arthur 124
  Mary 124
  Ray 124
LITEL, Matt 54
LITTLE ANTELOPE 107,167
LITTLE BEAR 44
  Thomas 254
  Tom 107,191
LITTLE BLAZE 288
LITTLE BULL 27,28,87,149,214
LITTLE BULL #1 284
LITTLE BULL #2 281
LITTLE CHIP MUNK 215
LITTLE DIVER 108
LITTLE DOG 31,80,148,239,287
  Eliza 80,148
  Harrison 80,148,287
  Irene 28,183
  John 31,80
  Mary 31,148,239
  Micheil 85

331

Index

Mike 28,183,199,249
Oliver 31
Sam 50
LITTLE FOX 119,165,202,
.... 209,252,253
LITTLE GIRL 285
LITTLE HAWK 95
LITTLE HAWK WOMAN 290
LITTLE MINK 17
LITTLE OTTER ... 14,95,148,230,284
LITTLE OWL 31,82,148,180,
.... 214,269
   Maggie 31,82,148,180
   Mary 82,148,180,269
LITTLE PECK 71
LITTLE PERSON 214
LITTLE PETRIFIED ROCK 277
LITTLE PLUME .. 27,86,148,213,286
   Annie 287
   Cora 27
   Irvin 27,87,203,250
   Irwin 176
   James 148,213,287
   Jessie 176
   Joe 148
   John 250
   Joseph 287
   Josephine 27,214,287
   Louis 148,214,287
   Mary 27,176,214,287
   Millie 287
   Mollie 148
   Peter 27,214,287
   Susie 27,148,214
LITTLE PLUME MOTHER 27
LITTLE RAIN 50,110
LITTLE RAM 192
LITTLE ROCK 148,284
LITTLE SNAKE 57
LITTLE STAR 232
LITTLE STINK TEAT 188
LITTLE WHITE WOMAN 286
LITTLE YOUNG MAN 52,115,
.... 180,199,258
LIVERMORE
   Clara 37,180,207,255
   Joe 180
   Joseph 37,207

Leggins 180
Lillie 207,255
Lilly 37
Lily 180
LIVINMORE
   Clara 124
   Jos 123
   Lilly 124
LODGE, Harrison T 16
LODGE POLE
   Louisa 193
   Louise 266
   Peter 71,136,241
LODGE POLE CHIEF 7,107,179
LODGEPOLE, Lousia 107
LOGAN, W R 132
LOMG T M PIPE 86
LONE BEAR, Thos 201
LONE CHIEF
   Dan 19,91,141,289
   Ellen 19,141,244,289
   Jas 244
LONE CHIEF #1, Dan 243,289
LONE CHIEF #2, Dan 243
LONE CHIEF #3, Dan 244
LONE CROW 255
LONE CUT 5,68,148,157,
.... 233,238,279,294
LONE MOUSE 199,260
LONE ROCK 82,143,239,279
LONE RUSHER 211
LONE WARRIOR 58
LONE WOLVERINE 241
LONE WOMAN 48,119,194,
.... 215,266
LONE YOUNG MAN 203
LONG BEAR 108,181
LONG FACE 30,185,210,270
LONG FISH 86
LONG TIME BEAR WOMAN ....
.... 197,258
LONG TIME BIRD 11,265
LONG TIME BLACK BIRD 293
LONG TIME BUFFALO STONE .....
.... 293
LONG TIME BULLALO STONE .....
.... 289
LONG TIME CALF 23,232,281

Index

LONG TIME CHICKEN 89,138,
.... 202,232
LONG TIME GOOD 101,194
LONG TIME HAWK 290
LONG TIME MEDICINE PIPE ...203
LONG TIME MEDICINE PIPE
  WOMAN 272
LONG TIME OLD WOMAN 262,295
LONG TIME OTTER 65,160
LONG TIME OWL 52,108
LONG TIME OWL WOMAN 200
LONG TIME RED SQUIRREL ...203
LONG TIME ROCK 6,17,70,
.... 148,235,277
  Annie 289
  George 289
  Joe 70
  Nellie 70
LONG TIME SINGING 200
LONG TIME SLEEPING 19,148,
.... 242,295
  Joe 243
  Joseph 295
  Lohn 295
  Mary 243
  Wm 243
LONG TIME SQUIRREL 288
LONG TIME STANDING ROCK
  SIOUX 206
LONG TIME STAR 50
LONG TIME WOLVERING 281
LONG TIME WOMAN 9,10,65,
.... 74,156,160,233,239,244,286
LONG WOLVERENE 78
LONG WOLVERINE 15,148
LONGTIME OWL 180
LONGTIME SLEEPING 81
  John 81
  Johnny 81
  Julia 81
  Mary 81
LOOKING FOR SMOKE 113,180,
.... 204,260
  Louis 204,260
LOOKING GLASS 262
LOOKS AT, Annie 231
LOOKS LAST 242
LOOKS PLENTY 93,147

LOST HER FINGER 119,165
LOTS MASSACREE 10
LOUIS 211
LOWER WOMAN 84
LUCERO, Dick 115,180,217,269
LUCY 285
LUKEN
  Dora 222,270
  John 222
  Mary 222,270
  Peter 222,270
LUKENS
  Dora 179
  John 179
  Mary 179
  Peter 179
LUKIN
  Dora 118
  John 118
  Mary 118
  Peter 118
  Victoria 118
LUKINS
  Albert 55
  Dora 55
  John 55
  Mary 55
  Peter 55
  Victoria 55
LUVERO, Rosa 126
LYNX WOMAN 137
LYTLE
  James 271
  Katie 223,271
  Matt 223,271
M B RIBS
  Emma 104
  Maggie 104
M BONES
  Likes 26
  Mrs 26
M BULL, Thos 94,228
M C WEATHER
  Joe 47,110,181
  Julia 110,181
  Mary 47
M CALF
  Chas 46

Index

John 111
Mary 46
Sam 46
M CHIEF
   Anthony 9
   Emma 9
   John 9
   Thelsa 9
M GUN
   Chas 228
   Joe 228
   Minnie 228
   Thos 228
M GUNS
   Joe 92
   Josephine 32
   Thos 8,92
M HIDES 112
   Maggie 112
M PLUME
   Albert 14
   Geo 94
   John 3,94
   Julia 4
   Mack 3
   Maggie 14,94
   Mike 94
   Susie 14,94
M RIDER
   Fred 84
   Levi 84
   Mary 84
M SIGNS, Louise 184
M T FEATHERS
   James 181
   Jas 108
   Josephine 265
M W HORSES
   Crow 51
   Gun 51
   John 51
   Lone Girl 51
   Thos 51
   Young 52
M WOLF
   Charley 109
   Henry 109
MAD BEEN YELLING 214
MAD MAN, Steve 276
MAD PLUME 3,94,150,239,290
   Albert 94,150,230,290
   Charles 291
   Geo 3
   George 150,239
   James 150
   John 3,150,239
   Joseph 230,290
   Julia 239,291
   Maggie 150,230,290,291
   Mary 290
   Medicine 150
   Michael 150
   Mike 239
   Mollie 231
   Richard 239,291
   Susan 290
   Susie 150,230
MAD PLUME NO 2 3
MAD WOLF 49,109,181,210,265
   Charles 265
   Chas 181,210
   Henry 182
   Joseph 210
   Mark 265
MADE A MEDICINE LODGE
   SUDDENLY 279
MAGEE
   Annie 128
   Dewey 114,183
   Geo 56,114
   George 183
   Henry 56,114,183
   Joe 114,183
   Joseph 56
   Julia 56,114,182
   Mary 56,114,183
   Thos 56
   Tom 114,183
   Walter 56,114,183
MAIN
   Alice 33,96,181,220,261
   Elizabeth 33
   Henry 33,96,181,220,261
   Isabel 96,181
   Isabella 261
   Isabelle 220

Index

Issabella 33
Lizzie 96,181,261
Mary 181,220,261
MAKES COLD WEATHER 47,85,
.... 110,181,207,255
   Joe 255
   Jos 207
MAKES FIRST TREATY 203
MAKES GUN BY MISTAKE 52
MAKES NOISE 60,169
MAKES SIGNS 184,252
MAKES SINGS AT ONE ANOTHER
.... 205
MAKES TWO GUNS 56
MAKING SIGNS 122
MALAT ROCK 42
MANDAN WOMAN 222,270
MANS FACE 298
MANY BOYS 51
MANY CATS 102
MANY CUTS 183,223,271
MANY DIFFERENT PETRIFIED
   WOMAN 212
MANY GUNS 8,32,82,92,141,150,
... 188,204,239,242,244,272,276,292
   Jas 239
   Joe 8
   John 151
   Josephene 82
   Josephine 150,239,292
   Thomas 151
   Thos 242,276
MANY HIDES 112,182,215,256
   Maggie 182,256
   Mary 215
MANY MASSACRE 12
MANY MORNING GUN 77
MANY NECKLACE 149,183,
.... 216,269
MANY NECKLASS 76
MANY OWLS 58,209,262
MANY PETRIFIED 12
MANY PIPES 213,258
MANY SHEILDS 122
MANY SHELLS 28
MANY SNAKES 52,116,165,197,259
MANY STARS 19
MANY TAIL FEATHERS

.... 45,108,181,197,213,258
   Bertha 258
   James 198,265
   Jennie 258
MANY TAIL FEATHERS #2 263
MANY VICTORIES 295
MANY WHITE HORSES
.... 51,101,194,200,262
MANY WHITE HORSES 2 51
MANY YELLS 204,269
MARCEAU
   Agnes 239
   Alex 72,149,239,287
   Anna 72,149,287
   Annie 239,265
   Charles 271
   Chas 39,219
   Frank 39,222,271
   Henry 197,259
   Josephine 149,240,293
   Lizzie 199
   Louie 149
   Louis 72,240,278
   Louise 72,149,239,287
   Mabel 271
   Mable 222
   Margaret 293
   Mrs 149
   Pete 149
   Pete #1 72
   Peter 293
   Rosa 72,149,240,278
   Thereca 72
   Theresa 149,239,287
MARCERD
   Alex 18
   Josephine 18
   Louise 18
   Peter 18
   Theresa 18
MARCEREAU
   Chas 183
   Frank 183
MARCERO
   Chas 99
   Frank 99
   Louie 22
   Rosa 22

Index

MARROE BONES, Felix 231
MARRORBONES, Felix 7
MARROW BONES 94,150
   Anna....................................143
   Annie.....................................78
   Fannie 231
   Fanny 286
   Felix 143,286
   Lucy 231
   Maggie 226
MARROWBONES
   Felix 78
   Willie 7
MARTAIN
   Charles 249
   Floyd 249
   Rena 249
   Ross.....................................249
MARTIN
   Chas 40,118,180,225
   Maud 40,225
   Rena 181
   Ross.....................40,118,180,225
MASSACRE WOMAN 6
MATT
   Ada.................................112,182
   Adaline...........................112,182
   Adeline................................44
   Albert 267
   Alice.....................................44
   Frances 182
   Francis........................44,112,267
   Julia................................112,182
   Julia Alice 267
   Lena 267
   Lewis...................................44
   Louis 112,182,267
   Machiel 267
   Matchell 218
   Michael 182
MAY SITS UNDER 166
MCGOVERN
   Jas 208
   John.....................................208
   Sophia 208
MCGOWAN
   Eliza....................................274
   Georgiani 274

   Jeanette Marie.........................274
MCGOWEN
   Eliza....................................208
   Georgia 208
   Jocie....................................208
MCKNIGHT
   Aaron 226,298
   Anna 24
   Irene.............. 24,73,149,226,298
   James 149
   Joe 24,73,149,226
   Joseph 298
   Lucy.............. 24,73,149,226,298
   Nancy 298
MCMULLEN, Ellen.. 75,149,241,243
MEDICINE 23,88,199,253
MEDICINE BEAVER......... 16,23,69,
   91,146,227,282,297
MEDICINE BIG HEAD..............283
MEDICINE BLACK BIRD... 215,294
MEDICINE BOSS RIBS...... 104,182,
  201,271
   Maggie................................271
MEDICINE BULL 26,94,149,
  228,281
   Mary 149
   Thomas 149
   Thos................................26,281
MEDICINE CHILD 200,210,262
MEDICINE GIRL 284
MEDICINE GRINDER...................44
MEDICINE HAWK 95,153
MEDICINE HOLLERING WOMAN
  277
MEDICINE LODGE 238
MEDICINE M PLUME...................94
MEDICINE O WOMAN.................70
MEDICINE OLD WOMAN.........256
MEDICINE OTTER.....................285
MEDICINE OWL 52,116,184,
  197,259
MEDICINE PINE WOMAN......... 159
MEDICINE PIPE 30,89
   Sallie...................................174
MEDICINE PIPE WOMAN..... 10,21,
   28,143,236,286,293
MEDICINE RATTLING RUNNING
  287

Index

MEDICINE RIPE WOMAN.........228
MEDICINE ROAD................212,271
MEDICINE SHEILD......................84
MEDICINE SINGER..............85,183,
................................200,249,250
MEDICINE SMOKE WOMAN ...277
MEDICINE STAB....................24,79,
................................150,232,284
MEDICINE STAR........11,92,139,236
MEDICINE STONE..........31,166,242
MEDICINE SUGAR......................30
MEDICINE TIE........................8,226
MEDICINE TOP..................106,165
MEDICINE WEASEL............21,109,
................................184,212,260
   Theresa.....................................260
MEDICINE WOMAN........65,93,138,
................................139,144,232,240
MELLEGAN, Wesley....................179
MERCHANT
   Emma................................202,256
   Henry..................124,183,202,256
   John.....................107,181,203,269
MESTAS, John...............124,181,210
MIDDLE CALF
   Agnes..263
   John................46,111,177,213,254
   John, Jr......................................177
   Mary...254
   Mollie...213
   Mrs John....................................213
   Sam......................................213,263
MIDDLE PERSON..........................21
MIDDLE RIDER.............................29
MILLER
   Jack..................43,104,182,200,252
   Josephene...................................124
   Julia.................43,104,182,200,252
MINER..57
MINK..28,239
MINK CALF ROBE.....................283
MINK WOMAN......156,243,277,290
MITTENS..............11,78,149,231,288
   Anna....................................149,232
   Annie..78
   Charles...78
   Chas..149
   James..288

   Jas..................................11,78,231
   John............................11,232,288
   Joseph..149
   Minnie..232
   Sophia...11
   Susie..78,149
MOMBERG
   Bessie...219
   Jacob...182
   Julia..182,219
   Julis..270
   L J...219
   Lewis Jacob.....................................270
   Mabel..182,270
   Mable..219
   Maud..219,270
MONEY...108,190
MONIAC...224
MONROE
   Angus...124
   Antoine..182
   Campbell...184
   Carrie.................120,182,211,273
   Christina..124
   Donald...183
   Francis...121
   Frank...182
   Frezoni...184
   Frizini..222
   Grinnell....................................211,273
   Hanks...183
   Henry...183
   Henry C...184
   Isabel..183
   Jesse...273
   Jessie....................................120,182,211
   Joe..273
   John...124,183
   Jos..120,211
   Joseph..182
   Louis...................................124,182,183
   Mabel..................120,182,211,273
   Mary..182
   William...183
MOONIC...121
MORGAN
   Agnes...246
   Albert..127

Index

Alice	127,201
Claude	201
Dave	258
David	202
Davis	35,122,183
Elizabeth	246
Fannie	246
Fanny	127
Geo	127
George	246
Infant	122
Ire	122
Jesse	246
Jessie	127
Joe	202
John	35,122,183,202,246,258
Joseph	35,183,258
Katie	127,246
Lizzie	127,201
Louis	246
Lucy	35,122,183,202,258
Mack	246
Mary	127,183,202,246,258
Millie	201
Nellie	127,246
Robert	201
Wilber	201
Wm	201

MORNING GUN, John 77
MORNING EAGLE 30,81, 151,204,269
   Geo 30,81
   George 151
   John 81,151
MORNING GUN 14,77,150, 228,284
   Emma 14,284
   John 14,150,284
   Joseph 284
   Mary 150
   Rosa 284
MORNING OWL 17,243
MORNING OWL WOMAN 279
MORNING PLUME 55,109, 181,200,262
MORNING STAR 53,128
MORNING WOMAN 10,152, 244,284

MOUNTAIN, Thekla 278
MOUNTAIN CHIEF 9,71,150,278
   Amy 150
   Anna 71,150
   Antoine 71
   Antone 278
   Arthur 150
   John 29,150,178,203,249
   Louie 150
   Louis 71
   Thakla 71
   Thekla 150
   Walter 71,150,278
MOUSE GIRL 93
MOUSE WOMAN 8,92,150, 242,276
MUD HEAD 85,182,203,258
   Joe 85,182
   Tarlow 203
MULE RIDER 102,169
MUMBERG
   Julie 105
   Louis J 105
MUMBURG
   Julia 42
   L J 42
MUMMY 31
MUNRO
   Alfred 50
   Antoine 57
   Ben 50
   Campbell 50
   Carry 54
   Francis 58
   Frank 57
   Frank, Jr 58
   Frezen 50
   Guss 58
   Henry 50
   Jessie 54
   John 58
   Joseph 54
   Justine 58
   Lewis 57,58
   Mable 54
   Mary 57
MUNROE
   Alice 225

Index

Amelia 225
Angus 266
Antoine 112,271
Antone 212
Campbell 101,222
Donald 223
Eliza 225
Francis 222
Frank 112,212,215
Frank, Jr 259
Frezine 101
Henry 101,223
Isabel 223
Isabelle 222
Jennie 223,225
John 222,266
Joseph 225
Joseph H 225
Louis 112,212,271
Louise 260
Louize 215
Mary 112,212,225
Sarah 225
Wm 223
Wm Wallace 223
MUNROEJOHN 211
MUNROW, Frank 271
MURPHY
Albert 38,99,181,222
Albert H 276
Hamlin 38,99,181,210
Hamlin H 276
Harlem 222
Harlin 276
Holland 99,181
Holond 38
Mary 38,99,181
William 38
Willie 99,181,210
Wm D 276
N GUN
Samuel 57
Susan 57
N SHOOT
Geo 104
Jos 104
NAVARO, Louis 278
NEQUETTE
Charles 257
Chas 109,216
Joe 109,257
John 216,257
Josephene 109
Josephine 216
Mary 216
NERIS
Daniel 15
Rachel 15
Rosa 15
NEUQUETTE, Mary 109
NEW BREAST 30,86,184,210,270
Mary 185
NEW COMER EAGLE CHILD ... 198
NEW CROW 7,69
NEW ROBE 24,79,151,238,291
Annie 79
Chas 238
James 79
John 24
Joseph 24,151,291
NICE LOOKING GIRL 181
NICE LOOKING WOMAN 109
NICE SNAKE 172
NICHOLS
Cecil 75,151,246
Edith 151
Maggie 75,151,246
Olive 151
Ollie 246
NIEQUETTE
Chas 184
Joe 184
Joseph 210
Josephine 184
Mary 184
NIGHT CUT 29
NIGHT GUN 56,151,229,296
John 119,177,204,229,268
Joseph 296
Josephine 268
Lucy 268
Mary 194,199,263
Minnie 268
Stella 151,229,296
Wallace 194,199,263
NIGHT KILLS 50,217

Index

NIGHT RIDER 13,76,151
   Mrs 236
NIGHT SHOOT 104,184,201,263
   Geo 201
   George 184,263
   Joe 201
   Joseph 184,263
   Maggie 184,263
NIGHT SHOOTS, Maggie 201
NO BEAR
   Henry 145,229,286
   Mary 145
   Rosa 229,286
   Thomas 145,286
   Thos 229
NO CHIEF 29,86,184,249
   Gertrude 29,177
   Grace 29,85,177
   Harry 57,82,176,276
   Jim 29,85,86,177,200,249
   John 86
   Mary 85
   Rachel 85
NO CHIER, Harry 236
NO CHILD 49
NO COAT 23,95,151,231,285
   Anna 23,95,151
   Annie 231,285
   Charles 285
   Chas 11,89,138,231
   Jennie 138
   Jimmie 89
NO HOME 216
NO OWL 83
NO OWL SPRING 61,166
NO OWL WOMAN 269
NO PETRIFIED ROCK 255
NO RUNNER 31,82,151,238,292
   Tim 32
NO SNAKE 145
NOBODY LIKES 212
NORMAN
   Adolph 184,221,274
   Adolphas 36
   Adolphus 100
   Alfred 184,221,274
   Lena 36,184,221,274
   Mary 36,100,184,221,274

   Valina 100
NORRIS
   Daisy 95,205
   Dan 95,184
   Daniel 34,205,253
   Dora 253
   Mary D 184
   Rachel 33,95,184,205,253
   Rosa 95,184,205,253
   Rose 33
NOTHING GUN 278
NUT WOMAN 32
O CHIEF
   Daniel 10
   Jas 10
   John 88
   Mary 10,88
   Paul 88
   Robert 88
O CHILD
   (Infant) 7
   Annie 7
   Isabella 7
   Joe 7
   John 7
   Louie 7
   Mary 7
   Susie 7
O M CHIEF
   James 152
   John 152
   Lucy 152
   Mary 14
O T FEATHERS
   John 18
   Mary 18
OARS 119
OKTIGA 184
OKTIYA 104
OLD BEAR 45
OLD CHIEF 10,88,152,244,284
   Arthur 244
   Cecil 244
   John 10,152,244,284
   Mary 152,244
   Paul 152,244,284
   Robert 284
   Robt 152

Index

OLD COYOTE 16,70,151,227,279
   Mary 16,70,151
   Philip 16,70,151
OLD FORM 281
OLD LONE CUT 234
OLD MAN 293
OLD MAN BEAVER 112
OLD MAN CHIEF 14,77,152,
.... 245,285
   Annie 245
   James 14,285
   Jas 77,245
   John 77
   Lucy 14,77
   Rosa 285
   Thos 245,285
   Wm 245
OLD MOUSE 278
OLD PERSON 29,36,45,97,
.... 185,206,259
   Addie 45
   Anthony 259
   Edna 259
   Grace 29
   Jennie 185,259
   Jenny 45
   John 45,185
   Juniper 259
OLD PERSON WOMAN 278
OLD ROCK
   Peter 17,71,152,236,293
   Rosa 236,293
OLD RUNNING CRANE 14
OLD TIME WOMAN 4,5
OLD WHITE WOMAN 32,152
OLD WHITEMAN 83
OLD WOMAN 47,81,84,89,
.... 135,136,282,293
OLD WOOD, Chas 167
ONE GIRL 188
ONE STRIKE 87,158,294
ONLY GIRL 101,194
ONLY SMOKES 213
ORPHAN WOMAN 279
OSCAR 106
   Peter 185,225,268
OTTER 209
OTTER WOMAN 14,77,150,
.... 228,284
OWL
   Fanny 170
   Ignace 170
OWL CHIEF 7
OWL CHILD 68,151,232,280
   Anna 69,233,280
   Annie 151
   Isabel 280
   Isabella 151,233
   Issabella 69
   Joe 233
   John 67,152,233,280
   Joseph 67,152,280
   Louie 152
   Louis 67,233,280
   Mollie 69,151,232,280
   Susan 280
   Susie 69,151,233
   William 152,280
   Wm 233
OWL CRY 58
OWL FACE 67,228
OWL ON TOP 258
OWL SQUIREL 49
OWL SQUIRREL 123,191
OWL TOP 234
   Mable 234
OWL TOP FEATHERS 18,73,
.... 152,279
   Fannie 73
   Fanny 152
   Jennie 152
   Jenny 73
   John 73
   Julia 18
OWL WOMAN 73,145,152,212
P A BUFFALO
   Annie 186
   Isabel 186
   Joe 186
P CHICKEN
   Cecil 24,144,236
   George 24
   Hannah 236
   Jessie 24
   Johannah 144
   Thomas 144

Index

Thos 236
P PEPION, Cecil 75
P WINGS, Susie 232
PABLE, Mary 277
PABLO
    Agnes 186,208,249
    Christina 186,207,249
    Emma 208,249
    Eva 208,249
    Genevieve 249
    George 106,186,207,249
    Maggie 106,186,207,249
    Mary 106
    Nellie 186
    Susan 106
PAINTED WINGS 20,76,152,
.... 232,288
    John 20
    Lucy 76,152
    Susie 20
PAISLEY
    Allen 55,125,186,212,269
    Chauncey 55,125,186
    Chauncy 212,269
    Geo 55,125
    George 186,212,269
    Lou 55,269
    Louise 125
    Louize 212
    Mattie 55,186,212,269
    Paisley 55
    Walter 125
PAISLY, Lou 186
PAMBRANE
    Jas 43
    Thressa 38
PAMBRUM, Theresa 98
PAMBRUN
    Annie 98,225,253
    Davd 253
    David 98,225
    Dora 225,253
    Eddie 98,225
    Edw 253
    Geo 98,253
    George 225
    Isabel 98
    Isabella 225,253

James 185,222
Jas 112
Louis 98,225,253
May 98
Percy 225
Theresa 186,253
PAPER WOMAN 47
PARRINE, Jas 37,224
PATTERSON
    Fred 221,259
    Helen 259
    Malcolm 259
    Oscar 221
PAUL 10,90,161,237,281
    Albert 36,100,185,221,275
    Celina 275
    Eddie 36,101,185,221,275
    Louisa 36
    Louise 100,185,275
    Louize 221
    Oliver 36,101,185,221,275
    Philip 36,101,185,221,275
    Rosa 185,221
    Rosena 36
    Rosina 101,275
    Salina 185,221
    Selena 36
    Selina 101
    Solomon 36,100,185,221,275
    William 36,275
    Willie 101,185
    Wm 221
PAYES PLENTY 80
PAYS FOR HER TROUBLE 4
PAYS PLENTY 157
PEMBRANE
    Ammie 55
    Davis 55
    Eddie 55
    Geo 55
    Isabel 55
    Lewis 55
PENDERGRASS
    George 201,261
    Julia 39,201,261
    Mellie 39
    Millie 201,261
    Phil 261

Philip...201
PENDERGRAST
  Emily.......................................74
  George.....................................74
  Julia..74
PENDERGREST
  Emily.....................................186
  George...................................186
  Julia..186
PEPION
  Cecil....................15,76,235
  Cecile....................................285
  Chester............15,76,236,294
  Frank.................15,76,236,294
  Jesse..15
  Jessie....................76,236,283
  Joe..76
  John.......................15,235,285
  L 15
  Louis.....................................236
  Louise..................76,236,285
  Lousese...................................15
  Lucius...................................283
  Thos.........................15,76,236
  Tom.......................................283
  Victor.........................236,283
PEPPION
  Cecil.............................152,153
  Chester.................................153
  Frank.....................................153
  Jessie.....................................152
  Joe..153
  John.......................................152
  Louise...................................153
  Michael.................................153
  Thomas.................................153
PERRIN, Jas......................121
PERRINE
  Annie.....................................267
  Florence................................267
  James.....................................267
  James A................................185
  Stella.....................................267
  Wm..267
PERTTY STAR...................143
PETER AFTER BUFFALO..........186
PETERSON
  Frank..............37,100,185,208,269
  Maggie...........37,100,185,208,268
  Melvin...........37,100,185,208,269
  Michael.................................185
  Mitchel.................................100
  Mitchell....................208,269
  Oscar.............37,100,185,208,268
  Walter............37,100,185,208,269
PETRIFIED..........33,92,152,226,290
PETRIFIED ROCK.....................207
PETRIFIED STONE......233,235,236
PHEMISTER
  George........................91,153,241
  Mary............................91,153,241
PIAS
  Aggie.....................................298
  Dan.............................152,242
  Daniel...................19,75,298
  Kate.......................................223
  Katie....................19,75,152
  Reuben..................................152
  Ruben......................................75
  Ruth..19
  Susie............................75,152
PIEGAN, Ezra.............216,268
PIPE GIRL.............................43
PIPE STONE, Mary.........49,122,176
PIPE WOMAN..........................127
PITTIFULL..............................30
PLENTY HAIR................109,184
PLENTY IRON WOMAN...........139
PLUME..................................7
  Sam..53
PLUME WOMAN.................207,272
POLITE PEPION, John..................75
POOR TOUNG MAN..................107
POOR WOMAN..........5,73,122,153,
 234,279
POOR YOUNG MAN...........166,202
POTTS
  Chas......................................225
  Johnny..................................251
POWEL
  Chas..96
  Jennie.....................................96
  Jessie......................................96
  Mary.......................................96
  Susie.......................................96
POWELL

Index

Charles 274
Chas 34,185,206
Clara 56,121
Frank 56,121
Hattie 207
Hunter 121,186
Jennie 185,206
Jenny 34
Jesse 34,274
Jessee 206
Jessie 185
Lizzie Ellen 257
Lorenza 211
Lorenzo 257
Lucy 34
Maggie 185,211,257,274
Mary 34,185,206,274
Sophia 56,121,186,211,257
Susan 274
Susie 185,207
William 186
Wm 121
PRAIRIE CHICKEN
   Cecile 276
   Geo 144
   George 236,276
   Johanna 276
   Thomas 276
PRARIE CHICKEN
   Cecil 77
   George 77
   Johanna 77
PRETTY BIRD 283
PRETTY BIRD WOMAN 197
PRETTY BUFFALO STONE 293
PRETTY SNAKE 57,204,261
PRETTY STEALING WOMAN .. 214
PRETTY WOMAN 11,96
PUSS 106
PUTS FACE FRONT 121
PUTS FACE IN FRONT 174
QUIET WOMAN 176
QUIVER
   Benj 241
   Josephine 241
   Maggie 241
   Minnie 241
R A DOOR

Dick 186
Frank 186
James 186
Louise 186
Mary 186
R A T DOOR
   Dick 117
   Frank 117
   Jas 117
   Louise 117
   Mary 117
R AT DOOR
   Dick 54
   Frank 54
   Louize 54
   Mary 54
R AWAY
   Mary 53,116
   Susan 53
   Susie 116
R CRANE
   Ed 14
   Eddie 95
   James 148
   Maggie 14
   Nellie 14,95
R FISHER
   Carrie 28
   George 85
   Mary 28
R HEAD, Daniel 19
R I MIDDLE
   Anna 29
   Fred 29,187
   Levi 29,187
   Mary 29,187
R OWL
   Agnes 12,88
   Joe 88
   Mary 88
   Rosa 88
   Susie 12
R PLUME
   John 87
   Pete 87
R RABBIT
   Julia 4
   Kate 4

Index

Mary 4
R WOLF
   Geo 18
   Herbert 18
   Homer 18
   John 18
   Miles 18
RABBIT 281
RABBIT OLD WOMAN 101,
.... 194,262
RABBIT WOMAN 200
RACINE
   Belle 154,234,298
   Frank 22,113,186,216,255
   Joseph 234,298
   Nettie 186,216,255
   Oliver 22,115,154,234,298
RAG WOMAN 284
RAGGED 272
RAGGED CLOTHES 107,179
RAGGED MAN 7
RAGGED WOMAN 165,213,254
RAGGID WOMAN 111
RAMSEY
   Jessie 153
   Mart 153
   Melvin 153
RANDALL
   Sam 155,238,283
   Sam'l 26
RANDEL, Samuel 78
RAPE WOMAN 279
RATION WOMAN 205
RATTING 84
RATTLER 14,77,154,239,277
   Elmer 14,77,107,154,239,277
   Louise 224
RATTLES RUNNING ON TOP ... 204
RATTLES WITH MANY 278
RATTLING 166,209
RATTLING BARRY CARRIER .. 253
RATTLING RUNNING ON TOP 269
RED BIRD TAIL 22
RED BOY 20,281
RED BUFFALO STONE 276
RED FOX 14,77,154,231,287
   James 154,287
   Jas 14
   John 14,77,154,287
   Jos 77
RED HEAD. 19,127,153,209,245,283
   John 68
RED HOLLER 262
RED HORN 30,78,154,240,285
RED HOWLING 209
RED MOUSE 199,260
RED PETRIFIED ROCK 203,250
RED PLUME 27,86,214,294
   Peter 294
RED ROCK 26,94,149
RED SQUIRREL 204
RED STAR 17
RED STONE 83,167
REEVIS
   Annie 272
   August 91
   Charles 204
   Chas 85,272
   Emet 91
   Emma 91
   Francix 272
   Frank 91
   Joe 85,272
   Joseph 204
   Julia 91,244,272
   Laureta 85
   Mary 85
   Sam 85
REMSA
   Jesse 6
   Mary 6
REVIS
   Chas 187
   Joe 188
   Julia 154
   Sam 187
RIDED AT DOOR 206
   Mary 206
RIDER
   Eli 58,84,210,266
   Elier 56
   Ely 172
   Frank 33,96,143,231,288
   Gretchen 33,96,174
   Henry 210,266
   Joe 243

Index

Maggie 231,288
Mary 266
Mollie 243
RIDES AT DOOR 54,186,206
    Louis 206
    Richard 206
RIDES AT THE DOOR 117,255
    Frank 255
    James 255
    Louise 255
    Mary 255
    Richard 255
RIDES BEHIND 48,80,126,
.... 187,211,255
RIDES GOOD HORSE 44
RIDES IN FRONT 28,84,166
RIDES IN MIDDLE 29,83,84,
.... 170,187
RIDES IN THE MIDDLE 209,250
    Joe 209
    Levi 250
RIDES YELLOW HORSE 42
RIPLEY
    Belle 22,69,153,242,286
    David 74,158,286
    Emma 22,69,153
    James 153
    Minnie 74,153,242,278
    Peter 242,278
RIPLY
    David 3
    Minnie 3
RISH 82
RISING FROM THE WATER 113
RISING FROM WATER 180
RISING SUN 228
RIVIS
    August 8
    Emet 8
    Emma 8
    Julia 8
ROBE, Jeanette 125
ROBINSON
    Ad 121
    Agnes 60,187,224
    Allen 4
    Annie 4
    Chas 4

Geo 60,121
George 187
Jas 4
Joe 121,187,224
Joseph 60
Louise 121,187,224
Louize 60
Mary 60,121
Vic 121,187
Victoria 60,224
ROCKING OWNER 212
ROLLING UP A CALF 254
ROMSAY
    Jesse 270
    Malvin 270
    Marry 270
RONDAN
    Baptist 187
    Isabel 187
    Louisa 187
    Mary 187
    Nancy 187
    Richard 187
    Sam 187
RONDI
    Bat 50
    Isabel 51
    Louize 51
    Mary 51
    Nancy 51
    Richard 51
    Sam 51
RONDIN
    Baptiste 109,211,260
    Isabel 109,260
    Louisa 109
    Louise 211,260
    Mary 109,211,260
    Nancy 109,211,260
    Philip 211
    Phillip 260
    Richard 109,211,260
    Sam 109
    Samuel 260
    Smuel 211
    Usabekka 211
ROOT DIGGER 119,186,202,261
ROSE

Agnes	93,154,241,296	Hester	65
Alice	59,93,154,241,296	Isabel	282
Annie	93,154	Isabelle	243
Charles	296	Julia	65,160,233,282
Chas	59,93,154,241	Katie	231
James	154	Mary	160,231
Jas	93,241	Susie	282

- Agnes 93,154,241,296
- Alice 59,93,154,241,296
- Annie 93,154
- Charles 296
- Chas 59,93,154,241
- James................................154
- Jas 93,241
- Jennie 93,241
- Jim.......................................59
- Julia.....................59,154,241,296
- Lorene 296
- Maggie 59,93,154,241,296
- Peter 59
- Susie..................................241
- William 154,296
- Wm 93,241
- ROTH, Rosa.....................................67
- ROUND, Lilly....................................49
- ROUND BUTTE 116,174
- ROUND FACE 206,250
- ROUND HEAD 215,282
- ROUND MAN 244
- ROUND ROBE............................283
- RUMSY
  - Jessie 117
  - Mary 117
- RUNING RATTLER 139
- RUNNING CRANE..........95,154,230
  - Eddie 153,230,287
  - James..................................284
  - Jas 14,230
  - John 5,67,160,233
  - Josephine............................233
  - Nellie 153,230,287
  - Paul 230,287
  - Peter 230,287
- RUNNING CRANE #1..........230,288
- RUNNING CRANE #2.................284
- RUNNING FISHER 28,85,187,199
  - Grace................................187
- RUNNING OWL 12,88,161,
  - 244,283
  - Agnes 161
  - Anna 244
  - Mary 161
  - Rosa 161
- RUNNING RABBIT
  - Esther 231,281
- RUNNING RATTLE 291
- RUNNING RATTLER........ 9,79,240
- RUNNING WOLF 18
  - Albert................................ 72,154
  - Geo 72
  - George 154,243,292
  - Herbert................................ 154,292
  - Homer 72,154,292
  - James 292
  - Jas 243
  - Joe 243
  - John 72,243
  - Mile 154
  - Miles.................... 72,243,292
  - Mrs 72,154
- RUNNISNG FISHER................... 268
- RUNS AWAY 53,73,116,
  - 140,186,197
  - Mary 187
  - Susie 187
- RUNS BACK 214
- RUNS BEHIND 137
- RUNS ON BOTH SIDES............. 211
- RUSHES HOME 30,276
- RUSHES LAST................................ 30
- RUSHES ON BOTH SIDES
  - 209,253,254
- RUSHING ALONE 199,268
- RUSHING HOME.......................... 11
- RUSHING ON BOTH SIDES 197
- RUSSELL
  - Cecil 33,91,154
  - First One.................................... 33
  - Geo 33,226
  - George 92,154,282
  - Henry 33,92,154,226,282
  - Isabel 203
  - Isabella 143
  - Isabelle 290
  - Joe 91,154,226
  - Joseph 33,203,282,290

Mary 33,91,154,226,282
William 91,154
Wm 33,92,226,282
RUTHERFORD
   Alice 24,65,153,226,297
   Dewey 298
   Edna 73,153,226,297
   Eliza 24,153,226,297
   Elizabeth 73
   George 226
   Henry 24,65,153,226,297
   James 24,153
   Jas 65,226
   Mary 24,65
   Richard 24,73,153,226,297
   William 153,297
   Wm 24,65,226
S A ANOTHER, Martha 155
S B MISTAKE
   Anna 155
   Peter 155
S CAP, Maggie 122
S CHIEF, Philip 94
S CLOSE
   Geo 41
   Jas 41
S DOWN
   Edward 190
   Peter 50
S EAGLE
   Jas 5,95
   Joe 5
   John 5
S EARS
   Maggie 58,120
   Susan 58
   Susie 120
S FIRST
   Calf 110,189
   Cecil 110,189
   Henry 110,189
   Louise 110,189
S FLINT, Louie 16
S MAN, Victoria 45
S ROBE
   Annie 108
   Cicell 44
   Emma 44,108

   Young 44
S TEAT, Edward 111
SAMPLE
   Annie J 208
   Florence E 208
   Jesse 263
   Mary 208
   Stella M 208
   Wm A 208
SAMPLES
   Annie 97,189
   Baby 189
   Elsie 35
   Florence 35,97,189
   Jess 190
   Jesse 219,220
   Jessie 97
   Mary 35,97,189
   Vine 34
   William 35
   Willie 97,189
   Wm 97,189
SAMPLES, Jesse 34
SANDERVILLE
   Agnes 20,72,80,116,155,
   190,229,280
   Bridges 229
   Bridget 280
   Cecil 116,190,197
   Cecile 263
   Edward 116,190
   Irene 20,72
   John 59,72,115,189,229,292
   Mary ... 59,72,115,155,189,229,292
   Nancy 20,72,229,280
   Oliver 59,72,115,189,229,292
   Richard 20,72,155,229,280
SARSEE WOMAN 11
SAUCY WOMAN 292
SAVAGE WOLF 228
SCABBY ROBE, Sam 272
SCATTERED GIRL 88
SCATTERED WOMAN .. 15,233,289
SCHELDT
   Andrew 188
   Augusta 188
   Harry 188
   Irene 188

Mary	188
Nellie	188
Stillman	188

SCHILDT
Andrew	122,271
Augusta	49,122,216,271
Harry	49,122,216,271
Henry	216
Irene	49,122,216,272
Joe	121
Joseph	216,271
Mary	49,122,216,271
Nellie	121,122,216,271
Nettie	49
Stillman	272

SCHMIDT
Alex	222,270
Geo	222
George	251
Karl	222,270
Margaret	221,270
Rosa	251

SCHUBERT, Agnes 276
SCHULTZ
Hart	156,237,282
Susan	156,237,282

SCISSORS WOMAN 33
SCRAPER WOMAN 20
SCRAPING HIDE 201,263
SEAL WOMAN 227
SETTING EAST 258
SETTING WEST 203
SHADDOW 249
SHARP 213
Julia	104,189,200,252
Rosa	104,189,200,252
Rose	43

SHARP NOSE 79,151
SHARPE FACED WOMAN 291
SHARPS 258
SHATTER 202
SHE CROW 184
SHEARS, Ora 217
SHEEP WOMAN 52,197,259
SHEILD WOMAN 93
SHERIFF
Ira	191
Orrie	271

SHERMAN
Alex	102,262
Alexander	189,201
Charles	198,261
Charley	190
Elix	42
Emma	42,102,189,201,262
Eva	262
Geneva	190
Genevieva	102
Genevieve	198,261
Geniveve	42
Martin	261
Mary	42,102,190,198,261
Robert	42,102,189,201,262
Sophia	42,102,189,201
Sophie	262
Susan	42,102,189,201,262
William	42,102,190
Wm	198,261

SHERRIF, Ora 105
SHIELD WOMAN 20,137,287
SHILDT, Nellie 49
SHINES AGAIN 285
SHOE CHICKEN 236
SHOOTING CLOSE 199
SHOOTS ANOTHER 285
Jennie	242
Joe	242
Mary	242

SHOOTS AT ANOTHER .. 16,70,155
Martha	70
Susie	155

SHOOTS CLOSE17,41,61,166,260,285
SHOOTS FIRST 110,189,197,258
Maggie	197,259

SHOOTS IN NIGHT 155
SHOOTS IN THE NIGHT 70
SHOOTS ONE ANOTHER 242
SHOOTS WEASEL 126,187
SHOOTS WEASLE 48
SHOQUETTE
Antoine	57
Chas	57
Henry	39
Josephene	57
Louisa	39
Louize	57

Index

SHORT FACE 24,25,94,
................................156,210,240,250
SHORT FACT 200
SHORT GUN............................94,160
SHORT MAN 45,215
   Mike............................181,206,256
   Sophronia........................206,256
SHORT NOSE 238
SHORT QUILL WOMAN............285
SHORT RIBS................................44
   Ammie 44
SHORT ROBE.........108,188,211,254
   Anna.......................................211
   Annie......................................188
   Cecil.......................................211
   Cecile.....................................254
   Emma.......................189,211,254
   Wm 211,254
SHORT WOMAN 12,29,119,177,
...........190,204,234,244,263,276,283
SHORTH, Samuel.........................201
SHORTMAN, Mike......................108
SHORTY
   Anna.......................................190
   Annie.................................48,110
   Cecil.......................................197
   Dick..111
   Joe 111,188,201,263
   John...............48,110,190,197,256
   Joseph....................................263
   Lizzie...............................111,188
   Louis 111,188
   Lucy 201
   Mary......110,111,188,190,201,263
   Rosa.......................................263
   Rosalie 201
   Sam 111,188
   Susan..........................111,188,201
   Susanna..................................263
SHULTZ
   Hart 9,91
   Susan 8,90
SIGNING 69
SIMON
   Chas 124
   Monic 120
SIMONS
   Moniac 295

Monic 185
Monnik 36
SING BY MISTAKE...................295
SINGING............17,86,155,234,282
SINGING INDISE.......................290
SINGING WATER 52
SINGLE WOMAN 250
SINGS HIGH 27
SINGS IN THE AIR...................280
SINGS ON TOP 86,160,215
SIPOTA..97
SITE UNDER..............................60
SITS AGAINST WIND...........85,182
SITS AWAY 49
SITS IN FRONT....................28,177
   Austin 28
   Joe 28
SITS UNDER..............................83
SITTING IN ROAD 155
SITTING IN THE ROAD 70,294
SITTING ON TOP 18
SITTING UNDER................203,250
SITTING UP 243
SITTING WITH FACE TOGETHER
....265
SKUNK CAP 122
   Abel................................135,285
   Able 10,65,238
   Alonzo 257
   Minnie 199
SKUNK WOMAN 210,283
SLASHED ON BOTH SIDES......199
SLEEPING WOMAN 111
SLIM TAIL 61,113,188,212,257
   Rosa.......................................257
SLIM WOMAN............24,79,84,187,
....................................209,232,250
SMALL BEADS 116,162
SMALL EYES............................104
SMALL FACE 15,61,79,83,156,
................216,217,243,264,269,282
   Mary 79,156
SMALL FOX 28
SMALL HEAD 50,123
SMALL LEGGINS 101
SMALL MINK............................289
SMALL MOUTH........................204
SMALL OTTER.........................264

Index

SMALL PETRIFIED 14
SMALL RAIN 206
SMALL ROCK 17
SMALL TEETH 262
SMALL WOMAN 13,30,33,66,
76,87,136,155,176,198,203,234,250,
.... 291
SMALL YOUNG MAN 289
SMITH
   Lizza 57
   Lizzie 190,203,260
   Mary 118
   Peter 57,190,213,258
   Sam 122,203,260
   Smithy 203
   William 57,190
   Wm 203,258
SMOKING FLINT 16,69
   Jas 16
   Peter 16
SNAKE GIRL 89,139
SNAKE LOOKING 15,147
SNAKE OLD WOMAN 290
SNAKE PEOPLE 200
SNAKE WOMAN ... 10,55,80,90,109,
.... 162,181,232,262,281
SNOW, Mary 234
SNOW FLAKE TAIL 47
SNOW GIRL 84
SOMETHING GOOD 109
SOPHIA 47,163
SORE BACK 26,94,149,228,281
SOUIX WOMAN 49
SPANISH
   Joe 117,189,294
   Joseph 236
   Margaret 236
   William 294
SPARKS 211,250
SPEAR WOMAN 14,47,48,77,154,
.... 207,239,255,258,277
SPEARSON
   Albert 200,254
   Alfred 114
   Frank 58,114,190,200,253
   Mary 58,254
SPIDER 96,143
SPLIT EAR

   Agnes 209
   Maggie 209
   Susie 209
SPLIT EARS 58,120,189,209,251
   Maggie 190,251
   Susie 190,251
SPOTTED BACK 212,265
SPOTTED BEAR 25,68,156,231
   Alice 25
   Anna 153,288
   Annie 153
   Jas 25,240
   Joe 68,156
   John 25,231,288
   Mary 25
   Mike 68,156
   Minnie 25,79,136,240
   Perry 288
   Peter 25,79,153,231,288
   Rosa 288
SPOTTED BEAR #1 288
SPOTTED BEAR #2 240
   Pete 240
SPOTTED BEAR NO 2 79
SPOTTED BERA
   Annie 231
   Rosa 231
SPOTTED CALF 28,156,243,277
SPOTTED EAGLE 4,95,155,
.... 230,284
   Birdie 167
   George 230
   James 156,289
   Jas 230
   John 156,230,284
   Mary 289
   Matilda 286
   May 46,178
   Thomas 156,286
   Thos 5,96,230
SPOTTED HEAD 33,82,156,
.... 212,231,271
SPOTTED HORSE GIRL 89
SPOTTED WOMAN 8,57,68,85,
.... 156,214,250,289
SPY GLASS 51
SQUEAL IN THE NIGHT 291
SQUIRREL 254

Index

SQUIRREL GIRL 209
SQUIRREL WOMAN 207,250
SQUIRRELL WOMAN 207
ST GODDARD
   Agnes 242,292
   Alamena 292
   Archibald 292
   Archie 242
   Lena 242
   Philamon 242
   Philomena 292
ST GODDERT
   Agnes 80
   Almma 80
   Philomine 80
STABBING 233
STABBING BY MISTAKE 20,71
   Anna 71
   Peter 71
STABING DOWN 50
STABS 78
STABS BUFFALO 135
STABS BY MISTAKE 155,281
   Louise 281
   Maggie 281
STABS DOWN 96,111,143,
.... 190,200,265
   John 265
   Wm 265
STABS HIM DOWN 289
STAR
   Christian 50
   Geo 50
   John 50
   Maggie 50
   Philip 50
   Pra 50
STAYS AT HOME 58
STEADY WOMAN 18
STEAL WOMAN 283
STEALS ALONE 289
STEALS FOR NOTHING 202
STEALS FROM ONE ANOTHER ....
.... 298
STEALS GOOD WOMAN 284
STEALS HORSE ALONE 106
STEALS IN DAYTIME 20
STEALS IN THE DAY WOMAN .....
.... 281
STEALS INSIDE 264
STEALS NOTHING 48
STEALS WOMAN 48
STEPHENSON
   Cecil 188
   Kate 188
   Laura 188
   Phoebe 188
STEVENSON
   Ammie 41
   Annie 102
   Cecil 102
   Cecile 264
   Dora 41
   Henry 41,102
   Katie 102
   Kattie 41
   Laura 102
   Orcella 41
   Phebe 41
   Phoebe 102
STEWARD
   Carrie 22,92
   Cecil 22,92
   Clara 22,92
   Jennie 22,92
   Maria 22
   Marion 92
   Mary 22,92
   Mollie 22,92
STEWART
   Agnes 220
   Carrie 156
   Cecil 156
   Clara 156
   Earl 51,115,189,216,273
   Geneva 51,115,189,216,273
   Isabelle 220
   James 189,216,273
   Jas 51,115
   Jennie 156
   Jesse 273
   Marion 156
   Mary 156
   Mollie 156
   Vera 115,189,216,273
   Virginia 189,216,273

Index

STILL SMOKING
- Joe 177,273
- Jos 212
- Minnie 177,273
- Susan 273

STINGY 47,108,190,220,265
- Mary 265
- Monac 220
- Wm 265

STINK TEAT 111,188
- John 221,265

STINK TIT 51
- Rose 51
- Ruth 51

STINK TOPKNOT 162
STINKS 207
STOLE INSIDE 112,193
STOLEN FROMM 51
STONE
- Frank 188,206,268
- Henry 35,98,188,205,268
- Joseph 98,188,206,268
- Mary 35,98,188,205,268
- Robert 35,98

STOPS FIRST 199
STRAIGHT RUNNER 7
STRANGE CUT 27
STRANGLE WOLF 84,253
STRANGLED WOLF 29,198
STRANGLES WOLF 190
STRECHED OUT 86
STRETCHED OUT 213,287
STRETCHES OUT 27
STRIKE BACK 291
STRIKE ONCE 5
STRIKES #3 211,255
STRIKES BACK ..26,28,32,57,82,86,
94,106,124,142,155,190,205,212,231,
235,245,258,279,290
- Anna 26

STRIKES BY MISTAKE 282
STRIKES CLOSE 231
- Susie 11

STRIKES DOWN 12
STRIKES EDGE 229
STRIKES EDGE WATER 10
STRIKES FIRST 56,112,204,215,
.... 262,272,277,283

STRIKES GOOD 4
STRIKES GUN 94,156
STRIKES HER SELF 53
STRIKES HER-SELF 201
STRIKES HERSELF 169,258
STRIKES IN AIR 89
STRIKES IN FRONT 29,197,203
STRIKES IN THE EDGE OF THE
WATER 296
STRIKES IN THE FRONT 249,
.... 258,271
STRIKES LAST 67,238
STRIKES NEAR 288
STRIKES ON THE FLOOR 282
STRIKES ON THE TOP 288
STRIKES ON TOP 20,30,96,
.... 204,269
STRIKES ONE ANOTHER 204
STRIKES TWICE 283
STRIKES TWO 127
STRIKES WIT GUN 60
STRIKES WITH A GUN 276,296
STRIKES WITH GUN 88,169
STRIKING FIRE 106
STRIPED ELK 102,169
STRIPED STONE 48
STUART
- Cecelia 297
- Cecil 245
- Clara 245,297
- Jennie 245,297
- Maggie 245
- Mary 245,297
- Mazie 297
- Mollie 245,297

SULLIVAN, Josephine 237,273
SUN WOMAN 5
SURE BUFFALO STONE 289
SURE CHIEF 26,94,155,230,296
- Geo 230
- George 296
- Philip 155
- Phillip 26,296
- William 296
- Willie 230

SURE WOMAN 91,150,156,
.... 229,286
SUSAN 119

Index

SWEET GRASS 104,235,255
SWEET GRASS GIRL 42
SWEET GRASS HILLS 207,209
SWEET GRASS WOMAN 12,77,
.... 159,295
SWIFT GIRL 214
SWIFT WOMAN 214
SWIMS UNDER ... 25,79,155,232,290
    Josephene 79
    Josephine 155
    Maggie 232
T BEARS
    Cecil 114,191
    Jos 114
    Joseph 191
T F COMING
    Cecil 90,162
    Mary 90
    Sicsie 90
T FEATHERS COMING, Mary ... 162
T G A NIGHT, Agnes 157
T G B SIDES
    John 158
    Pete 158
T G O TOP
    John 191
    Louise 191
T G ON TOP
    John 93
    Louise 94
T GUNS
    Florence 56
    Joseph 56
    Katie 104
TAIL, Carl 19
TAIL F COMING, Susie 162
TAIL F WOMAN 86
TAIL FEATHERS 16,17,71,
.... 157,236,289
    Charles 289
    Charley 157
    Chas 71,157,237
    Jane 71
    Jas 46
    Jennie 17,157
    Jenny 46
    Lucy 46
    Mole 45

    Peter 17,71,157,237
    Thos 71
    Walter 71,157
    William 289
    Wm 237
TAIL FEATHERS COMING
.... 10,90,162,237
    Cecil 237
    Cecile 281
    Mary 162,237
    Mollie 237
    Susie 237
TAIL FEATHERS COMING #1 .. 281
TAIL FEATHERS COMING #2 .. 282
TAIL FEATHERS WOMAN 148,
.... 213
TAKES ALONE 42,283
TAKES DOUBLE GUN 290
TAKES DOWN 246
TAKES FINE GUN 205
TAKES GOOD GUN 29,215
TAKES GUN 9,19,32,43,72,85,
86,104,128,148,191,194,204,210,240,
264,267
    Billy 264
    James 204
    Katie 191
    Minnie 204,264
TAKES GUN ALONE 29,85,183,
.... 191,200,249
TAKES GUN AT NIGHT . 10,89,157,
.... 294
TAKES GUN BOTH SIDES5,87,157,
.... 158,215,294
    Pussy 294
    Sophia 294
TAKES GUN FOR NOTHING ....
.... 29,198
TAKES GUN HIMSELF 290
TAKES GUN IN THE BRUSH 291
TAKES GUN IN THE MORNING ....
.... 12
TAKES GUN INDISE 270
TAKES GUN INSIDE 17,83,
.... 180,209
TAKES GUN ON TOP 52,93,191,
.... 213,250
    Louise 213

Maggie 213	TELLS IN WATER....................25
TAKES GUN UP 203,271	THE BITE 13,92,137,226,283
TAKES IRON GUN 31,82,158,	THE COAT 45
....................231,288	THE CROW 109
Lucy 158,231	THE HORN 25,94,145,230,294
TAKES LAST GUN 26	THOMAS
TAKES MEAT 172	Ada....................246
TAKES SHORT....................44,126	Geo 37,269
TAKES THE MAN....................203	George 100,190,219
TAKES TWO GUNS....................284	Ida....................109,187
TAKES-MEAT....................119	Isa Belle....................246
TAKING GOOD....................217	Isabel 126
TAKING GUN IN THE MIDDLE	John 109,187
....................200	Julia 37,100,190,219,269
TAKING IN THE BRUSH 198	Nora....................100,191,219,269
TAKING SOMETHING...............264	Sarah....................37,191,208
TAKS GOOD GUN 294	THREE BEAR....................57
TALK WOMAN 21,122	Cicell 57
TALKING WOMAN......119,191,215	Joseph....................57
TALKS 260	THREE BEARS 114,191,212,249
TALL HEAD 23	Joe 249
TALLOW MUD HEAD 258	Mary 191
TANS HIDES 41	THREE CESSORS 53
TATSEY	THREE CHIEVES 49
Anna....................21,156	THREE GUNS 76,123,136,
Annie....................75,225,298	191,217,254
Elixabeth 298	Agnes....................217
Elizabeth 225	Chas....................191
Hattie............21,75,156,225,298	THREE RIDERS....................119,172
Joe....................21,75,156,225	THREE SCISSORS....................119
John....................21,75,156,225,298	THREE SUNS, Chas................29,83
Joseph 225,298	THROWING DOWN 249
Josephene....................75	THROWS GUN....................25
Josephine..............21,156,225,298	THUNDER NEST 200,262
Mary....................157	THUNDER NEST WOMAN 101,194
Susan................21,75,157,225,298	THUNDER STAR....................202
TEARING LODGE....80,157,238,278	THUNDER WOMAN 13,76,151,
TEARING LODGE POLE..............41	292
TEASDALE	TIGER WOMAN 96,288
Annie....................227	James 291
Josephene....................75	Minnie 291
Josephine....................19,157	TIME ROCK
Mary................18,75,157,227,290	George 235
Nellie....................19,75,157,290	Jas 235
Rose 19,75	Nellie 235
TELESCOPE 101,194	TINGLEY
TELLING STORIES....................58	Daniel 230
TELLS IN NIGHT....................24	David 126

Elizabeth	230
John	124,230
Lizzie	126
Louise	126,230
Mose	230
Moses	126
Oliver	126,230
Robert	126
Rogert	230
TINGLY, Jogn	39
TOOK AFTER THEM HOME	284
TOOTH WOMAN	231

TOP
John	52
Louize	52
TOP KNOT, Antoine	207

TOPKNOT
Antoine	162
Philip	162

TROMBLEY
Alfred	92,158
Isaac	157
Isabell	92
Isabella	158
Joe	96,157
John	157
Joseph	157
Julia	96,157
Louie	157
Maggie	157

TROMBLY
(Infant)	3
Alfred	226,282
Cecelia	226
Cecile	282
George	229,286
Isaac	3,66,229,286
Isabella	230,291
Joe	22,243,291
Jos	66
Joseph	229,286
Julia	22,243,291
Lane	66
Louie	3
Louis	229,286
Maggie	3,66,229,286

TROMLY
Alfred	21
Isabella	21
TURNS BACK	101,170
TURTLE	32,82,158,244,295
Mary	32,244
Mary Ann	295
Minnie	82,158,244
TWO BEAR WOMAN	44,271
TWO BEARS	105,191,217
TWO CATCHES	47,50
TWO GUNS	27,47,81,87,95,111, 137,149,191,214,217,264
John	15,121,147,241,281
Joseph	47,217
Maggie	147,241
TWO GUNS S EAGLE	5
TWO HORNS	58
TWO IRON WOMAN	197
TWO IRONS	53
TWO OWLS	56
TWO RABBITS	81,151,204,269
TWO SPEAR	193
TWO SPEARS	30,114
Annie	30

TWO STABE
Joe	157
Joseph	68
Lawrence	68
Louie	157
Louis	68
Louise	157
Maggie	68,157
Mary	68
Thomas	157
Thos	68

TWO STABS
Joe	4
Joseph	229,288
Louie	4
Louis	229,288
Louise	288
Louize	229
Maggie	4,229,288
Thomas	288
Thos	4,229
TWO STRIKES	19,68,77,141,153, 191,216,245,270,293
UGLY GIRL	11
UNDER BEAR	39,108,122,170,

Index

.... 181,197,215,256
    Henry 216,257
    Maggie 187
    Mary 257
    Philip 187
    Rubert 187
UNDER BEAVER 16,69,143,277
UNDER BIRD 94,145
UNDER BULL 31
    Charles 291
    Chas 31,231
    Joe 80
    John 81,158
    Mary 31
    Mollie 80
    Peter 31,81,158,291
UNDER BULL #2 (STRIKES BACK)
.... 158
UNDER BULL NO 2 81
UNDER BULL WIDOW 80
UNDER CHICKEN 25,230
UNDER MINK 31,32,122
UNDER OTTER 7,67,158,227,282
UPHAM
    Emma 33,97,191,222,251
    Geo 192
    George 97
    Jack 97,191,251
    Joe Brown 273
    John 33,222
    Johnson 97
    Joseph 33
    Katie 33,34,191,222,251
    Kutie 97
    Mertie 97
    Murtie 33
    Myrtie 192,251
    Myrtle 222
    Rosa 33,222
    Rose 97,191
    William 34,192
    Winifred 222
    Wm 97,206,273
VAN SENDEN, Laura 276
VHOUQUETTE, Josephene 113
VICTORY BEFORE TIME 286
VIELLE
    Andrew 158

Andy 125
Anna 158,192,292
Annie 118,125,270
Ben 59
Francis 211,270
Frank 125,158,240,292
Jack 125,158,240,292
James 292
Jennie 211
Joe 118,192
John 59,118,192,211,270
Jos. 240
Joseph 59
Mary 59,118,192,270
Susie 240
Thos 224,273
Tom 59,118,192
William 59
Willie 118,192
Wm 270
VILLE
    Annie 12
    Frank 12
    John 12
W CALF
    Annie 23
    Minnie 111
W EAGLE, Geo 31
W GRASS
    Catches Two 192
    Eneas 110
    Joe 46
    Louis 47
    Lucy 47
    Mary 46
    Richard 49
    Ross 110
    Sam 46
    Susan 46
W GUN, John 65
W HEAD
    Jennie 90
    Joe 89
    John 13,90
    Lizzie 90
    Lucy 13
    Mary 89,90
    Pete 89

Index

Thos 13,90
W HORSES, Joe 101
W IN WATER, Lucy 15,95
W PLUME, Wesley 16
W QUIVER
   Benj 22
   Maggie 22
   Thos 22
W TAIL
   Annie 114
   Fred 114
   Gilbert 47,111
   Louisa 114
   Paul 47
   Thos 47
W UP LAST
   Jennie 88
   Mollie 88
W WOLF
   Baptist 50
   Barnett 50
   Clement 50
   Geo 50
   John 50
WADES IN 239
WADES IN THE WATER 230
   Lucy 230
WADES IN WATER 15,80,95,
.... 159,285
   Lucy 159
WAGNER
   Annie 127
   John 98,193
   Lilly 98
   Lily 193
   Mary 98,127,193
   Wm 127
WAITING ALONG TIME TO FLY..
.... 268
WAKES UP LAST 23,88,159,238,283
   Jennie 159
   Julia 283
   Mollie 23,159,238,283
   Stephen 238
WALKING BACKWARDS 262
WALKING SMOKE 59
WALKING TOGETHER 58
WALKS BACK 209

WALKS BACKWARD 193
WALKS BACKWARDS 120
WALKS IN WATER 287
WALL
   Joe 240
   Joseph 276,286
WALLEY, Annie 12
WALTERS
   Arthur 73,135,278
   Geo 73
   George 135,278
   Julia 73,135
   Mary 73
   Robert 73
WAR BONNET 5,66,88,
.... 158,231,286
   Anna 67
   James 158,286
   Jas 6,67,231
   Susie 231
   Thos 231,286
WARD
   Emma 121,192,223,273
   Geo 56,121,192
   George 223,273
   James 223,273
   Jas 121
   Jim 56,192
   Mary 121,192,223
   Mary Rose 273
   Rosa 121,192,223,273
   Rose 56
   William 274
   Wm 223
WATER BLACK BIRD 289
WATER CARRIER 108,188
WATER OTTER 21
WATER SNAKE 77,148,150
WAY LAYING 214
WAY OFF IN SIGHT 250
WEASEL FAT 118,193,213,263
   Mrs 213
WEASEL HEAD 13,89,159,
.... 237,281
   Charles 281
   Chas 13,227
   James 159
   John 13,159,237,238,281

Index

Lizzie 159,237
Mary 13,159,237
Peter 13,159,237,281
Thomas 159
Thos 237,281
WEASEL TAIL 81,114,159,
.... 194,215,249
  Amy 194
  Anna 215
  Antoine 194
  Emma 249
  James 249
  John 215,249
  Louise 249
  Louize 215
  Minnie 194
WEASEL TAIL WOMAN 23,233,
.... 298
WEASEL WENT 294
WEASEL WOMAN 21,172,204
WEASLE FAT 49
WEASLE TAIL 45
  Amie 45
  Antoine 45
  Louize 45
  Minnie 45
WEATHER WAX
  Joe 70
  Josephine 70
  Mary 70
WEATHERWAX
  Joe 16,155
  Joseph 285
  Josephine 16,155,242,285
  Mary 16,155
WELLS, Phillip 279
WENT IN BY MISTAKE 294
WENT IN FIRST 292
WENT IN HERSELF 107,109,
.... 193,224,266
WENT TO WAR 21
WEST WOLF
  Anna Shorty 199
  Annie 260
  Baptist 171
  Baptiste 112,199,260
  Bernard 112,171
  George 112,171,260

John 112,171,200,260
WET TEETH 288
WETXEL, Pearl 37
WETZEL
  Daizy 37
  Maggie 37,192,207,255
  Pearl 100,192,207
  William 37,192
  Willie 100
  Wm 207,255
WETZIL, Maggie 100
WHIPS ON BOTH SIDES 23
WHITE
  Cora 3,74,158,297
  Garret 194,297
  Garrett 242
  Lorenza 3
  Lorenzo 74,158,297
  Malinda 74
  Mary J 3,158
  Mary Jane 297
  Mary Jean 74
  Melvina 3,158,297
WHITE ANTELOPE 256
WHITE ARM RIDE 32
WHITE CALF 47,111,193,214,266
  Anna 159,233
  Annie 81
  Blanche 193,222
  James 111,214,266
  Jim 47,193
  John 23,47,81,159,233,298
  Josephine 233
  Mary 47,214,266
  Minnie 47,193
  Rosa 266
  Susie 160
  Thos 47
WHITE CALF #2 214,264
WHITE DOG 21,70,159,228,286
  Henry 70,159
  Mollie 70,159
  William 159
  Wm 70
WHITE GRASS 50,110
  Angeline 263
  Eneas 192
  John 263

Index

Minnie 206
Ross 49,193,206,263
Shorty 192,206,263
WHITE H RIDER 182
WHITE HIDE 47,108,190
WHITE HORSE RIDER 85,203,
.... 209,258,270
WHITE HORSES
   Garret 125
   Joe 194
   Joseph 200
WHITE MAN 12,77,159,235,295
   Adam 13,135,237
   Anna 135
   Annie 13,237
   George 12,77
   James 295
   Jas 235
   John 12,77,159,235,295
   Louie 159
   Mary 295
   Peter 12,78,159,235,295
WHITE PETRIFIED ROCK 256
WHITE PETRIFIED WOMAN 197
WHITE QUIVER .. 22,78,158,241,289
   Ben 159
   Benj 289
   Benjiman 78
   Josephine 289
   Maggie 78,159,289
   Minnie 78,158
   Mollie 78,159
   Thomas 78,159
WHITE SHIRT 5
WHITE SKIN 220
WHITE SWAN
   Charles 292
   Chas 141
WHITE TAIL 7,69,142,234
WHITE TAIL FEATHERS 278
WHITE WIMAN 95
WHITE WOMAN 14,31,82,151,
.... 154,230,238,288,292
WHITEMAN
   Adam 285
   Anna 285
WIDOW WOMAN 203
WIFER

Isaac 13
Mary 13
WILD CAT 273
WILD GUN 4,65,158,211,
.... 232,253,255,288
   Arthur 158
   Big Tiger Woman 158
   Julia 232,288
WILLIAMSON
   Gertrude 246
   Henry 246
   Mary 246
   Susan 127,244,246
   Wm 246
WING 289
WINGS 22
WINNING WOMAN 88
WINS MANY GUNS 90,162,237
WIPE HIS EYES 267
WIPERT
   Isaac 159
   Issac 89
WIPES HIS EYES 128,194,203
WITE DOG, Mollie 70
WOLD TAIL 217
WOLF BITE 92,137,227
WOLF CALF 45,126,194,206,258
WOLF CHIEF 48,119,194,212,251
   Mrs 212,251
WOLF EAGLE 31,82,160,239,277
   Daniel 31
   George 82
   Rufus 82
WOLF GETTING UP 111
WOLF GIRL 42
WOLF HEAD 27,86,160,280
   Alex 280
   Pete 86,160
WOLF HEAL, Pete 27
WOLF HORN 215
WOLF MEDICINE 80,160,240
   Hazlet 160
WOLF PLUME 16,81,159,283
   Lizzie 283
   Wesley 81,159,240,283
WOLF SITTING UP 193
WOLF SPEAKING 217
WOLF TAIL 47,111,193

Cecile	217
Gilbert	193
Julia	264
WOLF TALKING	263
WOLF WOMAN	87
WOLVERINE	58,120,193,209,262
Joe	120,193,209,262
Joseph	59
William	120,193
WOMAN ALONE	114,193
WOMAN CHIEF	97
WOMAN IN CENTER	176
WOMAN IN THE CENTER	111
WOMAN SHAPE	43
WOMAN'S WORD	193
WOMANS WORD	30,114,203,250
WOOD CHIEF WOMAN	204,260
WOOD WOMAN	27,113
WORK WOMAN	104
WREN	
Baby	39
Dora	39,99,192,223,274
Geo	39,192
George	98,222,270
Ida	39,99,192,223,274
James	270
John	39,99,192,223,274
Katie	99
Kattie	39
Liby	39
Lillie	99,192,274
Lilly	39
Malinda	223,274
Melinda	99,192
Milenda	39
Nellie	223
Robert	99,192,223,274
Salina	223
Susan	39
Susie	98,192,222,270
William	39,99,192
William Wren	274
Wm	223
Y IN WATER, John	94
Y IRON	
Mary	126
Sand	126
Y KIDNEY	
Maggie	87
Mike	87
Y M CHIEF	
Cecil	21,238
Morgan	21
Y R CRANE, John	294
Y WOLF	
Agnes	53
Annie	116
Cicell	53
Emma	53
John	116
Mollie	116
YELLED THERE BEFORE	285
YELLING LAST	202
YELLOW BEAVER	114,190,200
YELLOW BIRD	52,93,110,163, 179,191,213,250
YELLOW BUFFALO ROCK	214
YELLOW FLY	293
YELLOW GRASS	53
YELLOW GROUND HOG	250
YELLOW HEAD	83,141,209
YELLOW HORSE RIDER	207
YELLOW IRON	88,126,160,215
YELLOW KIDNEY	87,160,214, 284,291
Maggie	284
Minnie	214
YELLOW LIGHT	280
YELLOW OTTER	215
YELLOW OWL	160,216,268
Margaret	160,216
YELLOW SPIDER	233,289
YELLOW SPOT	252
YELLOW SPOTTED WOMAN	197
YELLOW SQUIREL	56
YELLOW SQUIRREL	119,167
YELLOW SQUIRRL	83
YELLOW SQUITREL	177
YELLOW TOP KNOT	293
YELLOW WEASEL WOMAN	261
YELLOW WEASLE	57
YELLOW WOLF	53,116, 194,197,262
Agnes	197
Anna	197
Annie	194

Index

John..194
Mary.....................................194,197
Molley.......................................53
Mollie..................................194,263
Sam 116,187,197
Samuel 197
YELLS AT NIGHT 207
YELLS IN NIGHT..........................85
YELLS IN THE WATER 226,238
   George...............................226,280
   John....................................226,280
   Mary...226
YELLS IN WATER..................90,94,
....160,161,280
   John..160
   Thomas 160
YELLS LAST WOMAN 276
YELLS ON THE WAY HOME....285
YOUNG BEAR CHIEF 8,90,
....161,244,295
YOUNG EAGLE 28,122,212
   Joseph 213,265
YOUNG H BREAST 123
YOUNG MAN..............................289
YOUNG MAN CHIEF 21,80,
....161,294
   Cecil......................................80,161
   Cecile 294
YOUNG MOUNTAIN CHIEF 238
YOUNG RUNNING CRANE 5,67,
....160,233,293
YOUNG RUNNING RABBIT ...4,65,
....160,233,282
YOUNG TO GO IN 10

www.ingramcontent.com/pod-product-compliance
Lightning Source LLC
Chambersburg PA
CBHW020239030426
42336CB00010B/538